Speaking Spanish in the US

MM Textbooks

MM Textbooks bring the subjects covered in our successful range of academic monographs to a student audience. The books in this series explore education and all aspects of language learning and use, as well as other topics of interest to students of these subjects. Written by experts in the field, the books are supervised by a team of world-leading scholars and evaluated by instructors before publication. Each text is student-focused, with suggestions for further reading and study questions leading to a deeper understanding of the subject.

All books in this series are externally peer-reviewed.

Full details of all the books in this series and of all our other publications can be found on http://www.multilingual-matters.com, or by writing to Multilingual Matters, St Nicholas House, 31–34 High Street, Bristol BS1 2AW, UK.

MM Textbooks: 16

Speaking Spanish in the US

The Sociopolitics of Language

2nd Edition

Janet M. Fuller and Jennifer Leeman

MULTILINGUAL MATTERS
Bristol • Blue Ridge Summit

DOI https://doi.org/10.21832/FULLER8281
Library of Congress Cataloging in Publication Data
A catalog record for this book is available from the Library of Congress.
Names: Fuller, Janet M. - author. | Leeman, Jennifer, author.
Title: Speaking Spanish in the US: The Sociopolitics of Language / Janet M. Fuller and Jennifer Leeman.
Description: 2nd edition. | Blue Ridge Summit: Multilingual Matters, 2020. |
Series: MM Textbooks: 16 | Includes bibliographical references and index. |
Summary: "This textbook introduces readers to basic concepts of sociolinguistics with a focus on Spanish in the US. The coverage goes beyond a focus on language to examine how the Spanish language is embedded in history and politics, and both reflects and shapes societal views of the language and its speakers"— Provided by publisher.
Identifiers: LCCN 2019054057 (print) | LCCN 2019054058 (ebook) | ISBN 9781788928274 (paperback) | ISBN 9781788928281 (hardback) | ISBN 9781788928298 (pdf) | ISBN 9781788928304 (epub) | ISBN 9781788928311 (kindle edition)
Subjects: LCSH: Spanish language—United States. | Spanish language—Social aspects—United States. | Sociolinguistics—United States.
Classification: LCC PC4826 .F85 2020 (print) | LCC PC4826 (ebook) | DDC 306.442/61073—dc23
LC record available at https://lccn.loc.gov/2019054057
LC ebook record available at https://lccn.loc.gov/2019054058

British Library Cataloguing in Publication Data
A catalogue entry for this book is available from the British Library.

ISBN-13: 978-1-78892-828-1 (hbk)
ISBN-13: 978-1-78892-827-4 (pbk)

Multilingual Matters
UK: St Nicholas House, 31–34 High Street, Bristol BS1 2AW, UK.
USA: NBN, Blue Ridge Summit, PA, USA.

Website: www.multilingual-matters.com
Twitter: Multi_Ling_Mat
Facebook: https://www.facebook.com/multilingualmatters
Blog: www.channelviewpublications.wordpress.com

Typeset by Nova Techset Private Limited, Bengaluru and Chennai, India.
Printed and bound in the UK by the CPI Books Group Ltd.
Printed and bound in the US by NBN.

Contents

Tables and Figures		ix
Acknowledgments		xi
Chapter 1	**An Introduction to Speaking Spanish in the US**	**1**
	Objectives	1
	Introduction	1
	An Interdisciplinary Sociopolitical Approach	3
	Linguistic Variation and Language Varieties	3
	Social Constructionism	4
	Critical Approaches	5
	A Few Words about Terminology	6
	Overview of Chapters	7
	Notes	8
Chapter 2	**The Demographics of Spanish in the US**	**9**
	Objectives	9
	Introduction	9
	A Statistical Portrait of Spanish in the US	10
	National Origin Groups	11
	Statistics on Language Ability and Use	14
	The English-speaking Ability of Spanish-speakers and Latinxs	16
	The Desire to Maintain Spanish and the Sorrow of Language Loss	18
	Factors Impacting Language Maintenance and Shift	21
	Spanish Language Maintenance and Shift in the US	24
	Conclusions and Connections	29
	Discussion Questions and Activities for Chapter 2	30
	Note	31
	Further Reading and Resources	31
Chapter 3	**The History of Spanish and Spanish-speakers in the US**	**33**
	Objectives	33
	Introduction	33
	Spanish Colonization in North America and the Caribbean	36
	US Expansionism and Spanish in the US	40
	Black and White Legends, Hispanophilia and Oñate's Foot	45
	(Im)migration and Spanish in the US	49
	Conclusions and Connections	59
	Discussion Questions and Activities for Chapter 3	60
	Note	61
	Further Reading and Resources	62
Chapter 4	**Language Ideologies**	**63**
	Objectives	63
	Introduction	63
	Language Ideology Defined	64

	Hegemony and Symbolic Domination	65
	Language Ideologies: Bridging the Linguistic and the Social	68
	The Consequences of Language Ideologies: Power, Politics and Policy	71
	The Standard Language Ideology	73
	The One Nation–One Language Ideology	76
	Normative Monolingualism and the Zero-sum Ideology	80
	Monoglossic and Heteroglossic Ideologies	81
	Language Commodification and Instrumentality	83
	Differential Bilingualism	84
	The Relative Worth of English and Spanish	85
	Spanish as Essential to Latinx Identity versus Language as a Choice	86
	Conclusions and Connections	88
	Discussion Questions and Activities for Chapter 4	88
	Further Reading and Resources	89
Chapter 5	**Race, Racialization and Latinx Ethnoracial Identity**	**91**
	Objectives	91
	Introduction	91
	Race as a Social Construct	92
	Racialization	94
	The Racialization of Spanish	96
	Variability in the Construction of Race	97
	Race versus Ethnicity	99
	Race in Latin America	100
	Comparing Constructions of Race in Latin America and the US	103
	Migration and Racial Identities	106
	The Ethnoracial Identity of Latinxs in the US Census and Beyond	107
	Conclusions and Connections	117
	Discussion Questions and Activities for Chapter 5	118
	Further Reading and Resources	119
Chapter 6	**Language and Identity**	**121**
	Objectives	121
	Introduction	121
	Identities	121
	The Linguistic Construction of Social Identities	123
	Indexicality and Identity	132
	Multilingual Practices and Identity	134
	Multiple and Intersectional Identities	136
	Mock Spanish	141
	Conclusions and Connections	146
	Discussion Questions and Activities for Chapter 6	146
	Further Reading and Resources	147
Chapter 7	**Spanish and Spanish-speakers in US Media**	**149**
	Objectives	149
	Introduction	149
	Stereotypical Portrayals of Latinxs	150
	Latinxs and Spanish-speakers in English Language Media	152

Latinxs in English Language News 155
Representing Latinx Language Use: Monolingual Norms and Deviant Behavior 157
Constructing the Latinx Audience: Spanish Language Media and Beyond 162
Spanish in Linguistic Landscapes 166
Conclusions and Connections 169
Discussion Questions and Activities for Chapter 7 170
Further Reading and Resources 170

Chapter 8 Language Policy and Spanish in the US **173**
Objectives 173
Introduction 173
Language Planning and Policy 174
Orientations to Language in Planning and Policy 176
Historical Perspectives on Language Policy in the US 179
Language and Civil Rights in the US 184
Official English 192
Language Policy in Puerto Rico 195
Conclusions and Connections 196
Discussion Questions and Activities for Chapter 8 197
Notes 198
Further Reading and Resources 198

Chapter 9 Spanish in US Schools **201**
Objectives 201
Introduction 201
A Short History of Minority Language Schooling in the US 202
Educating English Language Learners: Program Types 205
Effectiveness of Bilingual and Dual Language Education Programs 208
Spanish as a Second or Additional Language 210
Spanish for Heritage Speakers 211
Language Ideologies in Education 212
Critical Pedagogical Approaches to Language Education 219
Educating Diverse Populations: Beyond Language Differences 221
Conclusions and Connections 222
Discussion Questions and Activities for Chapter 9 223
Further Reading and Resources 224

Chapter 10 Structural Aspects of Speaking Spanish in the US **225**
Objectives 225
Introduction 225
Varieties of Spanish in the US 226
Language Contact Phenomena 230
Spanglish 231
Language Contact Phenomena Defined 233
Convergence? Focus on Pronouns 238
Contact between Varieties of Spanish 240
Beyond English and Spanish 241

	Latinx Englishes	242
	Attitudes toward Varieties of Spanish and English	245
	Conclusions and Connections	248
	Discussion Questions and Activities for Chapter 10	249
	Note	250
	Further Reading and Resources	251
Chapter 11	**The Future of Spanish in the US**	**253**
	Objectives	253
	Introduction	253
	Demographics, Maintenance and Shift	254
	History and Immigration	256
	Language Ideologies	258
	Race and Ethnicity	259
	Identity	260
	Media	262
	Policy	264
	Education	265
	Linguistic Features	267
	Conclusions and Connections	268
	Discussion Questions and Activities for Chapter 11	269
	Note	270
Glossary		271
References		281
Index		325

Tables and Figures

Tables

Table 2.1	National origin in the Latinx population	12
Table 2.2	Racial make-up of the Latinx population	13
Table 2.3	English- and Spanish-speaking ability among Latinxs	26
Table 5.1	Racial classification in the US census 1790–2010	98

Figures

Figure 2.1	Percentage of the population age five and older that speaks Spanish at home	11
Figure 2.2	American Community Survey language question (2015)	14
Figure 3.1	A 1765 map of North America showing British and Spanish colonial possessions	34
Figure 3.2	Timeline of Spanish conquest and US annexation	35
Figure 3.3	San Xavier Mission outside Tucson, Arizona; the mission was founded in 1692 and the current structure was completed in 1797	38
Figure 3.4	Map of US territorial expansion	41
Figure 3.5	National origin groups (ACS 2017 One-year estimates)	52
Figure 4.1	Bumper sticker: 'Welcome to America: Now SPEAK ENGLISH!'	66
Figure 4.2	Bumper sticker: 'WELCOME TO AMERICA: NOW SPEAK CHEROKEE'	66
Figure 4.3	¡Yo ♥ U.S.A!	79
Figure 5.1	Unknown Artist, *De Indio y Mestiza sale Coyote* ('From Indian and Mestiza, Coyote'). Mexico, about 1750. Oil on canvas. 31 1/2 × 41 inches	101
Figure 5.2	Hispanic origin question from the 2010 census	108
Figure 5.3	Race question from the 2010 census	109
Figure 5.4	Race question for the 2020 census	112
Figure 7.1	Sign in Little Village, Chicago: 'American Family Insurance'	168
Figure 7.2	Sign in Humboldt Park, Chicago: *'Ay! Mami "Una cocina caliente"'*	168
Figure 10.1	*Tacos plis!* Billboard outside Los Angeles, California (September 2018)	234

Acknowledgments

We would like to acknowledge the anonymous reviewers as well as the following people for their generous and helpful feedback on previous drafts of this book: Joan Bristol, Yvette Bürki, Héctor Emanuel, Julio Torres, Claudia Holguín Mendoza, Galey Modan, Kim Potowski, Adam Schwartz, Randolph Scully, Ellen Serafini and Hai Zhang. Thank you for your insights and for your support. We are also grateful to Lalo Alacaraz for permission to reproduce the cartoon that appears in Chapter 4.

Chapter 1

An Introduction to Speaking Spanish in the US

Objectives

To present and explain the focus and approach of our book, provide a general background on the sociopolitics of language and provide a brief overview of the subsequent chapters.

Introduction

In the decades leading up to and following the turn of the 21st century, the presence of Spanish in the United States has become more salient. The most obvious reason is that the number (and percentage) of people who speak Spanish has increased significantly over the past few decades. According to the US Census Bureau, in 1990 roughly 17 million people aged five or older spoke Spanish at home, which was 7.5% of all persons over the age of five. That number increased to 28 million people (10.7%) in 2000 and 41 million (13.4%) in 2017 (American Community Survey 2017 one-year estimates). Spanish is by far the most common non-English language spoken in the US (the next most common language is Chinese, spoken at home by approximately 3.5 million people). These statistics, together with the long history of Spanish in what is now the US, make Spanish the de facto second language and part of the national fabric.

Even people who do not speak Spanish themselves and who do not regularly come into contact with Spanish-speakers are likely also to have become more aware of the presence of Spanish in recent decades. In other words, hand in hand with an increased number of speakers has come increased visibility of Spanish in the public sphere. Think, for example, of the expansion of Spanish language media and entertainment – including television channels, music, radio and internet programming – and the ubiquity of automated menus offering users the option of using Spanish at ATMs and on telephone customer service lines. In addition to both increased growth and increased recognition of Spanish-speaking populations in the US, these trends are also attributable to the proliferation of media outlets, audience segmentation, transnational programming, targeted and niche marketing and technological advances. In addition, outcry and activism surrounding the lack of **ethnoracial** diversity in television programming, Hollywood films and broader mainstream popular culture has brought increased attention to the underrepresentation of Latinxs[1] and Spanish-speakers in English language media (such as the #OscarsSoWhite campaign). So too, political dialogue and campaigns invariably discuss the growth and the potential impact of the Latinx electorate. Because Latinxs are linked to Spanish in the minds of many people in the US, public discourse about Latinxs often involves attention to Spanish, even when language is not discussed explicitly. Thus, politicians routinely use Spanish in efforts to attract Latinx voters, sometimes even in primarily English language contexts such as presidential candidate debates.

While the presence, visibility and attention to Spanish have been on the upswing in recent years, people have been speaking Spanish in what is now the US for hundreds of years. In fact, two-thirds of the present-day US was previously under the control of a country where Spanish was the official language (i.e. Spain or Mexico), and Spanish has been spoken continuously by a significant segment of the population ever since (Macías, 2014). Indeed, Spanish has long been and still is 'an American language' (Lozano, 2018).[2] In short, Spanish plays an important role in US society, whether you speak it or not, and this means that understanding what it means to speak Spanish in the US is critical to understanding the workings of US society. Further, understanding the case of Spanish in the US helps us to understand larger issues of multilingualism, so the concepts, themes and theories discussed in this book are also relevant for students who are interested in linguistic diversity more broadly.

Our primary emphasis is on social and political issues related to Spanish in the US. As such, we focus on the use and representation of Spanish rather than on its linguistic characteristics. Similarly, we are interested in language as social action, particularly the ways in which people use language to convey social and political meanings. For this extensively revised second edition of the book, we changed the title to better reflect this focus. The first part of the title is meant to emphasize speaking Spanish as an action and something that people do, rather than the language itself. The second part of the title similarly reflects our approach, and is also intended to make clear that we offer a broad introduction to the study of the sociopolitics of language, for which Spanish in the US can be considered an extended case study. In the next sections we will outline our theoretical orientation and then provide a brief overview of the chapters to come.

An Interdisciplinary Sociopolitical Approach

A key tenet of our approach is that language is inseparable from the people who speak it and the context in which it is situated; the sociopolitical context shapes the formal features of language, its use and its symbolic meaning. For this reason, our examination of speaking Spanish in the US covers a broad range of issues in language and society. Some of the questions we address are: Who speaks Spanish in the US and why? How is Spanish related to Latinx identity? How do people use language to express their identities? How are Spanish and Spanish-speakers treated in education? What public policies govern the use of Spanish and other minority languages? How is Spanish represented and utilized in the media? In order to answer these and other questions, we incorporate theory and research from a broad range of academic disciplines. Of course one of these is sociolinguistics, or the study of language in relation to society. However, the book is informed by social theory more broadly, and we also draw from anthropology, education, critical race theory, demography, history, law, media studies, political science and sociology, among other disciplines. Each chapter focuses on a different aspect or perspective, thus giving readers the opportunity to examine Spanish in the US from many different angles, even as we stress the interrelatedness of the topics we cover. In our view, it is only through this prism of perspectives that we can gain a full appreciation of what it means to speak Spanish in the US.

Just as language use is inherently social and political, the social and political world is also shaped by language. Indeed, language is at the heart of many of the issues discussed in this book, including individual and group identities, education and civil rights, as well as historical and contemporary understandings of national belonging. For this reason, our goals are not only to show how an interdisciplinary sociolinguistic approach can provide a multifaceted understanding of Spanish-speakers and Spanish in the US, but also to show how a consideration of what it means to speak Spanish can shed new light on those issues. Thus, our aim in writing this book is to make information about language in its social context accessible to readers from all academic backgrounds and interests.

Linguistic Variation and Language Varieties

One of the most striking characteristics of human language is its incredible diversity, and variation is inherent to all languages. One type of variation that is particularly salient to linguists and laypeople alike is geographic variation; differences in the ways in which people speak a shared language in different places is a frequent focus of humor and an occasional source of misunderstandings. To give just one example, *carro* is the word typically used for 'car' in Mexico and Puerto Rico, *máquina* is used in Cuba and *coche* and *auto* are used in other places. In Spanish, there is also significant geographic variation in subject pronouns; in some places including Mexico and the Caribbean the informal singular second person pronoun (i.e. 'you') is *tú*, while in others, including large parts of

Central and South America, *vos* is used, and in some regions people employ both forms. (We provide more examples of geographic variation in Chapter 10.)

Not only does language vary geographically; it also varies socially. That is to say, there is also variation across social groups within the same geographic location. To return to the example of *vos*, in some places members of all social classes use this pronoun, while in others it is more common among people of lower socio-economic status and/or educational attainment (Lipski, 1993). Further, individual speakers don't speak the same way all the time. Instead, they vary their language according to where they are, who they are with, what they are doing and how they want to present themselves, among other factors. Thus, there are three main types of variation: geographic, social and contextual or stylistic. Some linguists also cite a fourth type of linguistic variation, temporal variation (e.g. Penny, 2000). Temporal variation refers to language change, which is a natural aspect of all human language.

When we talk about variation being an inherent aspect of language, this means all levels of language. For instance, there is lexical variation (as in the different words for 'car' mentioned above), phonetic variation (such as whether the *s* at the end of a syllable is pronounced as 's' or aspirated as 'h'; for example the word *más,* which means 'more', might be pronounced 'mas' or 'mah'), and morphosyntactic variation (such as the different pronouns and their corresponding verb forms, discussed more in later chapters). There is also variation in the social norms regarding language use.

Although laypeople sometimes use the word *dialect* to refer to the ways of speaking associated with specific places, linguists generally prefer the term **varieties** for different ways of speaking, whether these are regional varieties or social varieties associated with particular genders, ethnic groups or other social categories. We generally prefer to avoid *dialect* because non-linguists sometimes use it disparagingly to refer to languages with less official recognition or social prestige, such as Mayan languages in Central America.

Social Constructionism

In contemporary social theory, **social constructionism** is the dominant theoretical approach to social structures, identities and behaviors. The underlying idea is that social categories (such as race, gender and social class), as well as the specific characteristics that we associate with them, are not naturally occurring or fixed. Instead, even though they may seem like objective facts, they are actually constructed through the social practices and beliefs of members of society. One important aspect of this theoretical perspective is that it recognizes that social constructions, such as the boundaries between categories or the characteristics associated with them, can change. To give an example, societal ideas about the category 'woman' have shifted over time (e.g. What age is the boundary between 'girl' and 'woman'? Must one have two X chromosomes to be a 'woman'?), as have societal assumptions about what women are like and how they should behave.

Another central aspect of social constructionism is that our identities are not the source of our social behavior but the outcome of it. This is not how we often use the word *identity* in our everyday lives, so it may take a while to get used to this idea. We will discuss these ideas in great detail in Chapters 5 and 6, but social constructionism is a thread that runs through the entire book. As we noted earlier, we see language as a type of social action, and in this book we explore how people use language in the construction of their own and other people's identities. In particular, we look at how speaking Spanish can be used to present oneself to the world – as well as how speaking Spanish impacts how people are perceived by others.

There is a constant interaction between our social behavior (including linguistic behavior) and our ideas about the world; they influence each other. To give one example: if speaking Spanish is perceived negatively, Spanish-speakers might avoid speaking it, in order to escape public stigma. However, if people speak Spanish publicly and proudly, this could contribute to a shift in perceptions of the language. The construction of the social meanings of particular language practices and the interactions between language use and perceptions of social reality are a major theme in this book.

Critical Approaches

Our final overarching theoretical theme in the study of speaking Spanish in the US is linked to critical approaches to the study of language and society. There are many different approaches under this umbrella term of *Critical Studies* (Critical Discourse Analysis, Critical Race Theory, Critical Philosophy, etc.), but all share the underlying goals of examining phenomena within their sociohistorical context, investigating the relationships between social and political structures and exposing inequalities in society. A major focus is the study of ideologies, and our taken-for-granted ways of thinking about the world, a topic we delve into in great detail in Chapter 4. Implicit in critical approaches is a social constructionist perspective, that is, the idea discussed above that social categories are not fixed but instead are based on social behaviors and societal beliefs. Critical approaches ask us to question unexamined social norms and social categories. When we do, and we look critically at things taken as 'common sense,' the underlying assumptions and biases become clear, as well as the ways in which these assumptions serve powerful interests and reinforce inequality.

An illustrative example can be found in examining the outrage expressed online and elsewhere about having to press 1 for English; for example, see the song 'Press One for English' by RivoliRevue (https://www.youtube.com/watch?v=sEJfS1v-fU0). The taken-for-granted assumption underlying this irritation and outrage is that English is the only legitimate language in the US. Thus, speaking Spanish is seen as a violation of the 'natural' state of affairs. A critical perspective brings these assumptions to light, examines their connection to **xenophobia** and racism, and analyzes how they contribute to inequality (we return to this topic in Chapter 4, and to this example in Discussion Question 2 in

Chapter 8). Once revealed, these assumptions can be understood and challenged, with the ultimate goal of promoting social justice. With this book we hope to help readers think critically about language and the world around them – in general as well as specifically with regard to Spanish in the US.

A Few Words about Terminology

We have adopted the use of *Latinx* (plural *Latinxs*)[3] as the generic term for referring to individuals and groups. We prefer these terms to the alternatives *Latino(s)* and *Latina/o(s)* or *Latin@(s)*, which either give preference to males or rely on a binary gender categorization of 'male' and 'female'. The term *Latinx*, and gender-inclusive language in general,[4] is not accepted by everyone, and in Chapter 5 we discuss some of the objections that have been put forth. Nonetheless, *Latinx* is an increasingly common term in academic and activist circles (see Vidal-Ortiz & Martinez, 2018, for further discussion). As we explore in depth later in this book, particular ways of using language allow people to position themselves in particular ways. We use the term *Latinx* in order to position ourselves, as authors, as inclusive and critical in our thinking. However, because we recognize that *Latinx* has some limitations, we will continue to engage with the heterogeneity of Latinxs and Spanish-speakers in the US and the marginalization of groups through language in our ongoing choice of labels. In instances where we (or authors we cite) are referring to specific individuals identified as male or female, we use *Latino* or *Latina* accordingly. In addition, when quoting research or official documents, we use whatever term appeared in the original.

Another less-than-perfect term that appears in this volume is *Anglo*, most commonly used to refer to non-Latinx Whites. This term is problematic in several ways, including its implication of Anglo (i.e. British) heritage, which is not the actual heritage of everyone referred to with the term. Nonetheless, as we have just explained, identity categories are socially constructed rather than based in objective facts. Further, the meaning of labels (and of words in general) does not reside in the words themselves, but in the ways in which they are used and understood in society. Thus, even though it doesn't reflect the historical meaning of the word, if *Anglo* has come to be used to refer to non-Latinx White people, that is what the word means, at least in some contexts, such as the Southwestern US, where it is more common than in other regions. Still, people don't often use *Anglo* to identify themselves. Thus, while we use the term, we do so sparingly.

We hope that this introduction has given you a sense of the philosophy and theoretical approach we take in this book. As we have said, two primary goals of this text are to help readers understand the historical, social and linguistic issues related to speaking Spanish in the US, as well as to appreciate the importance of taking language into account in other disciplines. While Spanish in the US is important in and of itself, it also serves as a valuable example or case study with which to gain a deeper understanding of the social and political aspects of language. Thus, a third goal is for readers to gain familiarity with the sociopolitics of language more broadly and throughout the book we have sought to introduce and explain key theoretical constructs in an easy-to-understand way. Finally, we aim to foster your critical analysis of taken-for-granted ideas about language, Latinxs and Spanish, as well as your ability to be critical consumers of public discourse popular culture. We hope to encourage you to be proponents of policies and practices that have a positive impact on the societies in which you live.

Overview of Chapters

While retaining the primary sociopolitical focus of the first edition, this extensively revised and expanded edition covers additional topics and includes a wealth of new material and activities. Each chapter begins with a short overview before introducing readers to key theoretical concerns, historical perspectives, empirical research and practical issues. We stress interdisciplinarity and common themes throughout the book and each chapter ends with a section highlighting connections to other chapters. We follow this with set of discussion questions and activities, many of which make connections to materials available online as well as to other chapters. Finally, each chapter has a brief list of suggested further readings and resources. After the last chapter is a glossary with important concepts for which readers might require definition beyond what appears in the main text; words contained in the glossary appear in bold on their first usage in each chapter. An index is provided at the end of the volume.

Chapter 2 is a brand new chapter that provides information about the demographics of speaking Spanish in the US and reviews theoretical and empirical research about Spanish language maintenance and shift. Chapter 3 is also completely new and focuses on the history of the Spanish language in the US, including colonization, conquest and historical and present-day immigration, as well as contemporary struggles regarding the representation of that history. This chapter provides the context for the contemporary situation of Spanish in the US, which is the primary focus in the rest of the book.

Language ideologies, a central topic of the book, is the focus of an expanded Chapter 4, which outlines how ideas about language are deeply embedded in societal norms and are often more about the speakers than the languages spoken. We then turn to address race and ethnicity in Chapter 5, emphasizing both the socially constructed nature of race and the role of language in its construction, comparing constructions of ethnoracial identity in Latin America and the US and examining the ethnoracial classification of Latinxs. The focus on identity is broadened and deepened in Chapter 6, where we present more detail on the theoretical underpinnings of research on language and identity, and we examine the connection of speaking Spanish to a broad range of identities, such as gender, sexuality, nationality and so forth. These chapters have been significantly revised and updated to include expanded theoretical frameworks and recent empirical research. This is also the case for Chapter 7, which addresses how Latinxs are portrayed in the media, and how these portrayals draw on ideologies about language, race and other identities in the construction of **Latinidad**. New sections examine Spanish-language media and language in the built environment.

Chapter 8, another new chapter, addresses language policies in the US, with a brief history of the rise of English in dominance as well as the persistent multilingualism of the US, and an examination of the role of ideologies in language policy. Chapter 9 focuses on policies and practices in one important sector of society, education, looking at the goals and effectiveness of different models for educating Spanish-speakers, and linking these pedagogical approaches to ideologies about multilingualism, Spanish and Spanish-speakers. We have expanded the treatment of the teaching of Spanish to **heritage speakers** and added a new section on teaching Spanish as a second or additional language.

Chapter 10 shifts to a more linguistic focus and looks at structures that result from the contact between English and Spanish, as well as other languages, in the US. Included in this new edition are discussions of different varieties of Spanish spoken in the US, language mixing and contact between Spanish and English, and Latinx Englishes. Finally, Chapter 11, another new chapter, provides an overview of important takeaway points from this textbook, future directions and a call to action.

Notes

(1) Later on, we will explain our use of this term; please see discussion below as well as in Chapter 5.

(2) By *American*, Lozano means 'of the United States.' It is worth noting that many people object to this usage given that America encompasses all of North, Central and South America, rather than just the United States.

(3) Usually pronounced like 'LaTEEnex' but also sometimes as 'LAtin-ex'.

(4) Another gender-neutral formulation gaining ground in Latin America replaces the *-a* and *-o* endings with *-e*.

Chapter 2

The Demographics of Spanish in the US

> **Objectives**
>
> To present quantitative data regarding the place of birth, national origins, geographic distribution and linguistic profiles of people who speak Spanish in the US, discuss some limitations of official statistics, and explain patterns of Spanish maintenance and shift as well as the factors that shape them.

Introduction

As we said in the previous chapter, the US Census Bureau reports that in 2017 there were over 41 million people in the US who spoke Spanish at home. In this chapter, we try to give a sense of who these speakers of Spanish are by providing statistics about their nativity (i.e. whether they were born in the US or abroad), their national origin or ethnicity and their geographic distribution within the US. We then turn to a consideration of patterns of language knowledge and use. Specifically, we address questions such as whether or not people who speak Spanish also speak English, whether Spanish can be seen as encroaching on English and whether Spanish–English bilingualism is the norm among US-born Latinxs. In order to answer these questions, we present statistics from the Census Bureau and we explain the limitations of that data. We then go on to examine statistics from other sources that can shed additional light on generational patterns of language knowledge. Finally, we discuss theoretical approaches to the study of language maintenance and/or shift, including a consideration of the societal and individual factors that have an impact and the ways in which they play out in the case of Spanish in the US.

A Statistical Portrait of Spanish in the US

In the US, many people think of Spanish as a foreign language and a common misconception is that people who speak Spanish in the US are primarily immigrants. Further, public discourse often portrays Spanish as a language not just of immigrants, but of unauthorized immigrants (Dick, 2011; DuBord, 2014; Leeman, 2012a). In reality, however, more than half (53%) of the people who speak Spanish at home were born in the US (American Community Survey 2017 Five-year estimates). These data, together with Spanish's long history within the current borders of the US (discussed in detail in the next chapter), make it clear that Spanish is not a foreign language (Alonso, 2006; Lozano, 2018). In addition to the implications for how we think about Spanish, these statistics also have concrete linguistic and sociolinguistic repercussions. Specifically, they mean that a majority of Spanish-speakers are either bilingual or dominant in English. Thus, it bears emphasizing that when we use the term 'Spanish-speakers' we don't mean people who are monolingual in Spanish; instead, we are referring to people who speak Spanish, regardless of whether or not they also speak English and of which language they use more frequently. The high rates of Spanish–English bilingualism and language shift to English (discussed below) have important implications for educational policy and language policy more broadly (discussed in Chapters 8 and 9).

Another common misconception is that all Latinxs speak Spanish. Some people even use the terms *Spanish-speaking* and *Latinx* interchangeably, as if they were synonyms. Further, some Latinxs believe there is an obligation to know Spanish and, among those who don't, feelings of shame or guilt are not uncommon (we will return to this issue later in this chapter). However, even though some people consider speaking Spanish to be a key part of 'authentic' Latinx identity (a topic we will return to several times later in this book), a look at the statistics reveals that roughly a quarter (27%) of Latinxs aged five and older speak only English at home (ACS 2017 Five-year estimates). The percentage of Latinxs born in the US who only speak English at home is even higher (41%). Because a growing share of Latinxs are US-born (66% in 2017; ACS 2017 Five-year estimates), the overall share of Latinxs who speak only English is also on the rise (López & González-Barrera, 2013).

So far, we have talked about the number and percentage of Spanish-speakers in the US as a whole, but we want to stress that there is a great deal of variation from state to state, county to county and city to city. As shown in Figure 2.1, the states with the highest percentage of Spanish-speakers in the population are in the Southwest, followed by Florida and then New Jersey and New York. In Maine, Spanish-speakers represent less than 1% of the population, while in Texas they comprise over 29%, demonstrating the tremendous range. There are also differences within states; taking Florida as an example, in the city of Miami roughly 67% of the population aged five and older speak Spanish at home, but in St. Petersburg city just 4% do. As we discuss in detail in the next chapter, the states with the highest percentages of Spanish-speakers are not just closest to Mexico; they were part of Mexico until the mid-19th century. Still, even though the percentage of Spanish-speakers is lower in some parts of the country, Spanish is the most commonly spoken non-English language in every state except Alaska, Hawaii, Louisiana, Maine, New Hampshire, North Dakota and Vermont (Blatt, 2014).

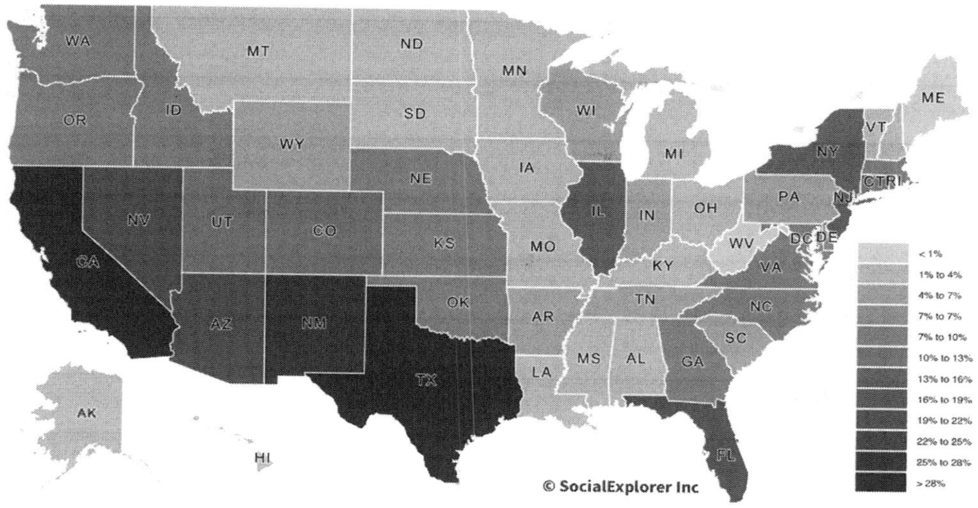

Figure 2.1 Percentage of the population age five and older that speaks Spanish at home
Data – ACS 2017 One-year estimate; Map – Social Explorer.

National Origin Groups

As we stress repeatedly in this book, people who speak Spanish are extremely diverse. In the previous sections we saw that Spanish-speakers include people born in the US as well as immigrants. We now look at the national origin groups that make up the Spanish-speaking population in the US. Because the US Census Bureau does not produce statistics on language use for specific Latinx subgroups, in Table 2.1 we present the relative size of the largest national origin groups as a way to approximate the make-up of the Spanish-speaking population (but it's not a perfect proxy, as we explained above!). The data are based on responses to the Census Bureau's question on Hispanic Origin (see Chapter 5). To be clear, *national origin* does not mean 'nationality,' but rather something along the lines of 'ethnicity' (we discuss ethnicity further in Chapter 5). Thus, the national origin groups listed in Table 2.1 and elsewhere in this book include people born in the US (whether offspring of immigrants or descendants of lands incorporated by the US) as well as people born elsewhere.

As can be seen in Table 2.1, Mexicans and Mexican Americans make up the largest share of Latinxs by far. However, this percentage has decreased since peaking in 2008, and the Latinx population has become increasingly diverse (Flores, 2017).

There is also a great deal of geographic diversity, and the proportion of each national origin group varies in different parts of the country. For example, in Arizona the vast majority (89%) of Latinxs are of Mexican origin, in Florida the most common Latinx national origin groups are Cubans (29%) and Puerto Ricans (21%), in New York they are Puerto Ricans (29%) and Dominicans (23%), and in Virginia they are Salvadorans (23%) and Mexicans (23%) (ACS 2017 One-year estimates). (Those interested in specific national origin groups

Table 2.1 *National origin of the Latinx population*

Mexican	62.3%
Puerto Rican	9.5%
Cuban	3.9%
Salvadoran	3.9%
Dominican (Dominican Republic)	3.5%
Guatemalan	2.5%
Colombian	2.1%
Honduran	1.6%
Spaniard	1.4%
Ecuadorian	1.3%
Peruvian	1.2%
Spanish[a]	0.8%
Nicaraguan	0.8%
Venezuelan	0.7%
Argentinean	0.5%
Panamanian	0.4%
Chilean	0.3%
Costa Rican	0.3%
Bolivian	0.2%
Uruguayan	0.1%

Note: [a]The categories here reflect the answers provided by respondents. As we discuss later in this chapter, as well as in Chapter 5, there are multiple possible meanings for the identity term *Spanish*. It is sometimes used as a pan-ethnic label roughly equivalent to *Hispanic* or *Latinx*, but can also refer specifically to origins in Spain.
Source: ACS 2017 One-year estimates.

or geographies, can perform customized searches using the US Census Bureau's online data tool at https://data.census.gov).

In addition to geographic distribution, demographic statistics also reveal other differences among Latinx national origin groups. For example, the poverty rate among Guatemalans, Hondurans and Dominicans is 28% but only 16% among Argentineans (vs. 25% for Latinxs overall and 16% for the general US population) (López & Patten, 2015). The percentage of Latinxs who were born outside the US is declining for all national origin groups, but the intergroup differences are notable: in 2013, 69% of Venezuelans and 65% of Peruvians were foreign-born while only 33% of Mexicans were (López & Patten, 2015). Finally, Mexicans had the lowest median age (26), while Cubans had the highest (40), which is higher than the mean both for all Latinxs (28) and for the general US population (37) (López & Patten, 2015). Demographic profiles for each of the 14 largest Latinx groups are available on the Pew Research Center's website (http://www.pewhispanic.org/2015/09/15/the-impact-of-slowing-immigration-foreign-born-share-falls-among-14-largest-us-hispanic-origin-groups). While these statistics reveal overall trends, we want to stress yet again that there are individual differences and variation within national origin groups.

Latinxs and Spanish-speakers in the US are also **ethnoracially** diverse, as a result of the multifaceted history of conquest, colonization, slavery and immigration across the Americas, as well as Latinxs' varied personal and family histories and life experiences within the US. Table 2.2 shows the Census Bureau's statistics on the racial make-up of the Latinx population. As we will discuss in depth in Chapter 5, the Census Bureau considers 'Latino' to be an ethnic, rather than a racial, identity. In that chapter, we critically examine the construct of race, the Census Bureau's race and ethnicity questions and the ethnoracial classification of Latinxs.

We want to note that, in contrast with the Census Bureau's ethnoracial statistics that show roughly two-thirds of Latinxs' racial identity as White, a recent Pew Center survey found that two-thirds of Latinxs consider their Latinx background to be part of their racial identity and roughly one-third consider themselves to be of 'mixed race' (González-Barrera, 2015). Further, despite the small percentage of Latinxs who identify themselves as Black or African American on the Census Bureau's surveys, approximately one-quarter of Latinx respondents on a recent Pew survey classify themselves as 'Afro-Latino, Afro-Caribbean, or Afro-[country of origin]' (López & González-Barrera, 2016). These discrepancies highlight the constructed, contextual and contested nature of ethnoracial and other identities, an issue we will return to in Chapters 5 and 6, as well as the impact of the question format on the responses and data collected.

The diversity of the Latinx population and the concentration of national origin groups in different parts of the country also point to the diversity of varieties of Spanish spoken within the US. The make-up of local Latinx populations shapes the Spanish spoken in different areas of the country, such that the Spanish one hears in El Paso, Texas is more likely to sound like Mexican varieties, whereas the Spanish heard in Washington Heights, New York is more likely to sound Dominican (see Chapter 10 for a discussion of some of these linguistic characteristics). Still, this is not to say that the Spanish spoken in these areas is just like what you might hear in Mexico or the Dominican Republic; not only do all language varieties change and develop in different ways over time, but contact with English, and with other varieties of Spanish, also has an impact on how Spanish is spoken in the US (see Chapter 10). Further, we want to stress that 'Mexican Spanish' and 'Dominican Spanish' are not monolithic, homogenous entities. Instead, there is significant geographic and social variation within nations and national origin groups (in Chapter 4 we discuss the ideologies linking language to nation).

Table 2.2 *Racial make-up of the Latinx population*

White	65.0%
Black or African American	2.1%
American Indian and Alaska Native	1.0%
Asian	0.4%
Native Hawaiian and Other Pacific Islander	0.1%
Some other race	26.7%
Two or more races	4.7%

Source: ACS 2017 One-year estimates.

Statistics on Language Ability and Use

In our overview of how many people speak Spanish at home we relied on official statistics from the Census Bureau. Before going further in our discussion of the patterns of language knowledge and use, let's stop to examine where those statistics come from and how they are produced. In particular, we'll describe the Census Bureau's question about language and the kinds of language data that the Census Bureau does and doesn't collect, and we'll explain how the Census Bureau's language question limits our knowledge about Spanish and Spanish-speakers in the US (Leeman, 2004, 2018c). In Chapter 5 we will explain and critically analyze the Census Bureau's statistics on ethnoracial identity.

Since 1980, the Census Bureau has produced statistics about language using a three-part question which is asked of persons aged five and older (see Figure 2.2). The first part of the question asks whether the person speaks a language other than English at home. If the answer is yes, the next part of the question provides a write-in box to identify the non-English language, and the third part asks how well the person speaks English, with four response options: Very Well, Well, Not Well and Not at All. This question does not appear on the census itself (which is conducted every ten years), but rather on the Census Bureau's American Community Survey (ACS). The ACS is an annual sample-based survey that collects a wide array of social, economic and other data from US households. The language data are used in decisions about where voting materials in Spanish and other minority languages are needed as well as in the implementation of other language policies (see Chapter 8).

There are several aspects of this language question, and the resulting statistics, that are worth noting. First, the ACS asks only about language *use*, not language *knowledge*, and only about *home* use. Thus, if a person knows another language but doesn't speak it at

14 **a. Does this person speak a language other than English at home?**

☐ Yes
☐ No → *SKIP to question 15a*

b. What is this language?

☐

For example: Korean, Italian, Spanish, Vietnamese

c. How well does this person speak English?

☐ Very well
☐ Well
☐ Not well
☐ Not at all

Figure 2.2 American Community Survey language question (2015)

home, this isn't recorded by the Census Bureau. For this reason, the actual number of people who know Spanish is certainly higher than the 41 million reported by the Census Bureau, since many people who know Spanish don't speak it at home (Leeman, 2004). Secondly, the question only provides one write-in box for a non-English language. As a result, there is no way of knowing whether respondents speak more than one non-English language at home. The proportion of immigrants from Latin America, and especially Central America, who speak indigenous languages (such as K'iche', Mixtec and Nahuatl) is growing (Bazo Vienrich, 2018). Some such individuals also speak Spanish, but others don't. However, because the ACS only provides space for one non-English language, multilingual individuals who answer that they speak an indigenous language (such as Aymara, K'iche', Mixtec, Nahuatl or Quechua) are omitted from counts of people who speak Spanish. On the other hand, if they answer that they speak Spanish, their use of indigenous languages goes unrecorded.

The third and fourth points we want to highlight are related to the English-speaking ability question. Rather than an objective assessment, the question relies on the respondents' subjective judgment about how well the person speaks English. Obviously, this raises some concern about the reliability and validity of the results, since people differ in the criteria they use, and notions about 'good' and 'bad' ways of speaking might impact responses (Leeman, 2015). On the other hand, it clearly wouldn't be feasible or desirable to give everyone a language exam! The fourth aspect of the ACS language question that we want to mention is that it doesn't ask about ability in the non-English language. Thus, while the question allows for classification people based on four levels of *English*-speaking ability, there is no way to know about their ability in *Spanish* (or any other non-English language). Some people who speak Spanish at home are completely fluent, whereas others have more limited ability, but there is no way to tell them apart in the ACS data (Leeman, 2004, 2018c).

A final limitation of the ACS is that, because it is based on a sample (rather than on the entire population, like the census), it isn't possible to calculate statistics for small areas. Thus, we can only use ACS data to compare the percentage of people who speak Spanish in different states or in large cities, but not in less populated counties, smaller cities or neighborhoods.

The reason that the Census Bureau's language questions are the way they are is related both to language policies and to language ideologies (Leeman, 2004, 2018c). As we discuss in Chapter 8, there are a few US language policies that require services in minority languages but these are designed for people with limited speaking ability in English (Gilman, 2011). In some cases (e.g. the Voting Rights Act), the requirement depends on how many such people live in a given area, and ACS statistics are used to make that determination. In contrast, there aren't any policies that require statistics about ability in non-English languages (Leeman, 2018c). Further, dominant language ideologies don't see minority languages as a particularly interesting social characteristic (Leeman, 2004), something we will delve into further in Chapter 4. For this reason, while the ACS provides invaluable statistics on home language use and English-speaking ability, corresponding statistics about knowledge of Spanish must come from other, non-governmental sources.

The English-speaking Ability of Spanish-speakers and Latinxs

One thing that the ACS statistics do allow us to determine is the English-speaking ability of people who report speaking Spanish at home, and thus to evaluate the oft-repeated claim that Spanish-speaking immigrants and their offspring don't learn English. The supposed failure to learn English, which is often framed as a refusal or unwillingness to do so, is a common trope on social media and in online comments, letters to the editor and everyday discourse, one that is often taken for granted or presented as fact without any evidence. For example, in a recent appearance on *Meet the Press*, former NBC news anchor Tom Brokaw answered a question about the high levels of support among residents of Wyoming and South Dakota for building a wall on the US–Mexico border as follows:

> And a lot of this, we don't want to talk about. But the fact is, on the Republican side, a lot of people see the rise of an extraordinary, important, new constituent in American politics, Hispanics, who will come here and all be Democrats. Also, I hear, when I push people a little harder, 'Well, I don't know whether I want brown grandbabies.' I mean, that's also a part of it. It's the intermarriage that is going on and the cultures that are conflicting with each other. I also happen to believe that the Hispanics should work harder at assimilation. That's one of the things I've been saying for a long time. You know, they ought not to be just codified [sic] in their communities but make sure that all their kids are learning to speak English, and that they feel comfortable in the communities. And that's going to take outreach on both sides, frankly. (NBC News, 2019)

There is a lot to unpack in Brokaw's statement, including his acknowledgement that support for a border wall is rooted at least in part in anti-Latinx racism and fears about the racial make-up of the nation, in addition to his implied claim that Latinxs do not ensure that their children speak English. In a particularly flagrant example of 'bothsidesism,' or the tendency of the press to treat both sides of a debate as equally valid, Brokaw framed Whites' racist opposition to intermarriage as if it were morally equivalent to Latinxs' supposed lack of effort to teach English to their children.[1] In Chapter 5 we examine the racialization of Spanish and in Chapter 8 we discuss the legal understanding of linguistic discrimination as a proxy for national origin or racial discrimination; here we focus on the false notion that Latinxs and Spanish-speakers refuse to learn English.

Despite the frequency with which it is repeated, both quantitative and qualitative research has shown that the myth of Latin American immigrants' refusal to learn English is just that – a myth. This myth actually consists of three interrelated notions, all of which are false: (1) they don't want to learn English; (2) they don't learn English; and (3) they don't make sure their children learn English. Let's start with the idea that immigrants don't want to learn English. In fact, a Pew Center survey found just the opposite: nine out of ten Latinxs think learning English is important (Taylor *et al.*, 2012). Like quantitative surveys, qualitative studies as well as memoirs have also consistently found that immigrants perceive learning English as valuable for both symbolic and practical purposes. For example, in DuBord's (2014) ethnographic study of Mexican immigrants at a day laborer center in Arizona, participants told her of the language barriers and difficulties they had faced prior to learning English, such as having less access to employment, being unable to stand up to abusive employers and needing to rely on others to go shopping. For those that had not learned English, it was not because they had rejected it. On the contrary, they saw knowing English as way to get better jobs, to have better relationships with supervisors, to earn more money and, in the following example, to open one's own company:

> *Yo no sé el inglés pero si supiera inglés ya anduviera en mi propia compañía porque hay muchos que no saben trabajar pero saben el inglés. Eso es lo que les ayuda a ellos.*
>
> I don't know English, but if I knew English I would already have my own company because there are many guys who don't know how to work but they know English. That is what helps them.

(DuBord, 2014: 69)

Although it is not at all clear in the context of DuBord's research that knowledge of English actually confers the imagined benefits, the key point here is that Spanish-speakers *want* to learn English and they perceive it as valuable for professional reasons (we discuss this emphasis on the economic value of languages in Chapter 4).

In addition to practical and labor market considerations, many Latinxs also see English as a prerequisite for full participation and legitimacy in US society. For example, when asked if there are any positive aspects to speaking English, a female participant in Velázquez' (2018: 74) research responded: '*Pues la comunicación, el no sentirse, el no sentirse como una sombra en todo lugar*' ('Well, communication, not feeling, not feeling like a shadow everywhere'). Another woman answered as follows:

> *Pues lo bueno de hablar inglés es para comunicarse con las demás personas de aquí [...] O para entenderles también [...] Para entenderles, eso es bueno porque [...] Si no hablamos no somos nada.*

(Velázquez, 2018: 74)

> Well, the good thing about speaking English is to communicate with other people from here [...] or to understand them too, that's the good thing because [...] if we don't speak [it] we're nothing.

Similarly, other scholars have also found that Mexican immigrants feel an obligation to learn English, as well as a sense of shame and/or emotional pain when they do not acquire it as fully or as quickly as they would like (García Bedolla, 2003; Relaño Pastor, 2014). Moreover, like many non-Latinxs, the US-born Mexican Americans in García Bedolla's study shared the belief that immigrants have a moral obligation to learn English. Along the same lines, Ullman (2010) described the sense of failure and personal inadequacy of Mexican migrants who had spent hundreds of dollars on the language-learning program *Inglés sin Barreras* ('English without Barriers'), but had not been able to master English as quickly as they had imagined (or been promised).

But it's not just that Spanish-speaking immigrants *want* to learn English; with time, they *do* learn it and so do their children and grandchildren, which disproves the second and third parts of the myth. Indeed, according to the Census Bureau statistics, more than three-quarters (76%) of people who speak Spanish at home are able to speak English either 'very well' or 'well' (ACS 2017 Five-year estimates). The percentage is even higher (95%) for Spanish-speakers who were born in the US, a statistic that includes people born in Puerto Rico. And even among foreign-born Spanish-speakers, 55% speak English 'very well' or 'well.' In other words, virtually all US-born Spanish-speakers speak English well, as do a majority of the foreign-born. And regarding the foreign-born, it's worth noting that this includes recent arrivals as well as people who came to the US as adults. Not surprisingly, childhood immigrants and people who have been in the US for many years are the demographic groups with the highest rates of English proficiency (ACS 2017 Five-year estimates; Portes & Rumbaut, 2001; Veltman, 2000), given that language learning tends to be more difficult for adults, especially for those with limited time and/or financial resources to devote to it.

Note that the statistics we have just presented are about the English-speaking ability of people who speak Spanish at home. But Brokaw didn't say that 'Spanish-speakers' need to make sure that their children speak English; he said that 'Hispanics' do. This is a clear example of the phenomenon we described at the beginning of this chapter – people using *Hispanic* and *Spanish-speaking* as synonyms and/or assuming that all Latinxs speak Spanish (we discuss this further in Chapters 5 and 6). Although we said it earlier, we'll say it again: not all Latinxs speak Spanish. In fact, 41% of native-born Latinxs only speak English at home (ACS 2017 Five-year estimates). And among all Latinxs (including both native- and foreign-born), more than three-quarters (81%) speak English 'very well' or 'well.' Brokaw's concern that Latinx immigrants and their offspring don't speak English – which is not unique to this newscaster but instead is representative of a broader public discourse that portrays Latinxs as a threat to English – is simply unfounded. English is not in danger. As we discuss in Chapter 4, the idea that people who speak Spanish don't also speak English is rooted in assumptions about monolingualism being the normal state of affairs. In fact, the issue for concern shouldn't be that the offspring of Spanish-speaking immigrants fail to learn English; it should be that they don't learn Spanish.

The Desire to Maintain Spanish and the Sorrow of Language Loss

As we saw in the previous section, despite common portrayals to the contrary, there is absolutely no evidence that speakers of Spanish (or Latinxs more broadly) fail to embrace or learn English. This does not mean, however, that they don't care about maintaining Spanish. In fact, 95% of respondents in the Pew Center's survey said it was important for future generations of Latinxs to speak Spanish (Taylor *et al.*, 2012). The desire of Spanish-speaking immigrants to pass Spanish on to their children is also evident in qualitative studies of language maintenance and family language practices (e.g. Schecter & Bayley, 2002; Torrez, 2013; Velázquez, 2018). Sometimes Spanish is framed as valuable for future employment opportunities (Schecter & Bayley, 2002; Velázquez, 2018), but more commonly it is seen as important for ethnoracial identity and/or necessary for familial communication either in the US or with relatives abroad. For example, a Mexican immigrant in Torrez's (2013) research explained her desire for bilingual Spanish–English educational opportunities for her children as follows:

> *Son perdidos porque no saben cómo hablar con sus familias. ... Porque en primer lugar, nosotros, con nuestros hijos, nosotros hablamos puro español porque nosotros no sabemos mucho inglés y nuestra raza es de México y por eso. Y si ellos hablan puro inglés pues no van a entendernos a nosotros. Por eso queremos que puedan hacer eso, que puedan poner español y inglés. Y pues la mayor parte se comunica uno con ellos en español. Y en español, español porque es nuestro lenguaje de nosotros. Y ellos ya es diferente porque ellos es otro nivel de vida que llevan ellos y ellos ya están aprendiendo otro idioma, y qué bueno.*
>
> They are lost because they don't know how to speak with their families. ... In the first place, with our children, we speak Spanish because we don't know English well and our people are from Mexico. And if they only speak English, well, they won't understand us. For that reason, we want them to [be able to] do that – learn both Spanish and English. For the most part, we communicate with them in Spanish. And in Spanish, because it is our language. And for them it is different, because they are taking a different level of life and they are learning a different language, and that is good.
>
> (Torrez, 2013: 282)

In her explanation, she underscores the importance of Spanish for group identity and familial communication and describes terrible emotional consequences of not learning Spanish ('*Son perdidos,*' 'They are lost'). Her commentary in support of Spanish is not a rejection of English, which she clearly wants her children to know. Instead, she advocates Spanish–English bilingual education, because she has no doubt that her children will learn English.

A similar desire to transmit Spanish to the next generation, a sense of its importance for parent–child relationships and a recognition of the universality of English acquisition are apparent in the case of Nilda, a participant in Schecter and Bayley's (2002) study of language socialization practices among Mexican migrants and their US-born offspring in Texas and California. Nilda was born in the US to Mexican parents. At age 15 she married a Mexican man with whom she had a child. Nilda explains her decision to speak Spanish to her son as follows:

> And I got pregnant, and it seemed inconceivable to me that I would teach my son anything else but Spanish. Because I *knew* that if he went into the school system, he'd learn English. And I spoke English so I could always help him out in that way. But to think that my son would lose out on all that I had learned and that was me. There was too much of me to say 'Well now you learn English so you can get ahead.' (Schecter & Bayley, 2002: 167, emphasis in the original)

Nonetheless, despite the widely expressed desire among Latinxs for subsequent generations to maintain Spanish (Taylor *et al.*, 2012), the unfortunate reality is that many children of immigrants are not fluent in the language of their parents, and the majority of the grandchildren of immigrants are monolingual English-speakers (we present detailed statistics on generational patterns of Spanish knowledge later in this chapter). Sometimes this is because parents and other caregivers decide to focus on English acquisition; in other cases children turn away from Spanish. Of course, adults and children alike are exposed to explicit and implicit societal messages that English is the key to fitting in and achieving success and that other languages are un-American and dangerous, and these messages play a role in shaping household language practices and individual choices (King & Fogle, 2006; Velázquez, 2018). The impact of these ideologies can be seen in the words of one participant in Zentella's ethnographic study of Puerto Ricans in New York, who reported that, 'I gotta let some of it go. If I start hanging on to my culture, speaking Spanish, it's gonna hold me back' (Zentella, 1997a: 142). In some cases, in addition to symbolic violence, Spanish-speakers have also been subjected to physical violence, and the memories and trauma of having been punished for speaking Spanish can lead them to prioritize English. For example, one woman in García-Bedolla's (2003: 269) research explained that in her grandmother's youth, 'they would hit them and stuff when they spoke Spanish in schools, so she didn't teach her kids how to speak Spanish.'

Spanish-speaking parents whose children don't speak Spanish sometimes express regret about not having managed to pass on Spanish. However, as Velázquez (2018: 77) astutely puts it, 'the transmission of Spanish [is] one of the many tasks in the constellation of child-rearing duties.' In a context in which there is little educational support for Spanish or other minority languages, the burden falls largely on the parents and other caregivers. For those who need to work outside of the home, this can be a challenge, as the following mother explained:

> I think a lot of parents are working and I don't think they have the time to get their kids. ... It's a lot of work. And I have to say that first hand that I wish I could sit and spend a couple of hours a day because I'm sure I could teach them as well as the school could and you know that's so expensive. We don't have the time. You know we are living at such a fast paced life. Everything is so expensive, two working parents, you are constantly going, so you basically just let it go, and they start to lose it. (Pease-Alvarez, 2003: 18)

It's not just parents who lament their children's lack of Spanish ability, but also the adolescents and adults that they become (García Bedolla, 2003; Goble, 2016; Villa & Rivera-Mills, 2009). For many Latinxs who don't speak Spanish, this comes with a sense of shame that has some similarity to the shame their parents or grandparents experienced if they did not speak English (García Bedolla, 2003). However, it is often accompanied by a sense of loss, as well as feelings of cultural insecurity or inauthenticity. Indeed, the ideology that sees speaking Spanish is a requirement of 'authentic' Latinx identity is widespread among Latinxs as well as non-Latinxs (see Chapter 6). These feelings are evident in the following quote from a Mexican American teacher interviewed by Goble:

> a huge barrier for me learning Spanish was also fear of shaming myself because, because Spanish is something that I am supposed to know, because I'm Mexican ... If I say it, and I mispronounce something, that would be really embarrassing to me. I was always afraid of sounding like a White girl, trying to speak Spanish. That was – that was a huge fear of mine, and so it was better to just not try at all. (adapted from Goble, 2016: 43–44)

In this excerpt we see how linguistic insecurity can lead to avoidance, which in turn can contribute to language loss. Further, some Latinxs who don't speak Spanish feel that it has impacted their relationships with those that do. For example, a participant in García Bedolla's (2003: 270) research reported that, 'some people think I'm snobby because I don't speak Spanish'.

In the next section we will examine in more detail, and in a more systematic way, the societal and individual factors that that shape language maintenance and shift.

Factors Impacting Language Maintenance and Shift

Having looked at the patterns of language knowledge and use among US Latinxs and Spanish-speakers, we now consider some group and individual factors that play a role. In this section we focus on social structures and societal values, and the practices that result from them, which can foster or inhibit the use of minority languages such as Spanish.

Ethnolinguistic vitality

One of the most well-known frameworks for the analysis of a minority language's chances of survival is Giles *et al.*'s (1977) model of **ethnolinguistic vitality**, which presupposes that the maintenance of minority languages and ethnic group identities go hand in hand. Although the ethnolinguistic vitality model has received a fair amount of criticism, it is still widely used to analyze language maintenance and/or shift in contact settings around the world (Velázquez, 2018; Yagmur & Ehala, 2011). Further, despite its limitations, one valuable aspect of the ethnolinguistic vitality model is that it takes three different kinds of factors into account, together with group members' subjective perception of those factors. The three types of factors that shape patterns of language maintenance are *demographic factors, status factors* and *institutional support factors* (Giles *et al.*, 1977; Harwood *et al.*, 1994).

Demographic factors include the overall number of speakers, their geographic distribution and density, and the degree to which they are isolated from each other as well as from the rest of society. Large, dense concentrations of ethnolinguistic group members isolated from other groups are thought to promote maintenance. A low rate of **exogamy** (i.e. marriage outside the group) compared to **endogamy** (i.e. marriage within the group) is also seen as contributing to maintenance. The potential impact of exogamy and endogamy rates is highlighted by a recent survey showing that 92% of Latinx parents with a Latinx spouse or partner say they speak Spanish to their children but only 55% of Latinx parents with a non-Latinx partner do so (Lopez *et al.*, 2018). This is particularly noteworthy given the rising rates of exogamy among Latinxs and especially US-born Latinxs; in 2015, approximately 39% of US-born Latinx newlyweds were married to non-Latinxs (Livingston & Brown, 2017).

Status factors are related to how the minority language is viewed both within the ethnolinguistic group and by the broader society, and they include social status or prestige, cultural status and sociohistorical status. Negative ideologies such as racism, linguistic subordination and **xenophobia** can also be considered to be status factors. Finally, *institutional support factors* include the availability of minority language media (such as websites, radio and TV as well as newspapers), religious institutions and/or services, and government services in the minority language.

One key type of institutional support factor is whether education is available in the minority language and if so, what kind of education. Does the public school system offer bilingual or dual immersion programs? Or are classes in the minority language limited to a few hours a week, available only in upper grades, or are they not offered at all (except perhaps by the local community in evening classes or weekend schools)? As we explore in Chapter 9, the importance of minority language literacy and education in promoting language maintenance is one reason why researchers call for more Spanish language educational opportunities (e.g. Valdés, 2015).

Of course, the three types of factors outlined by Giles *et al.* (1977) are not independent of each other. Demographic and status factors clearly play a role in the availability of institutional support: when there are a large number of speakers of a minority language concentrated in a particular area it is easier to establish community media and religious institutions (or get existing institutions to offer programming) in that language. Similarly, policies requiring local and national governments to provide services or materials in minority languages are sometimes contingent on the number or percentage of speakers in a particular area. For example, in the US, the Voting Rights Act only requires that minority language electoral materials be available in districts where a certain percentage of the population speak that language and have limited English-speaking ability (see Chapter 8).

There have been several critiques of the ethnolinguistic vitality model. For one, the various factors are difficult to measure. Moreover, no single factor is sufficient to explain patterns of language maintenance and loss, and it is not clear which ones should be considered most important, making the model extremely difficult to test (Husband & Khan, 1982). In addition, the model focuses only on the characteristics of minority groups, thus failing to take the power and practices of dominant groups into account (Tollefson, 1991). Further, societal ideologies about languages in general, rather than a specific language or ethnolinguistic group, can also have an impact on vitality. For example, the notion that monolingualism is the norm, and that multilingualism is divisive, can have an impact on patterns of language use (Valdés, 2015), just as attitudes towards any specific language can.

Other limitations of the ethnolinguistic vitality model are related to the assumption of a one-to-one relationship between group identity and language. While speaking a minority language is sometimes seen as key to 'authentic' group identity, this isn't always or automatically the case. Think, for example, of various ethnic groups in the US such as Italians and Polish; many people claim these identities despite being monolingual in English. Further, ethnolinguistic groups are not homogenous, and the model fails to consider factors such as social class, age, gender and/or subgroups (Husband & Khan, 1982). This critique is evocative of **intersectionality**, an analytic construct that we explore in greater depth in Chapter 6. Intersectional approaches stress that people don't belong to just one identity category (such as gender, class or race) but rather they belong to several different categories at the same time, and their experiences are shaped by the ways in which these categories interact with one another (Crenshaw, 1989). For example, it would be a mistake to lump all Spanish-speakers into a single category without also considering their race, class and gender identities, among others. In fact, in their longitudinal study of the children of immigrants from a variety of countries, Portes and Rumbaut (2001) found that these factors were predictors of language maintenance. A related limitation of the ethnolinguistic vitality model is that it focuses on factors impacting groups and is unable to explain differences among individuals belonging to the same group (Pauwels, 2016). It is likely as a result of these limitations that the ethnolinguistic vitality model doesn't always result in accurate predictions. In particular, minority languages are sometimes maintained in contexts where the model predicts shift (Velázquez, 2018; Yagmur & Ehala, 2011).

Social networks, family language practices and other individual differences

Because the ethnolinguistic vitality model focuses on factors impacting groups, some scholars have argued that **social network theory**, with its emphasis on individuals' relationships within and outside of groups, is better suited for explaining individual-level patterns of language maintenance and use (Pauwels, 2016). The premise of social network approaches to language is that individuals' patterns of language use derive from the people with whom they interact regularly. Thus, researchers adopting this approach examine individuals' social relationships and networks. While early research in this area looked at how relationships impacted the use and spread of linguistic features within social networks, subsequent research expanded the focus by looking at how social networks can play a role in patterns of minority language maintenance and shift (e.g. Raschka *et al.*, 2002; Stoessel, 2002).

Two features of social networks that have been the focus of analysis are density and multiplexity. Dense social networks are those networks in which lots of people in the network have ties to each other. Think, for example, of a close group of friends; everyone in the group is friends with each other. In a loose social network, in contrast, individuals have connections not shared by others, as in the case of a group of friends who come together at school or work, but outside of that context interact with a lot of other friends who don't know each other. Multiplex networks are networks in which people have multiple kinds of ties or relationships – for example, if your sister-in-law is also your colleague and your workout buddy. In the case of minority languages, it makes sense that the more a person uses the language, the more likely they are to maintain it. Thus, minority language speakers in dense, multiplex social networks that use that language are more likely to maintain it. Some research has found the make-up of individuals' social networks to be a more reliable predictor of language maintenance or shift than socio-economic status or gender (García, 2003; Milroy, 2002; Sallabank, 2010).

In recent years, scholars have noted that increased migration and mobility as well as new technologies make it easier for people to participate in dispersed networks and negotiate their identities transnationally (Coupland, 2003; De Fina & Perrino, 2013; Márquez-Reiter & Martín Rojo, 2014). The social networks of immigrants and their offspring connect them to people and languages in their countries of national origin as well as in the country where they reside, and they also consume media produced for transnational audiences. Increased mobility in recent decades means both that immigrants and their children are more likely to visit their countries of origin, and that they have a greater chance of coming into contact with more recent arrivals. Attending to these trends forces us to recognize that languages and social networks can't really be mapped onto specific locales, as people are so often on the move and may communicate with people thousands of miles away on a daily basis.

Some researchers have pointed out that in some sense, the decision about whether or not to use a minority language comes down to a series of everyday choices, both conscious and unconscious (Valdés, 2015; Velázquez, 2018). In most cases, even one's social networks involve some element of choice on the part of the individual. Thus, given that language maintenance depends on intergenerational transmission (Fishman, 1991), researchers have also begun to pay more attention to parents' and other caretakers' linguistic decisions and attitudes regarding their children's minority language maintenance (we discuss **family language policy** in more depth in Chapter 8). Still, it's important to stress that household language policies, including both adult and child language practices, don't take place in a vacuum. Instead, individual language choices are shaped by structural forces and societal ideologies (Grosjean, 1982; Valdés, 2015), and even positive attitudes toward the minority language are not sufficient to ensure maintenance (Velázquez, 2018).

Indeed, while it is crucial for parents and caretakers to understand the factors that can shape children's language acquisition and use, this doesn't mean that we should treat intergenerational or family language transmission as something that depends solely on the decisions of individual speakers, as doing so would ignore the structural constraints on parental agency. As Zentella (1997a) demonstrated in her landmark ethnographic study of language shift among Puerto Ricans in New York, racism, linguistic subordination and economic precarity are key factors constraining parental language decisions and impacting language shift. Similarly, a person's desire to maintain Spanish may not be sufficient to make that happen and, despite common feelings of guilt regarding language loss, individual agency is constrained by structural factors. Thus, in addition to looking at social networks, individual factors and personal decisions, we shouldn't lose sight of the ways in which societal language ideologies and policies impact groups as well as the people within them.

Spanish Language Maintenance and Shift in the US

Historically, immigrants to the US have largely followed a three-generation pattern of language shift to English, with the immigrant generation being mostly dominant in the non-English language, the second generation being bilingual, and the third (and subsequent) generations being monolingual in English (Alba, 2004; Rivera-Mills, 2012; Veltman, 2000). However, some observers have expressed doubts that these patterns would continue to hold for Spanish, given the large number of speakers of Spanish and their relative high density in certain parts of the country – demographic factors that the ethnolinguistic vitality framework posits should contribute to maintenance. In some cases, these doubts are rooted in racially inflected anxiety and entangled with the unfounded and inaccurate claims that Spanish-speakers do not want to learn English, such as we saw in the Tom Brokaw quote presented earlier in this chapter, as well as a broader discourse about Latinxs' supposed unwillingness and inability to assimilate (Chavez, 2013). Further, some people have suggested that greater 'tolerance' of multilingualism and multiculturalism makes it less likely that recent immigrants would assimilate linguistically. We examine patterns of Spanish maintenance and loss in the next sections.

Shift to English

In our earlier discussion of ACS data, we compared the English ability of immigrants and US-born Latinxs and Spanish-speakers, but we did not take into account how many generations someone's family had been in the US. In order to get a better sense of the intergenerational patterns of language transmission and use, Alba (2004) did just that. Specifically, he compared the ACS language data for first-, second- and third-generation immigrants (i.e. those who immigrated themselves, the children of immigrants and the grandchildren of immigrants). He found that virtually all US-born Latinxs speak English well, but he noted an important difference between the second and third generations in terms of their Spanish use: 85% of the second generation spoke Spanish at home but only 18% of the third generation did. Alba interpreted this as evidence of the endurance of the three-generation pattern of shift to English.

Based on the high percentage of people in the second generation reported to speak Spanish at home, Alba also concluded that second-generation bilingualism is widespread. However, while at first glance this conclusion seems reasonable, it must be taken with a pinch of salt. As we discussed above, the Census Bureau doesn't ask how well individuals speak Spanish (see Figure 2.2), and thus the count of 'Spanish-speaking' persons includes people with only limited Spanish-speaking ability as well as those who are completely proficient (or Spanish dominant), and there is no way of knowing the relative proportion of each. Because even individuals with very limited Spanish ability are included, Census Bureau statistics may give an inflated sense of Spanish maintenance and Spanish–English bilingualism (Leeman, 2018c). This is also the case for research that relies on the Census Bureau's statistics, such as the *Instituto Cervantes*' reports on the number of Spanish-speakers in different countries around the world (e.g. *Instituto Cervantes*, 2018). For this reason, in order to get a more accurate picture of patterns of language knowledge among the second and subsequent generations, we turn to data from the large-scale surveys of Latinxs carried out by the Pew Research Center, a non-governmental organization that conducts surveys and public opinion polls on a wide array of political and social issues.

In contrast with the Census Bureau's ACS, the Pew Center surveys ask how well respondents speak both Spanish and English. By inquiring about speaking ability in both languages, the Pew Center is able to compare respondents' ability in Spanish and English, and thus get a better sense of where they fall on the bilingual continuum. Regarding English, the Pew Center's findings mirror those of the Census Bureau in that they show that nearly all US-born Latinxs are proficient in English (Taylor *et al.*, 2012). But of greater interest for the question of Spanish maintenance are the data for the responses from the Spanish-speaking ability question. The results show that Spanish knowledge diminishes between generations; 82% of the so-called **second generation** (i.e. the US-born children of immigrants) speak Spanish 'very well' or 'pretty well,' but only 47% of the third generation do (Taylor *et al.*, 2012).

Lopez *et al.*'s (2017) analysis of a subsequent Pew Center survey shows a similar trend. In that analysis, researchers compared individuals' speaking ability in English and Spanish: respondents who reported speaking both languages 'very well' or 'pretty well' were considered bilingual, and the remainder were classified as either 'English dominant' or 'Spanish dominant' (so people classified as 'dominant' in a language also included monolinguals). The foreign-born were most likely to be Spanish dominant, although almost one-third of them were bilingual. In the second generation, almost everyone was bilingual or English dominant, and people in the third generation or higher were most often English dominant, with only a quarter reporting speaking both languages well (see Table 2.3).

Taking into account these data as well as the ACS statistics on English knowledge and home use that we presented earlier, we have seen that almost all Latinxs born in the US are proficient in English, and the vast majority are either English dominant or bilingual, while the grandchildren of immigrants are either monolingual in English or English dominant. This pattern is consistent not only in studies based on Census Bureau and Pew Center data (e.g. Alba, 2004; Lopez *et al.*, 2017; Taylor *et al.*, 2012; Veltman, 2000), but also ethnographic research (e.g. Schecter & Bayley, 2002; Zentella, 1997a) and studies using a combination of surveys and interviews (e.g. Bills *et al.*, 1999; Porcel, 2006; Portes & Rumbaut, 2001; Rivera-Mills, 2001). In other words, among the children and grandchildren of Spanish-speaking immigrants, the tendency for language shift to English parallels the linguistic trajectories of previous immigrant groups. This pattern holds even in Miami, with its high density of Spanish-speakers and their relatively higher socio-economic status (Carter & Lynch, 2015).

Table 2.3 *English- and Spanish-speaking ability among Latinxs*

	English dominant or monolingual	***Bilingual***	***Spanish dominant or monolingual***
Foreign-born	7%	32%	61%
Second generation	43%	51%	6%
Third or higher generation	75%	24%	–
All Latinxs	28%	36%	36%

Source: Lopez *et al.* (2017).

The well-documented pattern of language shift among the children and grandchildren of Spanish-speaking immigrants demonstrates that the apparent vitality and continued presence of Spanish has been the result of continued immigration, rather than intergenerational language transmission and maintenance (Jenkins, 2018; Rumbaut, 2009; Silva-Corvalán, 2004; Veltman, 2000). Further, in addition to disproving the enduring myth that Spanish-speaking immigrants and their offspring don't learn English, the pattern of intergenerational shift makes it clear that it is Spanish, not English, that is at risk. Nonetheless, despite the universality of English acquisition and the predominance of language shift, we don't want to suggest that Spanish language loss is universal or inevitable, as we'll see in the next section.

Spanish maintenance against the odds

As we discussed earlier in this chapter, the usefulness of the Census Bureau's statistics about Spanish in the US is constrained by the questions that they don't ask as much as by the ones that they do (Leeman, 2004, 2018c). In particular, we saw that the lack of a question about how well respondents speak non-English languages prevents us from gauging the degree of bilingualism among home speakers of Spanish. Another gap in the data is that the ACS doesn't ask respondents what language(s) they *know*, but only whether they speak a language other than English at home (see Figure 2.2). As a result, people who know Spanish but don't speak it at home are invisible in the Census Bureau's statistics and thus some Spanish maintenance goes unrecorded (Leeman, 2004).

In fact, various researchers have found evidence of Spanish maintenance (in addition to English proficiency) into and past the third generation. For example, Alba (2004) found that in some border communities, such as Laredo, Texas, more than 40% of the third generation report speaking at least some Spanish at home. And in their research examining language maintenance among the children and grandchildren of immigrants in Southern California, Rumbaut *et al.* (2006) found that 17% of third-generation Mexican Americans surveyed spoke Spanish fluently. More anecdotally, Carter and Lynch (2015) attest that it is not hard to find third-generation bilinguals with high levels of Spanish proficiency in Miami, while Rivera-Mills (2012: 28) reports a 'resilient use of Spanish into the fourth generation' in her Arizona study. So too, in Anderson-Mejías' (2005) Texas research, there were several fourth- and fifth-generation participants fluent in Spanish. Some Spanish-speakers actively resist the pressure to assimilate to English monolingualism by using Spanish in their public and private lives. For some, the anti-Spanish and anti-Latinx policies and discourse of recent years have strengthened their resolve to do so (Sánchez-Muñoz & Amezcua, 2019). One manifestation of this resistance on social media is the hashtag #stillspeakingspanishyque.

García *et al.* (2001) also point to the ongoing use of Spanish by Puerto Ricans in New York. Their work challenges the binary conceptualization of language knowledge and use in studies of language maintenance (i.e. either you know a language or you don't; either you're speaking English or you're speaking Spanish), as well as the assumption that language shift is a one-way street. Instead, García and her colleagues describe Puerto Ricans' patterns of language use as a *vaivén* ('swaying, back-and-forth'), emphasizing not only the back-and-forth connections and mobility of Puerto Ricans in New York and Puerto Rico, but also the continued use, and symbolic importance, of Spanish even among people who more traditional, binary models might consider to have undergone shift to English.

Factors impacting Spanish maintenance or shift

In our discussion of the ethnolinguistic vitality framework we outlined the three kinds of factors that shape patterns of language maintenance and shift. In the previous sections, we saw that while favorable demographic factors can contribute to somewhat higher rates of Spanish maintenance, they are insufficient to buck the overall trend of shift to English. In particular, areas with greater numbers and density of Spanish-speakers do tend to have more Spanish maintenance, but members of the third and subsequent generations who have maintained Spanish are still in the minority.

As for status factors, language ideologies constructing the US as an English-speaking nation, the negative portrayal of Spanish and the racialization of Latinxs are all aspects of the subordination of Spanish that contribute to its intergenerational loss. These ideologies and processes (which we discuss in Chapter 4) also shape institutional support factors. Generally speaking, there is little governmental support for Spanish maintenance, and educational policies also favor shift to English. Indeed, for the children of immigrants who learn Spanish at home, the start of school often also marks the transition to English dominance. In contrast, when educational policy promotes **additive bilingualism**, this has been shown to have a positive impact on Spanish maintenance (see Chapter 9).

In addition to these group factors and societal trends, researchers have also examined individual factors. For example, there are differences among siblings based on birth order. Specifically, first- and/or second-born children are more likely to retain Spanish than their younger siblings (Beaudrie & Ducar, 2005; Parada, 2016; Valdés, 2005). Gender has also been seen to play a role in some cases, with girls showing higher levels of proficiency than boys (Arriagada, 2005; Lutz, 2006; Portes & Rumbaut, 2001; Zentella, 1997a). Some of these gendered patterns might be accounted for by social networks; among the Puerto Rican children in Zentella's (1997a) study, girls were expected to help around the house and stick close to home, and thus were more likely to interact with other Puerto Ricans. In contrast, boys were allowed more freedom to go out of the neighborhood and thus developed more friendships with children who did not speak Spanish. Further, mothers seem to play a more important role in intergenerational transmission than do fathers (Arriagada, 2005; Velázquez, 2018). Cashman's (2017) research on patterns of language use among queer Latinxs (discussed further in Chapter 6) offers an important reminder both that gender identities are not binary (i.e. there are more identities than just 'male' and 'female'), and that there is a need to take intersectional identities into account. Along these lines, Cashman found that for some of her participants, the homophobia of their biological families led to severed ties and reduced participation in Spanish-speaking networks.

Although societal forces work against Spanish maintenance, parents' and caretakers' efforts to use and pass their language on to children can serve as a counter-balance (Fishman, 2001). As we noted above, parents are not always successful in their efforts to transmit their language to their children, and for this reason researchers have sought to investigate the language maintenance success stories in order to identify the specific behaviors and language practices that have had a positive impact (e.g. Schecter & Bayley, 2002; Velázquez, 2018). One finding emerging from such research is that the desire to pass on Spanish is not enough on its own. Instead, language socialization through shared activities and sustained interactions in Spanish was important as was participation in language-focused and literacy-related events, whether these were centered on religious activities, schoolwork, movie watching or pleasure reading (e.g. Schecter & Bayley, 2002; Velázquez, 2018).

It is not only parents and caretakers who make decisions for their children; children themselves and the adults they become also obviously play a role. People also change over time, and some who reject Spanish as children later make a conscious effort to recover and strengthen their ability. Silva-Corvalán (1994) uses the phrase '**cyclical bilingualism**' to refer to the phenomenon of people learning Spanish at home from their parents, undergoing shift to English after entering school, and then seeking to reacquire Spanish in their teens or twenties. It's likely that some such individuals are included in the reports of fourth- and fifth-generation Spanish-speakers cited above. Relatedly, Villa and Rivera-Mills (2009) use the phrase 'reacquisition generation' in reference to **heritage speakers of Spanish** who enroll in Spanish courses and, like Silva-Corvalán, they stress the motivation as being to (re)connect with ethnolinguistic heritage. Just as the loss of Spanish is often accompanied by shame and regret, maintaining Spanish and/or passing it on to one's children is often associated with pride and satisfaction as well as other positive social indicators (Portes & Rumbaut, 2005; Schecter & Bayley, 2002; Velázquez, 2018).

Conclusions and Connections

In this chapter we delved deeper into the statistics about Spanish and Spanish-speakers in the US and used these statistics to demonstrate their great diversity. Speakers of Spanish claim a vast range of racial identities and national origins, and they include recent immigrants as well as people whose families have been in the US for many generations. So too, they live in many different kinds of places across the country, with some living in communities where a majority of people speak Spanish at home, and others in communities where Spanish is quite rare. The next chapter will offer a deeper exploration of this diversity, as well as a review of the history of Spanish and the people who have spoken it in what is now the US since Christopher Columbus arrived in the Americas more than five centuries ago.

The statistics on language knowledge and use that we examined in this chapter show that while not all Spanish-speaking immigrants are proficient in English (especially recent arrivals), essentially everyone in the second and subsequent generations is. Spanish maintenance, in contrast, is more variable. On one hand, the children and grandchildren of Spanish-speaking immigrants largely follow the three-generational pattern typical of earlier European immigrants. In other words, although about half of the second generation is bilingual (with most of the remainder dominant in English), by the third generation English is the norm. On the other hand, exceptions to this rule demonstrate that Spanish maintenance or reacquisition is possible. In Chapter 4 we critically analyze the language ideologies that work against Spanish maintenance, while in Chapters 5 and 6 we delve deeper into the role of Spanish in Latinx identities. Chapter 9 examines the role of ideologies in educational policies and the ways in which English-only policies contribute to language shift, as well as alternative approaches that can allow multilingualism to flourish. Of course, one goal of this book is to help make that possible.

Discussion Questions and Activities for Chapter 2

(1) Read Daniel José Older's 'I rejected Spanish as a kid. Now I wish we'd embrace our native languages,' published in the 2019 volume, *The Good Immigrant: 26 Writers Reflect on America* (available online via *Time Magazine* at https://time.com/5528434/daniel-jose-older-spanish). Analyze his childhood rejection of Spanish and the societal factors that influenced it, as well as his sense of loss. What made him want to recover and strengthen his ability in Spanish and how did he go about doing so? Additionally, you may wish to compare Older's experience with the myth that immigrants and their children refuse to learn English.

(2) In recent years, various organizations have pointed out that there are now more Spanish-speakers in the US than in many Latin American countries. Along the same lines, the *Instituto Cervantes* (2018) has suggested that US will surpass Spain in the number of speakers of Spanish (see, for example, 'Number of Spanish speakers tops 577 million' from the newspaper *El País*, available in English at https://elpais.com/elpais/2018/07/05/inenglish/1530780465_701866.html?fbclid=IwAR2k3wy1fLg_8czqbxhALxFqIeQhA0TgQuL71pjbo1zaTw8gz-ag7-iPUZA and in Spanish at https://elpais.com/cultura/2018/07/03/actualidad/1530619272_823616.html). What is this prediction based on? What factors might limit the growth in the US' Spanish-speaking population? How are Spanish-speakers and the status of Spanish in the US different from other countries? Finally, why might the *Instituto Cervantes* (which receives funding from the government of Spain) be interested in publicizing and celebrating the number of speakers of Spanish in the US?

(3) In our discussions of demographics and patterns of language knowledge and use, we have made reference to different 'generations' of immigrants and their offspring. Consider the connotations of labeling someone as a 'first-generation American' versus a 'second-generation immigrant.' Which makes the most sense and why? In some discussions of immigration, people use the term 'generation 1.5' to refer to people who immigrated to the US as children. In what ways is generation 1.5 similar to and different from first- and second-generation

immigrants? What patterns of language knowledge and use would you predict for generation 1.5? Are there any pros or cons to using this term?

(4) One issue that we return to repeatedly in this book is the role of Spanish in the construction of Latinx identity. In other words, can someone 'really' be Latinx without speaking Spanish? Can you think of examples from public discourse or interactions with friends in which the issue came up? Watch Remezcla's *Do you have to speak Spanish to be Latino?* (https://www.youtube.com/watch?v=yKmrVdF17Lw), Mitú's video *Are you a REAL Latino if you DON'T speak Spanish?* (https://www.youtube.com/watch?v=BNxPuQaGmNM) and BBC Mundo's video of rapper Andrew Figgy Baby Figueroa (https://www.bbc.com/news/av/world-us-canada-50395013/i-m-hispanic-but-can-t-speak-spanish). Discuss your examples and/or the videos in light of the statistics and patterns of language maintenance and shift discussed in this chapter. Do you think demographic trends will have an impact on how people understand the relationship of Spanish to Latinx identity?

(5) In this chapter we identified several challenges in using Census Bureau data to determine how many people speak Spanish in the US. Sum up these challenges (as well as any others you might identify) and consider how they could be addressed. If it were up to you, how would you change the Census Bureau's language questions (see Figure 2.2)? Are there any other language-related questions you would want to add? If you couldn't make any changes to the Census Bureau's language questions, what other methodologies might you use to complement the data and gain a better sense of how many people speak Spanish in the US?

Note

(1) Moreover, Brokaw seems to simultaneously suggest two contradictory 'problems': (1) a high rate of intermarriage; and (2) a failure of Latinxs to integrate and assimilate.

Further Reading and Resources

García Bedolla, L. (2003) The identity paradox: Latino language, politics and selective disassociation. *Latino Studies* 1 (2), 264–283.

Leeman, J. (2004) Racializing language: A history of linguistic ideologies in the US census. *Journal of Language and Politics* 3 (3), 507–534.

Schecter, S.R. and Bayley, R. (2002) *Language as Cultural Practice: Mexicanos En El Norte*. Mahwah, NJ: Lawrence Erlbaum.

Velázquez, I. (2018) *Household Perspectives on Minority Language Maintenance and Loss: Language in the Small Spaces*. Bristol: Multilingual Matters.

Zentella, A.C. (1997a) *Growing Up Bilingual*. Oxford: Blackwell.

Chapter 3

The History of Spanish and Spanish-speakers in the US

> **Objectives**
>
> To examine the history of Spanish in the US, including Spanish exploration and conquest in North America and the Caribbean, US territorial expansion and the annexation of lands inhabited by Spanish-speakers, and the migration of Spanish-speakers to the US, and to analyze how history and the ways in which it has been represented shape the current status of Spanish and Spanish-speakers, as well to consider symbolic implications of the representation of that history.

Introduction

In Chapter 2 we challenged the myth that people in the US who speak Spanish are primarily immigrants by pointing out that the majority of people who report speaking Spanish at home were born in the US are US-born. Further, while there is no denying that immigration to the US has played (and continues to play) a key role in the presence of Spanish in the US, it would be a mistake to classify Spanish exclusively as an immigrant language. Although conventional accounts of US history typically start with the English colonies at Jamestown, Virginia in 1607 and Plymouth, Massachusetts in 1620, the Spanish government had established a settlement in Virginia 80 years earlier (Taylor, 2002; Weber, 2000).[1] Thus, Spanish was spoken in what is now the US before English was, and it has been spoken continuously since that time (Gonzalez, 2011). Advocating for the study of Spanish, Thomas Jefferson referenced the long presence of Spanish in North America, as well as Spanish-speakers' arrival prior to English-speakers, and observed that 'the antient [sic] part of American history is written chiefly in Spanish' (Jefferson, 1787, cited in Boyd, 1955). Jefferson's remark is even more accurate today than at the time he wrote it because in the following century the US annexed thousands of acres of land that were under Spanish rule in Jefferson's time. Like Jefferson, we believe that knowing the history of Spanish and Spanish-speakers is crucial for a full understanding of US history. Even more relevant for this book, we argue that it is crucial for the understanding of Spanish in the US, as the sociolinguistics and sociopolitics of Spanish (as well as its linguistic characteristics) are rooted in this history.

The version of history typically taught in US schools frames the development of the US as a westward expansion of English colonial settlers and their descendants, largely downplaying the role, and in some cases even the existence, of Native peoples, enslaved Africans and other European colonists (Taylor, 2002). As a result, many people in the US are unaware that large swaths of North America were claimed by the Spanish long before they became part of the US. For this reason, this chapter gives a brief history of the Spanish colonial possessions that were eventually incorporated into the US. These possessions include essentially all of the present

Figure 3.1 A 1765 map of North America showing British and Spanish colonial possessions
Source: Library of Congress, Geography and Map Division.

territory of the US west of the Mississippi River, as well as Florida and Puerto Rico (see Figure 3.1). This colonial history is reflected in the names of hundreds of US rivers, mountains, towns and even several states (including Arizona and Colorado), although the Spanish origin of these names is not always recognized by present-day inhabitants (Gonzalez, 2011). The US' annexation of these lands via military force, as well as the broader intervention in the Caribbean and Central America, are what transformed the US from 'an isolated yeoman's democracy into a major world empire' (Gonzalez, 2011: 28). In this chapter, we explain the Spanish conquest in North America and the subsequent annexation of lands by the US; key moments in this history are shown on the timeline in Figure 3.2.

In the past few decades, historians and other scholars have sought to correct the Eurocentric and Anglocentric triumphalist versions of US history by paying more attention to all that they leave out or downplay. In particular, researchers, educators and activists have forcefully dispelled the myth that European colonists encountered 'virgin' lands by pointing to the many millions of Native peoples that lived in North America prior to European arrival. While the exact size of the pre-contact population is a matter of some debate, the prevailing academic view puts it somewhere between 7 and 18 million people (Daniels, 1992; Gonzalez,

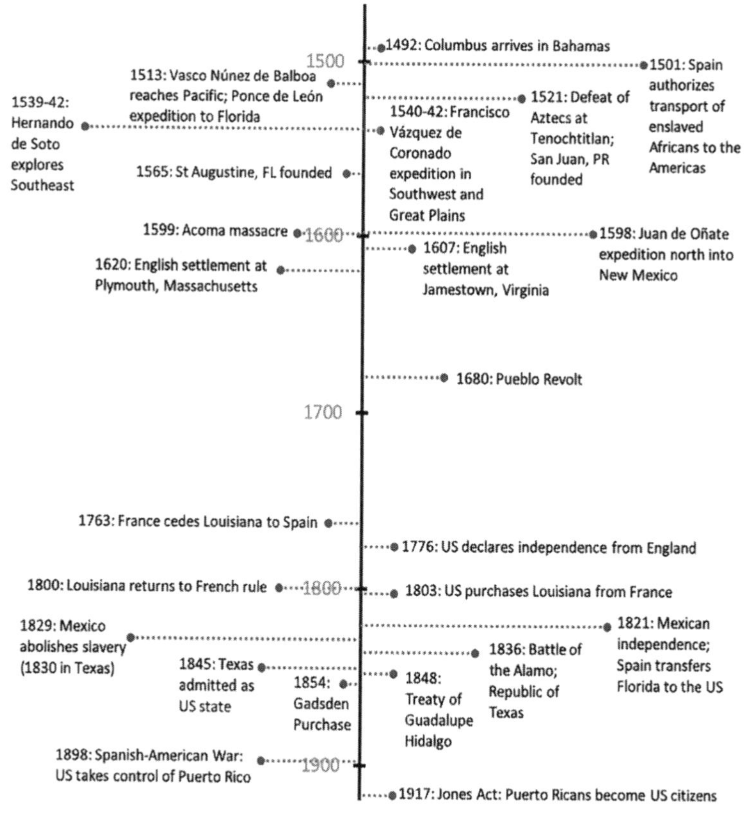

Figure 3.2 Timeline of Spanish conquest and US annexation

2011; Taylor, 2013). The war, slavery, torture, disease, starvation and murder that resulted from European colonization caused the death of 100 million Indigenous people in the Western hemisphere over the next 400 years, which has been called the biggest genocide in the history of the world (Stannard, 1993). Scholars have also brought new attention to the centrality of slavery in the English colonial project and ultimately in the development of US wealth and power (e.g. Baptist, 2016; Beckert & Rockman, 2016). In addition, historians have also sought to include other European colonies in North America, including those of the Dutch, French and Spanish, within accounts of the history of the US (e.g. Taylor, 2002).

Efforts to offer a more complete picture of US history represent a welcome correction to the more traditional whitewashed accounts. However, attention to the Spanish colonial history of the US is not exclusively a recent phenomenon. In fact, since the early 20th century, various social actors have sought to highlight the Spanish history particularly of the Southwest but also of Florida. Later in the chapter we explore this celebration of Spanish colonization, its connection to specific economic and political interests and the ways in which it also glosses over the brutality of European conquest and the subjugation and decimation of Native peoples and cultures. We will also look at protests against the romanticized portrayal of Spanish conquistadors and colonists, drawing parallels to recent challenges to the racist glorification of Confederate leaders. Our discussion emphasizes the continued relevance of history, and of historical representation, to current debates about national identity and belonging.

US intervention in Latin America did not end with the annexation of the lands that now comprise the Southwestern US and Puerto Rico. Instead, the US continued to exert economic, political and military power in the Caribbean as well as Central and South America. Whereas 19th and early 20th century intervention was focused on allowing US businesses to maximize profit, primarily by supporting repressive governments that kept workers in line, in the second half of the 20th century Cold War concerns (i.e. stopping communist movements) also played a crucial role. US policies and involvement have contributed to economic and political instability, as well as social unrest, which in turn have led to increased migration to the US. The need for workers in the US has also attracted immigrants, sometimes as the result of active recruiting efforts by businesses. Thus, despite the long history of Spanish in the US, immigration has been a key factor in its continued presence and strength, given the pattern of language shift that results in the third generation being likely to be predominantly or exclusively English-speaking. For this reason, in the second half of chapter we look at the history of Latin American migration to the US, and we briefly consider current immigration policy.

Spanish Colonization in North America and the Caribbean

With the arrival of Christopher Columbus in the Bahamas in 1492, the Spanish began a centuries-long period of exploration, conquest and colonization in the Caribbean and throughout the Americas. Columbus and his men claimed the islands of Cuba and

Hispaniola (shared by the present-day countries of Haiti and the Dominican Republic). After returning to Spain and impressing the Spanish monarchs Isabelle and Ferdinand with tales of gold and riches, Columbus again sailed to the Caribbean, bringing more ships, men, and livestock, as well as plans to create a Spanish empire in the Americas.

In the Caribbean the Spanish colonists enslaved the Indigenous Taíno population, forcing them to work on sugar plantations and ranches as well as in the mines. As a result of the brutal treatment and exploitation they suffered at the hand of the conquerors, together with the devastating effects of exposure to European diseases, hundreds of thousands of Taínos died. According to Taylor (2002), the number of Taínos on Hispaniola dropped from at least 300,000 in 1492 to just 500 in 1548, a 98% reduction in just over 50 years. Others put the original number higher and the speed of the devastation even faster (Gonzalez, 2011). With the decline of the Taínos, their Arawak language was lost. A few Arawak **borrowings** into Spanish (and English via Spanish) have endured, including *huracán, tabaco* and *guayaba* ('hurricane, tobacco, guava'). And many Puerto Ricans of all ethnoracial backgrounds refer to the island as *Boríquen* or *Borínquen*, and to themselves as *Boricuas*, all of which derive from Arawak terms. In recent years there has been a growing movement to reclaim and reconstruct Taíno identity, and to recognize the endurance of some aspects of Taíno and other Native Caribbean cultures (González, 2018).

Spanish explorers used their Caribbean settlements as the point of departure for expeditions northward up the Atlantic Coast, through the Gulf of Mexico, up the Mississippi River and westward to Central America. In 1513 Ponce de León led the first European expedition to the Florida Peninsula, which was inhabited by the Apalachee, Calusa and Timuca, among other Native groups. In the same year, Vasco Núnez de Balboa crossed Panama and became the first European to see the Pacific Ocean, which he claimed, together with all the lands touching it, for Spain. On their expeditions, Spanish explorers ravaged villages and captured Native peoples to replace the Taínos in the Caribbean colonies. These newer captives also proved susceptible to European diseases such as measles, smallpox and influenza, and the Spanish slavers took captives from increasingly distant villages all around the Gulf of Mexico (Taylor, 2013). In 1501 they had also begun to bring enslaved Africans to toil in the Caribbean.

The Native peoples of North America included a multitude of different groups with tremendous cultural and linguistic diversity. They spoke at least 375 distinct languages and differed in their rituals, beliefs and social organization (Mithun, 2001; Taylor, 2002). For example, in the Southwest, the Acoma, Hopi, Zuni, and other groups collectively known as the 'Pueblo Indians,' lived in sedentary agriculture-based societies. In contrast, the diverse Native groups along the Northern Pacific coast relied on hunting, fishing and gathering (Taylor, 2002). Native peoples did not think of themselves as belonging to 'a common category until named and treated so by the colonial invaders' (Taylor, 2002: 12). Enslaved Africans were also culturally and linguistically diverse; they included Ashanti, Fulani, Ibo, Malagasy, Mandingo and Yoruba people, among other groups (Taylor, 2002). In Chapter 5 we discuss **racialization**, the sociopolitical and ideological process in which people are lumped together within a single category, assigned a shared racial identity and treated as inherently different and inferior to dominant groups.

In 1521, Hernán Cortés, accompanied by thousands of Indigenous troops who were enemies of the Aztecs, took Tenochtitlan (now Mexico City), the center of the Aztec empire.

Amazed by the incredible riches of the Aztecs, and having heard rumors of gold farther north, Spain sent Hernando de Soto to explore Florida and the Southeast, while Francisco Vázquez de Coronado headed north from Mexico into the Southwest and the Great Plains. Everywhere they went, death and destruction went with them in the form of massacres, exploitation and/or disease. By the mid-16th century, the Spanish empire encompassed lands and peoples deep into North America, as well as in the Caribbean and South America. However, Spain did not settle all their newly claimed possessions to an equal degree. For example, although they explored the Mississippi River basin and claimed Louisiana for Spain, no permanent settlements were established. And despite Spain's early 16th century claim to all lands touching the Pacific, Spanish settlement of the coast of present-day California didn't begin until much later, in the 18th century.

Both in Spain and in its colonies, the monarchy and the Catholic Church were closely intertwined, and the conversion of Native peoples to Catholicism went hand in hand with their subjugation to the Spanish Crown. As such, and in light of the perceived need for loyal Spanish subjects, Spanish missions also played a key role in the Spanish colonial project. Spanish authorities hoped that Franciscan friars could help consolidate Spanish power as effectively, and less expensively, than could be done through military force (Taylor, 2002). The Franciscans established missions in Florida, California and the Southwest, in many cases close to existing Native villages. Present-day US cities that were founded by Catholic missionaries include San Antonio, El Paso, San Diego, Los Angeles and San Francisco, among others (Gonzalez, 2011). Many missions are still standing today (see Figure 3.3, and visit the California State Parks' webpage for information about the 21 Franciscan missions in the state, at https://www.parks.ca.gov/?page_id=22722).

Figure 3.3 San Xavier Mission outside Tucson, Arizona; the mission was founded in 1692 and the current structure was completed in 1797
Source: ©Jennifer Leeman (2012).

In some cases, Spanish and Native peoples formed alliances, but it was not a relationship of equals. Instead, Spaniards tried, often successfully, to subordinate Native Americans through a variety of forced labor systems and tribute arrangements, and colonists and missionaries vied for control of Native labor and souls (Taylor, 2002). Yet Native peoples resisted in a variety of ways, including outright revolt. For example, in what is commonly referred to as *The Pueblo Revolt*, almost 17,000 Native people participated in a well-coordinated uprising against the continued exploitation and abuse by the Spanish. This late 17th century act of resistance was the 'greatest setback that natives ever inflicted on European expansion in North America' and it forced the Spanish to show somewhat greater restraint in their exercise of power and domination (Taylor, 2002: 89).

In contrast with England's North American colonies, which were made up largely of family units that segregated themselves from Native communities, most Spanish colonists were single men (Gonzalez, 2011). Sexual unions between colonists and Native women were common, and ***mestizos*** (their 'mixed' offspring) became a new social category, as did ***mulatos*** ('mulattos'), the Spanish-language term that was used for the offspring of Europeans and Africans. In the Caribbean, racial 'mixture' was typically the result of Spanish colonists fathering children with the enslaved Africans who had replaced Indigenous slaves. In Mexico, Central America and the Southwest, Mestizos and Native people were more common than people with African heritage, but all groups are attested in the historical record (Bristol, 2007; Nieto-Phillips, 2000). In contrast with the more rigid racial categories of New England, 'the increasing racial and cultural complexity of New Spain challenged the stark and simple dualities of the conquest: Spaniard and Indian, Christian and pagan, conqueror and conquered' (Taylor, 2002: 61), as well as the Black/White binary. Spanish colonial society incorporated the notion of racial mixture into social and political hierarchies via the ***castas***, the ranked racial classifications that determined everything from perceived social worth to legal and political privileges (see Chapter 5).

The encounters among peoples from Africa, the Americas and Europe obviously had, and continue to have, tremendous cultural, demographic, economic and political impact in all three places and around the world. In North America, despite the gross inequality among them, all three groups influenced the cultures of the others. For Taylor (2002: xii), 'in such exchanges and composites, we find the true measure of American distinctiveness, the true foundation for the diverse America of our time.' Because this is a book focused on language, we want to mention that some of these influences are also manifested linguistically. Numerous borrowings from various Native and African languages were incorporated into the Spanish spoken in North America and/or the Caribbean and, in some cases, around the world. Many of these are related to food, flora and fauna, or cultural expressions. African origin words include *banana* and *chango* ('monkey') (Megenney, 1983). In addition to the Taíno (Arawak) origin words mentioned earlier, others include *aguacate, cacao, chocolate* and *elote* ('avocado, cacao, chocolate, corn') of Nahuatl origin, as well as *cancha, choclo* and *puma* ('field/court, corn, puma') from Quechua. Scholars have also investigated the influence of Indigenous and African languages on the grammar and sound system of Spanish and the development of Spanish-based creole languages among African descendant populations in the Americas, as well as the impact of Spanish on Native languages (e.g. Lipski, 2005; Stolz *et al.*, 2008).

The brief history of Spanish exploration and conquest in the Caribbean and North America that we have presented in this section is, of course, also the history of the Spanish language in these same places. We want to point out that under Spanish colonial rule Spanish was the language of power, wielded by those who spoke it as another way to maintain their social and political privilege. Further, post-independence governments throughout Latin America continued to privilege Spanish and Spanish-speakers at the expense of Indigenous, African and African-descendant languages and peoples. In Chapter 5 we will focus more specifically on questions of ethnoracial identity and racialization. Here, we call attention to the elevated position of Spanish in order to highlight the broader principle that a language's status is not a characteristic of the language itself but is instead tied to the status and power of its speakers. Further, the ongoing discrimination against Indigenous peoples and their languages in Latin America shapes the experiences of Indigenous Latin American immigrants in the US. In the next section we will explain how the formerly Spanish lands, together with the Spanish-speakers who inhabited them, came to be part of the US. This annexation also marks a shift in Spanish's status in North America from a colonizing to a colonized language. Of course, the impact of that new status endures in the present-day subordination of Spanish in the US.

US Expansionism and Spanish in the US

During the 17th and 18th centuries, European powers competed for control of North American colonies while Native peoples struggled for sovereignty, resulting in various shifting alliances and armed conflicts. Following US independence from England, these conflicts continued to play out, but the new nation eventually achieved dominance over much of North America. In the 19th century, US expansionism led to tremendous territorial growth and the incorporation within the US of large swaths of land that were previously ruled by Spain, as well as territories controlled by other European powers (see Figure 3.4).

US expansionist policy was rooted in both material and ideological concerns. It reflected the geopolitical and economic ambitions of the US as a nation as well as the financial interests of bankers, merchants and speculators (Acuña, 2015; Duany, 2017; Gonzalez, 2011). There was money to be made by the US acquiring more territory and expanding the frontier, and expansion would enrich individuals while also solidifying US power. In addition, the doctrine of **Manifest Destiny** framed it as inevitable, desirable and even divinely ordained that the US would expand across North America, a view that was tied to racist notions about Whites' supposed political and cultural superiority to Indigenous and 'mixed race' people (Horsman, 1981).

Incorporation of lands previously held by the Spanish happened in three phases: Florida and the Southeast were annexed at the beginning of the 19th century; Texas, the Southwest and California in the mid-century; and Puerto Rico at the century's end (Gonzalez, 2011). These three phases, and the ways in which lands and peoples were incorporated, not only provide the historical backdrop for the current status of Spanish and Spanish-speakers in the US but they also shape that status; the roots of the racialization of Spanish can be traced back to this

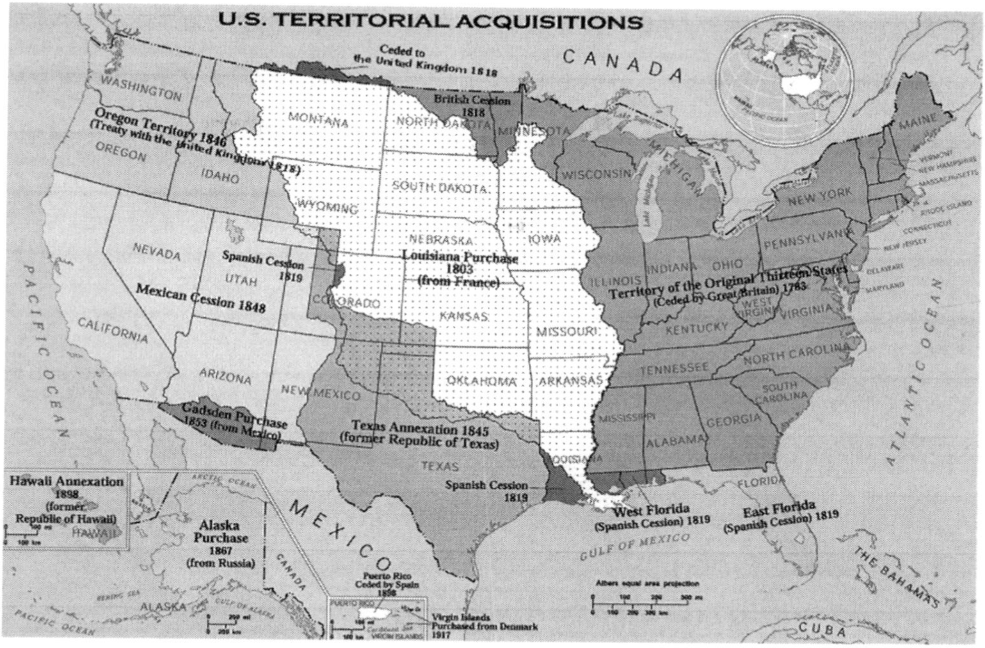

Figure 3.4 Map of US territorial expansion

period. We include key dates in the following discussion; more details are presented on the timeline in Figure 3.2 as well as on the map in Figure 3.4.

Phase 1: Florida and the Southeast

As we have seen, the Spanish were the first Europeans to explore and/or claim much of what is now the Southeastern US. However, the French and the British also had designs on the region and the control of various areas switched hands several times among the three of them. Here, we focus on how these lands were incorporated by the US.

The French laid claim to the Louisiana territory, which in addition to the present-day state of Louisiana, also comprised all or part of what is now Arkansas, Colorado, Iowa, Kansas, Missouri, Montana, Nebraska, North Dakota, Oklahoma, South Dakota and Wyoming. At the start of the 18th century, French outposts reached all the way from the Gulf of Mexico to Hudson Bay, in present-day Canada. These lands were inhabited by numerous Indigenous peoples including the Caddo, Choctaw, Crow, Lakota, Natchez and Osage, among others.

France ceded Louisiana to Spain in the second half of the 18th century, took it back again roughly 40 years later, and ultimately sold it to the US in 1803 in what is commonly known as the Louisiana Purchase. During the period of Spanish colonial rule, Spain had recruited thousands of settlers to Louisiana; thus, the Louisiana Purchase 'brought the first group of Spanish-speaking people under the U.S. flag' (Gonzalez, 2011: 35). People from the Canary

Islands were predominant among the Spanish settlers and their language variety shaped the *isleño* Spanish that was spoken in several isolated Louisiana communities well into the 20th century (Lipski, 2008).

In contrast with Louisiana, the Spanish not only explored Florida but also established various settlements and missions there fairly early on. For example, St. Augustine, the oldest city in what is now the continental US, was founded in 1565. Colonial control of Florida shifted hands several times between the Spanish and the British, and it was returned to the Spanish in the late 18th century. Following US independence, tensions with Spain mounted as a result of US expansionist designs and of Spanish colonies' provision of refuge to African Americans escaping from slavery and Native peoples fighting the US (Gonzalez, 2011).

The US annexed Florida via a type of rebellion called a *filibuster*, which was used or attempted throughout the borderlands. The way in which filibusters worked was that large numbers of **Anglo** settlers and speculators moved from the US into sparsely populated areas held by the Spanish. Next, the settlers declared independence from Spain; US troops were sent in and Congress eventually approved incorporation of the newly Anglo-settled lands. Under the pressure of repeated filibusters, Spain transferred ownership of Florida to the US in exchange for just 5 million dollars (equivalent to about 100 million dollars in 2019), in the hopes that this might quench the US thirst for more and more land and allow Spain to retain its empire (Gonzalez, 2011). It did not.

Phase 2: Texas, the Southwest and California

In the same year that the US took Florida from Spain (1821), the end of the Mexican War of Independence brought the close of Spanish colonialism in continental North America. As a result, Texas, the Southwest and California were now all part of an independent Mexico.

The Spanish had not established many settlements in Texas and thus the population remained predominantly Apache, Caddo and Comanche. Following independence from Spain, Mexico sought to attract White settlers who would provide a 'counterweight' to Texas's Native population (Massey, 2016: 161). Once in Texas, the settlers who poured in from the US, many of them adventurers and land speculators, became increasingly rebellious toward the Mexican government (Gonzalez, 2011). They were unhappy with various aspects of Mexican law and religious culture, but Mexico's 1829 abolition of slavery was the biggest point of contention (Gómez, 2007; Massey, 2016). When Mexican authorities sought to enforce the ban, Anglo settlers declared Texas's independence, and war broke out. While the Army of Texas lost the mythologized Battle of the Alamo in 1836, they went on to defeat the Mexican army and establish the independent Republic of Texas later that same year. Texas's admission to the US was delayed as Congress debated the balance of slave and free states, but it was eventually admitted (as a slave state). As Ramos (2019) explains, despite the still common portrayal of the Texas Revolution as 'an organic uprising' and of the Battle of the Alamo as a heroic stand for freedom, 'the Alamo was in Mexico – its seizure [and Texas's] was precisely an act of American expansion.' Further, the role of slavery in Texas's independence and its eventual admission to the US, as well as the references to race in arguments both in favor of and against annexation (Gómez, 2007), illustrate that 'race was at the core of the earliest attempt to define a clear symbolic boundary between Anglo-America and Latino lands to the south' (Massey, 2016: 162).

Following the incorporation of Texas, the US sought to continue its territorial expansion. It sent troops into Mexican territory, initiating what is generally known in the US as *The Mexican-American War* (1847–1848). What is frequently referred to in Mexico as *La Guerra de la Intervención Estadounidense* ('The War of US Intervention') was brutal, with tremendous losses on both sides. US troops advanced far into Mexico, eventually capturing and occupying Mexico City. (The alternate names for the war underscore the role of language in historical representation.)

The 1848 Treaty of Guadalupe Hidalgo officially ended the war and established the Rio Grande as the border between the two nations. Under the terms of the treaty, Mexico ceded over half of its pre-war territory to the US and gave up all claims to Texas. The roughly 525,000 square miles of land transferred from Mexico to the US included all or part of present-day Arizona, California, Colorado, Nevada, New Mexico, Utah and Wyoming. While some US politicians had argued for annexing more Mexican territory, opponents, who objected to adding so many non-White or racially mixed people to the US, ultimately prevailed (Gómez, 2007; Gonzalez, 2011). A few years later, the US paid Mexico 10 million dollars for roughly 30,000 additional square miles of land in present-day Arizona and New Mexico in what is known as the Gadsden Purchase.

Post-annexation, Anglo migrants from the eastern US quickly outnumbered the former Mexican citizens who remained north of the new border (Massey, 2016). The influx was especially rapid in California following the 1848 discovery of gold, with devastating effects for Native peoples, who were driven out and, in many cases, slaughtered. The linguistic and racial make-up of the population played a role in debates about whether territories should be admitted as states (Gómez, 2007; Nieto-Phillips, 2000). For example, one Cincinnati newspaper editorial opposed statehood for New Mexico by characterizing the residents as 'aliens to us in blood and language' (Gomez, 2007: 72). As the influx of Anglo migrants Whitened the population, statehood gained more support, especially in territories that had received more immigration, such as California (Baron, 1990; Crawford, 1992).

On paper the Treaty of Guadalupe Hidalgo granted full citizenship to the residents of the formerly Mexican territories, but in practice the **treaty citizens** (i.e. people who became US citizens as a result of the Treaty of Guadalupe Hidalgo) were racialized and treated as second-class citizens. They were subjected to segregated and inferior schools, housing and public facilities, and were often denied the right to vote (Gómez, 2007; Gross, 2008; Lozano, 2018; Olivas, 2006). In addition, under Mexican rule Indigenous groups such as the Pueblos had been citizens, but under US rule their rights were severely restricted. Further, promises to respect Spanish and Mexican land grants were often broken, and land was routinely appropriated by speculators or awarded to Anglo homesteaders arriving from the East (Acuña, 2015; Gonzalez, 2011).

In addition to the denial of rights and the seizing of property, Mexicans and Mexican Americans were also the target of mob violence, and thousands were lynched in the period from 1848 to 1928 (Carrigan & Webb, 2013). Lynchings were a tool of subjugation as well as a reflection of racism. They occurred throughout the Southwestern states as well as far from the border such as in Nebraska and Wyoming, but they were 'greater in scope and longer in duration' in Texas (Carrigan & Webb, 2013: 56). The early 20th century was a period of particularly brutal violence against Mexicans and Mexican Americans, some of it carried out by the Texas Rangers, an official law enforcement agency. (See the website *Refusing to Forget* at https://refusingtoforget.org, for more information on this racial violence, its lasting impact, and efforts to increase public awareness.) Some see parallels between the early 20th century anti-Mexican violence and recent anti-Latinx attacks, including the 2019 mass shooting at a Walmart in El Paso, Texas in which the shooter is believed to be have been motivated by anti-immigrant, anti-Mexican and White supremacist racism (Beckett, 2019).

Phase 3: Puerto Rico

In the 19th century, and coinciding with independence movements throughout Latin America, Puerto Ricans seeking greater self-determination carried out a series of revolts against Spanish colonial power. At the end of the century, Spain did concede some autonomy and local control (but not full independence) to Puerto Rico, but the new status was short-lived. In 1898, the Spanish-American War broke out, with US troops battling the Spanish in Cuba and the Philippines. At the war's end that same year, Spain was forced to cede Puerto Rico, Guam and the Philippines, as well as temporary control of Cuba, to the US. At first, many Puerto Ricans celebrated, optimistic that US control would bring democratic values and improved labor conditions (Duany, 2017). However, that optimism didn't last long; the US granted Puerto Ricans even less autonomy and political rights than they'd had under Spanish colonial rule.

As it did in westward expansion, Manifest Destiny and the treatment of the inhabitants of the Southwestern territories, racism also played a crucial role in decisions about Puerto Rico's political status (Gelpí, 2011; Gonzalez, 2011; Rivera Ramos, 1996; Torruella, 2007). In particular, opposition to extending citizenship to Puerto Ricans centered on notions regarding their supposed unsuitability for representative democracy and self-government. For example, Senator Albert Beveridge of Indiana (who also opposed statehood for the Southwestern territories) argued that God had 'been preparing the English-speaking and Teutonic peoples for a thousand years' to be 'the master organizers of the world' and to 'administer government among the savage and servile peoples' (Gelpí, 2011: 22). So too, President Theodore Roosevelt described US democracy as 'unsuitable' for the people of Puerto Rico (Gelpí, 2011: 22).

In the midst of World War I, the Jones Act (1917) extended US citizenship to Puerto Ricans, which granted them some additional rights but also made them eligible for the military draft. Even with citizenship, however, Puerto Ricans were not granted full political representation or legal rights. For example, Congress retained the ultimate say over bills passed by Puerto Rico's legislature, most appointed officials were from the continental US, and Puerto Ricans did not have the right to trial by jury (Ayala & Bernabe, 2009; Cruz, 2017; Duany, 2017). Further, in a series of early 20th century cases, the Supreme Court ruled that inhabitants of Puerto Rico were not entitled to the same constitutional protections as other citizens. The official decisions, which still stand, include references to 'alien races' presumed to be so different from (White) Americans in 'religion, customs, laws, methods of taxation, and modes of thought' that 'Anglo-Saxon principles' could not be applied (Cruz, 2017: 46).

Eventually, in the mid-20th century, Puerto Ricans did gain the right to elect their own governor and to draft their own constitution, but to this day residents of the island, despite being US citizens, do not have representation in Congress and are not allowed to vote in presidential elections. Puerto Rico's status as a Commonwealth (*Estado Libre Asociado*) with limited rights in comparison to US states stands in stark contrast to the earlier pattern of US territorial expansion, in which annexed lands were incorporated and set on a path to eventual statehood. The ongoing status of Puerto Rico as an unincorporated territory, and of Puerto Ricans as second-class citizens, as well as the notion that Puerto Rico's current economic crisis results from cultural or political inadequacies rather than structural issues or federal policies, are all rooted in this racist past.

In this section we have examined the three phases of the Spanish conquest of North American and Caribbean lands, as well as the subsequent annexation of these territories by the US. In the 16th century, Spanish arrived in what is now the US as a language of colonizers, but over the course of the 19th century it increasingly became a colonized language. As such, Spanish became subordinated to English in language ideologies (discussed in the next chapter) as well as language policies (discussed in Chapter 8). Of course, these ideologies and policies were not just about language per se; rather, they were part of a broader subordination of Spanish-speakers in which language was a tool for the exercise of power. Just as the racialization of African and Native peoples can be traced to colonial encounters and the slave trade, the **Othering** of Spanish-speakers and Latinxs is rooted in the period leading up to and following US territorial expansion (Vélez-Ibáñez, 2017).

Black and White Legends, Hispanophilia and Oñate's Foot

At the outset of this chapter we noted that the historical presence of Spanish in the US is often overlooked. But while the periods of Spanish and Mexican rule are often omitted or downplayed in traditional accounts of US history, this does not mean that they are universally ignored. In this section we discuss the portrayal of the Spanish history of the Southwest, and of New Mexico in particular. History is never just a neutral description of the past, and historical accounts of the US' Spanish colonial past are no exception. As we'll show, these accounts are tied up with various political, economic and social interests, as well as with debates over the construction and representation of ethnoracial and national identities.

The 16th and 17th centuries were a period of intense competition among European imperial powers and religious institutions for dominion in the Americas and around the globe. In addition to military force, imperial rivals also used political and religious propaganda to convince their subjects of the righteousness of their efforts. One such effort is known as the **Black Legend**, the inaccurate portrayal of Spanish colonialism as more brutal than that of other European powers (Taylor, 2002). The Black Legend was popularized by the British, who sought to justify their own imperialism by claiming moral superiority over the Spanish (Nieto-Phillips, 2004). While there is no question that Spanish colonizers committed horrible atrocities, such atrocities were also carried out by the British in equal measure. Nonetheless, the Black Legend endured, and in the years following US independence many Americans held negative views of Spaniards, who they saw as authoritarian, bloodthirsty, corrupt and fanatical (Weber, 2000).

In contrast with this negative view of the Spanish represented by the Black Legend, a new literary and cultural movement, sometimes referred to as *Hispanophilia*, emerged toward the end of the 19th century (Nieto Phillips, 2004). Hispanophilia celebrated Spain's colonial presence in the Southwest, with novels, magazines and films of the era portraying the Spanish conquistadors not as cruel fanatics but as romantic, noble adventurers and missionaries (see Chapter 7 for a discussion of such representations in film). This new glorified account of the Spanish conquest, which Nieto-Phillips (2004) calls 'the White Legend,' framed Spaniards as 'civilizing' the 'primitive' Native peoples, thus minimizing genocide, enslavement and oppression. Not only were the Spanish portrayed as heroes, but **mestizaje** (i.e. racial 'mixture' between Spanish and Native peoples) was downplayed or denied. In this way, Spanish-speakers were represented as the 'racially pure' descendants of Europeans.

According to Nieto-Phillips (2004), the White Legend and the downplaying of mestizaje served various ideological and discursive purposes for both New Mexicans and Anglos. In particular, the narrative that framed the Spanish colonizers as courageous and chivalrous gentlemen didn't just represent resistance to the Black Legend; it was also a counterpoint to the racist portrayals of Mexicans (including New Mexicans) as members of a 'mongrel race' (Gómez, 2007; Nieto-Phillips, 2000, 2004). According to the dominant racist views of the time, Whiteness was the ideal and interracial unions were degrading. Further, these views had political implications; as we noted earlier, anti-Mexican and anti-Indigenous racism was central to arguments against New Mexican statehood. Representing New Mexicans as the descendants of Europeans, rather than Native people and Mestizos, was a way to 'Whiten' the state's population and thus make a claim about fitness for self-government, even without the huge influx of Anglos which had altered ethnoracial and linguistic demographics in California and Texas (Gómez, 2007; Nieto-Phillips, 2004).

Language and linguistics – in particular the existence of a unique New Mexican variety of Spanish – also played a supporting role in discourse about New Mexicans' purported Spanish origins. Multiple factors contributed to the development of New Mexican Spanish, but some researchers focused primarily on the linguistic and social isolation of New Mexican communities (Lipski, 2008). For example, New Mexican linguist Aurelio Espinosa's early 20th century research emphasized similarities of New Mexican varieties of Spanish, as well as popular sayings and folksongs, to those found in Spain. Just as New Mexicans' language supposedly showed little African or Indigenous linguistic influence, the implication was that New Mexicans themselves were also racially 'pure' (Nieto-Phillips, 2004; Wilson, 1997).

During subsequent periods of immigration from Mexico, some treaty citizens sought to distinguish themselves from new arrivals by virtue of their proficiency in English and/or their assertions of European ancestry (Gonzales-Berry & Maciel, 2000; Lozano, 2018). Whiteness claims were a way to resist racial discrimination, segregation and disenfranchisement. However, rather than challenging anti-Mestizo and anti-Indigenous racism, many such claims focused on improving the status of the individuals who were able to successfully make them and thus they have been sharply criticized.

New Mexico's Bureau of Immigration also deployed a romanticized depiction of the Spanish colonial past in its efforts to attract tourists and potential migrants from the East (Nieto-Phillips, 2004). In contrast with earlier images of hostile 'savages' and 'cruel, swarthy Mexicans,' the Bureau's marketing materials painted a picture of New Mexico as a an 'enchanting' landscape where 'peace-loving Pueblo Indians and noble Spaniards had co-existed for nearly three centuries' (Nieto-Phillips, 2004: 119–120). While on the surface this might seem like a positive portrayal of the Spanish and Pueblo peoples, it relied on exotification, as well as the implication that these cultures were less developed or sophisticated than the supposedly more modern and industrious Anglo Americans. As such, it sought to attract Eastern tourists by offering them a nostalgic escape from industrialized urban centers (Nieto-Phillips, 2004).

As early as the late 19th century, the recognition of the tremendous economic potential of tourism and the **commodification** of ethnicity and culture played a role in the promotion of a sanitized colonial past and, in turn, of an emerging Spanish-American identity. In addition to tourist brochures, travelogues, movies and the like, Hispanophilia and the celebration of 'Old Spain' could be found in architectural motifs, as well as New Mexican souvenirs and cultural artifacts (Nieto-Phillips, 2004; Wilson, 1997). Language was another way to construct an exotic, romantic Spanish ambience; the same period saw an increased use of Spanish in business names and real estate, such as hotels named *El Conquistador* and *La Hacienda*, as well as housing developments with *plazas* and streets named *Alameda* and *Camino*. In many cases, Spanish was both used by Anglos and directed toward Anglos (often with little regard to Spanish grammar rules) (Hill, 2008: 131). As we discuss in Chapter 7, Spanish is still sometimes used by businesses to create a particular sense of place or to convey exotic flavor or cultural authenticity.

The celebration and commodification of an imagined Spanish colonial past has endured through the 20th century and into the 21st. As was the case earlier, the symbolic meaning and discursive implications of the emphasis of Spain's role in the history of the area are multifaceted. The existence of multiple, competing and contradictory meanings is evident, for example, in the controversies surrounding several statues of Spanish conquistador Juan de Oñate, who became the first governor of colonial New Mexico at the end of the 16th century. Oñate led a brutal massacre of approximately 800 Acoma men, women and children as punishment for having violently resisted demands that they turn over their food to Spanish soldiers. Following the massacre, Oñate sentenced the survivors to forced servitude and ordered the amputation of the right foot of all men over the age of 25.

Despite this brutal history, in New Mexico there are numerous businesses, schools and streets named for Oñate and other conquistadors, as well as a variety of Spanish-themed celebrations and pageants. For example, a reenactment of the *Entrada*, the Spanish reoccupation of Santa Fe after the Pueblo Revolt, was a central part of the city's annual festival until very recently. The reenactment was created in the early 20th century as a tourist attraction designed to capitalize on the region's cultural history (Rael-Galvéz, 2017). Similar motivations shaped late 20th century plans for official commemorations of the 400th anniversary of Oñate's arrival in New Mexico. A larger-than-life bronze equestrian statue of Oñate was built for the new visitors' center in Alcalde, New Mexico, and others were planned for Albuquerque and El Paso (Texas), which Oñate founded.

Although the promotion of tourism was a key impetus, there were also non-economic motivations to commemorate the Spanish conquest. Indeed, some advocates of Oñate monuments saw them as 'an opportunity to help correct a deficiency of Spanish history in New Mexico public education' (June-Friesen, 2005). In other words, the monuments and the visitors' center were a way to provide what they believed was a long overdue recognition of the presence and cultural contributions of the Spanish and their descendants, as well as to challenge to the traditional teaching of US history as having progressed from east to west. Interest in Oñate may also have been related to New Mexicans' 'insecurities over losing their language, culture and political and demographic dominance' as a result of intergenerational language shift to English and the influx of Anglos from the East (Brooke, 1998). Thus, for some, recognition of Oñate and Spanish colonial history was a way to reclaim a non-Anglo past, more than a celebration of the Spanish conquest itself.

However, for many people, the Oñate monuments and conquistador-themed commemorations of the quadracentennial did not simply represent the recognition of a long-overlooked history. Instead, the celebrations of Spanish colonial history replaced one historical **erasure** and whitewashing with another, by focusing exclusively on Europeans and their descendants, and failing to acknowledge and address the atrocities that the Spanish committed against the Acoma and other Native peoples. For this reason, activists demonstrated and spoke out against the statues. In one high-profile act of protest, a group calling themselves 'Friends of Acoma' cut off the right foot of the Oñate statue at the Alcalde visitors' center. They sent a letter to the local newspaper explaining their motivation by stating: 'We see no glory in celebrating Onate's fourth centennial, and we do not want our faces rubbed in it' (Alcorn, 2018).

In the years since, opposition to Oñate monuments and conquistador-themed celebrations has grown, much like the growing objections to statues of Confederate generals. Regarding the previously mentioned plans for new Oñate monuments in Albuquerque and at the El Paso airport, numerous public discussions were held, newspaper editorials were published and letters to the editor were written. Ultimately, the El Paso airport statue was installed, but it was renamed 'The Equestrian' in an effort to allay opposition. In Albuquerque, planners modified the original design by adding a second monument depicting the land before European arrival (Alcorn, 2018). In the wake of the White supremacist violence at rallies defending Charlottesville, Virginia's statue of Confederate General Robert E. Lee in 2017, protests and opposition intensified. In 2018, the city of Santa Fe suspended the *Entrada* reenactment, and held the Fiesta de Santa Fe without it (you can read some reactions to the change in the *New York Times* article, 'New Mexico grapples with its version of Confederate tributes: A celebration of Spanish conquest' at https://www.nytimes.com/2018/09/08/us/new-mexico-la-entrada.html, accessed 1 February 2018).

(Im)migration and Spanish in the US

As we have seen, the earliest historical presence of Spanish in the US was due to colonization and conquest, rather than immigration. However, while some descendants of treaty citizens may have managed to retain or reacquire Spanish, the overwhelming force of linguistic shift to English means that migration has been a key factor in Spanish's continued presence in the US. Spanish-speaking migrants hail from a variety of countries, and they have myriad personal, professional and political reasons for coming to the US. Some come as refugees escaping violence or persecution, whereas others come to pursue educational, economic or professional opportunities. They also encompass people from a wide range of socio-economic statuses and educational backgrounds.

Scholars emphasize that migration patterns are shaped by both **push factors** and **pull factors**. Push factors are conditions in migrants' countries of origin that contribute to migration, such as natural disasters, political violence, gangs or high unemployment. Pull factors, on the other hand, are rooted in the receiving country and include political or religious freedom, labor demand (and recruitment of migrant workers) and educational opportunities. These societal and structural factors condition overall patterns, but of course people's individual circumstances also play a role in their decisions regarding migration.

The demographics of immigration

In the last chapter, we noted that many people in the US erroneously think that all Latinxs as well as all speakers of Spanish are immigrants, but the actual percentages are just 38% and 47%, respectively (ACS 2017 Five-year estimates). Similarly, and similarly inaccurately, public discourse often equates immigration with Mexican immigration. In reality, while Mexico is the most common country of origin among immigrants, the rate of new immigration from Mexico has slowed. In fact, more Mexicans now leave the US than come to it, resulting in a net decrease in the number of Mexican immigrants living in the US (Zong & Batalova, 2018). Moreover, in most years since 2010, more Asians than Latinxs have migrated to the US and in 2017 the top country of origin of new arrivals was India (Radford, 2019).

So too, many people seem to assume that a majority of immigrants are in the US without authorization. In reality, it is less than a quarter – 23% (Radford, 2019). Further, almost half of all immigrants in the US are naturalized citizens and a little over a quarter are legal permanent residents (Radford, 2019). Moreover, the overall number of unauthorized immigrants has declined steadily since peaking in 2007, with the 2017 numbers representing a 14% reduction (Radford, 2019). In addition, the category of unauthorized immigrants includes people with Temporary Protected Status (TPS) and Deferred Action for Childhood Arrivals (DACA). TPS allows migrants from certain countries to stay in the US when the government designates it too dangerous for them to return home because of armed conflict or natural disaster. DACA, a program created via Executive Order by President Obama in 2012, grants temporary status (without a path to citizenship) to certain individuals brought into the US as children before 2007. Essentially all the research has shown DACA to have had positive impacts on the overall economy as well as on participants and their families, and not to have negatively impacted job prospects or wages for the rest of the population (Kurtzleben, 2017).

In 2017, President Trump suspended DACA as part of a broader effort to reduce both authorized and unauthorized immigration. The Trump administration also terminated TPS protections for most countries and instituted a ban on migrants from certain Muslim-majority countries. These changes to immigration policy have faced numerous legal challenges based on claims that they are discriminatory, and the ongoing court battles are expected to take years to resolve. As this book goes to print, DACA is no longer accepting new applications but renewals are being processed for the 700,000 people already enrolled. However, the status of DACA and TPS are subject to further policy changes and judicial decisions; for up-to-date information, see the National Immigration Law Center website, https://www.nilc.org/issues/daca.

The terminology of immigration: Unauthorized immigrants and the *i*-word

Given that public discourse often makes reference to 'illegal immigration' and sometimes includes claims that one's grandparents came to the US 'the right way' in contrast with today's 'illegal immigrants,' we want to problematize this notion as well as the use of the word *illegal*. In so doing we will also highlight a few key moments in the history of US immigration policy.

For more than a hundred years following US independence, immigration was largely unrestricted. Thus, essentially anyone who wanted to come to the US could do so. This open immigration policy began to change in the late 19th century, as **nativists** expressed opposition to the growing number of immigrants, especially those they considered different from immigrants who had arrived earlier (much like contemporary nativists, although the 'new immigrants' of the early 20th century are the 'old immigrants' of today). Congress imposed various race-based restrictions on who was allowed to come to the US; Asians were excluded, and in the 1920s immigration from southern and eastern Europe was strictly limited. Thus, the possibility of immigrating legally was sharply curtailed.

The new immigration laws of the 1920s did not establish limits for Latin American countries, primarily in order to allow US businesses a continued supply of migrant labor from Mexico. However, people wishing to enter the US via Mexico were subject to literacy and health tests that were sometimes administered arbitrarily and they had to pay a fee, which was prohibitive for many (Hernandez, 2017; Ngai, 2004). Thus, many migrants continued to cross the border as they had done previously, without going through an official port of entry. In 1929, Congress passed a law designed specifically to impact Mexicans; for the first time, entering the country outside an official port of entry was made a crime, one that could be punished with fines and imprisonment as well as deportation (Hernandez, 2017). This change has had a dramatic impact not only how cross-border migrants are treated in the legal system but also on how they are portrayed in policy debates and broader public discourse; with 'entering the country unlawfully' constituted as a criminal act, migrants are framed as criminals.

Regardless of whether they entered the country unlawfully or they committed the civil infraction of overstaying their visa, we reject the use of the label 'illegal' to refer to people who are in the US without authorization, just as we would not apply this label to drivers who violate speed limits or even to convicted felons. In other words, we reject the idea that any person is 'illegal.' As we stress throughout this book, language is inseparable from the sociopolitical world, and the ways in which we talk about people have real-world consequences. Like a growing number of scholars, activists and journalists who want to 'drop the *i*-word' in media coverage and public debate (see Race Forward's website at https://www.raceforward.org/practice/tools/drop-i-word or ABC New's coverage at https://abcnews.go.com/ABC_Univision/linguists-york-times-illegal-neutral-accurate/story?id=17366512#.UGoRvhwsGiw), we believe that calling people 'illegals' is not only inaccurate, it is dehumanizing and part of a broader racializing discourse that portrays migrants as inherently unwelcome and detrimental to the country. We opt to use the more neutral term *unauthorized* to describe the migration status of people in the US (or any other country) without official permission.

As we discussed above, the overwhelming majority of Latinxs are either US citizens or immigrants who are authorized to be in the country. Nonetheless, like the false notions that all Latinxs are immigrants and all Latinxs speak Spanish, the myth that most immigrants are unauthorized endures, despite its inaccuracy. These three interrelated tropes, together with the discursive criminalization of unauthorized immigration discussed above, contribute both to the portrayal of Latinxs as 'perpetual foreigners' who are in the US illegally and to the representation of Spanish as an 'illegal' language (Leeman, 2012a, 2013).

National origin groups and (im)migration

In the previous chapter, we presented quantitative data on the national origins of the Latinx population, including the specific percentage comprised by each group (see Table 2.1). Based on the same data, we show the relative size of different Latinx national origin groups in Figure 3.5. In the following sections we look at the migration history of the five largest national origin groups: Mexicans, Puerto Ricans, Cubans, Salvadorans and Dominicans (due to space limitations, we cannot cover all groups). Our discussion focuses on the time periods in which members of these groups migrated to the US and where they settled, as well as the push and pull factors that promoted migration.

Mexicans

Mexicans are the largest Latinx national origin group by far, comprising roughly 62% of the Latinx population in the US (see Figure 3.5). People born in Mexico also make up the largest share (approximately 25%) of all immigrants currently in the US (Migration Policy Institute, n.d.). However, as we have discussed, in addition to immigrants and their children, Mexicans and Mexican Americans also include the descendants of treaty citizens (people living in Mexican lands that were annexed by the US) as well as the descendants of immigrants from long ago. In fact, less than one-third of people of Mexican origin are immigrants; more than two-thirds were born in the US.

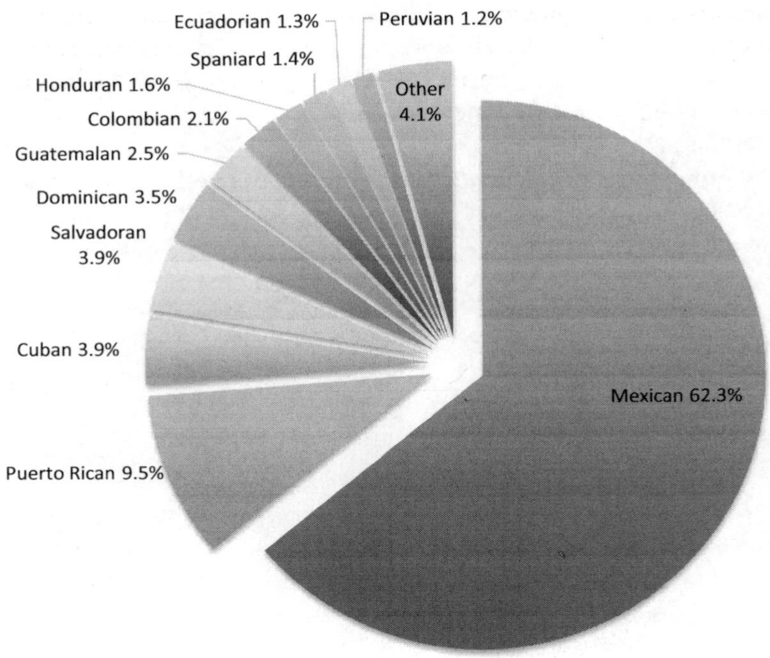

Figure 3.5 National origin groups (ACS 2017 One-year estimates)

Mexicans and Mexican Americans are most densely concentrated in the Southwest, where they have the longest history, which is closest to Mexico, and where they form a clear majority of the Latinx population (and in some places of the entire population). However, there are also longstanding Mexican and Mexican American communities in the Midwest (especially Chicago) and the Northwest, as well as newer communities in the Southeast. Indeed, there are Mexican communities all across the country, including the Northeast as well. It's also worth noting that there are thousands of people living in Mexico who cross back and forth across the border every day, either to study or to work.

Immigration from Mexico has ebbed and flowed depending on political and labor conditions in the two countries. One significant period of migration occurred in the early 20th century, spurred in part by the repression and violence leading up to and during the Mexican Revolution (1910–1920), as well as the devastation that followed. However, another key factor was recruitment by US employers after the prohibition on Japanese immigration resulted in labor shortages (Lozano, 2018; Massey, 2016). Immigrants arriving in the early 20th century far outnumbered the treaty citizens living in Mexican lands annexed by the US (Lozano, 2018).

Mexican immigration continued to increase in the 1920s but in 1929 the start of the Great Depression brought it largely to a halt. Together with the unemployment crisis, nativism and racism 'pushed anti-Mexican sentiment to a fever pitch' throughout the country (Lozano, 2018: 145). Not only were Mexicans stopped from crossing the border, but somewhere between 600,000 and a million US citizens of Mexican descent were deported to Mexico, together with almost as many Mexican citizens, most of whom had authorization to be in the US (Balderrama & Rodriguez, 2006; Hoffman, 1974). These so-called repatriations sought to, in the words of President Hoover, keep 'American jobs for real Americans' (Gonzalez, 2011; Malavé & Giordani, 2015), a discursive framing that has reappeared in subsequent calls for immigration restrictions and/or deportations. Such calls are more frequent during economic downturns and periods of high unemployment, but they can also occur in times of economic growth and near full employment, such as the present.

The US entry into World War II in 1940 precipitated a labor shortage which again led to the recruitment of Mexican workers, this time through the Bracero Program, a federal guest worker program that brought laborers from Mexico to the US for temporary jobs, primarily in agriculture. Originally envisioned as a wartime measure, the Bracero Program was expanded and renewed as the post-war boom created growing demand for labor among US employers. Even when the economic slowdown of the 1950s brought another round of deportations, this time under the derogatory official name 'Operation Wetback,' the Bracero Program was simultaneously expanded. This ensured a continued source of cheap labor from guest workers who were not allowed to settle in the US permanently, since Braceros were required to return to Mexico at the end of each 12-month contract. The specifics of the program, including the temporary nature of the visas, left participants vulnerable to abuse, and they were often subjected to harsh and inhumane conditions. Moreover, the failure of employers and government agencies to keep contractual promises regarding wages and retirement benefits has been well documented (Mize & Swords, 2010). As a result of activism by Mexicans and Mexican Americans, especially in the context of the Civil Rights movement, the Bracero Program was increasingly recognized as exploitative, leading Congress to end it in 1965 (Massey, 2016).

Another Civil Rights Era policy change was also hugely significant for immigrants from Mexico as well as other places. Specifically, in 1965 Congress carried out a major overhaul of immigration policy by eliminating race-based exclusions and national origin quotas, and instead established preferences for migrants with family members in the US or with needed skills. However, caps were put on the number of immigrants per country (including Latin American countries), as well as the overall number (see the American Immigration Council's website for overviews of the immigration system at https://www.americanimmigrationcouncil.org/topics/immigration-101). As a result of the changes, Mexicans went from having access to half a million permanent and temporary visas before the law to just 20,000 (permanent) visas in 1976, yet the push and pull factors of labor supply and labor demand continued as before (Massey, 2016). Thus, Mexicans continued to migrate to the US, but far more of them did so without authorization, leading to anxiety about border security and ultimately resulting in the US' militarization of the border (Massey, 2016). In turn, this led to more and more apprehensions of migrants, a trend which both fed and was fed by increased anti-immigrant and anti-Mexican sentiment as well as the discourse of criminality and danger that increasingly surrounded immigration and especially Mexican immigration (Dick, 2011; Massey, 2016; Ngai, 2004). This discourse has become a driving force in US politics, reflected for example in President Trump's racist portrayals of Mexicans as rapists and murderers, despite statistics that consistently show that immigrants are less likely to commit crimes than are US-born citizens.

Since 2010, immigration from Mexico has been declining due to improvements in the Mexican economy and dropping birth rates (Zong & Batalova, 2018). In fact, more Mexicans return to Mexico than migrate to the US, the overall number of unauthorized Mexican immigrants has declined since 2007, and border apprehensions of Mexicans reached a 40-year low in 2017 (Gonzalez-Barrera & Krogstad, 2018; Zong & Batalova, 2018). There has also been a change in the demographic characteristics of Mexican immigrants: they are now more likely to be college graduates and they have greater English proficiency than was the case in the past. Most Mexican immigrants have been in the country for a long time: 60% arrived before 2000; another 29% between 2000 and 2009; and only 11% in 2010 or later (Zong & Batalova, 2018). Mexicans also make up the largest share of DACA participants – approximately 80% (US Citizenship and Immigration Services, 2018).

Puerto Ricans

Unlike Mexicans, Puerto Ricans are US citizens (as we discussed above), and thus they do not need visas to migrate to the US. This, together with the geographic proximity of Puerto Rico to the US, allows for the *vaivén* ('back-and-forth') cited by García *et al.* (2001). Not surprisingly, migration from Puerto Rico has been influenced by labor market forces in the US as well as conditions on the island. Push and pull factors converged at the turn of the 20th century when two hurricanes devastated Puerto Rico's sugar industry; plantation owners recruited newly jobless Puerto Rican workers to Hawaii (then a US territory) as they sought to meet the new market demand for Hawaiian sugar (López, 2005). As a result, Puerto Ricans are the largest Latinx subgroup in Hawaii (ACS 2017 Five-year estimates).

According to Whalen (2005), Puerto Rican migration has followed a general pattern in which US occupation caused economic changes and displacement, Puerto Ricans were recruited as a cheap source of labor (but not always welcomed where they settled), and then the existence of Puerto Rican communities served to attract new migrants to those areas. For example, despite earning high profits, Puerto Rican sugar plantations cut wages, which together with high unemployment and the ensuing social and political unrest, pushed migrants to head for the US (Gonzalez, 2011). By the 1920s large Puerto Rican neighborhoods had been established in New York, and in the 1930s and 1940s communities were established elsewhere in the Northeast, including Philadelphia and Boston (Lipski, 2008). So too, Puerto Rican communities were established in Lorain, Ohio and Chicago, largely as a result of labor agencies recruiting workers in Puerto Rico and offering airfare and jobs on the mainland (Gonzalez, 2011). During the 'Great Migration' of the 1950s, approximately 470,000 Puerto Ricans (over one-fifth of the population) migrated to the US mainland (Culliton-Gonzalez, 2008). In the 1960s Puerto Ricans were recruited to work on farms in the Midwest, upstate New York and throughout the Northeast (Gonzalez, 2011), but New York has remained the cultural heart of mainland Puerto Ricans, with Nuyoricans maintaining a prominent symbolic position in the imaginary of the Puerto Rican diaspora (Lipski, 2008).

In the 21st century, long-standing economic problems were exacerbated by deindustrialization, austerity and changes to federal tax policy, as well as constraints on debt restructuring related to Puerto Rico's status as a territory rather than a US state or an independent country. In Puerto Rico, 45% of the population live below the poverty line, more than twice the rate for Mississippi and almost three times the national average (ACS 2017 Five-year estimates). Given the difficult conditions, and an unemployment rate more than twice that of the mainland US, almost half a million people left Puerto Rico for the mainland between 2006 and 2014 (Mora *et al.*, 2017). To make matters worse, in 2017 Hurricane Maria devastated Puerto Rico and left much of the island without electricity for months. In Maria's wake, over 400,000 Puerto Ricans (approximately 6% of the island's population) departed (Echenique & Melgar, 2018). Many headed to established Puerto Rican communities in the Northeast and Chicago, but over half went to Florida, especially the Orlando area. Political prognosticators have debated the potential impact of Puerto Rican voters on Florida elections, and this remains to be determined. Further, in 2018 as many as three-quarters of those fleeing Hurricane Maria had returned, although the infrastructure problems and financial situation were far from resolved (Echenique & Melgar, 2018). Updated information (in Spanish and English) on the political situation in Puerto Rico can be found on the Centro de Periodsmo Investigativo's website at http://periodismoinvestigativo.com.

Cubans

The first Cuban settlements in the US date to the early 19th century, not only prior to the Spanish-American War (1898) but also before Spain ceded Florida to the US. In other words, Cubans began settling in Florida when both Cuba and Florida were both still under Spanish control. Immigration accelerated in the period leading up to and following the war, with 100,000 people, almost 10% of Cuba's population, leaving for the US (Gonzalez, 2011). As we discussed earlier, at the end of the Spanish-American war in 1898, Spain ceded Cuba to the US. Although the US granted independence to Cuba in 1902, it remained involved in Cuban affairs and imposed several conditions, including permission to build several naval stations (the one at Guantanamo Bay is still in operation) and a permanent right to intervene in Cuba. US forces occupied Cuba from 1906 to 1909.

In the early 20th century, at the same time as a romanticized version of the Southwest's Spanish past was being marketed to tourists and newcomers (as we discussed earlier), Florida also promoted an exotic tropical version of its Spanish history and architecture (Lynch, 2018). US tourists saw Miami almost as an extension of Havana and they regularly visited both cities on the same trip (Lynch, 2018), while elite Cubans came to the US for vacations, medical treatment and to attend college (Gonzalez, 2011). But things were less sunny for regular Cubans, who endured inequality, corruption and increasingly repressive governments, such as the 1950s dictatorship of Fulgencio Batista. Batista, who had earlier served as elected president, returned to power through a military coup with the support of the US. The corruption and violence of the Batista regime led another 63,000 Cubans to emigrate; like their predecessors they settled primarily in Florida (Lipski, 2008).

In 1959 the Cuban Revolution toppled the Batista regime and brought Fidel Castro and his communist party to power. This led to an even greater exodus, as the revolutionary government nationalized land, housing and businesses, and violently cracked down on dissent. Despite the restrictions on emigration imposed by Castro's regime, in the 1960s almost half a million people left Cuba for the US, settling primarily in the Miami area.

Miami's Calle Ocho became the symbolic center of Cubans in the US and is still considered an obligatory stop for national as well as local politicians trying to garner their support. Roughly three-quarters of Cubans and Cuban Americans live in Florida, but there are also significant Cuban communities in New York and New Jersey (Batalova & Zong, 2017).

People who left Cuba in the wake of the revolution tended to be wealthier, Whiter, more educated and to have more technical skills than the general Cuban population as well as in comparison to other Latin American immigrants (Alfaraz, 2014; Gonzalez, 2011). Their affluence and ethnoracial identity gave them a leg up upon arrival in the US, as did the preferential treatment they received from the US government as a result of their status as refugees from communism. Specifically, until the mid-1990s, Cubans who reached US waters were allowed to stay in the US and were put through an expedited process that gave them permanent residency after just a year, as well as other kinds of assistance (Batalova & Zong, 2017). Thanks to the socio-economic advantages they brought with them from Cuba, combined with the support they received once in the US, as a group Cubans achieved greater prosperity than other Latinx groups (Gonzalez, 2011).

Like other communist regimes, the Castro government sharply restricted emigration. Nonetheless, in 1980 approximately 125,00 people seeking political freedom and economic opportunities were allowed to leave. Because they left Cuba in a boatlift from Mariel Harbor, they are commonly referred to as *Marielitos*. As a group, the Marielitos were poorer and darker skinned than earlier Cuban arrivals and as a result they faced class and race prejudice from both Cubans and Americans. In addition, whereas earlier Cuban migrants had arrived at the height of the Cold War and were warmly welcomed as political refugees, the Marielitos arrived at a time of increasing nativism, making their experience more like that of other Latinx immigrant groups (Gonzalez, 2011). This was also the case for the *balseros* ('raft people') who began arriving in large numbers in the 1990s. Under President Clinton, the US stopped allowing Cubans intercepted at sea to come to the US but continued giving those who reached US soil a chance to stay, a policy known as 'Wet Foot, Dry Foot.' As part of a move toward normalizing US–Cuba relations, President Obama ended the Wet Foot, Dry Foot policy in 2017. When President Trump took office that year, some restrictions on travel and investment in Cuba were reinstated.

Salvadorans

Although Cubans have long been the third largest Latinx national origin group in the US, since the 21st century there are almost as many Salvadorans. The almost 1.4 million immigrants from El Salvador are equivalent to one-fifth the population in El Salvador (Menjívar & Gómez Cervantes, 2018). Salvadorans are concentrated around Los Angeles and the Washington, DC metropolitan area (which includes Northern Virginia and suburban Maryland). Within the DC area's diverse Latinx community, Salvadorans are the largest national origin group (approximately 33%), while in Los Angeles there are roughly five times as many Mexicans as Salvadorans (ACS 2015 Five-year estimates). Other areas of high concentration are in Texas, Nevada and New York.

Central American immigration to the US surged in the 1980s, the result of what Gonzalez (2011: 129) calls 'intervention com[ing] home to roost.' In other words, the large-scale exodus from Central America was precipitated by civil wars and social chaos, 'and in each case, the origins and spiraling intensity of those wars were a direct result of military and economic intervention by [the US] government.' Throughout Latin America, the US has a long history of supporting repressive governments that have engaged in political disenfranchisement as well as violence, torture and murder of their own citizens. Early US interventions and support for dictatorial regimes were meant to install or prop up governments that defended the economic interests of US investors, plantation owners and corporations, who were typically aligned with a local ruling class. In the mid-20th century, Cold War politics also played an important role. Specifically, US politicians framed popular uprisings against repressive US-backed regimes in places like Guatemala, Nicaragua, Chile and elsewhere as communist revolutions (whether or not they had support from Cuba or the Soviet Union), and thus suppressing them was seen as a broader containment of the Soviet interests in the region.

After gaining independence from Spain in 1821, El Salvador faced a growing reliance on coffee as the sole export, increasing the concentration of land in the hands of a small oligarchy, and escalating economic hardship among peasants (Menjívar & Gómez Cervantes, 2018). When Salvadorans called for political freedom, land redistribution and economic reforms, they were met with brutal repression, including *La Matanza* in 1932, a government-ordered massacre of thousands of mostly Indigenous peasants (Gonzalez, 2011; Menjívar & Gómez Cervantes, 2018). The pattern of popular protest and military repression continued for decades, with the military staging coups whenever it seemed like the leftists were on the verge of winning elections (Gonzalez, 2011).

In 1979 the Salvadoran military again sought to preempt a leftist electoral victory by staging another coup. Civil war broke out between US-supported government forces and various leftist guerilla groups, with right-wing death squads murdering thousands of union organizers and civilians. Approximately 75,000 people were killed during the war, around 85% of them by the government, according to a UN Truth Commission report (Menjívar & Gómez Cervantes, 2018). Particularly brazen was the murder of Catholic Archbishop Oscar Romero, who was gunned down by death squads as he was giving mass, in retaliation for having spoken out against poverty, social injustice and torture (the story is recounted in the movie *Romero*). Under President Reagan, the US continued to supply the Salvadoran government with military and financial aid, even after government soldiers raped and killed four American nuns in 1980. As the war became increasingly violent, more and more Salvadorans fled, many of them to the US.

Like the violence that contributed to them leaving, Salvadorans' reception in the US was also colored by the Cold War; unlike Cuban migrants who were fleeing a communist regime, Salvadorans were fleeing from an anti-communist government that the US supported. Thus, they did not receive refugee status or benefits and they entered the US largely without authorization. In 1986, as part of a new US law that made it more difficult to hire unauthorized immigrants, Congress passed a limited amnesty to long-term residents with a clean record and knowledge of English, as long as they paid back taxes and a fine. This allowed many Salvadorans in the US to gain authorized status. However, new unauthorized immigrants continued to arrive.

In 1992 the civil war came to an end, but 'El Salvador was left awash in weapons and [...] psychosocial trauma' (Menjívar & Gómez Cervantes, 2018). Further, the unequal social structure was not addressed and neoliberal austerity policies were imposed, and thus economic conditions worsened for most Salvadorans. As a result, gangs thrived, due to the post-war poverty, violence and lack of opportunity, as well as the arrival of deportees who had been in gangs in the US. In 2001 a series of catastrophic earthquakes and aftershocks brought further suffering and worsened conditions, leading the Bush administration to grant TPS to almost 200,000 Salvadorans. Although the Trump administration sought to end TPS protections for Salvadorans, this was overturned by the courts in 2018.

Levels of violence in El Salvador are worse now than during the civil war and migration has continued to increase (Menjívar & Gómez Cervantes, 2018). In 2014 there was surge in migration by unaccompanied minors not just from El Salvador but from all of Central America. In some cases minors travel to reunite with parents already in the US, and in others they are sent by their parents to escape the violence and lack of opportunities at home. On paper, US immigration law allows people to enter or stay in the country if they have been persecuted or have a reasonable fear of persecution on the basis of race, religion, nationality, membership in a particular social group or political opinion, but in practice a smaller and smaller percentage of applications is approved. Further, the law stipulates that people can apply for asylum at a point of entry or inside the US, but the Trump administration has refused to accept applications at the border, and has detained or deported asylum seekers who are already in the US. These actions, together with a family separation policy in which thousands of children have been taken from their parents and held in separate detention centers, have caused a humanitarian crisis. (Up-to-date investigative journalism on immigration policy can be found on ProPublica's website at https://www.propublica.org/topics/immigration.)

Dominicans

As is to be expected, Dominicans have some similarities to, as well as some differences from, other Latinx groups. Dominicans began arriving in the US in the 1960s. Almost as numerous as Cubans and Salvadorans, Dominicans are concentrated in many of the same places as Puerto Ricans: New York, and the cities of the Northeast. There is also a large Dominican community in the Miami area. Rhode Island is the only state where Dominicans are the largest Latinx subgroup, but they also predominate in parts of eastern Massachusetts and Connecticut (ACS 2017 Five-year estimates).

Given the historical legacy of African slavery in the Caribbean, many Dominicans have African ancestry, as do many Puerto Ricans and Cuban migrants who arrived after 1980. According to Gonzalez (2011: 117), both Puerto Rican and Dominican migrants 'went largely unnoticed at first [because] New Yorkers tended to mistake them for Blacks who happened to speak Spanish.' Another similarity is that both Dominicans and Puerto Ricans tend to maintain close connections to their home societies, thanks to the geographic proximity to the eastern US and the availability of inexpensive transportation and telecommunications (Guarnizo, 1994; Roth, 2012). However, because Dominicans are not US citizens by birth, their ability to travel back and forth is far more restricted than Puerto Ricans'.

Like other Latin American countries, especially in the Caribbean, the Dominican Republic has been the object of US economic, political and military intervention. The US involvement in the Dominican Republic has been so continuous and intense that in the mid-19th century the Dominican president requested annexation by the US. Although annexation never happened, the US has been actively involved in Dominican political and internal affairs (Lowenthal, 1970). In the 20th century, US Marines occupied Santo Domingo three times, at least partially to protect US commercial interests in fruit and sugar production. The background for the most recent occupation, in 1965, was the assassination of dictator Rafael Trujillo, a brutal strongman who had ruled the Dominican Republic for 31 years. Trujillo's democratically elected successor was overthrown by a military coup, which led to a popular uprising. Fearing that the Dominican Republic was on the brink of a Cuban-style revolution, the US sent troops to help the military crush the revolt. This allowed a former aide of Trujillo to come to power, and to continue the right-wing violence and repression of human and civil rights (Gonzalez, 2011).

During Trujillo's reign, the Dominican government had made it extremely difficult to leave the country. His death, and the violence that surrounded it, led to a large-scale outmigration in the mid-1960s. That first group of Dominican migrants included members of the well-educated urban upper middle class, as well as people of lower socio-economic status from cities and rural areas (Guarnizo, 1994; Zong & Batalova, 2018). They were more likely to be political refugees rather than economic migrants (Gonzalez, 2011) but, like Central American migrants escaping civil wars, Dominican arrivals were fleeing a government backed by the US, and thus they did not receive the same assistance provided to refugees from communist Cuba. Subsequent Dominican migrants have been economically diverse and have included urban professionals as well as the rural poor (Zong & Batalova, 2018).

Conclusions and Connections

The history of the annexation of Mexican lands by the US is the basis for a saying common among Mexican Americans that 'we didn't cross the border; the border crossed us,' which is typically given as a rejoinder to anti-Mexican commentary or the portrayal of Mexican Americans as out of place and unwelcome. Macías (2014) points out that most of the current US once belonged to nations that had Spanish as an official language, whereas English has never been the country's official language (see Chapter 8). In addition, Macías (2014) argues that Spanish is different from so-called immigrant languages because, despite its history as a language of colonizers, most Spanish-speakers in the US today are descendants of colonized peoples (as a result of mestizaje, linguistic subordination of Indigenous languages and language shift to Spanish). The implication is that Spanish has more in common with Indigenous languages than it might first appear, and that this should be taken into account in the treatment of its speakers.

In our examination of the annexation of formerly Spanish territories, we saw that race and racism were key factors not just in US expansionism but also in the treatment of the people living in the annexed lands. Issues of race and racial identity as well as claims about racial purity and/or superiority also played a role in struggles for political representation and statehood, and in efforts to attract tourists. While we critiqued the downplaying of the historical presence of Spanish (an issue we return to next chapter, when we discuss the portrayal of the US as a monolingual English-speaking nation), we also showed that efforts to reclaim and celebrate the Spanish colonial past are not simply a straightforward attempt to counter Anglo-dominant narratives. Instead, they are intertwined with particular social, political and racial agendas and identity claims. Because representations of history have both symbolic implications and concrete, real-world consequences, they were – and still are – hotly contested. The claims to European heritage and Spanish identity we have discussed in this chapter will also be relevant for our discussion of race and racialization in Chapter 5. In that chapter we will examine the ways in which conquest and colonization, and the encounters among Europeans, Native peoples and Africans, have shaped understandings of race and racial identity in both Latin America and the US. These issues also come to the fore in our discussion of the history of US language policy in Chapter 8.

In our discussion of the most numerous Latinx national origin groups we hope to have given some sense of the diversity both of Latinxs and Spanish-speakers and of their reasons for coming to the US, while also emphasizing that the majority of Latinxs are not in fact immigrants. The diverse national origins of Spanish-speakers will be crucial in our discussion of the linguistic characteristics of Spanish in the US (Chapter 10). By looking at the unique histories of Mexican, Puerto Rican, Cuban, Dominican and Salvadoran migration, we showed how a combination of push and pull factors have led people to leave their homes in search of a better life in the US for themselves and their children. And while each place of origin is different, we saw that a common thread running through them all is the role of US political and economic policies and military involvement. In recent years, Latin American immigration has been at the center of political debate in the US. We hope to have given readers the background they need to be thoughtful participants in such debates, as well as the motivation to stay informed and engaged.

Discussion Questions and Activities for Chapter 3

(1) In his *Lines and Lineage* series (https://tomasvh.com/works/lines-and-lineage), photographer Tomas Van Houtryve combines 21st century landscapes and portraits to represent the Southwest prior to its 1848 annexation by the US. View the work (and possibly also listen to his 30-minute artist talk linked from that page). What are some of the themes that connect Van Houtryve's work, the Hispanophilia of the early 20th century, and the controversies surrounding Oñate? How do

representations of the past impact our understanding of the present? To what extent is our understanding of history shaped by popular culture and/or art, and to what extent can they be used to revise or 'correct' inaccurate understandings?

(2) Joshua Fishman (2001) identified three types of minority languages: Indigenous, colonial and immigrant. Consider how each of these labels might apply to the case of Spanish in the US. Next, discuss whether and/or how language type should impact a minority language's status or the rights of its speakers.

(3) Review the history and migration patterns of the largest Latinx national origin groups in the US and identify similarities and differences among them. At a minimum, you should consider: the historical timing of migration; push and pull factors; citizenship and immigration status; the ethnoracial make-up of the groups; and location within the US. In addition to the information in this chapter, you may wish to consult the demographic profiles available on the Pew Research Center's website (http://www.pewhispanic.org/2015/09/15/the-impact-of-slowing-immigration-foreign-born-share-falls-among-14-largest-us-hispanic-origin-groups) or Census Bureau data available online (https://data.census.gov)

(4) Read ProPublica's reporting on the treatment of unauthorized immigrants recruited to work in chicken-processing plants in North Carolina and Ohio (https://www.propublica.org/article/case-farms-chicken-industry-immigrant-workers-and-american-labor-law) and on their home town in highlands Guatemala (https://www.propublica.org/article/photos-returning-to-guatemala-roots-of-case-farms-workers). What are some of the push and pull factors that have contributed to Guatemalan immigrants coming to the US? What role did US foreign policy play? In what ways are unauthorized immigrants especially vulnerable to unethical employers? How might language and language barriers play a role?

(5) Informally interview someone you know about their own or their family's (im)migration history, as well as their minority language maintenance/loss (or analyze your own). What were the individual and group factors that led them to migrate? How easy or difficult was it for them to get authorization to do so? Does the person have regular contact with people in their country of origin? If the person has maintained a minority language, what were the group factors and individual decisions that helped make that possible? If the person underwent language loss (or never learned their family's heritage language), what were the contributing factors and how does the person feel about having lost (or never acquired) their heritage language?

Note

(1) It is also important to remember that prior to the arrival of both the English and the Spanish, there were approximately 15,000 Native people living in the Tidewater area (Hedgpeth, 2019).

Further Reading and Resources

Acuña, R. (2015) *Occupied America* (8th edn). New York: Pearson Longman.

Alcorn, S. (2018) Oñate's Foot. *99% Invisible Podcast*, 4 December. See https://99percentinvisible.org/episode/onates-foot/.

Duany, J. (2017) *Puerto Rico: What Everyone Needs to Know*. Oxford: Oxford University Press.

Gonzalez, J. (2011) *Harvest of Empire: A History of Latinos in America* (2nd edn). New York: Penguin.

Nieto-Phillips, J.M. (2004) *The Language of Blood*. Albuquerque, NM: University of New Mexico Press.

Chapter 4

Language Ideologies

Objectives

To define language ideologies, explain how language ideologies connect language to social meanings and power, and examine various language ideologies related to Spanish in the US.

Introduction

In this book we are particularly interested in the ways in which language, and Spanish in the US in particular, is tied up with social identities, culture and power. In previous chapters we made reference to the inaccurate assumption that people who speak Spanish don't know English, as well as to the portrayal of Spanish and Spanish-speakers as out of place in the US or even a threat to national identity. Where do these ideas come from and what assumptions undergird them? Why do people assign different kinds of social meaning to different languages and different ways of using language? How are these notions tied to broader social processes and how do they reproduce social hierarchies? In this chapter we address these questions through an examination of **language ideologies**, which at the simplest level can be defined as ideas about language structure and use (Errington, 2000). As we will see, there are also other, more complex, definitions.

Language ideologies can be about language in general, specific languages, specific language **varieties** or specific ways of using language. An example of a language ideology relevant to Spanish in the US is the idea that each nation 'naturally' has a single language and that the presence of multiple languages causes divisions (we discuss this ideology in more depth later in this chapter). Another common set of beliefs about language is the **standard language ideology**, which imagines that there is a single correct and unvarying way of speaking that is 'better' than 'non-standard' varieties, which are often denigrated as illogical or sloppy. The standard language ideology is inconsistent with a basic premise within the field of linguistics: all languages and language varieties are equally systematic and there is no objective linguistic reason for any variety or language to be considered 'better' than another.

If no variety is really better than the others, how does one way of speaking get chosen as the standard? Typically, the variety of the socio-economic elite, which is generally also the one associated with written language norms, is selected as the standard (Lippi-Green, 2012; Piller, 2015). Clearly, then, beliefs about the value or correctness of different language varieties and practices aren't only about language; they are also about other things, such as the status of the speakers of those varieties. Language ideologies are also shaped by other non-linguistic issues including societal understandings of national belonging (e.g. who is a 'real' American), the perceived intelligence or cultural 'value' of different groups, as well as other ideas about the people who speak different languages and language varieties (Woolard, 1998). Further, language ideologies don't just reflect ideas about people, groups or social and political issues; they also have an impact on them. For example, language ideologies undergird discussions and debates about whether English should be the official language of the US, whether someone is 'really' Latinx if they don't speak Spanish, what language(s) should be taught in schools, and if it is 'ok' to combine English and Spanish in conversation.

In the following sections we provide an introduction to the study of language ideologies and the ideological processes that give language social meaning. In addition to examining how language ideologies work, we show how they are inseparable from questions of power as well as how they allow linguistic difference to serve as a mechanism for maintaining social inequality. In the second half of the chapter we present some key language ideologies related to Spanish in the US. As we'll show, language ideologies are both reflected and reinforced in various kinds of public discourse and language policies, and they have 'real-world' impact.

Language Ideology Defined

Within the fields of sociolinguistics and linguistic anthropology, scholars emphasize that ideas and beliefs about language are a bridge between language and the social world. Language ideologies are what give social meaning to particular ways of using language and they allow us to judge people based on the way they speak. This notion is reflected in Woolard's (1998: 3) definition of language ideologies as 'representations, whether explicit or implicit, that construe the intersection of language and human beings in a social world,' as well as Irvine's (1989: 255) definition of language ideology as 'the cultural system of ideas about social and linguistic relationships, together with their loading of moral and political interests.'

Another important element of Irvine's definition is her description of language ideologies as 'cultural systems.' In this way, she makes it clear that language ideologies are not just individual opinions or impressions held by individual people; instead, different language ideologies are related to each other, and they are tied to societal values and norms. In other words, we don't come up with ideas about language completely on our own, in isolation from the world. Quite the opposite, people's beliefs about language (and other things) are shaped by our families and our communities, as well as the institutions and socio-economic and political structures with which we interact. Further, language ideologies can vary from society to society and culture to culture.

By pointing out that language ideologies are intertwined with 'moral and political interests,' Irvine makes it clear that they are not inconsequential opinions or preferences; rather, they benefit particular people or groups of people. As we noted above, when the standard language ideology portrays the way that the educated elite or dominant groups speak as better than other ways of speaking, this is not simply a neutral aesthetic preference; it reflects the higher status and power of the dominant group. But it's not just that that the dominant group's socio-economic or political status plays a role in determining that their way of speaking will be seen as better; the standard language ideology also plays a role in helping the dominant group maintain that status. People who speak 'standard' varieties are portrayed as intellectually and morally superior to speakers of 'non-standard' varieties – who are portrayed as ignorant or lazy – and they are offered more educational and professional opportunities (we return to this issue later in the chapter). For this reason, research on language ideologies emphasizes that they are part of the production and reproduction of social inequality. In other words, linguistic and social practices do not merely reflect social norms but also perpetuate and shape them.

Hegemony and Symbolic Domination

The concept of **hegemony** is a useful one for thinking about the role of language ideologies in the reproduction of social inequality and power. The basic definition is a simple: hegemony means that one entity (usually a social group or nation state) is dominant over another. The concept of hegemony also references the cultural and/or ideological influence of the dominant group in shaping broader societal norms and beliefs. With language ideologies, we are concerned not only with the way that certain ideologies help establish or sustain the hegemony of certain groups, but also with the hegemony of certain ways of thinking about language.

Hegemonic ideologies aren't always stated explicitly; in many cases they are **naturalized** and taken for granted (Kroskrity, 2004). *Naturalization* implies that an idea is not recognized as a specific cultural value or viewpoint, but is instead seen as common sense, an inevitable truth or something inherent to the human experience. For example, in the US there is widespread acceptance of the **one nation-one language ideology** (i.e. the notion that each nation is defined by single language and vice-versa) and of the hegemony of English. These ideologies are largely taken for granted, such as in the 'Welcome to America: Now SPEAK ENGLISH!' bumper sticker shown in Figure 4.1. Nowhere in the bumper sticker's text is there an *explicit* claim that nations should have just one language, that speaking English is a key part of US national identity or that other languages are unwelcome; however, the text only makes sense if the reader/viewer has access to these hegemonic ideologies. In addition to the belief that immigrants have an obligation to assimilate

Figure 4.1 Bumper sticker: 'Welcome to America: Now SPEAK ENGLISH!'

linguistically, the bumper sticker's message also rests on the (inaccurate) presupposition that immigrants to the US don't speak English (discussed in Chapter 2); otherwise they would not need a directive to do so.

Hegemonic ideologies can be so powerful and can become so naturalized that even when people reject arguments based on them, they sometimes inadvertently participate in and reproduce the same ideologies (Gal, 1998; Kroskrity, 2004; Silverstein, 1996). For example, take a look at the bumper sticker in Figure 4.2, which reads 'Welcome to America: Now speak Cherokee.' This bumper sticker offers a tongue-in-cheek rebuttal to the message in the bumper sticker in Figure 4.1 by reminding the reader/viewer that English is a relatively new arrival in what is now the US. As such, the apparent intention is to reject the disparagement of speakers of languages other than English and, on the first reading, it may seem like a challenge to the dominant **English-only** ideology. Nonetheless, this apparent challenge actually embodies some of the same assumptions inherent in that ideology. Indeed, the Speak Cherokee bumper sticker doesn't reject the one nation-one language ideology or celebrate multilingualism but instead upholds the idea that there is a single 'legitimate' language; it simply replaces English with Cherokee. By ignoring the linguistic and cultural diversity of Native peoples as well as implying that they would have felt the same way about the linguistic obligations of new arrivals, the bumper sticker inadvertently reinforces hegemonic ideologies as timeless common-sense notions. Moreover, having Native peoples offer a welcome to 'America' projects its existence backwards in time and naturalizes it.

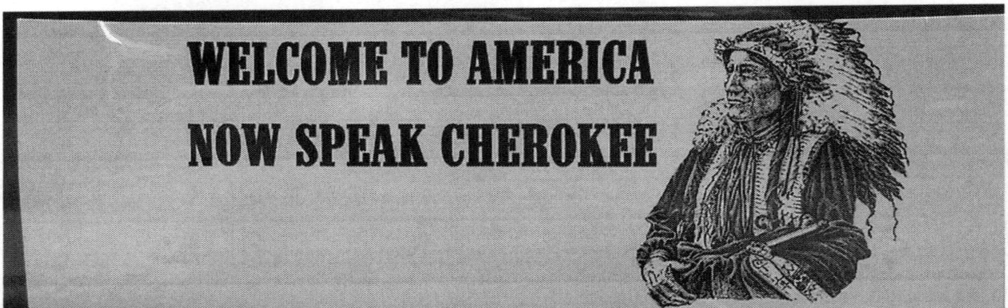

Figure 4.2 Bumper sticker: 'WELCOME TO AMERICA: NOW SPEAK CHEROKEE'

Further, this bumper sticker seems to suggest a false equivalence between contemporary immigration to the US and the historical colonization and conquest of the Americas by Europeans, thus obscuring the genocide and political domination we discussed in Chapter 3.

The two bumper stickers we have just analyzed illustrate the ways in which public discourse is influenced by language ideologies. But this relationship is two-way, or circular, in the sense that this kind of discourse also reinforces specific language ideologies. Taking the case of the Speak English bumper sticker, a person might put this on their car because of their beliefs regarding the role of English in the US and immigrants' supposed moral obligation to speak it. But presumably, the person who puts this bumper sticker on their car also hopes that it will influence other people to think the same way. In this way, discourse doesn't just reflect language ideologies; it also disseminates and promotes them to other people. Language ideologies are similarly disseminated and reproduced in everyday interaction, in the statements of public figures, in news media, television shows and movies and in a range of governmental and non-governmental policies. And this is generally the case for linguistic and social policies and practices too: they don't just reflect social norms or ideologies; they also perpetuate and shape them. In other words, the relationship between ideologies and practices is circular and mutually reinforcing. The hegemony of English, and especially 'standard' English, leads to its dominance in education and government. It then becomes associated with these domains, and people use it in order to convey status and authority. This, in turn, further strengthens those associations and the symbolic value of standard English, and the cycle continues.

Ideologies are sometimes conscious and expressed openly. However, in other cases they may circulate below the level of consciousness (Kroskrity, 2004) and their reproduction can also be more subtle, such as when television programs or movies use 'foreign' or 'non-standard' accents as a way to portray characters as unintelligent (Lippi-Green, 2012). Even when language ideologies have negative consequences for non-dominant groups, people who belong to those groups also often take them for granted. In other words, both socially dominant and dominated groups see hegemonic ideologies as natural and universal, or they don't even notice them (Woolard, 1998). For example, the hegemonic ideology that languages other than English are un-American and/or interfere with the acquisition of English is not limited to monolingual English-speakers. People who speak other languages (whether monolingually or in addition to English) also sometimes believe this (especially if told as much by their children's teachers), and this can lead them to speak to their children exclusively in English (Zentella, 1997a). (This is a pervasive but false notion. Spanish language maintenance does not interfere with English acquisition, as we saw in Chapter 2. Further, it is positively correlated with academic achievement and overall upward mobility; see discussion in Chapter 9.)

Scholars of social inequality sometimes use Bourdieu's (1991) notion of **symbolic domination** to refer to dominant groups' ability to convince dominated groups that existing social hierarchies are fair and just, and they point to schools as a key place where this happens (see Chapter 9). Let us again use the example of the standard language ideology which, as we saw, elevates the language variety spoken by the dominant group. By portraying speakers of the standard variety as smarter or more hardworking than the 'ignorant' and 'lazy' speakers of other varieties, the standard language ideology doesn't just favor the dominant group; it also portrays them as intellectually and morally deserving of higher status. Bourdieu stresses that the hegemony of one language or variety rests in part on the complicity of speakers of other languages or varieties. Thus, in the case of language ideologies, symbolic domination consists of getting people to take up or accept the hegemonic language ideologies that disadvantage them.

Although certain language ideologies achieve hegemony within a given society, there are also always competing ideologies that co-exist with them (Kroskrity, 2004). For example, in the one nation-one language ideology, language is considered a defining characteristic of national identity, societal monolingualism is seen as promoting national unity, and multilingualism is considered divisive. However, there is also a competing ideology that portrays multilingualism as a national resource for global competitiveness or national security. Competing ideologies regarding multilingualism also operate at the individual level. One ideology sees monolingualism as the normal state of affairs and minority language maintenance as a hindrance to English acquisition, but another ideology constructs multilingualism as a valuable resource for intellectual development as well as professional success (we discuss these ideologies in more depth later in this chapter). In some cases different members of society subscribe to different ideologies, but in other cases individuals shift back and forth between different ideologies depending on the context. The fact that counter-hegemonic ideologies can co-exist with hegemonic ideologies underscores that it is sometimes possible to resist dominant ways of thinking. Moreover, it suggests that ideologies can change over time and thus that hegemonic ideologies should not be considered permanent or intractable.

Crucially, language ideologies also play a role in how we think about or categorize individuals and groups of people. To understand this, let us look again at the examples of ideologies we've mentioned thus far. As we noted, the standard language ideology doesn't just reflect a group's relative prestige and power. Instead, by framing certain ways of speaking as better than others, it also plays a role in social differentiation, or the classification and evaluation of people and groups. Along the same lines, in the US the one nation-one language ideology contributes to the portrayal of people who speak languages other than English as un-American (even if they also speak English). In the next section we look more closely at how language ideologies allow linguistic forms and practices to take on social and symbolic meanings, and to justify social practices on the basis of linguistic difference.

Language Ideologies: Bridging the Linguistic and the Social

One key way in which language expresses social meaning is through a process called **indexicality**. When a linguistic feature (or language, language variety or linguistic practice) is associated with a specific **stance**, social category or characteristic, the feature is said to 'index' or 'point to' that category or characteristic (Ochs, 1992; Silverstein, 1996). In order to grasp this notion, remember that it is not only the content of our speech that has meaning, but also the *way* we talk. Just as we can say something about ourselves by the way we dress or style our hair, we can also enact certain identities by speaking in a particular language or style, or even just by choosing to use certain words. Indexicality is the process that allows us to do this. For example, in her research with Latina gangs in northern California, Mendoza-Denton (2008) found that the color red was an index of the Norteña gang while the color blue was an index of the Sureñas, such that dressing in these colors was a way to signal membership in one gang or the other. Feathered hair and the numbers 14 and 4 were also indexes of Norteña identity, whereas vertical ponytails and the numbers 13 and 3 were indexes of the Sureñas. Language was another way through which girls signaled their membership in one gang or the other: speaking Spanish (and minimizing or denying proficiency in English) indexed the Sureñas, while speaking English and downplaying or avoiding Spanish indexed the Norteñas.

Indexical meanings are not intrinsic, but instead depend on context; clearly, the color blue doesn't index the Sureña gang everywhere. Similarly, linguistic features and practices don't always mean the same thing in every context, or even to everyone with in a given context. Obviously, Spanish doesn't index Sureña identity universally; in many US contexts it is an index of Latinx identity, an issue we return to later in this chapter and throughout the book. For another example of the contextual nature of indexicality, let us consider the use of English words in a primarily Spanish conversation, which has different social and symbolic meanings in Latin America and the US. In many Latin American contexts, incorporating a few words in English can serve to index internationalism and sophistication, but in the US the exact same practice is sometimes interpreted as linguistic sloppiness or seen as evidence of deficient Spanish knowledge.

One framework for looking at the role of language ideologies in social differentiation, or how language ideologies allow for linguistic differences to be used in assigning people to different social categories or identities, has been put forth by Irvine and Gal (2000). They identify three key processes: **iconicity**, fractal recursivity and **erasure**. Iconicity is an ideological process in which linguistic features not only index certain groups or activities but are seen as iconic representations of them, and reflections of the group's 'inherent nature or essence' (Irvine & Gal, 2000: 37). In other words, the linguistic feature or language doesn't just 'point to' the social group; it is seen as inherent to the group. Further, with iconization, the linguistic feature and the group associated with it are perceived as being similar or sharing certain characteristics. Taking the case of Spanish in the US, in many contexts Spanish has become an icon for Latinxs, such that the perceived characteristics (and stereotypes) of Latinxs map onto perceptions of Spanish. For example, the Spanish language is commonly viewed as 'easy' (Lipski, 2002: 1248), which parallels racist attitudes about the cultural and intellectual achievements of Spanish-speakers.

Similarly, the **Mock Spanish** practice of adding *-o* endings to English nouns (e.g. *no problemo, el cheapo*) and the treatment of Spanish as if it weren't a 'real' language with its own words and complex grammar parallels the devaluing of Latinx peoples and cultures

(Barrett, 2006; Hill, 1995, 2008; we discuss Mock Spanish further in Chapter 6). In these cases, the perceived shared characteristics of Latinxs and Spanish are negative, but that isn't always the case in iconization. When a website selling online language classes states that 'Spanish tops off our list as one of the world's most romantic languages because of its passionate, sensual sound' (https://www.rocketlanguages.com/blog/the-languages-of-love-the-5-most-romantic-languages, accessed 12 September 2018), passion and sensuality are perceived as shared characteristics of the language and its speakers. Of course, even when presented as positive attributes, these are still stereotypes that can have negative implications (see the discussion in Chapter 7 on such stereotypes in media representations of Latinxs).

Fractal recursivity is the term that Gal and Irvine use to describe the tendency of social and linguistic distinctions to operate on multiple levels. Specifically, ideological features that are used to differentiate *between* groups are often also used to differentiate *within* groups recursively. Recursivity in US language ideology can be found in the hierarchy of languages that positions some languages as better than others and the pervasive idea that there is just one right way of speaking that is superior to other ways. In the dominant linguistic hierarchy, English is intellectually superior to Spanish. However, similar distinctions are also made *within* English, such that northern US varieties are seen as 'smarter' than southern varieties. Thus, the perception of one 'correct' way of speaking and multiple inferior ways of speaking is seen both on the level of language as well as on the level of variety. Similar types of fractal recursivity also operate in Spanish among national varieties and within them. For example, a common belief among Spanish-speakers is that Colombian Spanish is 'better' than other national varieties. However, within Colombian Spanish, Bogotá Spanish is often seen as superior to varieties spoken along the coast and, within Bogotá, the varieties spoken by the elite are seen as better than those of the working class.

Finally, *erasure* is the phenomenon of ignoring or rendering invisible any information or practice that would contradict the hegemonic ideology. The one nation-one language ideology frames monolingualism within a national territory as the natural and right way for a country to operate, and thus portrays multilingualism as divisive, an impediment to participation in mainstream America, and a characteristic of impoverished immigrant communities. In order for this ideology to stand, several sociolinguistic realities undergo erasure. To wit, there are many multilingual nations throughout the world, and the majority of the world's people are believed to be multilingual. In the case of the US, many bilinguals were born in the US, fully participate in all aspects of US society and are members of the middle and upper socio-economic classes. In addition, Spanish language maintenance (i.e. Spanish–English bilingualism) correlates with academic achievement and success (see Chapter 9). These facts constitute counter-evidence to the prevailing ideology but go largely unseen by those that subscribe to it. Similarly, the image of the US as a monolingual English-speaking nation involves selective erasure of various aspects of the linguistic history of the US, including the multilingual nature of early settlements and the maintenance of immigrant and Indigenous languages. And of course, it also erases the fact that English itself is not native to what is now the US.

The Consequences of Language Ideologies: Power, Politics and Policy

As we noted, language ideologies are opinions or beliefs, but they have real-world consequences. By influencing the public portrayal and perception of people and groups, language ideologies also shape the treatment of those people and groups. This can happen at the level of individual interactions, such as when someone yells at or attacks people for speaking languages other than English. There have been numerous videotaped examples of this in recent years, some of which are listed together with other examples of linguistic prejudice and discrimination on the webpage http://potowski.org/resources/repression. Here we will discuss one representative example which received a lot of attention in the media and public discourse, the case of a New York man who became enraged that employees of a Manhattan eatery were speaking in Spanish (Robbins, 2018; https://www.nytimes.com/2018/05/16/nyregion/man-threatens-spanish-language-video.html, accessed 15 September 2018). The one nation-one language ideology is clearly reflected in the man's outrage that 'staff is speaking Spanish to customers when they should be speaking English,' his explanation that 'It's America,' and his subsequent assumption and threat: 'I will be following up, and my guess is they're not documented. So my next call is to ICE [Immigration and Customs Enforcement] to have each one of them kicked out of my country.' For this man, the ideological linking of English and the US is so strong that he doesn't just demand that other people know English; he feels entitled not to have to even *hear* Spanish when in the US. Further, he sees Spanish as so illegitimate that he assumes that employees speaking it must be unauthorized immigrants (and threatens to call ICE), and he suggests that 'they' do not belong in '[his]' country.

It's important to note that there was a tremendous public outcry in response to this incident, again demonstrating the multiplicity of ideologies that can co-exist, as well as the possibility of resistance to hegemonic and/or racist ideologies. Particularly interesting is the response of one bystander who challenged the man; she can be heard on the video saying, 'It *is* America,' thus seemingly rejecting the one nation-one language ideology in favor of a construction of US national identity tied to the recognition (and perhaps celebration) of pluralism. And as we noted in Chapter 2, speaking Spanish in public can in and of itself constitute a form of resistance to anti-immigrant and anti-Latinx discourses (Sánchez-Muñoz & Amezcua, 2019).

Language ideologies also impact how people are treated in more subtle, but just as damaging, ways. For example, when schools treat one language or one language variety as the only 'correct' one, this tells students who speak differently that their way of speaking is wrong or bad and that, by extension, so are their ways of being, their identity, their family and their community. This denigration can be considered a type of symbolic violence (Bourdieu, 1991; Zentella, 2017) or 'linguistic terrorism' (Anzaldúa, 1987). The negative impact is not only symbolic, emotional and psychological, but also academic. For one thing, there are added challenges of being asked to do schoolwork, and take tests, in a variety different from one's own, especially if teachers don't recognize that students are learning an additional variety. Consider how much harder it is for you to do well in school if lessons, instructions and recess all take place in a language you have not yet learned and, further, you are graded in part on how well you manage the grammar rules of that language. Moreover, language ideologies sometimes lead teachers to assume that certain students aren't as smart as others based on the way they speak, which also impacts academic outcomes.

Just as language ideologies undergird negative assumptions about students who don't speak 'correctly,' they also undergird employers' decisions not to hire someone because they don't sound 'professional.' Importantly, the use of the standard language ideology as a gate-keeping mechanism doesn't just impact *individual* students or job-seekers, but instead contributes to structural inequality, in which disfavored *groups* are discriminated against (Fairclough, 1992, 2001; Flores & Rosa, 2015; Leeman, 2005, 2018b). In this way, as we noted earlier, hegemonic language ideologies play a role in the reproduction of social inequality. In the US, the hierarchy of languages portrays English as superior to Spanish (and other 'foreign' languages) and positions middle-class and White ways of speaking at the top; ethnoracial varieties (such as **African American English**, or AAE) as well as varieties associated with poor and/or rural people are positioned at the bottom. Thus, the standard language ideology plays a role in the socio-economic and political exclusion of these groups. However, because this same ideology portrays the favored variety (aka 'standard English') as inherently better, language discrimination is often naturalized, and not seen as discrimination at all. As we discuss below, ways of speaking are often portrayed as a choice, and this portrayal bolsters the view that negative consequences for speaking a particular variety or language are deserved, because the speaker could simply speak the standard. In turn, this allows people to express racist or discriminatory views while appearing (and claiming) to be defending common-sense views about 'proper' or 'correct' speech, or about English being the national language of the US. And because specific ways of speaking are linked to specific groups (i.e. AAE to African Americans, and Spanish to Latinxs), language ideologies contribute to structural racism without making reference to ethnic or racial identity (see Chapter 5).

Language ideologies can also become codified in language policies and laws. For example, the one nation-one language ideology and the related idea that monolingualism is the norm shape language-in-education policies such as the lack of bilingual education. As we discuss in more depth in Chapter 9, in the US, educational policies for speakers of minority languages (including speakers of Spanish) typically prioritize the acquisition of English over the development of students' home languages, and even the learning of academic subjects. In the relatively rare cases where education in Spanish (or another minority language) is provided, this is usually only a temporary measure, as a way to teach English or content. Further, speakers of Spanish who also know English are generally not provided with any academic support to maintain or develop their abilities in Spanish. These same ideologies also explain why less than 20% of K-12 students in the US are enrolled in a 'foreign' language course, a percentage that is even lower at the elementary school level (American Councils for International Education, 2017; we discuss language-in-education policy in Chapter 9).

Thus far in this chapter we have given an overview of language ideologies and the ideological processes that mediate between language and the social world, and we have outlined some of the emotional, academic, professional and political consequences of language ideologies. In the second half of the chapter we will present various language ideologies that have an impact on Spanish in the US.

The Standard Language Ideology

We have used the standard language ideology as an example several times in our discussion of language ideologies above but now we want to provide a definition and make a few additional points. Lippi-Green (2012: 67) defines the standard language ideology as 'a bias toward an abstracted, idealized, homogenous spoken language which is imposed and maintained by dominant bloc institutions and which names as its model the written language, but which is drawn primarily from the spoken language of the upper middle class.' She points out that variation is inherent to all languages and language varieties, and thus languages are never actually 'homogenous'; no two people speak exactly alike, and everybody speaks differently according to where they are, who they are with, what they are doing and what they are trying to express. For this reason, Lippi-Green describes the standard as 'abstracted' and 'idealized.' Nonetheless, the ideology sets up uniformity as a goal (Milroy & Milroy, 1999), and because certain ways of speaking are represented and perceived as being standard, they are seen as better than other varieties.

Despite favoring upper middle-class speech, the standard language ideology presents the standard variety as if it were neutral and equally accessible to everyone, thus erasing the unequal power relationships it reflects and reproduces (Woolard, 2005, 2016). This allows blame to be placed on people who 'choose' not to speak the standard. This is problematic for (at least) two reasons. First, people don't just choose to speak one way or another; people's languages, linguistic varieties and accents are obviously closely tied to their identities and their surrounding communities (Lippi-Green, 2012). Secondly, the standard language ideology makes it seem that subordinated groups could improve their status simply by speaking the standard variety. But this makes it seem as if language were the *cause* of social differences, when in reality language hierarchies are the *mechanism* by which inequality is reproduced. For example, let us take the case of AAE and **Chicanx** English. These varieties are often considered 'non-standard' and their speakers are frequently disparaged or discriminated against. If language were really the cause of this discrimination, then all the African Americans and Chicanxs who speak standard English would never face discrimination. However, this isn't the case; institutional and interpersonal racism continue to operate, regardless of how people speak (Bartolomé & Macedo, 1999; Macedo, 1997).

But who chooses the standard and how do people know which variety is preferred? Who makes the rules? One way that language subordination (which goes hand in hand with the standard language ideology) plays out is that language is 'mystified' and speakers of the language are portrayed as not being able to use their own language without 'expert guidance' (Lippi-Green, 2012: 70). Regular people are delegitimized regarding how to speak their own language, and linguistic authority is assigned to 'experts' who are assumed to know more than 'mere' speakers of the language. In some countries, and for some languages, there are official language academies. Spain's *Real Academia Española* (RAE; Spanish Royal Academy) was founded in 1713, and there are now affiliated national language academies throughout Latin America. With membership comprising prestigious members of the arts and sciences including well-known authors, and with the official motto of *Limpia, fija y da esplendor* ('cleanse, fix, and give splendor'), the RAE produces dictionaries, orthographies (i.e. spelling rules) and grammar books describing 'correct' usage.

In addition to promoting 'good' language use, the RAE seeks to ensure the unity of Spanish not only within Spain, but also internationally (Mar-Molinero & Paffey, 2011; Paffey, 2012; Villa & Del Valle, 2014). Although the RAE collaborates with Latin American academies of Spanish and the international *Asociación de Academias de la Lengua Española* (AALE) in the promotion of 'Pan-Hispanic' norms that recognize some regional variation, the RAE remains very much at the center of this endeavor and seeks to maintain Spain's symbolic ownership of Spanish (Mar-Molinero & Paffey, 2011). Along with Spanish government-funded institutions like the RAE and the *Instituto Cervantes* (which promotes the study of Spanish around the world), private business interests and corporations (such as the telecommunications giant *Telefónica*) have also sought to maintain Spain's leadership in defining international language norms, highlighting the intertwining of linguistic, political and economic concerns (Mar-Molinero & Paffey, 2011; Villa & Del Valle, 2014; Zentella, 2017). The involvement of these institutions in the definition of language norms and standards also includes the publication of Spanish-as-a-second-language teaching materials, as well as sponsorship and promotion of the *Servicio Internacional de Evaluación de la Lengua Española* ('International Spanish Language Evaluation Service') (see https://siele.org), a proficiency evaluation and certification service.

One of the most recent Spanish language academies to join the AALE is the non-profit *Academia Norteamericana de la Lengua Española* (ANLE), founded in 1973 and headquartered in New York. The ANLE's website (http://www.anle.us, accessed 15 September 2018) defines their mission in part 'to study, develop and execute the normative rules of the Spanish of the United States of America,' as well as to establish and promote 'the criteria of proper and correct usage' and 'to ensure that, in its constant adaptation to the particular needs of Spanish speakers,' the Spanish used in the US 'does not affect the unity and understanding of the language in the Hispanic world.' Like the RAE and the policy of pan-Hispanism, the ANLE has been criticized for its privileging of European norms and the subordination of local varieties and practices, especially those that reflect influence from English (Lynch & Potowski, 2014; Zentella, 2017).

While the standard language ideology disparages the language varieties associated with disfavored groups (such as those with less education or lower socio-economic status, or who belong to **ethnoracial** minorities), this rejection of social variation sometimes co-exists with an acceptance of geographic variation. For example, acceptance of geographic variation is reflected in descriptions of Spanish as a **pluricentric** language. *Pluricentrism* means that instead of a single, international standard, each 'Spanish-speaking' country has its own standard variety (Lope Blanch, 1986, 2001). However, this recognition of multiple standard varieties does not challenge the disparagement of 'non-standard' varieties. Indeed, while pluricentrism implies equality among different *geographic* varieties, it reproduces the hierarchies among *social* varieties (Leeman, 2012b). This is exemplified in the following quote from linguist Lope Blanch:

> *Es evidente que en cada país hispanohablante existe una norma lingüística ejemplar, paradigmática, a la que los habitantes de cada nación tratan de aproximarse cuando de hablar bien se trata. Suele ella ser la norma culta de la ciudad capital: la madrileña para España, la bogotana para Colombia, la limeña para el Perú, etc.* (Lope Blanch, 2001: n.p.)
>
> It is clear that in ever Spanish-speaking country there is a paradigmatic, exemplar linguistic norm that the inhabitants of each nation try to approximate when their trying to speak well. It is usually the educated norm of the capital city: Madrid's for Spain, Bogota's for Colombia, Lima's for Peru, etc. (Our translation)

Here, the description of Spanish as pluricentric goes hand in hand with reproduction of the standard language ideology and the naturalizing of the privileging of the educated elite in the definition of standard varieties.

The notion that each 'Spanish-speaking country' has its own standard is consistent with the existence of a language academy in each one, and it seems to suggest equal status for all of them. However, this is not always the case. As we discussed above, the RAE exerts significant influence in shaping the norms of the member academies of the AALE. Moreover, the standard language ideology and the associated belief in linguistic 'purity' contribute to ideas about the relative 'quality', 'correctness' and/or 'value' of different national varieties of Spanish. Sometimes, these linguist hierarchies are based on racist understandings about the superiority of language varieties spoken in countries perceived to have populations with less African and Indigenous ancestry (Alfaraz, 2002, 2014; Niño-Murcia, 2001; Valdés *et al.*, 2003). The relative wealth of different nations and the socio-economic status of the speakers can also shape attitudes toward different national varieties (Carter & Callesano, 2018). Linguistic purism also plays a role, such as in the longstanding subordination of Puerto Rican Spanish to the supposedly superior varieties spoken in Spain, as well as in the ANLE's denigration of words and expressions typically used by Spanish-speakers in the US (Zentella, 1997a, 2017). The ideological intertwining of ethnonational identity, socio-economic status, education and linguistic authority, as well as resistance to linguistic subordination, are evident in the following statement by the elderly matriarch of a family in rural Michigan:

> *No hablamos español, nunca hablamos español. Nuestra lengua es del campo, no de la escuela. Si yo hablo con alguien de España, no me va a entender. Ellos nos [dicen] que somos pobres, que no [podemos] hablar nuestra lengua. Pero sí [podemos], mexicano es nuestra lengua.*
>
> We don't speak Spanish, we never spoke Spanish. Our language is from the [migrant] camp, not from school. If I were to speak to someone from Spain, they wouldn't understand me. They say that we are poor, that we can't speak our language. But we can, Mexican is our language. (Torrez, 2013: 291)

We discuss research on attitudes toward different varieties of Spanish in Chapter 10.

As for English, Noah Webster's late 18th century efforts to create an American language academy were unsuccessful (Lepore, 2002). Nonetheless, there is no shortage of linguistic authorities, powerful institutions and experts who seek to set norms of proper and correct usage of American English. The standard language ideology is explicitly reproduced in grammar books, dictionaries, newspaper style guides and language columns and a host of other sources. Importantly, ideologies are also reproduced in linguistic usage as well as in the implicit linking of social identities to specific ways of talking (Woolard, 1998). Along these lines, in her research on the use of different accents and language varieties in Disney films, Lippi-Green (2012) found that 'non-standard', non-White and 'foreign' accents were typically associated with villains, while positive characters tended to speak 'standard English.' On one hand, this shows that the association of non-standard varieties with negative characteristics is so naturalized that these varieties can be used as an index of moral shortcomings. On the other hand, it signals the role of popular culture and the media in reproducing language ideologies. We analyze this further in our discussion of the use and representation of Spanish in the media in Chapter 7, paying particular attention to the use of accents and language in the portrayal of Latinx characters.

Lippi-Green's research has also shown that judges and judicial decisions reflect a bias against people who speak non-standard varieties and/or have 'foreign' accents, even though language-based discrimination is prohibited when it is related to other kinds of illegal discrimination (such as discrimination based on race or national origin). We discuss the legal prohibitions against language-based discrimination more fully in Chapter 8, our chapter on language policy in the US.

The One Nation–One Language Ideology

Without getting into a lengthy discussion of nations, nation states and nationalism, we want to mention that countries are not naturally occurring entities based in the physical or geological world. Instead, they are created and sustained through a series of sociocultural, historical and political processes that rely in part on naturalizing their existence and convincing the people within them that they belong to the same nation. (Before continuing, you may wish to take a moment to reflect on the Speak Cherokee bumper sticker we discussed earlier.) Anderson (1991) refers to nations as 'imagined communities' because members of these communities do not know most of the people in them, but nonetheless imagine shared values, practices, etc. By producing feelings of shared identity among large numbers of people who have never met, and who differ from each other in numerous ways, nations are able to achieve emotional attachment and loyalty among citizens – sometimes even including the willingness to sacrifice one's life for one's country or nationalist cause (Anderson, 1991; Billig, 1995).

The one nation-one language ideology sees language as a key element for defining national identities. On one hand, the existence of a shared language among people can serve as a justification for nationalist demands, such as when minority language groups seek autonomy or independence (Anderson, 1991; Billig, 1995). And on the other hand, linguistic diversity is seen as an impediment to national unity. As a result, people are expected to speak the national language in order to belong, speakers of other languages are seen as outsiders, and their social and/or political exclusion is naturalized. Because languages often index particular ethnic or cultural groups, ideas about which languages belong within a nation are often inseparable from ideas about which kinds of people belong.

It's worth noting that the one nation-one language ideology goes both ways; just as a shared language participates in the construction of a national identity, the existence of a nation associated with a particular way of speaking contributes to that way of speaking being considered a language rather than a regional variety or 'dialect,' an issue we return to later in this chapter. Further, as Woolard (1998: 17) points out, minority language speakers seeking governmental recognition and support often rely on the same 'nationalist ideology of language and identity' that is used to subordinate them to the majority language.

In the US, English is seen as central to national identity and national unity. Although the notion that the US is and has always been a (monolingual) English-speaking nation is naturalized and taken for granted, it is not consistent with the historical record, and it relies on the erasure of both past and present multilingualism in the English colonies as well as in the US. In Chapter 3, in addition to examining the long history of Spanish in what is now the US, we also noted that hundreds of Native languages were spoken in North America prior to European conquest. Although many languages disappeared as a result of genocide and forced assimilation, other Native languages, such as Cherokee and Navajo, continue to be widely spoken and in some cases are being revitalized (McCarty, 2016). Enslaved Africans also spoke numerous different languages, as did colonizers and immigrants who arrived from Europe and Asia (Schmid, 2001; Schmidt, 2000). In some areas of the country, French and German were dominant and were retained even after English became the de facto national language (Wiley, 1998, 2010). Immigrants from around the world have continued to bring new languages and have refreshed ones long spoken here. Thus, a multitude of languages have always been spoken in the area now known as the US (Kloss, 1977; Potowski, 2010).

Although English has long been dominant in the US, and despite some early efforts to establish an American language that would unify the nation (Lepore, 2002), linguistic diversity was not generally considered problematic before the mid-1800s. Until that time, US national identity was constructed primarily around race (i.e. Whiteness) and a commitment to democratic principles, rather than language (Painter, 2010; Pavlenko, 2002; Wiley, 2000). As immigration increased in the lead-up to the 20th century, and a greater percentage of immigrants came from southern and eastern Europe, concerns were raised about the arrival of people perceived as inherently different from the existing population. Much like today, at the turn of the 20th century, **nativists** worried that immigrants weren't assimilating, and that the country was undergoing unwelcome change (Bonfiglio, 2002;

Leeman, 2013). Around that time, the idea that immigrants not only should learn English, but also should give up their native languages, became hegemonic (Pavlenko, 2002; Schmidt, 2000; Wiley, 1998). Twenty-first century complaints about today's immigrants often portray earlier immigrants as having learned English shortly after arrival, but in reality it took many much longer and some never learned English at all (Wiley, 2010; Wilkerson & Salmons, 2008). This fact, as well as the suffering of those who were subjected to public stigma and discrimination based on their accents or lack of English, is another example of erasure (Pavlenko, 2002).

The early 20th century emphasis on English monolingualism, as well as the ideological linking of political philosophy, national identity and language, are manifested in a frequently cited letter written by President Theodore Roosevelt:

> There can be no divided allegiance here. Any man who says he is an American, but something else also, isn't an American at all. We have room for but one flag, the American flag, and this excludes the red flag which symbolizes all wars against liberty and civilization just as much as it excludes any foreign flag of a nation to which we are hostile. We have room for but one language here and that is the English language, for we intend to see that the crucible turns our people out as Americans, and American nationality, and not as dwellers in a polyglot boarding house; and we have room for but one soul [sic] loyalty, and that is loyalty to the American people. (Roosevelt, 1919: 1–2)

It is striking to note the parallels Roosevelt draws here between the American flag, US national identity, freedom, civilization, the English language and loyalty to the American people. Language is unambiguously made into a symbol of belonging, and speaking English – and only English – is portrayed as representing a choice to be American. English monolingualism is portrayed as a transparent representation of American identity, and bilingualism as reflecting a divided allegiance. The alternative to English monolingualism, Roosevelt suggests, is a 'polyglot boarding house' (Roosevelt, 1919: 2) – implying that multilingualism brings with it a certain working-class transience.

The ideology that US national identity requires English monolingualism is one source of the hostility toward Spanish (and other non-English languages) in the examples we presented earlier. This hostility also is reflected in a range of federal and local language policies including the scarcity of bilingual education, the English requirements for naturalization as a US citizen and the limited public services available in Spanish and other minority languages (see Chapter 8). Anti-Spanish, anti-Latinx and anti-immigrant discourses occur in a wide range of contexts from daily interactions to the speeches of political candidates and elected officials, including President Trump. Anyone spending a few minutes on the comments section of pretty much any English-language newspaper or website discussing language or immigration in the US will find numerous examples. Although such rhetoric has been directed at a wide range of languages, and speakers of various non-English languages have been subjected to verbal and physical abuse, Spanish and Spanish-speakers seem to be the most frequent target. This is probably due in part to the demographic prominence of Spanish compared to other minority languages in the US, but it is also surely related to the indexical relationship between Spanish and Latinx identity, which allows anti-Latinx racism to be expressed through reference to Spanish language.

Hostility toward Spanish has been particularly intense when it is used in conjunction with national symbols, such as the pledge of allegiance or the national anthem, suggesting that it is rooted in ideas about national identity. For example, there was a tremendous public outcry in response to the 2006 release of *Nuestro Himno*, a Spanish-language version of the US national anthem. The issue was all over the English-language and Spanish-language news and talk radio, with numerous politicians and even the President and the descendants of the author of the original *Star-Spangled Banner* weighing in. One common theme in responses was that the Spanish language was 'offensive,' a sentiment expressed even by long-time defenders of immigrant and Latinx rights, such as Antonio Villaraigosa (then Mayor of Los Angeles), who told CNN that 'I was offended, because, for me, the national anthem is something that I believe deserves respect.' He went on to explain his position by stating that 'the Spanish and Mexican anthems should be sung in Spanish; the French anthem in French,' underscoring both the strength and the naturalization of the one nation-one language ideology.

At the time, public opinion polls found that 69–78% of adults in the US thought the anthem should be sung only in English, and an article in the *Washington Post* explained that: 'Transforming the musical idiom of "The Star-Spangled Banner" is one thing, argue the skeptics, but translating the words sends the opposite message: "We are not Americans"' (Montgomery, 2006). In contrast to this understanding of the song's message, the title of the album on which the song appeared is *Somos americanos* ('We are Americans'), and the producer stated that his intentions were patriotic (Walters, 2006). Thus, if people really interpreted the song as denying American identity, it seems that the indexical relationship of English monolingualism to US national identity is so strong that it overpowered the content of the song. In Figure 4.3, cartoonist Lalo Alcaraz comments on this idea that speaking in Spanish is inherently anti-American, regardless of what you say, even if it is 'I ♥ U.S.A.'.

Figure 4.3 ¡Yo ♥ U.S.A!
Cartoon appears courtesy of Lalo Alcaraz & Andrews McMeel Syndication © 2019.

A different interpretation of the outcry around *Nuestro Himno* suggests that people understood the singing of the national anthem to be a claim to national belonging, and they were unwilling to consider Spanish-speakers as truly American (Butler & Spivak, 2007; Cepeda, 2010). Either way, the controversy shows the power of the one nation-one language ideology and the disparagement of Spanish (and speakers of Spanish, as well as anyone indexically linked to Spanish) as un-American. Such ideologies play a key role in the **racialization** of Spanish and Latinxs, as we discuss in Chapter 5.

We also want to note that although we have presented them as two distinct ideologies, the standard language ideology and the one nation-one language ideology are intertwined. National standard languages, and the language academies created to 'protect' and disseminate them, are one way of reinforcing the sense of a shared identity within a nation's borders. In fact, the motivations for 18th century calls for the creation of an academy of 'American language' that would establish uniform US-based linguistic norms and spelling conventions were both to foster national unity within the new nation and to distinguish it from England (Lepore, 2002). Regarding Spanish, the RAE has played an ideological role in solidifying the dominance of Castilian over other languages within Spain, such as Catalan and Galician (Paffey, 2012). Even the taken-for-granted assumption of distinct 'national varieties' is based on a false premise that language variation follows political borders. In reality, people on opposite sides of national borders sometimes have more in common with each other linguistically than they have with people in their corresponding capital city; talk of 'national varieties' obscures these cross-border similarities as well as the geographic (and social) variations within each country.

Normative Monolingualism and the Zero-sum Ideology

As we have seen, the one nation–one language ideology conceptualizes monolingualism as the normal or preferred state of affairs, an ideology which we refer to as **normative monolingualism**. As we have made clear throughout this chapter, normative monolingualism also applies to individuals. In both cases, languages are seen as existing in a state of competition, where knowledge of one language implies less knowledge of another, as if there were limited space available, and any space taken up by one language reduces the space available for other languages (Wiley, 2000). This **zero-sum ideology** operates both at the societal level (as in the Roosevelt quote above) and at the individual level, where bilingualism is seen not only as an exception to the norm but as inherently problematic. At both levels, maintenance of a minority language is seen as impeding acquisition of the majority language, and parents who speak Spanish (or other non-English languages) are often told to speak to their children in English, in order to avoid confusing them (Zentella, 1997a).

Contrary to the zero-sum ideology and normative monolingualism, a growing body of research now shows that there are significant cognitive advantages to early bilingualism

(Bialystok, 2011), as well as a correlation between bilingualism, minority language retention, academic achievement and upward economic mobility outcomes (García, 2009a; Linton, 2004; Portes & Rumbaut, 2005). Nonetheless, these ideologies are hard to overcome. As we saw earlier, even people negatively affected by such ideologies sometimes share in them, as we can see in the following explanation from a participant in Zentella's (1997a) ethnographic research with Puerto Ricans in New York: 'If I start hanging on to my culture, speaking Spanish, it's gonna hold me back' (Zentella, 1997a: 142). Children who do not have the opportunity to acquire their parents' language can feel a great sense of loss or resentment in later life, but while it might be tempting to 'blame' parents for not passing on their language, they are exposed to the same monolingual ideologies and they may also have suffered discrimination or shame if they struggled with English or had an accent.

Monoglossic and Heteroglossic Ideologies

How many languages are there in the world? It isn't really possible to know, not because we don't have time to travel around the world to count them, but because languages aren't clearly defined countable objects (Blommaert, 2010; Makoni & Pennycook, 2005). In this book we have been using the terms *English* and *Spanish* as if they had clear, well-defined referents, and for the sake of convenience we will largely continue to do so. But what exactly is English, or Spanish, or any other language? Like standard varieties, languages themselves are idealized abstractions as well as sociopolitical constructions. No two people who speak the same language speak in exactly the same way. Instead, everyone has their own **linguistic repertoire**, or the collection of linguistic resources – such as national and regional varieties, accents, social varieties, registers, linguistic styles and norms of linguistic interaction – that they know. Thus, there is no easy (or even any difficult) way to determine just what any 'language' includes. In fact, the idea that languages are definable, countable entities with clear boundaries between them is the reflection of a particular way of thinking about linguistic behavior (Heller & Duchêne, 2007; Makoni & Pennycook, 2005). This is sometimes referred to as a **monoglossic ideology** of language.

In contrast with these monoglossic ideologies that view languages as distinct, bounded linguistic systems, **heteroglossic** approaches see languages as consisting of multiple and varied systems that overlap and intersect with each other. Further, heteroglossic approaches recognize that individuals' linguistic repertoires often include resources associated with different named 'languages' (Blommaert, 2010). For example, the linguistic repertoires of bilingual Spanish-speakers in the US include some varieties, styles, words and other linguistic resources associated with English as well as some associated with Spanish. When speaking (or writing), people draw on the different linguistic elements in their repertoires, depending on the context, who they are talking to, what they want to express, how they want to present themselves, the relationship they want to establish with their **interlocutor** (i.e. the person they are talking to), and so on. In some cases, multilinguals may combine elements associated with different languages within a single conversation, a single utterance or even single word. The following examples are adapted from Fuller's unpublished transcripts of interactions in a bilingual elementary school program.

(1) *¡Déjala! ¡Déjala! Porque luego te metes en* problems.
'Leave it leave it because then you get in trouble.'

(2) *¿Por qué no se enseña qué queremos saber?* Open that!
'Why don't they teach us what we want to know? Open that!'

(3) **Student 1**: *No puedo leer porque es demasiado pequeño.*
'I can't read because it's too small.'

Student 2: Okay, I'll read.

In these examples, some elements are associated with Spanish and others with English, so it's easy to see how speakers combine resources from different languages. However, heteroglossic approaches to language rest on the idea that even 'monolingual' discourse (i.e. discourse that is associated with a single language, such as English or Spanish) contains a multitude of registers, styles, genres and varieties (Bailey, 2007; Bakhtin, 1981; García, 2009b). In Chapter 6 we discuss how people draw from their linguistic repertoires to portray themselves in particular ways, and in Chapter 10 we discuss grammatical patterns in multilingual discourse and we explain how combining languages can be a conversational strategy.

You may have heard the term **codeswitching**, which many linguists use to refer to the alternation or combination of different languages or varieties within a conversation or utterance. This term may be used somewhat differently by laypeople, who sometimes use it to refer to people's ability to speak differently in different contexts, and especially to use 'standard' English and a 'non-standard' variety such as AAE depending on who they are with. This seems to be the meaning of the title of National Public Radio's *Code Switch*, a program and podcast focusing on race and identity, which sometimes covers issues related to language and/or Latinx identity (https://www.npr.org/sections/codeswitch). Rather than *codeswitching*, linguists would likely describe this ability simply as choosing different elements from one's linguistic repertoire depending on context (something that everyone does).

But in any case, as scholars have come to reject the idea of languages and varieties as distinct bounded entities, many have grown skeptical of the term *codeswitching*, because it relies on the idea that there are distinct languages or codes: How could you switch back and forth between two things if they were not separate? Further, it seems to rely on the notion of language as code, rather than a way for people to communicate social meanings, such as who they are, how they feel about each other, etc. For these reasons, in place of codeswitching, some researchers have adopted the term **translanguaging** (García, 2009b; García & Wei, 2014). *Translanguaging* is meant to reflect a heteroglossic conception of language by recognizing that in interaction, people may draw from linguistic resources distributed across the boundaries of what have traditionally been labeled as distinct languages (Wei, 2018). In addition, it shifts the focus from formal features of language to the social and symbolic aspects of language use. Nonetheless, not everyone likes the new term (e.g. Auer, forthcoming; Bhatt & Bolonyai, 2019), an issue we return to in Chapter 10.

In addition to the fact that people who speak the same 'language' all have different linguistic repertoires, which makes it impossible to delineate languages, further evidence that languages are not bounded objects is that there is no objective way to draw a line between one language and another at the societal level. By this, we mean that there is no linguistic criterion by which we can say that two different ways of speaking should be classified as different varieties of the same language or, alternatively, as two different languages (Penny, 2000). Instead, such classifications depend on social or political considerations, such as being spoken in different nations or being associated with different orthographies or writing systems, rather than some sort of quantifiable amount of linguistic difference. The non-linguistic basis of such distinctions is reflected in the adage, 'A language is a dialect with an army and navy,' attributed to Max Weinreich, a scholar of Yiddish sociolinguistics.

One corollary of monolingual and monoglossic ideologies is the notion that languages should be kept strictly separate (García, 2009b; Zentella, 2017). Within this ideological system, languages are valued only as distinct, pure entities; codeswitching or translanguaging, as well as other signs of language contact (discussed in Chapter 10), are considered signs of deficiency or not to be taken seriously. As a result, bilinguals are expected to speak each language like monolinguals do, which Heller (1999, 2002) refers to as 'parallel monolingualism' and others have called **dual monolingualism** or **double monolingualism**. Further, people who combine languages are framed as not really knowing either language and they are sometimes described as 'semi-lingual' (Rosa, 2016b; Walsh, 1991; Zentella, 1997a, 2017). This ideology is also partly responsible for negative portrayals of Spanish in the US in comparison with monolingual varieties linked to nation states. However, it doesn't depend on actual linguistic practices; speakers of Spanish in the US are often perceived as mixing languages or speaking a non-standard variety, because their ethnoracial identity shapes how people 'hear' them, no matter how they actually speak (Flores & Rosa, 2015; Zentella, 2017). The disparagement of codeswitching or translanguaging ignores the vast body of research demonstrating the naturalness of multilingual discourse (e.g. Fuller, 2009; García, 2009b; Heller, 1999; Toribio, 2004). Further, it fails to recognize that multilingual discourse is a useful interactional resource, an important way to express one's identity, and a reflection of linguistic creativity. We return to these issues in Chapters 6 and 10.

Language Commodification and Instrumentality

In the previous sections we spent a fair amount of time explaining normative monolingualism and the monoglossic language ideologies that construct bilingualism as a problem. While some of the attitudes and discourse that we have described may have sounded familiar, and our descriptions accurate, you may also have been thinking about times when you have seen more positive representations of multilingualism. For example, you have likely heard people say that speaking a second language is valuable for getting a job. **Instrumentalist** discourses of language emphasize their value for doing something, rather than in their own right. A related discourse portrays multilingualism as a commodity, something of economic value that can be 'bought' and 'sold.' This **commodification** of language reflects the influence of capitalism and neoliberal policies on language ideologies (Duchêne & Heller, 2011). Rather than focusing on languages as primordial characteristics of ethnolinguistic groups (Silverstein, 2003), the emphasis is on their market value.

In addition to being portrayed as a key element of US identity, English is often framed – by immigrants and native-born Americans alike – as a way to increase one's economic opportunities. For example, in her research at a day laborer site in the Southwest, Dubord (2014, 2017) found that workers who didn't speak English felt that knowledge of English conferred advantages on their bilingual peers, although the bilinguals themselves didn't agree. Discourses about the economic value of English, and its supposed ability to open doors and provide new opportunities to immigrants who learn it, are also reproduced in the marketing of language learning programs such as *Inglés sin barreras* ('English without Barriers') (https://inglessinbarreras.co). The actual value of English–Spanish bilingualism (in contrast with either Spanish or English monolingualism) varies geographically within the US, but it is often less than commodifying discourses might have us believe (Dubord, 2017; Subtirelu, 2017).

Similar arguments about job opportunities are often used as a selling point to convince students to take 'foreign' language courses, especially Chinese and Spanish. These days, language commodification and an emphasis on the economic value of language can be seen in the RAE's and the *Instituto Cervante's* promotion of the 'language industry,' which includes Spanish teaching, proficiency testing and certification, pedagogical materials and study-abroad experiences, and which constitutes a significant sector of the Spanish economy (Bruzos Moro, 2017; Villa & Del Valle, 2014). In the US, the teaching of Spanish has long been linked to a discourse that portrays it as a useful language, while other European languages have more frequently been framed as prestigious vessels of high culture and literature (Leeman, 2007). In fact, in President Jefferson's comments advocating the study of Spanish that we cited in Chapter 3, he emphasized its instrumentalist value. By the 19th century it was common for Spanish to be portrayed as economically valuable, particularly for entrepreneurs setting up business ventures in Latin America (Lozano, 2018; Spell, 1927). More recently, advocates of bilingual education have increasingly emphasized the economic benefits of multilingualism for individuals as well as societies, rather than issues of educational equity or social justice (see Chapter 9).

Differential Bilingualism

Which view of bilingualism comes to the fore is often dependent in part on who the speaker is. While the Spanish–English bilingualism of US Latinxs too often is portrayed as a failure to assimilate or a problem, second language learners of Spanish are often praised. This **differential bilingualism** (Aparicio, 1998) underscores that the symbolic value or meaning of a language is not intrinsic to the language. Curtin (2007) documented the impact of this ideology in her interviews with Latinx and Anglo students at a US university.

Whereas the Latinx students recounted being ashamed of speaking Spanish as children and of their 'imperfect' Spanish as young adults, the Anglo students' narratives focused on their sense of accomplishment for acquiring even limited communicative ability in Spanish. In a related discussion, Duchêne (2019) points out that contemporary discourse broadly touting the economic value of multilingualism often fails to acknowledge that benefits accrue differently based on the languages and speakers in question.

The Relative Worth of English and Spanish

While the previous section discussed how multilingual language practices are stigmatized, it is important to recognize that even 'standard' monoglossic varieties of English and Spanish are assigned different symbolic values. English is often portrayed not only as central to national belonging, but also as a language that naturally leads to being successful in school and life. This view of English can be seen in the following comment in an online debate about educational policies for minority language speakers in Oregon:

> For the first 200 years of our republic people have come from all over the world and immigrated to America. They spoke every language on earth. With the exception of few isolated exceptions there were no ELL, ESL or dual language programs, just English immersion. Because immigrants were forced to learn English they became better citizens, more productive people and better educated. (http://www.answerbag.com/debates/oregon-pass-english-immersion-measure_1855505, accessed 20 August 2010; link no longer available)

This comment offers another example of the discursive erasure of the fact that not all early immigrants learned English or did so quickly, as well as of the historical existence of education in minority languages (Fishman, 2001; Wiley, 2010), which we discussed earlier. Here, our focus is on the portrayal of English, which the commenter claims was key to immigrants becoming 'better citizens, more productive people and better educated.' In other words, speaking English is framed as providing moral, political and intellectual benefits. In his analysis of newspaper coverage of a California referendum on bilingual education, Santa Ana (2002) also found that English was portrayed differently from (and better than) other languages; where English was framed as a transparent language that is easily learned, other languages were constructed as 'barriers' to communication. Such positive portrayals of English are not limited to the US; researchers have found that in the international sphere discourses surrounding English often link it to modernity, democracy and civilization (Horner & Weber, 2018; May, 2001).

There is a great deal of negative public discourse surrounding Spanish in the US that revolves around the notion that Spanish is a not only an immigrant language, but that it is spoken primarily by the underclass (Schmidt, 2002). Examples include the Tom Brokaw quote we discussed in Chapter 2, former Speaker of the House Newt Gingrich's description of English as 'the language of prosperity' and Spanish as 'the language of living in a ghetto' (Hunt, 2007), and the following quote from Harvard Professor Samuel Huntington:

> There is no *Americano* dream. There is only the American dream created by an Anglo-Protestant society. Mexican Americans will share in that dream and in that society only if they dream in English. (Huntington, 2004: 45)

In this ideology, English is portrayed as the only language of success, and Spanish is seen as linked to poverty. Further, this portrayal frames language as the cause of inequality and Spanish as inherently detrimental and subordinate. Thus it erases the status of Spanish as a global language that is used for business, diplomacy and politics (sometimes in ways that subordinate other languages). There is also erasure of the use of Spanish by middle-class and elite groups within the US as well as the fact that retention of Spanish is correlated with higher socio-economic status (Portes & Rumbaut, 2005). As we saw, attitudes toward languages and language varieties are inseparable from attitudes toward the *speakers* of those languages, and hostility to Spanish results from a broader animosity toward speakers of Spanish and Latinxs.

These negative portrayals of Spanish also spill over into discourses surrounding the teaching and learning of Spanish to second language speakers (Schwartz, 2008). Such discourses denigrate Spanish by portraying it as easy, not really important, or useful only for talking to domestic help.

Parallel to this denigration, however, is an ideology that celebrates Spanish – at least in certain contexts. Since the late 20th century, there has been talk of a 'Latino Boom' in popular music and culture (Cepeda, 2000). In fact, this fixation with Latin American and Spanish cultural elements can be traced back at least to the early 20th century (Lynch, 2018; Nieto-Phillips, 2004), as we discussed in the last chapter. While these discourses may appear celebratory, in many cases they rely on stereotypical notions about passionate, hot-blooded people, which actually serve to reinforce notions about purportedly more rational (and hence superior) Anglos. In addition, as we discussed in Chapter 2, such representations are complicit in the elevation of Spanish (i.e. European) ancestry and Whiteness (Cepeda, 2000; Nieto-Phillips, 2004). In Chapter 7 we consider how movies and television programs link Spanish to a range of negative characteristics, such as criminality, promiscuity and old-fashioned or outdated values.

Spanish as Essential to Latinx Identity versus Language as a Choice

Two contradictory language ideologies are reflected in: (1) the idea that Spanish is an essential part of Latinx identity; and (2) the idea that immigrants should choose to speak English. We have already noted that in the US, Spanish often indexes Latinx identity, and we delve further into this ideological relationship in Chapters 5 and 6; for now, we just want to mention the widespread expectation (among Latinxs and non-Latinxs alike) that Latinxs speak Spanish. This is manifested, for example, in the pressure within Latinx communities for Latinxs to speak 'flawless' Spanish in order to demonstrate their 'authenticity' (García Bedolla, 2003; Shenk, 2007), as well as the media's frequent interchangeable use of *Latinx* and *Spanish-speaking* as if they were synonyms. The ideological construction of Spanish as an inherent part of Latinx identity is so strong that Spanish language often serves as a proxy or index for all Latinxs, even those who are monolingual in English (Leeman, 2013).

In contrast with this ideology about a primordial or **essentialized** relationship between language and identity (and specifically between Spanish and Latinx identity), a co-occurring ideology sees languages and language varieties as separate from identity and equally available to everyone. This ideology is reflected in the standard language ideology as well as the neoliberal commodifying discourses we discussed above. The delinking of language and identity portrays language as an individual *choice*, rather than the consequence of identity and life experience, or of structural factors. As such, learning English is discussed as if it were a matter of individual agency; people who don't speak English are portrayed as simply having chosen not to do so. Indeed, many people believe that immigrants *refuse* to learn English, and public opinion surveys have found that a majority of respondents (58%) think immigrants don't learn English 'within a reasonable amount of time' (Pew Research Center, 2006). Of course, what counts as 'a reasonable amount of time' is a subjective (and ideological) question, but it's worth remembering that immigrants and their children both value English and learn to speak it, as we discussed in Chapter 2.

This conception of language as choice is apparent in complaints about recent immigrants not assimilating and in calls to make English the official language of the US (see Chapter 8). English-only proponents depict assimilation as egalitarian: if English were the official language, the privileges of being an English-speaker would be available to all (Schmidt, 2007: 202). Of course, this erases the time and effort needed to learn a language, and the lack of opportunities for people to do so. Nonetheless, the notion of language as choice has an important discursive impact because it makes it possible to blame people who make 'bad choices,' rather than recognizing structural marginalization. Given the discursive elevation of English and the negative portrayal of Spanish, speakers of Spanish are thus portrayed as choosing an impoverished life and constructing their own barriers to socio-economic and/or political integration. Moreover, when language is constructed as a choice, linguistic discrimination seems less problematic than discrimination based on characteristics seen as permanent and unchangeable, such as gender or race (Cameron, 1997; Schmidt, 2002; Urciuoli, 2009). Because overt racial prejudice has come to be seen as socially undesirable, people find more indirect ways to express prejudice (Sniderman *et al.*, 1991). In this 'new racism,' racial differences become coded as culture or language, allowing people to express prejudice without being labeled (or seeing themselves) as racists (see Chapter 5 for a discussion of race and racialization). This is even more insidious regarding Latinxs, who are often perceived as Spanish-speaking and as choosing not to speak English, regardless of their actual linguistic practices (Leeman, 2012a, 2013).

Like other hegemonic ideologies, the idea that learning English is a matter of individual choice is also sometimes taken up by immigrants, some of whom report feeling shame or guilt for not having learned English, as if it reflected a moral failing on their part (Relaño Pastor, 2014; Ullman, 2010).

The notion of language as choice applies not only to learning English, but also to learning or maintaining Spanish and passing it on to one's children. The idea that individuals simply choose what languages they speak contributes to Latinxs blaming themselves if they don't speak Spanish as well as they think they should (García Bedolla, 2003; Sánchez Muñoz, 2016; Urciuoli, 2008), rather than looking at broader structural issues like the predominance of English-only educational models (see Chapter 9) or the hegemonic ideologies that undergird them.

Conclusions and Connections

From our discussion in this chapter it should be clear that language ideologies play a tremendously important role in people's lives. They shape how we think about language, but even more importantly, they shape how we think about people, and they are what lend social meaning to particular ways of talking and using language. The theoretical framework that we outlined in this chapter, as well as the examination of some of the most prevalent language ideologies surrounding Spanish in the US, can be considered the foundation for the remaining chapters.

In the next chapter we'll see how language ideologies are intricately bound up with ideologies of race and racial classification and how language ideologies play a role in the **racialization** of Latinxs. In Chapter 6 we'll build on that discussion of race and racialization by examining a broader array of identities and the ways in which they are enacted through language. Our discussions of language and identity will rely on an understanding of indexicality (explained in the present chapter) and of the ideological nature of the relationship between particular ways of speaking and particular identities. In Chapter 8 we'll look at how language ideologies shape language policies, and we'll focus on educational policy in Chapter 9. As we'll see, policies both reflect and reinforce language ideologies, a two-way relationship that is also apparent in our discussion of the representation of Spanish and Spanish-speakers in the media in Chapter 7.

Discussion Questions and Activities for Chapter 4

(1) Ask a friend to define and describe 'Standard English' or 'Standard Spanish,' and follow up with questions about who speaks it, and who decides what is 'good' and 'bad' English or Spanish. What ideologies do their responses reflect?

(2) Do an internet search for where the 'best' English or Spanish is spoken. What ideologies do the answers reveal?

(3) Make a list of all the languages, varieties, registers, etc. that are in your **linguistic repertoire.** In addition to any 'named' resources you may come up with (e.g. AAE, 'standard' American English, 'standard' Peruvian Spanish), think about the different styles you use in different domains and with different people. Try to describe these linguistic resources even if they don't have established names. Next, compare your list with a friend's list. How are they similar and/or different? What does this say about the status of languages as bounded, uniform entities?

(4) What do you think is the social value of Spanish in the US? Is it prestigious to speak Spanish, and if so, in what contexts/which varieties/by whom? What other kinds of social meaning does speaking Spanish have?

Further Reading and Resources

Bruzos Moro, A. (2017) 'De camareros a profesores' de ELE: La mercantilización del español y de su enseñanza como lengua extranjera. *Spanish in Context* 14 (2), 230–249.

Cepeda, M.E. (2000) *Much loco* for Ricky Martin or the politics of chronology, crossover, and language within the Latino(a) music boom. *Popular Music and Society* 24 (3), 55–71.

Fuller, J.M. (2019) Ideologies of language, bilingualism, and monolingualism. In A. De Houwer and L. Ortega (eds) *The Cambridge Handbook of Bilingualism* (pp. 119–134). Cambridge: Cambridge University Press.

Kroskrity, P. (2004) Language ideologies. In A. Duranti (ed.) *A Companion to Linguistic Anthropology* (pp. 496–517). Malden, MA: Blackwell.

Leeman, J. (2012b) Investigating language ideologies in Spanish as a heritage language. In S.M. Beaudrie and M. Fairclough (eds) *Spanish as a Heritage Language in the United States: The State of the Field* (pp. 43–59). Washington, DC: Georgetown University Press.

Lippi-Green, R. (2012) *English with an Accent: Language, Ideology and Discrimination in the United States* (2nd edn). London: Routledge.

Pavlenko, A. (2002) 'We have room but for one language here': Language and national identity at the turn of the 20th century. *Multilingua* 21, 163–196.

Chapter 5

Race, Racialization and Latinx Ethnoracial Identity

Objectives

To examine the social construction of race in Latin America and the US, introduce the notion of racialization, discuss the racialization of Spanish in the US and critically analyze constructions of ethnoracial identity among US Latinxs.

Introduction

In our discussion of the history of Spanish and Spanish-speakers in the US in Chapter 3, we saw that race and racism were central in European conquest and colonization in Africa and the Americas, in the organization of Spanish and British colonial societies and in US territorial expansionism. Anti-Indigenous and anti-Black racism shaped the subsequent treatment (and abuse) of Mexicans, Puerto Ricans and other Latinxs in the US, as we will discuss in our consideration of language policy and education in Chapters 8 and 9. This history, as well as ongoing racism, continue to play a role in the experiences of Latinxs today. Language is intricately tied up with ethnic and racial identities, and Spanish plays a central role in the construction of Latinx identity. Further, as the discussion of language ideologies in Chapter 4 made clear, language subordination is one mechanism for the reproduction of social hierarchies and inequality. For these reasons, it is impossible to talk meaningfully about the sociolinguistics of Spanish in the US without examining race and **racialization**, the focus of the present chapter.

In line with current scholarship, we understand race to be a social construct while also recognizing the very real social, political and material consequences of race and racism. After providing an introduction to race and racialization, we look at the racialization of Spanish and its portrayal as inherently foreign and threatening to US national identity. Next, we explore how racial ideologies and social constructions of race are situational and vary over time as well as from place to place. This leads to an overview of race in Latin America and a comparison of social constructions of race in Latin America and the US. After examining the blurry boundaries between race and ethnicity, we turn specifically to current understandings of Latinx **ethnoracial** identity (this term signals the lack of a clear distinction between the two constructs). In the last section of the chapter, we examine the Census Bureau's classification of Latinxs both in order understand how it contributes to the official racialization of Latinxs and as an organizational tool to discuss the shifting and contested nature of Latinx identity. Language-oriented topics that we address in the discussion of the census include the ways in which Spanish is constructed as an inherent, quasi-biological characteristic, the multiple and contested meanings of identity labels, the power of language to challenge dominant understandings of racial identity, and current debates regarding gender-neutral language.

Race as a Social Construct

People often think of race as a visible, physical characteristic rooted in genes and biology that remains constant throughout a person's life. Further, people who belong to the same race often are believed to share certain physical characteristics that distinguish them from people in other racial groups. However, as a recent article in *Scientific American* points out, 'the mainstream belief among scientists is that race is a **social construct** without biological meaning' (Gannon, 2016). But what does it mean to say that race is socially constructed rather than biological? In the last chapter, we discussed how nations and languages, and the boundaries between them, are not based on objective characteristics but rather are socially and politically influenced ways of imagining and thinking about them. Similarly, race isn't an objective physiological property but an ideology about human difference, or a particular way of thinking about physical characteristics and giving them social and political meaning. Part of the ideology of race is the belief that humans can be divided into distinct, objectively defined groups on the basis of either genotype – a person's genetic make-up – or **phenotype** – their physical appearance including skin and eye color or hair texture. Ideologies about race and racial difference are so powerful that they become **naturalized** and seem like facts rather than social constructions.

If race is a social construct, where did it come from? Historically, the emergence of modern understandings of race is inseparable from European conquest in Africa and the Americas. In particular, diverse African and Native American peoples were lumped together in categories as a way of **Othering** them. As we noted in Chapter 3, religious institutions were integral to colonization and domination, and religious difference was often used by Europeans as a justification for the enslavement and exploitation of 'heathens.' Over time, racial discourses came to describe differences as biological, with some 18th and 19th century scholars even suggesting that different races belonged to different species (Nobles, 2000; Omi & Winant, 1994; Painter, 2010). Nowadays, racial ideologies and the concept of race are reproduced in social, economic and political structures as well as everyday practices that assign people to different categories used in the organization of society (Omi & Winant, 1994).

To say that race is a social construct is not to deny physical or genetic variation, nor to say that people don't have different phenotypical features – obviously they do. However, despite the widespread belief in the existence of distinct races with clear boundaries, different physical features don't correlate or neatly line up with racial identities. Thus, two people with different racial identities sometimes have more genetic material in common with one another than they do with people considered to be of the same race. In fact, researchers have found that over 84% of physical variation occurs within, rather than between, races (Jobling *et al.*, 2016; Mersha & Abebe, 2015).

While we are on the topic of genetics, we want to say a few words about home DNA testing services like 23andMe. Based on a saliva sample that a customer mails in, these services produce an 'ancestry composition' report purporting to show the exact percentages of that person's ancestry that can be traced to specific continents, regions or countries. Home DNA testing has become a multibillion-dollar industry, but scientists have identified numerous limitations and problematic assumptions. For one, the reference databases used for comparison to customer samples do not capture the actual genetic diversity of the regions or groups they supposedly represent. Secondly, they are based on recent samples; even if they show where genetically similar populations are found *now*, this does not mean that those populations are *from* there (Bolnick *et al.*, 2007). Thirdly, when a genetic marker is found to be most common in a given population, it is treated as an indicator of that population. But even though some genetic markers are more likely in particular population groups, this doesn't mean that everyone with that marker belongs to that group (Jobling *et al.*, 2016). According to Bolnick and her colleagues (2007), these shortcomings can lead to absurd test results, such as those from AncestryByDNA suggesting that high percentages of people from the Middle East, India and the Mediterranean region of Europe have Native American ancestry, which obviously conflicts with the archaeological and historical record. But even more important than the fact that the technical aspects of ancestry tests are inherently unreliable and misleading is that they reinforce the common misperception that genetics is the source of racial identity (Bolnick *et al.*, 2007; Jobling *et al.*, 2016). As we have explained, identity is a social and cultural phenomenon, not a biological one, so DNA tests can never identify someone's 'true' race. And in fact, the frequent mismatches between self-reported race and DNA test results actually provide further evidence that genetics are not the source of identity (Mersha & Abebe, 2015; Roth & Ivemark, 2018).

To be clear, when we say that race is a social construct rather than a biological fact, we are not saying that it isn't 'real.' On the contrary, race, like other social constructs, has very real individual and societal significance as well as wide-ranging material consequences. Let us return to the case of nations. Even though nations are socially constructed, there is no doubt that they really exist, as is evidenced by their ability to produce emotional attachment and loyalty among citizens, as well as feelings of shared identity among people who have never met (Anderson, 1991; Billig, 1995). Further, national governments have incredible power to regulate and influence the lives of people and to make the rules about who is allowed in and how they are treated, all of which have very real material consequences. Thus, even though borders are political boundaries that don't correspond to actual lines on the earth, crossing from one side to the other can have a significant impact on what someone is allowed to say or do, whether someone is considered a member of society or an undesirable outsider, and whether one is left alone or detained. So even though they don't correspond to a physical reality, we can certainly say that nations are 'real.' Similarly, race is also 'real,' and it has tremendous impact not only on people's understanding of their own and others' identities, but also on their physical wellbeing, their rights and legal standing and their access to a wide range of goods and services. Of course, the history of the US provides numerous examples of how race and racism have been officialized in law with very real consequences, such as enslavement, denial of citizenship and voting rights, and racial segregation, to name just a few. Although racial discrimination is now prohibited by law, in practice the legacy of history together with enduring personal and structural racism mean that race continues to impact people's socio-economic status, living conditions, health outcomes and life expectancy.

Racialization

Many scholars and activists use the term *racialization* in order to highlight that the social construction of race is a process and an ideological project, rather than a static fact. Not all researchers use the term in exactly the same way, but one commonly cited definition is 'the extension of racial meaning to a previously racially unclassified relationship, social practice or group' (Omi & Winant, 1994: 64). One aspect of racialization involves the construction of racial categories and the ideological linking of particular physical characteristics to racial identity, even though the specific features can vary from place to place. As we know, race in the US is constructed primarily with reference to skin color, although hair type and facial features are also seen as racial indicators. But racialization isn't just the construction of particular phenotypical features as racial; it also includes the **essentialist** treatment of social and moral characteristics, such as ambition, laziness or criminality, as if they were inherent to particular racial groups, as well as the use of race as an explanation for perceived cultural, intellectual and behavioral differences among people. Thus, racialization is not a neutral process of classification or categorization. Instead, it is a way of Othering and subordinating non-dominant groups. Or, as Schmidt (2002: 158) aptly puts it, 'Racialization is a social process whose point is inequality.'

As we have said, European conquest was a key historical moment in the construction of racial categories and the conferral or denial of status, rights and privileges based on those categories. However, racialization is an ongoing project, in the sense that race is continually reproduced. One place where the notion of distinct races is reinforced is in official racial classifications such as the census, which we discuss later in this chapter. In addition to institutional and official policies and practices, racializing ideologies and racism are also reproduced through language, including news coverage and other media discourse and official policies, as well as the everyday talk of individuals (Van Dijk, 1993, 2005). For example, Santa Ana (2002) showed how newspaper coverage of unauthorized immigration relies heavily on racializing and dehumanizing metaphors that portray migrants as invaders and/or animals.

Scholars have used the theoretical framework of racialization to analyze 'the processes by which racial meanings are attached to particular issues – often treated as social problems – and with the manner in which race appears to be a, or often the, key factor in the ways they are defined and understood' (Murji & Solomos, 2005: 3). In the US, crime is racialized and discursively linked to African American and Latinx men, such that some people presume criminals to be people of color (even when no mention of racial identity is provided) and stereotype African American and Latinx men as 'thugs' (Welch, 2007). So too, racialized understandings of criminality and drug use are used to justify racial profiling and increased surveillance in African American and Latinx neighborhoods, and they contribute to harsher prison sentences and greater rates of incarceration for Latinxs and African Africans than Whites, despite the statistically lower likelihood of members of these groups having used illegal drugs (Knafo, 2013).

Language itself is a social and cultural practice that is often racialized. For example, the portrayal of Spanish and other non-English languages as un-American and threatening to US national identity is part of the portrayal of the speakers of those languages as 'so foreign or "alien" that it is impossible to conceive of being equal members of the same political community with [them]' (Schmidt, 2002: 158). Similarly, in many Latin American contexts, speakers of Indigenous languages historically have been framed as being outside the imagined national collective (French, 2008; Koc-Menard, 2017). It isn't just specific languages that are racialized, but also language varieties and practices that don't conform to the 'standard.' In the US, linguistic varieties associated with Latinxs and African Americans are routinely portrayed as incorrect, sloppy and generally inferior to 'standard' varieties (see Chapter 4), which is one element of the racialization of these groups. Focusing on linguistic and other cultural practices, rather than physical characteristics, in the disparagement of racialized groups is one (sometimes unconscious) strategy to avoid the appearance of racism. Think, for example, of a job candidate who pronounces the word *ask* as 'ax,' which is common in **African American English**. There is nothing inherently wrong with this pronunciation, but framing it as 'unprofessional' or 'ignorant' means that an African American job candidate can be rejected for reasons purportedly unrelated to race (Lippi-Green, 2012).

In the example of *ask*, racialization involves discriminating against people based on linguistic features associated with specific groups, but the linking of specific characteristics, social practices and linguistic features to specific racial identities is also ideological. Like the portrayal of illicit drug use as if it were more common among African Americans and Latinxs than non-Latinx Whites, many people in the US associate stigmatized 'double negatives' (e.g. 'I don't have none') with African American speech, even though members of other groups also use this grammatical structure (Chun & Lo, 2016). Thus, the racialization of double negatives is not based only on how speakers speak, but also on how listeners hear that speech and assign social or racial meaning to it (Chun & Lo, 2016; Inoue, 2006). Listeners' preconceived notions about racialized speakers can be so strong that they 'hear' them as non-standard no matter how they actually speak (Flores & Rosa, 2015). Flores and Rosa (2015) demonstrate the power of racializing discourses in their discussion of Latinx students being constructed as linguistically deficient despite the complexity and richness of their translingual repertoires and language practices. This racialization impacts how students are treated in everyday interaction and it also shapes educational policy, as we discuss in Chapter 9.

The Racialization of Spanish

The racialization of Spanish involves both its treatment as a quasi physical or racial characteristic of Latinxs as well as its subordination and denigration (Leeman, 2004, 2013; Rosa, 2019; Rosa & Flores, 2017). Historically, this includes the linking of 'blood' and 'language' in explicit refusals to grant statehood to southwestern territories based on the percentage of Spanish-speakers (Gómez, 2007; Leeman, 2013), the use of English as a gatekeeping mechanism for political participation (see Chapter 8), and the segregation and exclusion of Mexican American children from public schools (see Chapters 8 and 9). The negative portrayal of Spanish in the public sphere, including politicians' condemnation of *Nuestro Himno* (see Chapter 4), former Speaker of the House Newt Gingrich's description of Spanish as 'the language of living in a ghetto' (Hunt, 2007), and newscaster Tom Brokaw's on-air comments (see Chapter 2), all contribute to the vilification of Spanish as harmful for individuals and the nation. Spanish and Spanish-speakers are also racialized by the actions of low-level officials, such as the Montana Border Patrol officer who detained two women for speaking Spanish (see Chapter 8), the high school teacher who admonished her students to stop speaking Spanish by telling them that 'the brave men and women' are 'not fighting for your rights to speak Spanish; they're fighting for your rights to speak American' (Stevens, 2017), and educators who require Latinx children to adopt 'American' names, such as Juan Gonzalez' first-grade teacher, who told him, 'Your name isn't Juan. In this country it's John. Shall I call you John?' (Gonzalez, 2011: 90–91). So too, the myriad comments and aggressions of everyday citizens who insult people for speaking Spanish or demand that they speak English or 'go back where you came from' also participate in the racialization of Spanish (see Chapter 4).

Official and unofficial policies and discourses disparaging Spanish are part and parcel of the racialization not only of Spanish but also of Latinxs (regardless of their actual linguistic practices). Hegemonic US racial ideologies portray Latinxs as biologically linked to Spanish, much like phenotypical characteristics. This notion is reflected in off-hand comments about who does or doesn't 'look like they speak Spanish.' Because Spanish is simultaneously portrayed as out of place and un-American, and prototypical American identity is often imagined as White, Latinxs are constructed as perpetual foreigners who can never fully assimilate (Leeman, 2013). However, by portraying language as a choice, even while constructing it as an essential characteristic of Latinxs, people who disparage

Spanish claim not to be racist (Cameron, 1997). Moreover, these two ideologies (i.e. language as a choice and Spanish as inherent to Latinx identity), lead to the portrayal of Latinxs as unwilling to assimilate no matter what language they actually speak (such as in the quote from Tom Brokaw in Chapter 2) (Leeman, 2013).

Another way in which Spanish and Latinxs are racialized is by conflating immigration, and especially unauthorized immigration, and being Mexican. In contemporary public discourse, 'illegal aliens' has largely become code for 'Mexicans' (Dick, 2011; DuBord, 2014) and all Mexicans are portrayed as immigrants. In addition, as we discussed in Chapter 3, the use of the word *illegal*, rather than a more neutral term like *undocumented* or *unauthorized*, stigmatizes and dehumanizes people (some of whom have committed the civil, rather than criminal, violation of overstaying their visa). Further, because Mexicans and other Latinxs are constructed as natural Spanish-speakers, these negative associations also attach to Spanish, which is portrayed as an 'illegal' language (Leeman, 2012a). In the next chapter we discuss another racializing discourse, **Mock Spanish**, which both relies on and reinforces negative stereotypes about Latinxs while simultaneously devaluing Spanish.

Variability in the Construction of Race

Because race is socially constructed, different cultures can have different ways of dividing the world into categories and assigning people to those categories. As a result, it's sometimes possible to 'change' race simply by getting on a plane or moving from one place to another. It's not that the person's physical characteristics change, of course; instead, the sociocultural understanding of those characteristics, and thus the person's racial identity, are different in the two places. Contextual differences in the social construction of race are at the heart of a comedy routine by talk show host Trevor Noah in which he contrasts his racial identity in South Africa and the US (https://www.youtube.com/watch?v=vi7SeBI7z9A). Born to a Black mother and a White father during South Africa's apartheid regime, Noah was officially considered 'Coloured' (i.e. neither Black nor White, but 'mixed'). This contrasts with the dominant view in the US, where 'mixed race' people with any trace of African ancestry are often considered Black. In the routine, Noah describes his decision to come to the US in order to be seen as Black. In addition to the situational nature of race, Noah's routine also illustrates several other aspects of identity that we will return to later, including the association of particular ways of speaking with particular identities, and the possibility of mismatches between people's own sense of their identity and the identity that others ascribe to them.

In order to see the instability of constructions of race and racial identity over time, let us look at the history of racial classification in the US census, the official count of all persons living in the country. The US census has always classified the population by race, but the specific categories used and the ways in which people are assigned to them have changed numerous times, as shown in Table 5.1. Census categories are a kind of official discourse, and thus the changes both reflect and reinforce changes in societal understandings of

Table 5.1 *Racial classification in the US census 1790–2010*

Year	***'Race' and 'color' categories***
1790	Free Whites (by sex); All other free people (by color); Slaves
1800–1810	Free Whites (by sex); All other free people except Indians not taxed (by color); Slaves
1820–1840	Free Whites (by sex); Free colored persons (by sex) (including all other persons except Indians not taxed); Slaves (by sex)
1850–1860	White; Black; Mulatto
1870	White; Black; Mulatto (including quadroons, octoroons and 'anyone with a trace of African blood'); Chinese; Indian
1880	White; Black; Mulatto (including quadroons, octoroons and 'anyone with a trace of African blood'); Chinese; Indian
1890	White; Black (three-quarters or more 'Black blood'); Mulatto (three-eighths to five-eighths 'Black blood'); Quadroon (one-quarter 'Black blood'); Chinese; Japanese; Indian (specify 'full bloods or half-breeds')
1900	White; Black; Chinese; Japanese; Indian (specify 'full or mixed blood')
1910	White; Black; Mulatto; Chinese; Japanese; Indian (specify 'proportion of White, Indian & Negro blood'); Other (specify)
1920	White; Black; Mulatto; Chinese; Japanese; Indian; Filipino; Hindu; Korean; Other (specify)
1930	White; Black; Mexican; Chinese; Japanese; Indian; Filipino; Hindu; Korean; Other (specify)
1940	White; Black; Chinese; Japanese; Indian; Filipino; Hindu; Korean; Other (specify)
1950	White; Negro; Indian; Japanese; Chinese; Filipino; Other (specify)
1960	White; Negro; American Indian; Japanese; Filipino; Hawaiian, Part Hawaiian, Aleut Eskimo, etc.; Other (specify)
1970	White; Negro or Black; Indian American; Japanese; Chinese; Hawaiian; Korean; Other (specify)
1980	White; Black or Negro; Japanese; Chinese; Filipino; Korean; Vietnamese; Indian (Amer); Asian Indian; Hawaiian; Guamanian; Samoan; Eskimo; Aleut; Other (specify)
1990	White; Black or Negro; Indian (Amer); Eskimo; Aleut; Asian or Pacific Islander (API); Chinese; Filipino; Hawaiian; Korean; Vietnamese; Japanese; Asian Indian; Samoan; Guamanian; Other API (specify); Other race (specify)
2000, 2010	White; Black, African Am., or Negro; American Indian or Alaska Native; Asian Indian; Chinese; Filipino; Japanese; Korean; Vietnamese; Other Asian (specify); Native Hawaiian; Guamanian or Chamorro; Samoan; Other Pacific Islander (specify); Some other race (specify) Multiple responses to the race question accepted and tabulated

Source: Gauthier (2002); Nobles (2000).

racial identity (Nobles, 2000), much like discourses about language both reveal and reproduce language ideologies (see Chapter 4). For example, the categories '**Mulatto**,' 'Quadroon' and 'Octoroon,' as well specific fractions of 'Black blood' were used in the late 1800s, a period in which scholars and policymakers alike sought to examine the implications of race 'mixing' by investigating the relationship between specific **blood**

quanta and various social indicators, such as number of children and life expectancy (Nobles, 2000). These 'mixed race' categories were subsequently eliminated with the institutionalization of rigid racial segregation and the legal officialization of the **one-drop rule**, which considered anyone with any African heritage to be Black. Since 2000, respondents to the census have been able to choose multiple race categories, reflecting another shift in dominant understandings of race and a new salience and recognition of multiracial identities (Nobles, 2000).

As can be seen in Table 5.1, national origin has often been used as a synonym for race and in 1930 the census had a 'Mexican' racial category. This addition, which followed an influx of Mexican immigrants to the US Southwest after the Mexican Revolution of 1910, reflected a growing anti-Mexican sentiment. The category was removed in response to protests by US activists as well as the Mexican government (Rodríguez, 2000). (As we will discuss in detail later in the chapter, the US government now considers 'Hispanic or Latino' to be an ethnic, rather than a racial, category.) In the next section we examine ethnicity and how it differs from race.

Race versus Ethnicity

Ethnicity is a social category having something to do with descent or heritage, although scholars have struggled to define just what it means, as well as how it differs from race. Ethnicity is often talked about as tied to cultural practices and traits, such as religion, language, foodways and music, while race is seen as rooted in biological characteristics. However, this distinction doesn't really hold up in common usage. For example, the Merriam Webster dictionary lists 'nation,' 'nationality' and 'race' as synonyms of *ethnicity* (https://www.merriam-webster.com/dictionary/ethnicity). Similarly, ethnicity and culture are constructed as having genetic roots in Ancestry.com's promise to 'connect you to the cultures, cuisines, and traditions of your heritage in a deeper way,' and to let you 'Discover your ethnicity' based on their home DNA test (https://www.ancestry.com/dna/ethnicity, accessed 12 August 2018). And another DNA testing company, MyHeritage.com, links genetics, ethnicity and geography in its promise to let you discover 'what makes you unique and learning where you really come from' (https://www.myheritage.com/dna, accessed 2 November 2019).

Like race and other social constructs, ethnicity does not have a stable meaning. Similarly, the distinction between ethnicity and race, as well as the classification of group identities as one or the other, has fluctuated over time. For example, prior to WWII, national origin groups that in the US are now generally referred to as *ethnicities*, such as Irish, Italian and Polish, were commonly referred to as *races*. Moreover, scholarly work from the time explicitly defined these 'races' with reference to physical characteristics (Ignatiev, 1995; Jacobson, 1998; Leeman, 2004). However, racial difference was constructed as a two-tier system: racial distinctions among people of European descent did not have the same social or legal significance as the distinction between people classified as White and those classified as non-White (Jacobson, 1998; Painter, 2010). In the wake of the genocides of Nazi

Germany, the construct of ethnicity gained in popularity as a way to talk about group difference without ascribing it to biology (Omi & Winant, 1994; Zelinksy, 2001). Crucially, however, *ethnicity* did not replace *race* as a way of talking about *all* difference. Instead, in the US *ethnicity* was used primarily in regard to European immigrant groups, and it implied the possibility of assimilation to mainstream Whiteness over time (Jacobson, 1998; Omi & Winant, 1994). In contrast, US racial ideologies constructed *race* as enduring difference passed on from one generation to the next forever.

While race and ethnicity have a significant degree of overlap, and both constructs are used to mark some groups of people as Others, they express different kinds of social difference, different trajectories of absorption into US racial hierarchies and different possibilities of national belonging (Urciuoli, 1996). Urciuoli argues that racialized groups, such as the Puerto Ricans in her ethnographic research, are constructed as dangerous and threatening, whereas groups constructed as ethnic, such as Italian Americans, are portrayed as relatively safe and even picturesque or charming, especially when their expressions of ethnicity take place at festivals, parades and other such spaces. As we'll discuss later in this chapter, racialized understandings of Latinx identity and Spanish don't align with the US government's official classification of 'Hispanic or Latino' origin as an ethnic identity.

Race in Latin America

A comprehensive examination of race in Latin America is clearly beyond the scope of this book. However, because Latin American immigrants bring with them notions of race that are different from understandings dominant in the US (Roth, 2012), and given that roughly two-thirds of the US was at some point under Spanish colonial rule, we do want to give an overview of the social construction of race in Latin America. First, it is important to stress that there is no single Latin American conceptualization of race; the diversity of Indigenous populations, the specifics of conquest and colonization, the particulars of labor practices, economics, wars of independence, immigration, social movements and politics, and a vast array of other factors have impacted the construction of race and racial identities and thus there are important differences across Latin American contexts. To give just one example, in the Caribbean the decline of the Indigenous population was followed by the early and continued importation of enslaved Africans, leading to larger Afrodescendant populations in that region than in highland regions of Central and South America. Still, while the relative proportion of each group and the extent of 'mixing' varied from place to place, one thing that characterizes much of Latin America is the historical intermingling of Indigenous populations, Portuguese and Spanish colonialists and Africans (and Afrodescendant persons born in Spain). The term **mestizaje** is often used to refer to racial and cultural mixing (especially among Indigenous and European peoples).

Latin American colonial understandings of social and racial difference were also influenced by the conflicts and hierarchies of medieval and early modern Spain and, in particular, the centuries-long battles between Christians and Muslims for control of the Iberian Peninsula, which culminated with the 1492 capture of the Emirate of Granada by Catholic Kings Isabel and Ferdinand. Spanish colonizers in the Americas brought with them a racial ideology that bundled together religion, cultural practices (including language) and parentage or descent, in which *limpieza de sangre* ('blood purity,' or lack of Jewish or Muslim ancestors) was key to social standing and national belonging (Alcoff, 2015; Bristol, 2007; Nieto-Phillips, 2004). In the Americas, they expanded racialized social, legal and political hierarchies to include Indigenous and African people, who they considered inferior and who they subjected to systems of forced labor and enslavement, as well as genocide.

As we discussed in Chapter 3, racial identity was a crucial determinant of rights and social position throughout Spain's American colonies including those colonies that would later be annexed by the US. Europeans were at the top of the hierarchy, followed by *criollos* (the American-born offspring of Europeans), and Indigenous and Afrodescendant people in the bottom two tiers (Bristol, 2007; Nieto-Phillips, 2004). Colonial ideologies of race also made social and legal distinctions among various *castas* ('mixed race' categories). Such ideologies, as well as anxiety about racial 'mixing,' are reflected in early 18th century Mexican *casta* paintings, such as the one in Figure 5.1 (Katzew, 2005). These paintings provided illustrations and labels for the offspring of 16 different interracial unions. Although many of the labels and categories of the casta paintings, such as the fantastical and derogatory *torna atrás* ('throwback') and *tente en el aire* ('hold yourself in the air'), were never really used (Katzew, 2005), several casta identities are reflected on 18th century New Mexican censuses, which had separate categories for *mestizo* (offspring of Spanish and Native parents), *coyote* (offspring of Mestizo and Native parents), *genízaro* (enslaved Native person) and *mulato* (offspring of African and Spanish parents) (Nieto-Phillips, 2004).

Figure 5.1 Unknown Artist, *De Indio y Mestiza sale Coyote* ('From Indian and Mestiza, Coyote'). Mexico, about 1750. Oil on canvas. 31 1/2 x 41 inches

Gift of the Collection of Frederick and Jan Mayer, 2014.218.

Photography ©Denver Art Museum.

As for contemporary racial identities, many but not all of the categories from the colonial period have faded from use. Large segments of the population can be considered to be of 'mixed' race and mestizaje has sometimes been presented as evidence of a supposed lack of racism, as well as the national ideal, in some countries such as Mexico and Peru. However, in reality, Indigenous and Afrodescendant populations have not been fully incorporated, Whiteness is still associated with economic and social status, and racism and racial inequality are enduring aspects of Latin American societies. In addition, the historical and contemporary presence of Afrodescendant groups is often downplayed or erased (Andrews, 2004), Indigenous peoples are often excluded from constructions of national identity (French, 2008), and there is an ongoing myth of rapid and universal acquisition of and assimilation to Spanish which does not match the reality of the centuries-long endurance of Indigenous languages and cultures into the present (Kamen, 2008).

Despite these commonalities, racial identities, the labels applied to them and the meaning of different labels vary greatly across Latin America, depending in part on the historical make-up of the population. For instance, in Puerto Rico the phenotype-based identities of 'Black,' 'Brown' and 'White' are primary (Duany, 2005), whereas in Guatemala the primary social boundary is between '*ladinos*' (people of European and Indigenous ancestry, called *mestizos* in other places) and '*indios,*' which subsumes 21 different Mayan ethnolinguistic groups under one label (French, 2008). In the Caribbean, *indio* is used to refer to people of African and European heritage. There is also variation within nations. For example, in Mexico, '*moreno*' (which in the US might be called 'Black') is a significant category on the southern Pacific coast (Lewis, 2000), but is less frequent in the interior, where there are fewer people with sub-Saharan ancestry and a more salient distinction is based on Indigenous ancestry (Farr, 2010). In her research in Michoacán, Mexico, Farr (2010) found the primary racial distinction to be between Indigenous and non-Indigenous identities. Participants in her study, who had a range of phenotypes, described themselves as having mixed Indigenous and European ancestry, but none categorized themselves as '*mestizo.*' Instead, they self-identified as '*ranchero*', which literally means 'rancher.' However, in this context the term signified more than occupation – it was a way to distance themselves from the Indigenous community and claim a non-Indigenous identity, even if their phenotype suggested Indigenous heritage. Another way they enacted a non-Indigenous identity was by downplaying or denying their knowledge of Purépecha, the local Indigenous language, another example of the relationship of language to ethnoracial identity.

Since the 19th century, immigration from Asia, Europe and the Middle East has brought additional diversity and new ethnoracial identities. To cite just a few examples, there is a large Japanese-heritage population in Peru, often referred to as *Nikkei*, which traces its history to the late 19th century, a well-known Italo-Argentinean community dating to the same period, and numerous Lebanese descent communities throughout Latin America especially in Argentina, Colombia and Venezuela.

We want to emphasize that racial categories are not homogenous and, like other identity categories, they always include individuals with a range of physical characteristics and experiences. Nor is race necessarily the most salient aspect of identity in every context or situation. Further, race intersects with other categories such as gender and socio-economic status, among others. For instance, whether considering racialized labor conditions or racial stereotypes, it is important to keep in mind that there are often important differences for men and women. Moreover, even individuals from the same place and with similar backgrounds don't always conceptualize race and racial identity in the same way (Dowling, 2014; Roth, 2012).

Comparing Constructions of Race in Latin America and the US

Spanish and English histories of colonialism and racialization in the Americas have some obvious similarities: Europeans colonized lands already inhabited by Indigenous peoples and brought enslaved Africans against their will, with racialization being a key ideological and administrative mechanism to maintain power. Throughout the Americas, sexual unions between people of different races led to 'mixed' offspring. Further, racism, racial inequality and the elevation of Whiteness have been lasting aspects of both Latin American and US societies. Nonetheless, there are important differences. For one, the specific cultural and linguistic groups within those three broad categories were not the same, and Native populations were more numerous in the Spanish colonies (Gonzalez, 2011). Today, a far higher percentage of the Latin American population still speak Indigenous languages (either monolingually or in addition to Spanish), although throughout the Americas many Indigenous languages have disappeared or are endangered. In both the US and Latin America, Indigenous and Afrodescendant groups have led social and political movements resulting in greater recognition and political rights. Since the 1990s, constitutional reforms carried out in numerous Latin American nations have formally recognized pluralism and cultural diversity, and established new Indigenous rights including official status for Indigenous languages and bilingual education (Yrygoyen Fajardo, 2015).

Another salient difference between the US and Latin America relates to ideologies and practices of racial 'mixing.' At least in part as the result of a predominance of men among Spanish colonists, interracial sexual unions and marriage were more common in the Spanish colonies than in the English ones (Gonzalez, 2011; Taylor, 2002). Post-independence Latin America is also characterized by higher rates, and greater social acceptance, of intermarriage (Telles & Bailey, 2013). Further, even as inequality and racism have persisted, many Latin American countries have incorporated elements of Indigenous and African cultures, as well as a celebration of mestizaje, into national folklore and artistic expression. As Telles and Bailey (2013: 1560) explain, 'although racial hierarchies in Latin America and the United States are roughly similar, Latin American national projects of mestizaje, or racial and cultural mixing, stand in stark contrast to the United States' historic emphasis on segregation and White racial "purity".'

A related distinction between US and Latin American ideologies of race is that, in contrast with the US racial ideology which tends to see 'Black' and 'White' as distinct either/or categories, many Latin American societies conceptualize race as a continuum. For example, in the Caribbean there are numerous identities between 'White' and 'Black' including '*trigueño*' (loosely 'olive-skinned'), '*indio*' and '*mulato*' (Duany, 2005; Roth, 2012). Further, in some Latin American contexts, children are not always classified in the same way as their parents, suggesting that more weight is given to phenotype than ancestry in some racial ascription. In addition, in Latin America the identity categories of 'race' and 'nationality' are sometimes used interchangeably, and it is not uncommon to hear references to, for example, the *Mexican race*, despite the diverse origins and cultures of the population.

Roth (2012) refers to the different ways of understanding of race, racial categories and how to assign people to them as 'racial schemas.' In order to get a better sense of the racial schemas prevalent in Puerto Rico and the Dominican Republic, she asked participants in her research to identify the race of people in photographs she showed them, as well as to describe their own racial identity. Many participants used what Roth refers to as a 'nationality schema'; they discussed race using nationality terms such as *Puerto Rican* or *Dominican*. However, other participants utilized a color-based 'continuum schema' and used terms like *blanco*, *trigueño* and *moreno*. In addition to variability among participants, Roth also found that some participants used different schemas according to the context; for example, some participants employed the nationality schema when describing the photos but the continuum schema when describing their friends or family.

In both the US and Latin America, race often correlates with socio-economic status, and there is a similar structural valuation of Whiteness above Blackness and Brownness, with race playing a role in shaping groups' wealth and status. A recent multiyear research project on race and ethnicity in Brazil, Colombia, Mexico and Peru utilizing sociological as well as anthropological data found that skin color, at least as much as racial categorization, is a predictor of socio-economic inequality and discrimination (Telles, 2014). In the US, scholars have also documented how skin tone stratification and discrimination (i.e. **colorism**) impact education, employment, criminal justice sentencing and mental health, among other aspects of life (Hunter, 2016). However, in the continuum of Latin American racial categories, social standing is not simply the result of racial categorization, but is also a key influence in how people are categorized (e.g. Hernandez, 2002; Roth, 2012; Wade, 2008). Thus, moving up or down on the social hierarchy can lead to changes in how one's racial identity is perceived. The colloquial expression 'money whitens' reflects the tendency for higher socio-economic status and prestige to result in a lighter classification (Roth, 2012: 20). The ideological elevation of Whiteness, the subordination of Blackness and the role of status in determining racial identity in Latin America are described by Hernandez as follows:

> In Latin American settings, social status informs formal racial classification, as illustrated by the common belief that persons of prominence should not be 'insulted' by referencing their visible African ancestry. Additionally, it is generally presumed that because no person of prominence could be Black, these persons should be designated distinctly. (Hernandez, 2002: 7)

Interestingly, recent research has documented that shifts in social standing also sometimes impact racial classification in the US (Saperstein & Penner, 2012). However, there is greater racial fluidity in Latin America than in the US, in the sense that people can 'move' more easily between categories not only over the course of their lifetimes but even from one context to the next. Indeed, in Latin America racial identity is relational and situational and thus categorizations sometimes shift based on the context. As Roth explains:

> Someone who is dark or has African features may refer to a man of medium skin tone as *blanco*. But that same man might be described as *trigueño* by someone of light color who has European features. In both Puerto Rico and the Dominican Republic, it is common for a child to be nicknamed *la blanquita* or *el negrito*, not because she or he is objectively White or Black but because she or he is the lightest or darkest in the family. Similarly, the same person may identify a woman as *trigueña* at one moment and as *morena* at the next, even in a single conversation, based on the context or the implicit comparison. (Roth, 2012: 20)

One thing that is surprising for many people coming to the US from Latin America (as well as other places) is that explicit racial classification is institutionalized and ubiquitous. In the US, people often take for granted that they will be categorized according to race: a person's racial identification is requested on bureaucratic forms and documents beginning in earliest childhood (although a newborn's race is no longer recorded on standard birth certificates, parental race is; see http://www.cdc.gov/nchs/data/dvs/birth11-03final-ACC.pdf, accessed 12 August 2018) and continues throughout one's life. This constant racial categorization is not as prevalent in Latin America, where people often find questions about their race to be strange (Alcoff, 2015; Duany, 2005). As a result of the infrequency of explicit racial classification in many Latin American countries, as well as the understanding of national identities as races, many Latin American immigrants to the US answer questions about their race with reference to their country of origin.

So why is all this racial data collected in the US? Doesn't it just strengthen the ideology of race and, thus, racism? This is certainly an argument that some people make. As we have seen, racial classification is one site or mechanism of 'race-making' and racialization, and it can reinforce the notions both that race is a key element of identity and that people fit neatly into race categories. However, eliminating such classifications would not be sufficient to eliminate structural racism. Further, classification is often used to combat racism. In fact, since the Civil Rights era, the primary reason that data on ethnicity and race are collected is to track and mitigate inequality and discrimination. Think, for example, about tracking the racial identity of people stopped by police or subjected to additional questioning by customs agents; in these contexts, racial classification allows the production of statistics used to prove that racial profiling takes place. Statistics and quantitative evidence are often seen as more objective than the first-hand experience of people who have been the target of profiling, and thus they can be useful in convincing authorities of the extent of the problem. So too, racial data are used to document income inequality, discrepancies in voter registration rates and life expectancy, among other social, political, economic and health indicators. They are also needed for the implementation of federal policies such as the Voting Rights Act (see Chapter 8). As Mora and Rodríguez-Muñiz (2017: 2) put it, 'statistical evidence of underrepresentation and inequality has been indispensable to racial justice campaigns.' In fact, nowadays calls for 'color-blindness' and the elimination of racial statistics most often come from political groups advocating an end to programs that are designed to reduce racial inequality (Omi, 2001). Moreover, in the case of the census, having an official category for a particular group identity offers symbolic recognition of that group within the nation. Further, it offers a way to document the size of the group and to demand increased attention and/or representation; as the adage says, there is power in numbers.

In recent years, Latin American countries that officially declare themselves multicultural or plurinational and seek to be more inclusive of Indigenous and Afrodescendant people have increased data collection on these populations and introduced new census questions (Nobles, 2000; Telles & Bailey, 2013). The fact that Indigenous and Afrodescendant social organizations themselves have demanded visibility in national censuses (Moreno & Benavides, 2019) highlights the modern-day connection between data collection, symbolic recognition, protection of minority rights and anti-discrimination efforts (Leeman, 2018c). Given the prominence of the census in defining and officializing racial categories and identities, we discuss the ethnoracial classification of Latinxs in the US census later in this chapter.

Migration and Racial Identities

As we have discussed thus far in this chapter as well as earlier in the book, the long history of racialization of Latinxs in the US can be traced back both to Spanish and English colonialism, as well as to the racial hierarchies enacted following the US annexation of the Southwestern territories in 1848. Thus, **treaty citizens** and other Mexican Americans were subjected to multiple layers of racialization. Although an 1896 federal court case established that Mexicans and Mexican Americans were legally White (Gross, 2008), society continued to treat them as non-White (Gómez, 2007). The racial status of Latinxs within US ideologies has long been ambiguous and shifting (Almaguer, 2012; Leeman, 2013; Rodriguez, 2000; Roth, 2012), but since the mid-20th century the arrival of greater numbers and greater diversity of immigrants from Latin America (as well as Asia, Africa and the Middle East) has raised new questions not only about how these new arrivals are classified but also about the broader social construction of race in the US.

Immigrants typically arrive with the racial ideologies of their home country and, as the previous section showed, racial categorization in Latin America is quite different from that in the US. In what circumstances do immigrants continue to rely on their existing understandings of racial identity and when do they adopt understandings dominant in the US? Will the presence of Latinxs (and other people whose identities do not fit easily within the existing categories) destabilize dominant conceptualizations of race? These questions undergird recent sociological research on ethnoracial identity and classification, including Roth's (2012) research discussed in the previous section. In addition to comparing the racial schemas of people living in the Dominican Republic and Puerto Rico, Roth also investigated the racial schemas used by Dominicans and Puerto Ricans who had migrated to New York, to see whether migration had impacted their understanding of race and racial identity. As we explained earlier, Roth found that participants in the Caribbean most frequently employed the nationality and continuum schemas. In contrast, participants who had migrated to the US were more likely to use what Roth calls the 'US schema,' by describing people as either Black, White or Hispanic/Latino. One key implication is that people can take up new, localized understandings of racial identity when they migrate. Another important finding is that people can have multiple, overlapping or competing schemas that they draw from according to the specific social context. In Roth's study, participants chose different schemas depending in part on whom they were talking to and what they knew or imagined about the people in the photos. For example, if they imagined the people in the photos were in New York, they were more likely to use US schema; if they imagined that the people in the photos were from outside the US, they were more likely to use the nationality schema.

One way in which immigrants learn about US racial schemas may be by answering those ubiquitous questions about race. Leeman's (2018a) study of Spanish-language interviews from the 2010 census, in which she analyzed the interactions between census interviewers and respondents surrounding the race and ethnicity questions, offers some evidence in this regard. Leeman found that many foreign-born respondents started off the interview by expressing confusion about how to classify themselves and other members of their household, but by the end of the interview they often took up a new classification system. Strikingly, the classification systems that respondents used at the end of the interview didn't always match the official Census Bureau definitions. Instead, they incorporated aspects of the interviewers' and the respondents' racial schemas, such as using nation of birth to define racial identity. Like Roth's (2012) research, Leeman's results indicate that migrants can acquire new racial schemas but also that the racial schemas that they bring to the US are not necessarily abandoned.

In fact, it is not just immigrants whose understandings of racial identity differ from the conventional US racial schema (Flores-González, 2017). In Flores-González' study, US-born Latinxs often utilized nationality labels, sometimes together with reference to phenotype, to describe their racial identities. Together with the other studies discussed in this section, Flores-González' research suggests that the growing Latinx population has the potential to challenge or destabilize the dominant US racial schema.

In the next section we look at how Latinxs have been classified in the US census, using some of the controversies surrounding the census classification as a way to talk more broadly about some key debates regarding Latinxs' ethnoracial identity.

The Ethnoracial Identity of Latinxs in the US Census and Beyond

Censuses are a key site of racialization and the production of official discourses about race in general, and about Latinxs in particular. For this reason, it is important to critically analyze how Latinx ethnoracial identity is constructed in the census (Leeman, 2013, 2018a; Nobles, 2000; Omi & Winant, 1994; Rodriguez, 2000). In addition, ethnoracial identity is expressed in the census explicitly, which makes the analysis of censuses a convenient way to look both at official constructions of identity and at individuals' identity claims. However, while labels are one language-based way in which ethnoracial categories are constructed and reproduced, it's important not to take these labels and categories as identities in themselves. In fact, as we'll discuss below, both the official categories and the ways in which people answer the questions sometimes contradict Latinxs' lived experience and their own sense of identity outside the context of the census.

As we noted, colonial censuses were an instrument of racialization and contributed to the discursive Othering of racialized groups (Anderson, 1991). Similarly, ethnoracial classification on early US censuses was tied to exclusionary and racist policies and ideologies (Leeman, 2004; Nobles, 2000; Rodriguez, 2000). However, in the mid 20th century, census classification and data began to take on new uses and symbolic meanings in the US and elsewhere (Leeman, 2018c; Loveman, 2014; Omi, 2001). In the US in particular, as a result of the Civil Rights movement, statistics on ethnoracial groups were utilized for documenting inequality and implementing anti-discrimination laws (such as the Voting Rights Act). Census categories, and the resulting statistics, were also a way for underrepresented groups to demand political and social inclusion. For these reasons, activists lobbied both for better data collection and for new ethnoracial categories.

Thanks to the mobilization of Mexican American and Puerto Rican activists, several ways of identifying the Latinx population were tested on the 1970 census (Mora, 2014; Rodriguez, 2000). A question about language was one method tested, but ultimately, because advocates and government officials wanted to include all Latinxs regardless of the language they spoke, the census added a self-identification question to the 1980 census (Leeman, 2018a; Mora, 2014; Rodriguez, 2000). The specific wording of what is often referred to as the 'Hispanic origin question' has varied slightly in the intervening years; the 2010 version is shown in Figure 5.2 (the 2020 question is almost identical, as we discuss below).

Although government documents, media coverage and the broader public discourse often construct the Hispanic origin category as linked to Spanish language, and sometimes use *Spanish-speaking* and *Latinx* interchangeably (see Chapter 2), the official definition does not

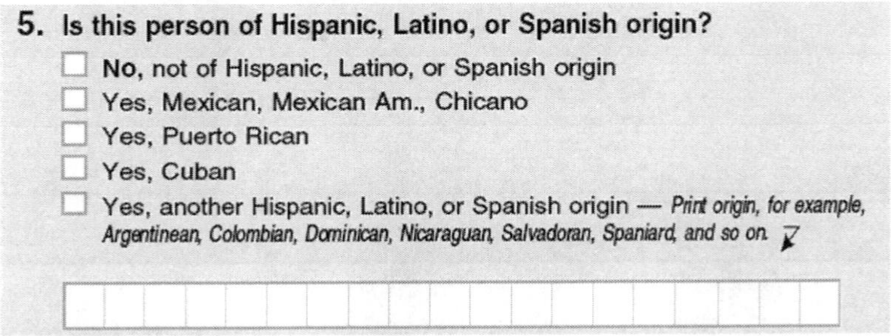
5. Is this person of Hispanic, Latino, or Spanish origin?

☐ No, not of Hispanic, Latino, or Spanish origin
☐ Yes, Mexican, Mexican Am., Chicano
☐ Yes, Puerto Rican
☐ Yes, Cuban
☐ Yes, another Hispanic, Latino, or Spanish origin — *Print origin, for example, Argentinean, Colombian, Dominican, Nicaraguan, Salvadoran, Spaniard, and so on.*

Figure 5.2 Hispanic origin question from the 2010 census

make explicit reference to language (Leeman, 2013, 2018a). Instead, the Office of Management and Budget (OMB), the governmental agency that establishes the guidelines for all federal statistics including the census, defines 'Hispanic or Latino' with reference to 'culture or origin':

> Hispanic or Latino: A person of Cuban, Mexican, Puerto Rican, South or Central American, or other Spanish culture or origin, regardless of race. The term, 'Spanish origin,' can be used in addition to 'Hispanic or Latino'. (OMB, 1997)

One frequent criticism of the Hispanic origin question, as well as of the terms *Hispanic* and *Latino* outside the context of the census, is that they lump together a vast array of very diverse people (Oboler, 1998) (although this is the case for all ethnoracial categories). Further, many people of Latin American heritage identify first by nationality or national origin, rather than a pan-ethnic label like *Hispanic* or *Latino* (Taylor *et al.*, 2012). Still, many Latinxs do feel a sense of shared identity or experience with other people in the category, suggesting that the category 'Hispanic or Latino' is meaningful, at least in some contexts and to some people. Given the use of ethnoracial statistics for documenting and combating inequality and discrimination, many people see the practical advantages as outweighing the limitations. We examine additional issues and concerns in the following sections.

Hispanic or Latino origin: Ethnicity versus race

Officially, 'Hispanic or Latino' is an ethnicity, not a race, and the Hispanic origin question is separate from the race question (shown in Figure 5.3). According to the OMB (1997), Latinxs can belong to any of the five officially recognized races: (1) American Indian or Alaska Native; (2) Asian; (3) Black or African American; (4) Native Hawaiian or Other Pacific Islander; and (5) White. The 2010 census questionnaire also included a space to

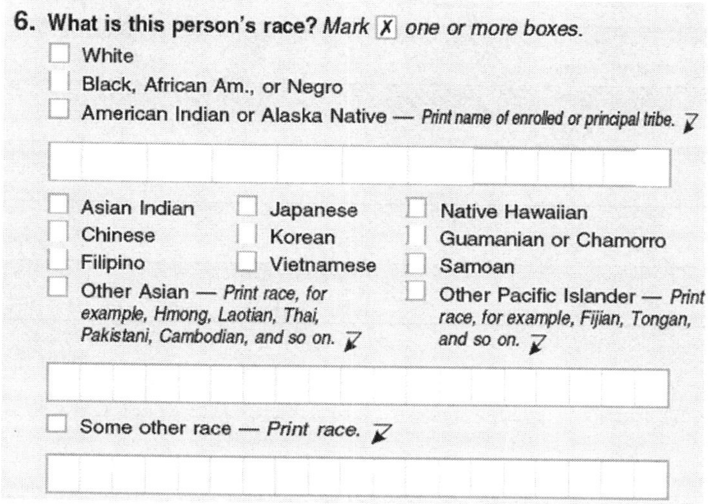

6. What is this person's race? *Mark* ☒ *one or more boxes.*

☐ White
☐ Black, African Am., or Negro
☐ American Indian or Alaska Native — *Print name of enrolled or principal tribe.*

☐ Asian Indian ☐ Japanese ☐ Native Hawaiian
☐ Chinese ☐ Korean ☐ Guamanian or Chamorro
☐ Filipino ☐ Vietnamese ☐ Samoan
☐ Other Asian — *Print race, for example, Hmong, Laotian, Thai, Pakistani, Cambodian, and so on.*
☐ Other Pacific Islander — *Print race, for example, Fijian, Tongan, and so on.*

☐ Some other race — *Print race.*

Figure 5.3 Race question from the 2010 census

write in 'some other race,' but there were no other officially recognized racial groups. For both ethnicity and race, the census relies on the principal of self-identification and classifies people according to whichever boxes they choose.

The OMB's official definitions notwithstanding, the census's ethnoracial classification system doesn't work very well for Latinxs, in that it doesn't seem to match Latinxs' own sense of their identity or how they are perceived by others. For one thing, as we saw, in Latin America it's common to think of national identities as racial, and many Latinxs in the US regard 'Dominican,' 'Puerto Rican' and 'Mexican' as racial categories (Flores-González, 2017; Rodriguez, 2000; Rosa, 2019; Roth, 2012). For example, US-born scholar and activist Gloria Anzaldúa explains:

> 'We say 'nosotros los mexicanos' ['us Mexicans'] (by mexicanos we do not mean citizens of Mexico; we do not mean national identity, but a racial one). We distinguish between 'mexicanos del otro lado' ['Mexicans from the other side'] and 'mexicanos de este lado.' ['Mexicans from this side']. Deep in our hearts we believe that being Mexican is nothing to do with which country one lives in. Being Mexican is a state of soul – not one of mind, not one of citizenship. (Anzaldúa, 1987: 62)

In addition, a recent Pew Center survey found that approximately two-thirds of Latinxs consider their Latinx background to be part of their racial make-up (González-Barrera & Lopez, 2015). This way of understanding identity explains why a significant proportion of Latinxs answer the census race question by checking 'some other race' and writing in either a specific national origin (like ***Chicano***, *Mexican*, *Puerto Rican* or *Salvadoran*) or a pan-Latinx label (like *Hispanic* or *Latinx*). Over 30% did so on the 2010 census, despite the explicit instructions that the census does not consider Hispanic origin to be a race (Ríos *et al.*, 2014). Similarly, a Pew Center telephone survey found that 51% of Latinxs chose 'some other race' or volunteered 'Hispanic' or 'Latino' when asked to identify their race using the census categories (Taylor *et al.*, 2012).

The notion that Latinx identity is racial is also reflected in Bailey's (2000a, 2000b) research with Dominican and Dominican American high school students in Providence, Rhode Island. Despite their African ancestry and phenotypical similarity to African Americans, participants in Bailey's study don't identify as Black. In contrast with the OMB's claim that someone can be both Hispanic or Latino (ethnicity) and Black (race), participants in Bailey's study frame these as mutually exclusive categories, as exemplified in the following data excerpt:

> **Wilson:** A lot of people confuse me for an African American most of the time. They ask me, 'Are you Black?' I'm like, 'No, I'm Hispanic.' And they'll be like, 'Oh I thought you were Black or something.' Most of the time I'll be talking with them, chilling, or whatever. They'll be thinking that I'm just African American. Because sometimes the way I talk, my hair, my skin color, it's just that my hair is nappy. I use a lot of slang. You can confuse a lot of Dominicans as African Americans by their color. (Bailey, 2000a: 565)

Further, language can play an even more prominent role in racial ascription than phenotype; when Dominicans who had been assumed to be African American were heard speaking Spanish, this triggered racial reclassification, as in the following data excerpt.

Wilson: Like for example, like I told you before, a lot of people confuse me like I'm Black. Yesterday I got that comment, on Sunday. I was at the park playing basketball ... there was this Spanish kid, he was Dominican, I was standing next to him and this other friend of mine, he's Dominican too, he was talking to me, and he heard me speaking Spanish to the other kid, he said, 'Oh I could've sworn he was Black' ... he asked me, 'Yo, you Black? You're not Black, huh?' I was like, 'Nah, I'm Spanish.' He was like, 'I could've sworn you was Black.' (Bailey, 2000b: 559)

Given that many Latinxs think of themselves as a racial group, together with the long history of racialization of Latinxs within the US, some people have called for the OMB to reclassify Hispanic origin as a race category (and to eliminate the separate Hispanic origin question). Respondents who identify as Latinx and another race (such as Black or White) could check multiple boxes, while those who see Hispanic or Latino to be their racial identity could check just that box. Advocates of doing this argue that it would better capture the lived experience of people who understand their Latinx identity as racial (Alcoff, 2000). On the other hand, people who prefer the two-question format argue that it is needed to capture the racial diversity among Latinxs, given that racial identities and racism play an important role in social differentiation within Latin America, and among Latinxs in the US (López, 2013). Because ethnicity and race are social constructions that vary not only geographically but also by situation and context, it's hard to imagine an ethnoracial classification system that could reflect everyone's understandings of race while also producing the data needed to examine racialization and combat racial inequity.

As part of the Census Bureau's ongoing research program on the race and ethnicity questions, the 2010 census included a test of 15 different ethnoracial classification question formats (Compton *et al.*, 2013). Based on the results, as well as input from experts and the public, Census researchers recommended using a single-question format, as well also adding a new 'Middle Eastern or North African (MENA)' category. However, these changes were not adopted and the two-question format was retained for the 2020 census. The 2020 Hispanic origin question is almost identical to that used in 2010; the only difference is in the examples provided for 'another Hispanic, Latino, or Spanish origin,' which in the 2020 version are 'Salvadoran, Dominican, Colombian, Guatemalan, Spaniard, Ecuadorian, etc.' In contrast, the format of the 2020 race question changed significantly from previous censuses. Specifically, on the format adopted for the 2020 census, each race category is accompanied by spaces for respondents to write in their specific ethnoracial identity (see Figure 5.4). (As this book goes to print, the 2020 census has not yet begun; updated information can be found at https://www.census.gov).

The instability of Latinx racial classification

Earlier in this chapter, we saw that racial categories in the census have changed over time, both reflecting and contributing to shifting societal understandings of race. Similarly, since the early 20th century the census has used a variety of mechanisms to categorize and quantify the Latinx population, including the 'Mexican' race category on the 1930 census, mother tongue, childhood language, surname, place of birth and parental place of birth, as

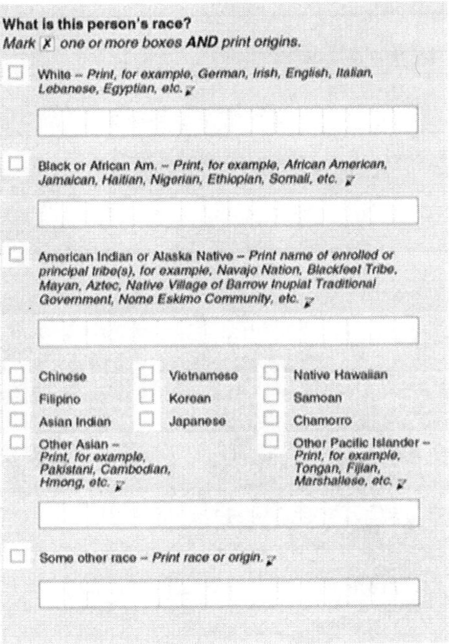

What is this person's race?
Mark X *one or more boxes* ***AND*** *print origins.*

☐ White – *Print, for example, German, Irish, English, Italian, Lebanese, Egyptian, etc.*

☐ Black or African Am. – *Print, for example, African American, Jamaican, Haitian, Nigerian, Ethiopian, Somali, etc.*

☐ American Indian or Alaska Native – *Print name of enrolled or principal tribe(s), for example, Navajo Nation, Blackfeet Tribe, Mayan, Aztec, Native Village of Barrow Inupiat Traditional Government, Nome Eskimo Community, etc.*

☐ Chinese ☐ Vietnamese ☐ Native Hawaiian
☐ Filipino ☐ Korean ☐ Samoan
☐ Asian Indian ☐ Japanese ☐ Chamorro
☐ Other Asian – *Print, for example, Pakistani, Cambodian, Hmong, etc.* ☐ Other Pacific Islander – *Print, for example, Tongan, Fijian, Marshallese, etc.*

☐ Some other race – *Print race or origin.*

Figure 5.4 Race question for the 2020 census

well as the current Hispanic origin question (Leeman, 2013; Rodriguez, 2000). In this section, we present some research that makes clear that individuals' ethnoracial classification can also be variable over time or across contexts.

In a large-scale study of more than 162 million anonymous Census Bureau records, Liebler *et al.* (2017) compared individuals' racial classification on the 2000 census to the same people's classification on the 2010 census. In contrast with dominant ideologies that see race as a permanent characteristic, Liebler and her colleagues found that almost 10 million people 'changed' race from one census to the next. The largest share of changes (37%) consisted of Latinxs who were classified as White on one census and 'some other race' on the other. Some scholars have predicted that Latin American immigrants and their offspring would assimilate into Whiteness (e.g. Alba, 2016), much as the southern and eastern European immigrants of the early 20th century 'became White' (Ignatiev, 1995; Jacobson, 1998). However, this prediction was not supported by Liebler *et al.*'s study. Instead, they found movement in both directions, both in and out of Whiteness. In other words, although some people who had been classified as 'some other race' in 2000 were classified as White in 2010, a similar number of people changed in the other direction. Although Liebler *et al.* identify the limitations of their study (for example, the impossibility of knowing whether it was the same household member who filled out the form in both censuses), the findings clearly show the fluidity of racial identity as captured by the census.

Not only can ethnoracial identities change over time, but they are also contextually dependent. Thus, the way someone thinks of their racial identity when answering the census may not match how they see themselves in other contexts or how they are treated by other people. For example, in Vargas' (2015) research, some Latinxs who checked the White box on the census reported that they were not perceived or treated as White in their daily lives. The conflicting results of two recent surveys also suggest a mismatch between census ethnoracial classification and respondents' sense of their identity in other contexts: as we noted in Chapter 2, a Pew Center survey found that a third of Latinxs consider themselves to be of 'mixed race' (González-Barrera, 2015), but on the 2010 census less than 6% indicated belonging to more than one race. Similarly, just over 2% of Latinxs reported their race as Black or African American on the 2010 census, but the on the Pew survey roughly 25% described themselves as 'Afro-Latino, Afro-Caribbean, or Afro-[country of origin]' (López & González-Barrera, 2016).

In some cases, the way in which people respond to the census questions can be strategic. In this regard, Dowling (2014) found that many Mexican and Mexican American participants in her study who identified themselves as White on the census question didn't really think of themselves as White. So why were they checking the White box? Based on follow-up interviews with participants, Dowling concluded that it was to claim societal and national belonging as Americans while also differentiating themselves from other racialized groups such as African Americans and Mexican immigrants. In contrast, some Mexicans and Mexican Americans who chose the 'some other race' category did so as a way of expressing solidarity with racialized groups. Dowling's results show that checking a box isn't always a simple matter of saying what race we belong to; instead it can be a way of expressing other aspects of our identity or beliefs.

The studies we have discussed in this section as well as earlier in the chapter show that census ethnoracial statistics are not a reflection of people's 'true' unwavering identities. Instead, they represent one particular expression of ethnoracial identity, at one particular place and time (Leeman, 2018a; Schiller *et al.*, 1995). This should not be interpreted as meaning that census statistics are inaccurate or wrong, but rather that we should take them with a pinch of salt and maintain a critical perspective about just what they mean. In addition to demonstrating the potential limitations of census statistics, the instability of census ethnoracial identification over time demonstrates the broader instability of ethnoracial identities in general; indeed, it's not just in the census that people's ethnoracial identities vary across contexts and change over time (Leeman, 2018a).

Hispanic or Latino or Spanish origin

As we have noted, two aspects of the Hispanic or Latino category that have received scholarly and popular attention are whether or not it makes sense to have a pan-ethnic category at all, and if so whether it should be considered an ethnic or a racial category. In this section, we address a third issue: the meanings and applicability of the different labels applied to the category.

As shown in Figure 5.2, the Hispanic origin question asks, 'Is this person of Hispanic, Latino, or Spanish origin?' The phrase *Spanish origin* has been included since the question was first tested on the 1970 census. This usage may seem strange and even offensive to some readers, but it should be noted that some Latinxs describe themselves as *Spanish*. In the US Southwest, especially New Mexico, some people use this term (as well as the Spanish-language term *hispano*) to describe descent from Spanish colonists who settled in the area in the 16th century (Nieto Phillips, 2004). As we discussed in Chapter 3, for some people this expression of Spanish or Spanish American identity amounts to a claim of European descent and Whiteness (Nieto-Phillips, 2000, 2004; Wilson, 1997).

However, other Latinxs, particularly those of Caribbean descent in the Northeastern US, sometimes also self-identify as *Spanish*, but with a different meaning from that in the Southwest. In the following exchange, Nanette, a Dominican American teenager in Providence, Rhode Island, explains what she means by *Spanish* to researcher Benjamin Bailey:

> **BB:** When people ask you what you are, what do you say?
>
> **Nanette:** I say I'm Spanish. I've had disputes over that one, 'What do you call Spanish, you're not from Spain.' When you're not Spanish, you don't really understand it, and I don't know if I really understand it myself. When people ask me, I'm Spanish. They're like, 'What's Spanish? Where are you from then if you're just Spanish?' Well, there's tons of different Spanish people, but we just come from all different places. But we all speak Spanish, so we're Spanish. And they're like, 'But no we speak English, and we're not all English.' But it's just so different. There's something different. We all say we're Spanish. (Bailey, 2000a: 199)

Rather than an ancestral connection to Spain, Nanette uses *Spanish* as a pan-ethnic label roughly equivalent to Latinx or Hispanic. In this usage, it is not a denial of Dominican origin or identity (nor a claim of European ancestry), but rather a pan-ethnic supra category of which Dominicans are a subgroup. As can be seen in Nanette's explanation, Spanish language plays a key role in the creation of this pan-ethnic identity. Bailey found that 'Spanish language is so central to identity for Dominicans in Providence that many use the term *Spanish* for their race, culture and ethnicity, even when active fluency in Spanish has been lost' (Bailey, 2000a: 204).

The fact that a single term (i.e. *Spanish*) is used by different groups to claim very different identities highlights an important fact about identity labels (and words in general): their meanings are socially constructed and can vary across contexts.

Hispanic versus Latino

The Census Bureau strives to use terms that align with the public's preferences and usage. It is for this reason that the 1997 OMB guidelines changed the official name of the category from 'Hispanic' to 'Hispanic or Latino' (while also authorizing the use of 'Spanish origin'). Officially, then, *Hispanic* and *Latino* are treated like synonyms. But do they really mean the same thing? The short answer is 'yes and no.' We provide the long answer below.

A quick internet search will turn up numerous videos and blog posts purporting to explain the difference between *Hispanic* and *Latino*. Such explanations typically say that *Hispanic* refers to people with a connection to the 'Spanish-speaking' countries in the Americas, and thus Brazilians are generally excluded. Nonetheless, people with Spanish (i.e. from Spain) ancestry are sometimes also included. In contrast, *Latino* is often defined as being inclusive of Brazilians, but is generally assumed to exclude people whose heritage is linked to the former French colonies in the Americas, as well as people from Spain. Many of these explanations explicitly claim, or implicitly suggest, that the differences between the terms are related to their etymology or origin, so let us examine those origins now.

The exact etymology of *Hispanic* is unclear but it seems to come from *Hispania*, the Romans' name for the Iberian Peninsula (where Spain and Portugal are located) (Gracia, 2000). It may have entered English via the Spanish-language word *hispanoamericanos*, which Oquendo (1995) defines as 'persons from the former colonies of Spain.' The different meanings in English and Spanish add an additional twist; New Mexicans who claim Spanish ancestry typically refer to themselves in Spanish as *hispanos*, but in English they often call themselves *Spanish* (which differentiates them from Mexicans and other Hispanics). There is somewhat more agreement about the origins of *Latino*, which likely derives from the Spanish word *latinoamericano* ('Latin American'), with *Latinx* being a more recent permutation. The phrase *Latin America* was first coined by the French to distinguish countries colonized by the British from those colonized by France, Portugal and Spain (Gracia, 2000).

However, while etymology is interesting, using word origins to distinguish the meanings of the present-day terms is problematic because language changes. The notion that a word's meaning is fixed and contained within the word reflects a referentialist ideology (Hill, 2008) that fails to take into account that the meaning of words depends on how speakers use and understand them. Or to put it simply, the origins of *Hispanic* and *Latino* matter less than how they are used now. These categories are socially constructed and it isn't possible to come up with a definitive definition.

Like the OMB, common usage and many dictionaries see the two labels as referring to the same people. For example, Webster's *New World College Dictionary* 4th edition defines both *Hispanic* and *Latino* as 'a usually Spanish-speaking person of Latin American birth or descent who lives in the US,' although it also provides 'a Latin American' as another meaning of *Latino* (http://www.collinsdictionary.com, accessed 12 August 2018). Note the linking of language and identity in the definition of *Hispanic* and *Latino*, as well as the exclusion of people of Latin American descent who live in other places (there are growing populations of people of Latin American descent in several European countries, including Spain, some of whom also identify as *Latino, Latina* or *Latinx*).

Webster's entries also note that *Latino* and *Latina* are now often 'preferred' to Hispanic, although they don't say by whom or why, so let us turn to that now. Even if they refer to the same people, *Hispanic* and *Latino* can have very different symbolic meanings and indexical values. For some people, using the term *Hispanic* represents a continuation of colonial ideologies and racism that elevate Spanish cultural heritage, and thus an erasure or denial of Indigenous and African heritage (Gracia, 2000; Oquendo, 1995). For example, Mexican American activist and writer Sandra Cisneros famously turned down an offer to appear on the cover of *Hispanic* magazine because of the title; as she put it, 'To me, it's like a slave name. I'm a Latina' (Fears, 2003). While the etymology of *Latino* is also rooted in colonial history (Oquendo, 1995), it is often seen as more inclusive of Indigenous and African heritage. Along these lines, for some people the use of *Latino* indexes political consciousness and resistance to racism, making it the preferred term in certain contexts, including many activist and academic circles (including this book!). Nonetheless, this preference is by no means universal. In fact, the Pew Center's nationwide survey of self-identified Hispanic/Latinos found that about half had no preference for either term, but those that did preferred *Hispanic* to *Latino* by more than two to one (Taylor *et al.*, 2012). It should now be clear why we hedged about whether *Hispanic* and *Latino* are synonymous. Ultimately, our answer has to be 'it depends on the context and the speakers.'

Gender inclusivity in labels: Latino/a, Latina/o, Latin@ or Latinx

Before leaving the topic of the terms *Latino* and *Hispanic*, we want to touch on the issue of gender. As reflected in the Webster's *New World College Dictionary* definition we discussed above, *Latina* is often used when referring to women, in accordance with gender-marking conventions in Spanish. In contexts where the referent is unspecified or includes both males and females, English and Spanish traditionally have used the masculine form, such as in the sentence: 'Latinos use a variety of labels to identify themselves.' However, many people consider this use of the male form as the generic to be an erasure of women and thus complicit in the reproduction of male dominance. For this reason, and in line with broader discussions about inclusive language that are taking place around the world, many people prefer *Latino/a*, *Latina/o* or *Latin@* to the traditional masculine generic *Latino*. While these forms recognize females as well as males, they reflect (and reinforce) a binary understanding of gender as either male or female, and thus they are not inclusive of queer, trans or gender nonconforming people who don't identify with the binary. Several alternative word endings have been proposed including *-e*, which is gaining ground in Argentina and Chile among other places, and *-x*, which is the most commonly used non-binary form in the US (in both Spanish and English). The use of *-x* (and other non-binary endings) extends beyond the term *Latinx*, with some people using it for all nouns and adjectives referring to humans (such as *amigxs* 'friends').

In September of 2018, *Latinx* was officially added to the Merriam-Webster (English-language) dictionary and defined as 'of, relating to, or marked by Latin American heritage – used as a gender-neutral alternative to Latino or Latina' (https://www.merriam-webster.com/dictionary/Latinx, accessed 1 December 2018). The most widespread use of *Latinx* is for the generic forms (i.e. when it doesn't refer to anyone specific) and for mixed-gender groups. However, some people also use *Latinx* in reference to specific individuals. Some people use it only for individuals who identify as non-binary or queer, but others use it for everyone, regardless of their gender identity, as a way to challenge gender categories and express a broader inclusivity that transcends ethnoracial, national and class boundaries (Torres, 2018). Nonetheless, some people reject the universal usage of *Latinx* because they see it as paradoxically erasing diversity by using a one-size-fits-all term for everyone (Trujillo–Pagán, 2018). For this reason, some people prefer a tripartite distinction between *-o/-a/-x* when referring to specific individuals, as this allows for the overt recognition of distinct gender and non-binary identities (e.g. *Latina*, *Latinx* and *Latino*).

While these more inclusive terms and word endings seem to be gaining traction, especially in academic and activist contexts, their use has also been critiqued, especially in Spanish. Opponents frame the *–x* as: artificial, unnecessary and unpronounceable; an imposition of English norms or trends on Spanish; and/or overly faddish or trendy (e.g. Guerra & Orbea, 2015; Martinez, 2017). These critiques undergird the rejection of *–x* (as well as other types of gender-inclusive language) by the *Real Academia Española* (RAE) in its style manuals and dictionaries.

The position of the RAE, which is consistent with its broader conservatism, provides clear evidence that the 'standard' is neither universally agreed upon nor politically neutral, despite its common portrayal as both (see Chapter 4). Further, like the controversies surrounding census classifications, the debates about gender-inclusive language underscore that debates surrounding identity labels, and language more broadly, are about much more than simply linguistic issues.

Conclusions and Connections

In this chapter we examined the social construction of ethnoracial identity in Latin America and the US, emphasizing the role of colonization and conquest in racialization. We saw how both of these processes, and the racial structuring of society in Spanish as well as English colonies, have left an enduring legacy in the ongoing racialization of Latinxs in the US. In Chapter 7 we will see how racial ideologies are reproduced in the media. In Chapters 8 and 9, respectively, we will look at the enactment and impact of racialization in language policy and education.

One recurring theme discussed in this chapter is the linking of Spanish to Latinx identities, which we also touched on in our earlier discussions of language shift (Chapter 2) and language ideologies (Chapter 4). Here, we focused on the construction of Spanish as part of the racial make-up of Latinxs by examining the notion that the ability to speak Spanish is a quasi-biological trait. As we saw, this ideology allows the vilification of Spanish to serve as a mechanism for the denigration of Latinxs, no matter what their actual language knowledge or practices are. In the next chapter we'll look at how this ideology also underlies Mock Spanish, a purportedly comical use of Spanish that covertly reproduces negative stereotypes about Latinxs. The indexical link between Spanish and Latinx identity also undergirds the power of language to trump phenotype in racial ascription, as was evident in Bailey's (2000a, 2000b) research, in which adolescents enacted different racial identities based on the language they spoke. Further, that research underscored the fact that despite the racialization of Spanish in some contexts, Spanish is nonetheless a powerful resource for constructing and expressing identity, which we will explore in greater detail in the next chapter.

Given the prominence of the census as a site for ethnoracial classification, and its role in disseminating official constructions of ethnoracial identities, we dedicated a fair amount of space to a discussion of the Hispanic origin and race questions. This discussion included a consideration of the reasons for collecting ethnoracial data and the challenges of determining whether Hispanic origin should be considered an ethnic or a racial identity, as well as the contested referential and symbolic meanings of the competing pan-ethnic labels. While explicit labels are one salient way in which people express and claim identities, we want to stress that they are not the only way people use language to index their identity or ascribe identity to others (as Bailey's research showed).

Although there is no question that ethnoracial identities have an important role in people's sense of themselves and their lived experiences, as well as in the structuring of society, these are not the only identities that matter. By highlighting how people's responses to census questions can change over time and/or differ from the identity claims they make in other contexts or from how other people see them, we made the broader point that ethnoracial identity is not a fixed, inherent part of who a person is. Instead, it is contextual and can fluctuate over time. In the next chapter, we'll see that this is also the case for other kinds of identity, as we explore the various ways in which people use language to construct, perform and negotiate a broad range of social categories.

Discussion Questions and Activities for Chapter 5

(1) Watch the New York Times Op-Doc, *A Conversation with Latinos on Race* (http://www.nytimes.com/video/opinion/100000004237305/a-conversation-with-latinos-on-race.html), and identify some examples of: (a) racial diversity within families; (b) a person's identity claims being challenged based on their language use; and (c) Spanish being the basis of for racial classification and/or racialization.

(2) Watch *Afro Latinos Get DNA Tested*, a Buzzfeed Pero Like video (https://www.buzzfeed.com/watch/video/62918?utm_term=.ewOXl6XX96#.ybLx4Zxx5Z). What are some of the assumptions about identity and DNA reflected in this video? How do the four people's comments reflect racial ideologies discussed in this chapter? Why do you think people are interested in doing ancestry tests? Do you think people's sense of themselves or their identity, or the ways in which other people treat them, change based on the results? When the results are different from people's lifetime experiences and beliefs prior to the test, which is the person's 'real' race?

(3) Do some internet searches on either the difference between *Hispanic* and *Latino*, and/or on the term *Latinx*. What kind of explanations do you find and what kind of ideologies do they reflect? Can you find any examples where the terms are used interchangeably or when only one is used? Analyze your findings, including any contradictory definitions or opinions, in light of our discussion in this chapter.

(4) Compare the ethnoracial and linguistic classification of the US census to that of another country, such as Cuba (http://www.one.cu/publicaciones/cepde/cpv2012/20140428informenacional/7_tematicas.pdf), Mexico (https://www.inegi.org.mx/programas/ccpv/2010) or Canada (https://www12.statcan.gc.ca/nhs-enm/2016/ref/questionnaires/questions-eng.cfm). What ethnoracial categorization

questions are included? What response options are provided? Who is 'invisible' in these censuses? What does this tell you about the social construction of race either in those places or in general?

(5) Read the following blog post (in Spanish) about a Mexican woman's difficulty answering the race question on the 2010 census: https://justanothergirlinthewall.wordpress.com/tag/census-2010. Analyze her account in light of the topics discussed in this chapter, including a consideration of her sense of her own ethnoracial identity, her interpretation of the choices offered and the guidance provided to her by the helpline operator. If you met the writer in person, what would you tell her regarding the issues and options? What overall insights does this give you into the meanings of labels as well as their relationship to identity?

Further Reading and Resources

Bailey, B. (2000) The language of multiple identities among Dominican Americans. *Journal of Linguistic Anthropology* 10 (2), 190–223. https://doi.org/10.1525/jlin.2000.10.2.190

Claudia Milian (2017) *Cultural Dynamics.* Special Issue 29 (3) on Theorising LatinX.

Gates, Jr., H.L. (2011) *Black in Latin America.* PBS. See https://www.pbs.org/wnet/black-in-latin-america/

Leeman, J. (2018). Becoming Hispanic: The negotiation of ethnoracial identity in US census interviews. *Latino Studies* 16 (4), 432–460.

Mora, G.C. (2014) *Making Hispanics: How Activists, Bureaucrats, and Media Constructed a New American.* Chicago, IL: University of Chicago Press.

Taylor, P., Lopez, M.H., Martínez, J.H. and Velasco, G. (2012) When labels don't fit: Hispanics and their views of identity. *Hispanic Trends,* 4 April. Washington DC: Pew Hispanic Center. See http://www.pewhispanic.org/2012/04/04/when-labels-dont-fit-hispanics-and-their-views-of-identity/

Chapter 6

Language and Identity

Objectives

To present a framework for analyzing the social construction and performance of identities in linguistic interaction, and to examine research on how Spanish-speakers in the US use language in the construction, performance and negotiation of identity.

Introduction

In this chapter, we will build on the discussion of race as socially constructed, as well as on the discussion of language ideologies and ideological processes, by looking at how many different types of identity – such as gender, social class, being a social activist or being someone's best friend – are constructed through language. We address how this theoretical framework can be applied to language use in general, and to speaking Spanish in the US in particular. As we will show, the ways in which we use language to construct and perform our identities are not limited to choices about speaking Spanish or English. People use many different linguistic features (including specific styles, words and pronunciations) to signal who they are or to position themselves in particular ways. We also discuss how identity is intertwined with the topics of other chapters in this book, because we are constantly constructing our identities through everything we do.

Identities

The word *identity* is used in many different ways in contemporary discourse; it is often used to talk about the seemingly objective, demographic-based essence of a person. The term is also used to talk about someone's official records and accounts, as in the phrase *identity theft*. Such usages imply that identity is static in nature, a set of characteristics, categories or even numbers. In this book we think about identity differently, in line with current understandings in the social sciences and humanities. In particular, identity is not a fixed category or unitary sense of self; instead, individuals' identities are socially constructed, and they are also fluid, varied and multiple. For one thing, just as **ethnoracial** identities are defined differently by different groups and in different contexts, other identities are also context dependent and rely on a shared understanding among people in that context. Identities such as 'woman,' 'professor,' 'cyclist,' 'politician,' 'friend,' 'nerd,' etc. are not constructed the same way, nor are they associated with the same characteristics, in all contexts. For example, the category 'friend' means very different things on social media and in real life, just as the identity 'cyclist' has very different meanings at a transportation planning meeting and at the Olympics. Secondly, individuals don't have just one identity, or one way of being and seeing themselves in the world and of being seen by others. Instead, different identities come to the fore based on where we are, who we are with and what we are doing. A key premise of social constructionist approaches to identity is that we do not act or speak in the ways we do as a result of our identities, but rather, our identities come into being through the ways we act, speak, dress, move, etc. Thus, social theorists talk about identity as something that people 'do' rather than something they 'have' and identity consists of performances of self in different contexts (Kroskrity, 2000: 111). The focus of this chapter is on how language is a symbolic resource that can be used to construct and perform identities, especially through interactions with others.

The concept of identities as performative is rooted in research on gender (Butler, 1990). The central idea in this work is that gender identities are based on culturally situated social behaviors rather than on biological sex, and that performances of identity draw on associations between particular behaviors and social categories. Thus, we enact our identities as members of those categories by doing the things associated with those identities in our cultural context. At the same time, doing so reinforces the associations of those behaviors with those groups. For example, **hegemonic** understandings of femininity in the US associate it with a particular set of attitudes, behaviors and ways of being, such as being emotional or nurturing. However, this notion of femininity is socially constructed rather than natural, and it is performative rather than an inherent or essential characteristic or the result of having two x chromosomes. When a person adopts these 'female' ways of being they enact and perform a feminine identity, while also reinforcing the idea that this is what it means to be feminine. Nonetheless, there are many potential ways of being feminine, and while we might have names for some of them (e.g. 'Girly girl,' 'tomboy'), it is also possible to construct a kind of femininity that does not fit into any named categories. This is, of course, true of all other aspects of identity as well, such as ethnic or national identities.

A good example of the social construction and enactment of identities not based on language involves clothing. In Chapter 4 we discussed Mendoza-Denton's (2008) research, and the ways in which members of the Norteñas and Sureñas used hairstyles and clothing colors to index or signal their gang affiliations. While we are perhaps not consciously aware of it, and we may not follow such strict color codes, most of us would likely agree that we also make choices about how to dress based on how we want to present ourselves. Those choices are constrained by societal norms and values; our ideas about how certain items of clothing indicate gender, sexuality, religious customs and ethnic or other group membership certainly inform our choices, and they are sometimes even made explicit by things like dress codes in schools and places of employment. But there is no inherent reason why skirts often are considered female and ties are considered male, just as there was no particular reason why the Norteñas would wear red and the Sureñas blue. The existence of exceptions (such as Scottish kilts) and the fact that clothing norms change over time provide further evidence that such norms are socially constructed.

Further, people don't automatically wear particular clothes *because* they are female, gay, a teenager or come from a middle-class background; they make choices. The clothes we choose are part of the performance of our identities, and here it is also easy to see that how we want to present ourselves is not always the same. In one context (such as an interview for an office job) you might chose particular clothing to signal to your potential employer that you are professional and understand the expectations of an office job, for example. Or, in the vocabulary from social theory, you might use the symbolic meanings of different clothing to construct and perform the identity of a middle-class professional. In other contexts, you might dress in the colors of your favorite team in order to perform the identity of a true fan, or wear clothing traditionally associated with the opposite sex as a performance of a non-binary gender identity or of a person who objects to hegemonic gender roles. It isn't that any one of these identities is any more 'real' than the others, or that you can only be one thing at a time. Instead, people perform different identities depending on the context, who they are with or what they wish to convey. But again, the crucial point is that a person's identity doesn't determine a person's behavior (or clothing choices). In fact, it's the opposite: people use symbolic resources and behaviors, including language, to construct and perform their identities.

In the last chapter we talked about ethnoracial identities such as 'Latinx,' which is obviously of particular interest. However, we will also address additional aspects of identity, including gender and sexuality, as well as identities not linked to named social categories. Although we sometimes use labels to construct, perform and/or explicitly claim identities, we want to reiterate that labels are not identities in and of themselves, and there are many other ways in which we use language to construct and perform our identities.

The Linguistic Construction of Social Identities

In this section we discuss how language is used to construct, perform and negotiate identities. This is an area where there has been a tremendous amount of theoretical research, not only in sociolinguistics and linguistic anthropology, but also in various subfields of linguistics (such as language acquisition and language teaching), as well as other disciplines. Here, we outline one model that is representative of contemporary understandings. Specifically, we present Bucholtz and Hall's (2005) framework for the study of how identities are produced in linguistic interaction, and we provide examples from research on Spanish in the US.

Bucholtz and Hall (2005) spell out five key aspects of the relationship of language and identity, which we will discuss below: (1) identity is interactionally constructed; (2) there are multiple levels of identity; (3) various linguistic means can be used to construct and perform identities; (4) identities are constructed in relationship to other people; and (5) there are multiple forces that play a role in the construction of identities.

The interactional construction of identity

Bucholtz and Hall (2005) argue that identity is not the source but rather the outcome of linguistic (and other social) behavior. The notion that language is a means to construct social meaning is not unique to their framework, and it is very much in line with recent research on linguistic variation. Early sociolinguistic studies looked at how different groups (such as men and women, or the affluent and the poor) used language differently, thus reflecting the idea that membership in a social category is correlated with language use, without focusing on intraspeaker variability or agency. More recent research on language variation, in contrast, looks at how people use language in order to construct and perform identities (Eckert, 2012). In this view, identity is social and cultural rather than an internal psychological state (Bucholtz & Hall, 2005).

Levels of identity

Perhaps the most obvious or salient aspects of identities are linked to macro-level demographic categories; these are named categories for gender, sexuality, ethnic, racial, age, social class, religious, national, etc. categories. For example, we might describe ourselves or others as 'Latinx,' 'straight,' 'Asian,' 'Catholic' or 'female' and we may be asked to use these categories to identify ourselves in official contexts (e.g. in the US it is common to fill out age, sex and race on forms to register for school). Further, macro-level categories often seem easy to define, although in reality they may be constructed differently in different contexts. Moreover, which categories we use to describe ourselves or others depend on the context: in some contexts nationality or religion may be salient; in others, gender and ethnicity.

There are also what Bucholtz and Hall (2005: 585) call 'local, ethnographically emergent cultural positions,' which are specific to the setting and situation. Such identities generally do not have official recognition and they only have meaning within a particular context. For example, the most salient identities in Fuller's (2007, 2009, 2012) research on children in bilingual classrooms were being a good or bad student, as well as identities related to linguistic proficiency. Often, being a good student was constructed in part by adhering to the language of the lesson, as each subject was explicitly taught in one language (e.g. math in Spanish, social studies in English). Further, sometimes speakers positioned themselves as bilingual by translating from English to Spanish and back again, and by constructing other speakers as monolingual.

In addition to macro-level and local identities, Bucholtz and Hall (2005: 585) note that there are 'temporary and interactionally specific **stances** and participant roles.' These micro-level identities include roles like 'evaluator' and 'engaged listener' which are embedded in the particular, ongoing interaction, while stances are positions regarding what is being said (we explain stance-taking in more detail below). Thus, in one conversational interaction a person might take on the role of devil's advocate or skeptic, but in another conversation they might enact an identity of sympathetic listener.

In sum, we have many different levels of identity. In any interaction, multiple levels are all present, although at any given moment one may be more salient than another. So, thinking of Fuller's research mentioned above, in one interaction a child can simultaneous enact her identity as a 'Latina girl' (macro-level), a 'good student' (local, ethnographic category) and an 'engaged listener' (interactional category). But how do we use language to do this? In the next sub-section we'll discuss some of the linguistic resources and strategies involved.

Linguistic means of constructing identities

There are many aspects of language that can be used in identity construction and performance. One seemingly straightforward means of claiming or assigning an identity is through the use of a label. This happens on the census, as we discussed in the last chapter, but it also takes place in other contexts. The use of labels in identity work is exemplified in Shenk's (2007) study of the identity constructions of three friends (Bela, Rica and Lalo) who all stake different claims to the category of 'Mexican.' As the three friends talk, they use the explicit label *Mexican*, as well as other terms, to construct their own (and others') identities. Like the census categories, the meaning of labels used in interactions is also socially constructed and contextual. In Shenk's study, Bela, who was born in Mexico, prioritizes birthplace and citizenship in the determination of authentic Mexican identity and tells Lalo, who was born in the US, that he is not 'original.' Lalo's implicit definition of Mexican identity as rooted in ancestry and 'blood purity' allows him to push back against Bela's challenge. Specifically, he claims that he is '*más original*' than she is, and '*puro*' because 'both of [his] parents are Aztec blood,' while one of Bela's parents is not Mexican (Shenk, 2007: 206–207). Finally, for Rica, being an authentic Mexican means being proficient in Spanish.

In addition to highlighting the negotiated and contested nature of identity categories, Shenk's study also points to other ways, in addition to labels, in which language is used in the construction and performance of identities. In particular, the participants in her study use the indexical linking of particular languages with particular identities in order to claim their own identities and challenge each other's. The essentialized link between speaking Spanish and being Mexican (or Latinx) that we have discussed previously allows language choice to function as another linguistic means of identity construction. At one point in Shenk's data, for example, Bela challenges Lalo's claims to Mexicanness – which he makes in English – by asking him where he was born and by switching to Spanish to do so. Clearly the content of what she says is important, as the point she is making is that he is less Mexican than her because he was born in the US and she was born in Mexico. However, given the connection of Spanish language to Mexican identity, Bela's use of

Spanish is a way to perform a Mexican identity and reinforce her claim. The indexical relationship between Spanish and Mexican identity also underlies Bela telling Rica, 'I'm going to revoke your Mexican privileges' when Rica mispronounces a Spanish word, thus turning Rica's own language-based construction of authentic Mexican identity against her.

It is not only different languages such as Spanish versus English that are used in identity construction and performance: accents, speech styles and particular words or structures can also be used to index identities. Even pronouncing words or names in a specific way can be an act of identity. For Latinxs with Spanish names, the decision to use either a Spanish or an anglicized pronunciation constitutes a particular position with regard to ethnolinguistic identity and belonging (Parada, 2016). Using the Spanish pronunciation can represent resistance not only to the symbolic violence of having to change one's name – a salient marker of identity – to fit in, but also to the underlying monolingual and assimilationist ideologies that construct the US as an English-speaking White nation.

Pronouncing one's own name in Spanish sometimes results in pushback. For example, in 2015 some viewers complained about Arizona newscaster Vanessa Ruiz's rolling of *R*s and other aspects of Spanish pronunciation in her reporting. Going beyond the growing trend of newscasters pronouncing their own names according to their native language norms, Ruiz also used Spanish pronunciation for local place names such as *Mesa*, the third largest city in the state. She responded on air to complaints by explaining that she was 'lucky enough to grow up speaking two languages,' continuing:

> So yes, I do like to pronounce certain things the way they are meant to be pronounced. And I know that change can be difficult, but it's normal and over time I know that everything falls into place. (https://www.nytimes.com/2015/09/04/us/latina-arizona-news-anchor-vanessa-ruiz-spanish-pronunciation.html, accessed 5 December 2018)

In a subsequent Facebook post thanking her colleagues for their support, Ruiz concluded: 'I am more proud now than ever to be an American, and also, a Latina. Thank you. Gracias.' (https://web.facebook.com/vanessaruiznews/posts/739128352886942?_rdc=1&_rdr, accessed 27 March 2019). Even without Ruiz's explicit commentary, the pronunciation itself, as well as saying *Gracias*, in Spanish, were part of her identity performance as a Spanish-speaker and a Latina. Moreover, the implications of Ruiz's pronunciation go beyond identity; by referring to cities by their Spanish names and framing her pronunciation as correct ('meant to be pronounced'), she discursively elevates Spanish vis-à-vis English and normalizes its presence in the US.

This attention to (or policing of) Ruiz's pronunciation is not an isolated incident; for example, in an interview on Fox News, New York Representative Alexandria Ocasio-Cortez was also criticized for her pronunciation of her own name, and accused of 'doing that Latina thing' – in other words, constructing herself as Latina and refusing to fully assimilate by relinquishing the Spanish pronunciation of her name. As Ocasio-Cortez's subsequent tweets pointed out, this criticism may be based on feeling threatened by multilingualism (https://www.nbcnews.com/news/latino/latina-thing-alexandria-ocasio-cortez-s-name-latest-culture-war-n985916, accessed 27 March 2019). However, changing or anglicizing someone else's name against their will is a kind of symbolic violence and forced assimilation (Bucholtz, 2016). Given the lack of understanding by Anglos, as well as negative reactions (we return to this below), the seemingly simple act of introducing yourself can be ideologically and emotionally fraught. Moreover, the negative reactions to names perceived as Spanish or Latinx are not 'just' rhetorical but also include employment discrimination and other material consequences. For example, *Business Insider* website recently ran a story of a man who changed his name from 'José' to 'Joe' on his résumé and immediately received more job interviews (https://www.businessinsider.com/job-seeker-changed-his-name-2014-9?international=true&r=US&IR=T, accessed 1 June 2019; we discuss linguistic discrimination in employment in Chapter 8).

These discussions of naming and pronunciation are also of interest here because they illustrate how people use language in stance-taking, and how stance is related to identity. Not everyone defines it in exactly the same way, but we like Jaffe's (2009: 3) straightforward definition of *stance-taking* as 'taking up a position with respect to the form and content of one's utterance.' Such positions can be about our feelings or emotions regarding what we are saying (affective stance), or about whether we think it is believable or true (epistemic stance). Stance is related to identity in that when people display their evaluation of what is being said, they portray themselves as specific kinds of people and/or (dis)align themselves with other speakers. When certain linguistic features are used repeatedly in particular stances and those stances are linked to specific identities, the features themselves can then become associated with identity categories (Jaffe, 2009; Johnstone, 2009).

One easy-to-grasp example of how language can be used to position oneself in a particular way is the identity label **Chicanx**. Until the 1960s, *Chicano* was used with a derogatory connotation, and *Mexican* or *Mexican American* were the terms more commonly used for self-identification. However, in the 1960s a new generation of activists gave *Chicano* new meaning. Rejecting dominant discourses that framed a lack of cultural assimilation as the cause of social inequality, these activists saw colonialism and racism as the cause of poverty and social problems in their communities. As part of a broader symbolic effort emphasizing that their presence in the Southwest predates the US and rejecting the notion that they must be either Mexican or American, they reclaimed the label *Chicano*. As a result, self-identifying as *Chicano* (and later, *Chicanx*), was one way to enact a specific social and political stance. (For more on this, listen to the podcast discussed in Question 5 in Chapter 9.)

Similarly, in the above example, Ruiz uses Spanish pronunciation not only to index and enact her identity as a Latina, but also to take a stance regarding the history of Mesa and, by extension, Arizona and the US. Further evidence of Ruiz's intent comes from her follow-up statement posted on the television station's website:

> Let me be clear: My intention has never been to be disrespectful or dismissive, quite the contrary. I actually feel I am paying respect to the way some of Arizona's first, original settlers intended for some things to be said. (https://www.nytimes.com/2015/09/04/us/latina-arizona-news-anchor-vanessa-ruiz-spanish-pronunciation.html, accessed 5 December 2018)

The link of stance to identity is evident in the fact that, by taking a specific stance about the history of Arizona, Ruiz positions herself as a particular type of person: someone who is appreciative of linguistic and cultural pluralism, and who both recognizes and wishes to draw attention to the historical erasure of the Southwest's Spanish and Mexican past that we discussed in Chapter 3 (we also note her simultaneous erasure of Native history). Similarly, Ruiz's use of both English and Spanish ('Thank you. Gracias') in her expression of patriotic pride is a way to take a stance regarding what it means to be an American and to challenge the monolingual construction of national identity. Further, her statement that she is an American 'and also a Latina' challenges the notion that these are incompatible identities and that 'real' Americans are Anglo/White. While Ruiz's on-air and online comments are helpful for understanding her intent, and providing additional evidence of it, normally this kind of stance-taking is not explicit. The positive response of some viewers, as well as the backlash from others, demonstrates that listeners understood the stance she was taking, as well as its broader challenge to dominant ideologies, even before she explained them.

Another example of stance-taking can be found in Showstack's (2016) analysis of how students in a Spanish course for **heritage language speakers** evaluated texts combining English and Spanish. Some students implicitly expressed disdain for English-influenced Spanish, such as when Aldo responded to the use of the **borrowing** *cora* ('quarter') by simply saying, 'Really. Wow.' (Showstack, 2016: 7), while others displayed a positive stance through appreciative laughter. Showstack's analysis reveals how these stances were part of students' positioning of themselves and others as either experts or novices. This research also sheds light on how purist ideologies (see Chapter 4) are reproduced and/or challenged in the classroom.

In order to show how word choice or grammatical structure can be an act of identity, we turn to Rivera-Mills' (2011) study of pronoun use among multiple generations of Salvadorans and Hondurans in the Western US. Specifically, she analyzed speakers' use of two second person singular pronouns: *tú* and *vos*. While *tú* is used throughout the Spanish-speaking world, *vos* is used primarily in the Southern Cone and Central America, where it coexists with *tú*. In Central America, *vos* is used to express particular interpersonal relationships and affective positions (such as intimacy or solidarity). In line with our discussion about how identities are enacted (not simply reflected) through interaction and the way people talk to each other, it's worth noting that pronoun choice (i.e. *usted* vs. *tú* vs. *vos*) is one way in which interlocutors construct their identities and their relationship to their interlocutor as, for example, more or less distant, deferential, formal, familiar, etc. (Raymond, 2016).

Among other findings, Rivera-Mills found that second- and third-generation Central Americans used *vos* less than immigrants, presumably influenced by the large Mexican American community (which typically only uses *tú*) (see Chapter 10 for a discussion of contact between different varieties of Spanish). But what is most relevant for our discussion here is the *way* third-generation participants in her study used *vos*. Third-generation Salvadorans actually used *vos* more than those in the second generation, but they used it without the accompanying verb form (e.g. '*Vos, ¿por qué no te compras unos zapatos nuevos?*' 'Hey [literally: you], why don't you buy some new shoes?') (Rivera-Mills, 2011: 100). Rivera-Mills explains that instead of a pronoun associated with distinct verb forms, *vos* has become one way to signal Salvadoran origin, as well as Central American identification more broadly. This can be seen in the following response of one second-generation participant to the question of whether he used *vos*, and if so, with whom.

> *Sí, en los EE.UU., las raras veces que conocí a un salvadoreño en la universidad que era de El Salvador, y con él usaba el vos, pero los otros eran de Panamá, o de Bolivia, o de Sudamérica, o de España, y con ellos no usé el vos, de vez en cuando, pero solamente para distinguir que yo era de otro país, con ellos era de usted o de tú.*
>
> Yes, in the US, the few times I met a Salvadoran in the university that was from El Salvador, and with him I used vos, but the others were from Panama, or from Bolivia, or from South America, or from Spain, and with them I didn't use vos, sometimes, but just to distinguish that I was from another country, with them it was usted or tú.
>
> (Rivera-Mills, 2011: 102)

The relational nature of identity

The last example from Rivera-Mills leads us to the next part of Bucholtz and Hall's framework: identities are relational. That is, people's identities are constructed in relationship to other people and they vary with the relationships that are co-constructed in interaction. In other words, the construction of an 'I' or a 'we' goes hand in hand with the construction of 'you' or 'them.' This was also apparent in Roth's (2012) research on ethnoracial classification among Caribbean migrants in New York that we discussed in the last chapter; participants classified people differently based on who they were comparing them to.

Bucholtz and Hall cite three particular relationships involved in identity construction: similarity/difference, genuineness/artifice and authority/delegitimacy. In the above example from Rivera-Mills (2011), we see that *vos* isn't only a way to establish connection (similarity) with Central Americans, it is also a way to differentiate oneself from Spanish-speakers of other national origins. The construction of similarity and difference is also illustrated in the examples from Bailey's (2000a, 2000b) work on Dominican Americans that we discussed in the previous chapter; when the Dominican adolescents in that study used **African American English** (AAE), it simultaneously enacted similarity to African Americans and difference/distance from White Americans. In other cases, they constructed difference between themselves and African Americans by using Spanish, while also expressing similarity and connection with Dominicans through the use of a Dominican variety of Spanish. Which of these differences or similarities were brought to the forefront through language depended on the individuals and the specific interactions, but in all cases the identities they constructed revolved in part around the relationship between self and other.

Shenk's work discussed above provides an excellent example of the role of authenticity, genuineness or 'enoughness' (Woolley, 2016) in the construction of identity. Lalo, Bela and Rica sought, through their conversation, to establish their own authentically Mexican identities based on the competing criteria of blood, birthplace and/or Spanish-language proficiency. One important element of Shenk's study is that she shows that the definition of authenticity was socially and interactionally constructed, rather than fixed. Another key point is that one way to establish one's own authenticity is by challenging other people's authenticity; in Shenk's study, Bela, Lalo and Rica sought to establish their bona fide Mexican identity not only by defining it based on their preferred criteria, but also by deauthenticating their friends' claims to Mexican identity. For example, Lalo didn't just claim to be 'pure' and 'original,' he made the point of being 'more original' than Bela, and her lack of 'originality' enhanced his.

In other research, we see attribution of ethnic authenticity based on a person's association with other group members. In Woolley (2016), two girls discuss whether there are any Latinx or Asian gay kids in their school, agreeing that a particular classmate doesn't 'count' (it's not clear if she is a candidate for being Latinx or Asian) because she hangs out with White kids. In his research at a Mexican restaurant in Austin, Texas, Barrett (2006) mentions being called a 'burrito' by some of his Anglo co-workers (that is, White on the outside but brown (Latinx) on the inside) because he spoke Spanish and hung out with some of the Latinx employees – which in their eyes made him less authentically White. In these examples, authenticity and artifice are based in part on the ways in which people are like, and different from, members of the identity group(s) in question.

Bucholtz and Hall's final dichotomy is authority and delegitimacy, which refers to the use of positions of power in the construction of identities. For instance, Bela's claim to being more Mexican than her friends based on her Mexican citizenship draws on the authority of the state to support her identity construction. Similarly, her claim that Lalo is less 'original' is an attempt to use this criterion to censor the identity construction of her friends (albeit in a playful manner), which reinforces her own identity claims. However, not all references to legitimacy in the service of identity construction are as explicitly linked to government authority; it may be simply what is considered normative in a particular context. In a study of English–Spanish speakers in Mexico, Holguín Mendoza (2018b) gives an example in which one speaker's use of an English word with a US American accent is (laughingly) criticized by her friend, who says, '*Mira Diana, nooo se dice así, estamos en México*' ('Look Diana, you don't say it like that, we're in Mexico').

Multiple sources of identity

Earlier we discussed the notion of identity as performance – something we do, rather than something we have. While the word *performance* may evoke a sense that the choices we make about who we are and how we speak are conscious, this can be the case, but it isn't always. The ways in which we speak are often habitual and unconscious, as well as limited by our ability to use different varieties. We are sometimes unaware of the linguistic features we use – and we may unconsciously switch from one language to another without even realizing it – whereas in some cases we may be well aware of the styles, varieties or accents we use. For example, many people who move from one region to another unconsciously begin speaking differently; it's quite common to adopt the accent around you without consciously trying to change the way you speak. However, in some cases you might make a conscious effort to speak like those around you. On the other hand, some people make conscious efforts to change their accents (as can be seen in the existence of various accent reduction programs), and this is notoriously difficult (Lippi-Green, 2012).

In other words, although we speak of 'choosing' specific languages, linguistic features and language practices (such as combining languages), this does not mean that we are cognizant of all of these 'choices' – or of all the social meanings layered in our words. Pronunciation features and word choices may be acquired without a speaker being attentive to that level of detail; although linguists can describe and analyze the features of speech, many such details are not apparent to speakers themselves. And not only are we not conscious of linguistic features, we are also influenced by ideologies without necessarily being able to understand or articulate what these ideologies are or whether we explicitly endorse them.

Further, we are not free to claim and enact any identity we wish. Instead, we are constrained both by the opinions of other people and by ideological and structural forces. For example, a middle-aged university professor may imagine themselves to be a super cool, with-it, hipster, and may dress the part while also using all the 'in' expressions. Is this performance sufficient to enact the corresponding identity? It depends on whether or not the professor is successful at getting other people to see them this way. Sadly (or not!), it's likely that the professor's students and colleagues alike will not see the professor's identity in the way they hoped, and will instead assign them to other identity categories. In fact, there is often tension between the identities we claim and those that others ascribe to us, and neither is sufficient to fully account for our identity.

The mismatch between the identities that we claim for ourselves and those that others ascribe to us sometimes leads to negotiation. Such mismatches were a recurrent theme in Bailey's (2000b) research with Dominican Republicans in Providence, in which many of the Dominican adolescents thought of themselves as Dominican or Spanish but were frequently considered Black by their classmates. This was apparent in the example we cited in the previous chapter, in which Wilson explained that he is often perceived as Black until he speaks Spanish. In Bailey's study, negotiation of identity took place through language, in part through explicit discussions but also through linguistic performance (e.g., speaking Spanish). This was also the case in Shenk's study; participants' identity did not rest solely on their own claims and performances; it was dependent in part on what their friends thought of them.

Interactional negotiation of identity was also evident in Leeman's (2018a) study of Spanish-language census interviews (discussed in the last chapter). In that study, respondents didn't simply report their existing sense of their own identity to census interviewers; instead, respondents and interviewers co-constructed the meaning of the categories (which didn't always match the official definitions), as well as the place of household members within them. Leeman's (2018a) study also points to the ways in which societal ideologies and institutional forces can limit our identity options. On one hand, the US government theoretically relies on the principle of self-identification in ethnoracial classification, but on the other hand, there is a limited set of response options, and people who provide an answer that doesn't match the official categories are asked to give a different response. Thus, we are not completely free to choose any identity we want, nor are our identities completely imposed upon us. This tension between our own sense of self and dominant ideologies occurs at multiple levels of identity (Benwell & Stokoe, 2006).

Structural racism also plays a role in the construction and ascription of identities, including those linked to language. For example, Flores and Rosa (2015) have shown that African American, Latinx and other racialized students are often 'heard' as speaking non-standard English, regardless of how they actually speak. It doesn't matter what the actual features of students' language are, the negative response is based on their racialized identities. As such, even when students of color use 'standard' language to perform identities as academically inclined members of the middle class, their ability to fully enact this identity and be perceived as such is constrained by individual and societal racism.

To sum up this section, then, we can say that our identity is made up of some combination of our unconscious or habitual actions, our intentional choices, the identities that others ascribe to us, and ideological and structural forces. Our linguistic performance of identity, and its effectiveness in enacting identity, is similarly constrained.

Indexicality and Identity

In this section we explore the notion of **indexicality**, introduced in Chapter 4, in greater depth. As we have discussed, the basic idea is that certain ways of speaking come to 'point to' particular social categories. For example, in the US speaking Spanish in is often seen as an index (and a requirement) of Latinx identity. Such indexical relationships between language and identity are not limited to Spanish in the US, however. In many Latin American contexts, for example, recognition as a member of an Indigenous group often depends on speaking the corresponding language. Along these lines, many nations use language as a proxy for ethnoracial identity in census classification (Leeman, 2017; Morning, 2008). Such practices both reflect and contribute to essentialist ideas about identity and language, as well as the assumption that people who do not speak 'their' heritage language have 'lost their culture.'

While the ideological linking of language to ethnoracial identity is common, languages can also index other identities and social attributes. In some cases this works as a indexical chain, in which a language points to a specific group, and if that group is associated with specific attributes, the language can index those attributes (Johnstone, 2010). In order to see the way in which language can index social or moral qualities, rather than social categories, let us look at another example from Bailey's research. As we noted, in some contexts the adolescents in his study used AAE to align themselves with African Americans and disalign themselves from Whites. In other contexts they used Spanish to differentiate themselves from African Americans and perform Dominican (or 'Spanish') identities. However, Spanish wasn't only or always an index of Dominican identity or **Latinidad**; the amount of Spanish adolescents used, and the ways they used it, served as an index either of Dominican American identity or of being a more recent arrival. This is apparent in a conversation between Isabella and Janelle about Sammy, a recent Dominican immigrant whom Isabella has been dating for about 10 days.

I: He's like – I don't know. He's- he's so jealous.
J: Oh
I: This kid is sickening! He- he tells me to call him before I go to the club. He- I'm like, I don't have time to call you, pick up the phone, call you while my friends are outside beeping the horn at me so I can jet with them to the club. And he's like- I don't know, he talks he's like a hick, he talks so much Spanish!

(Adapted from Bailey, 2000a: 210)

Isabella goes on to quote Sammy's using Spanish-language terms of affection (*'niña'* and *'loca'*) and reports her efforts to get him to speak to her in English. In this context, Bailey explains, Isabella and Janelle see the (over)use of Spanish and the use of Spanish terms of endearment as indexical of male possessiveness and jealousy, which they associate with heterosexual men from the Dominican Republic.

DuBord's (2017) research with Latin American day laborers in the US–Mexico border region also shows that the languages can index particular social attributes and moral qualities as well as categories. In this setting, bilingual laborers often translate for monolingual English-speaking employers and Spanish-speaking laborers. Monolingual Spanish-speakers imagined that the ability to use two languages was socio-economically advantageous (an opinion not shared by those who were actually bilingual and felt that they were economically exploited). But even though the monolingual Spanish-speakers associated English with opportunity, they also associated it with dishonesty. In fact, they often saw their bilingual peers as 'tricksters' who sought to take advantage of them. In addition to an example of how languages can be associated with moral attributes, DuBord's research is also a reminder that contradictory ideologies sometimes co-exist (see Chapter 4).

Indexicality is not just about the use of one language or another, such as English or Spanish; language varieties, styles and specific features of language can also index stances, specific attributes and identity categories. Negrón's (2014, 2018) research in New York City is informative in this regard. Negrón found that, although in some cases Latinxs of different national origins used Spanish to express a shared pan-ethnic Latinx identity, they also used national and regional varieties of Spanish to position themselves within 'a hierarchy of status and privilege' (Negrón, 2018: 187) by aligning or distancing themselves from different national origin groups. The intra-Latinx hierarchy and social perceptions of different national origin groups were linked to socio-economic status, labor sectors, immigration status and racial identity. In particular, Negrón explains that Mexican and Ecuadorian participants in her study were aware of anti-Indigenous prejudice from other Latinxs and thus, in some business-related interactions, they sought to associate themselves with other Latinx groups. For example, some Mexican participants either overtly claimed to be Puerto Rican or let others believe that they were. One Ecuadorian man reported purposefully changing his accent in order to be perceived as Colombian. By using a specific regional variety of Spanish, he constructed an identity that in New York City is associated with higher socio-economic status and Whiteness.

The ability of language styles to index a constellation of social identities and characteristics is evident in the research that Holguín Mendoza (2018b) conducted in Mexico, close to the border with the US. *Fresas* (literally 'strawberries'), a well-known Mexican social category and stereotype, are typically White, upper-class, consumer-oriented young women (although men can also sometimes be considered *fresas*). *Fresa* speech is characterized by the use of particular lexical items (e.g. *güey* 'dude') and discourse markers (e.g. *o sea* 'I mean'), profanity, and expressions in English. The association of this style with *fresa* identity is widely recognized and has been reproduced in the Mexican media since the 1980s. *Fresa* style is not simply indexical of social class, but also specific racial categories, cultural orientations, social attributes and stances; use of the style marks the speaker as affluent, cosmopolitan and geographically mobile. In Mexico, because having the opportunity to study English and/or travel is associated with having financial means, *fresa* style (and the use of English expressions) is also an index of upper middle-class status, which links the speaker to Whiteness. The numerous parodies of *fresas* and the way they speak also rely on indexicality. However, rather than worldliness and upper-class status, these parodies use *fresa* style to convey vapid consumerism. Because *fresas* are stereotypically female, these portrayals are gendered and they both rely on and reinforce specific understandings of female identity. But in either case, whether being used by the *fresas* themselves or to parody them, the linguistic style doesn't simply point to the group identity; instead it references (positive or negative) qualities associated with that group.

Multilingual Practices and Identity

Research on multilingualism has long focused on how speakers combine two (or more) languages in conversation. As early as the 1970s, researchers looked at grammatical patterns of Spanish and English bilingual discourse (e.g. Pfaff, 1979; Poplack, 1980), which will be discussed in Chapter 10; here we focus on **codeswitching** and **translanguaging** as resources for identity. Multilinguals' **linguistic repertoires** consist of resources distributed across what are traditionally considered different languages, for instance Spanish or English. These include registers, styles and a range of regional and social varieties. All of these ways of speaking carry social meanings. In other words, speakers do not simply choose Spanish or English but instead use features and elements of both in the performance of their identities. So too, despite some people's negative views of codeswitching and translanguaging, combining resources drawn from across languages is another resource for constructing and performing identities.

In the US, some Spanish-speakers' repertoires include 'non-standard' varieties associated with contact between English and Spanish. The connection of multilingual practices and contact varieties to identity is powerfully expressed by Chicana activist and scholar Gloria Anzaldúa in her well-known essay, 'How to tame a wild tongue':

> So if you really want to hurt me, talk badly about my language. Ethnic identity is twin skin to linguistic identity. I am my language. Until I can take pride in my language, I cannot take pride in myself. Until I can accept as legitimate Chicano Texas Spanish, Tex-Mex, and all the other languages I speak, I cannot accept the legitimacy of myself. Until I am free to write bilingually and to switch codes without having always to

> translate, while I still have to speak English or Spanish when I would rather speak Spanglish, and as long as I have to accommodate the English speakers rather than them accommodating me, my tongue will be illegitimate. (Anzaldúa, 1987: 81)

In addition to referencing the ideology linking language to ethnic identity, this excerpt makes clear that one's identities and sense of self-worth are also influenced by perceptions of one's language varieties and practices. So too, it highlights the power of hegemonic ideologies to be taken up by those hurt by them, but also the possibility of resisting those ideologies. In this quote and elsewhere, Anzaldúa points out that speakers of **Spanglish** are subjected to the denigrations of both English-language and Spanish-language purists (we discuss the term *Spanglish*, as well as attitudes toward Spanglish, in Chapter 10). Still, she underscores the privileged position of English, and English-speakers, who demand accommodation from speakers of other languages.

Work by Parra (2016) on heritage language classrooms underscores the value of multilingual practices in Latinx repertoires. Many of the Latinxs in her study were raised in families and communities in which there was a focus on and pride in ethnic heritage and Spanish maintenance. Of course, this does not mean that they rejected English; on the contrary, many were dominant in English. It should be unsurprising, then, to learn that for these students, English, Spanish and multilingual discourse were all resources for the performance of identity. While Spanish functioned as an index of community culture and belonging, and English as an index of alignment with the wider society, the combination of English and Spanish was used in the construction of dual or hybrid identities. The melding of two languages in the performance of identities has sometimes been analyzed as the construction of a 'third space' (Bhaba, 1990) in which both codes and cultures, and a mixture of the two, are valued. The connection of translanguaging to Latinx identities in the US is reflected in the comment from a participant in Zentella's ethnography of Puerto Ricans in New York: 'Sometimes I'm talking a long time in English and then I remember I'm Puerto Rican, lemme say something in Spanglish' (Zentella, 1997a: 114).

In Chapter 4, our discussion of indexicality stressed that Spanish does not have a single fixed or constant social meaning; instead, social meanings, like social identities, are locally constructed. Along these lines, Showstack (2018) shows that in some contexts in the US speaking contact varieties of Spanish is used to construct a localized identity which sets speakers apart from recent immigrants, but it may have different meanings in different contexts. She illustrates this with a vignette about a college student from Houston who speaks a local variety of Spanish with her parents and in the community. In this context, the local variety of Spanish indexes her membership in this Mexican American community. In contrast, when she visits extended family in Mexico, she is told she speaks like an American, and in an encounter with a girl from Spain she was told she spoke 'broken Spanish' (Showstack, 2018: 92), highlighting that the symbolic meaning of linguistic features and varieties are contextually dependent.

Cashman (2005) illustrates how codeswitching can be used to enact various social and micro-level identities. Like the 'lemme say something in Spanglish' example above, it is the shifts from one language to another, as opposed to language choice per se, that serves as the linguistic resource for constructing identities. For example, switching to English is sometimes a way of showing opposition to, or disalignment with, something said in Spanish, but not necessarily distancing the speaker from Spanish, or Latinx, identity. Fuller (2010) shows how the mixing of English and Spanish takes on gendered connotations among four children in a bilingual classroom based on their individual preferences and practices, with more use of English being part of two girls' best friend identities. These examples illustrate that the social meaning of language choices is often very specific to the context and community. In the subsequent section, we will continue to discuss the many nuanced social meanings of multilingual practices.

Multiple and Intersectional Identities

As we have made clear throughout this chapter, not only are there various levels of identity, but people can have multiple identities that they perform in different contexts, often through language. Moreover, people's identities can include not just many different layers, but also hybrid or even seemingly conflicting or mutually exclusive categories that vary situationally. For example, an individual might perform a masculine identity in one context and a feminine one in another, or a child identity in one situation and a parent identity in another. Perspectives from Queer Theory (e.g. Motschenbacher & Stegu, 2013) are relevant here. This theoretical approach not only addresses sexual identities, it also challenges the idea of rigidly constructed boundaries of social groups more broadly, as well as the assumed homogeneity of group members.

Another example of multiplicity involves national identities. When we label or think of people based only on their national identities, this hides the heterogeneity of people within a nation: in some cases, they may not identify with their national identity at all but rather with a regional or local identity; it is often only when one is outside of one's home country that national identification becomes important (Rodríguez, 2003). Thus, ideas about what it means to be Mexican, for example, may be different for Latinxs in the US than for people in Mexico, as well as being different for people in different communities within either nation. And as we have repeatedly noted, the meaning of *Mexican* is complicated, as it can be both an ethnoracial identity and a nationality identity.

National and other identities are often seen as mutually exclusive; that is, the question 'Are you Mexican or American?' assumes that you can be one or the other but not both, but in fact it is possible to be both. To be clear, we are not referring to the possibility of having dual citizenship, but rather to one's subjective sense of self, together with how one is seen by others. Because identity is socially constructed and contextual, someone can be Mexican *and* American, or Mexican American, or different things in different contexts. In some cases, claiming both a Mexican and an American identity is a means of pushing back against racist constructions of Americanness as rooted in (Anglo) Whiteness, as in the example of the newscaster Vanessa Ruiz, discussed earlier in this chapter.

The multiplicity of identities is apparent in García and Gaddes's (2012) discussion of the transnational identities of young Latinx writers in a writing program they developed. They describe these identities as additive; participants did not replace their ties to their countries of origin when they gained new cultural practices in the US, but added to them. Further, they used English and Spanish to express different experiences linked to these different contexts, as well as the sense of hybridity that comes with being what is sometimes referred to as a *hyphenated American* (e.g. Mexican-American, Cuban-American). The writing program they were involved in is described as a learning space where they are encouraged to 'explore the nature of that "hyphen"' (García & Gaddes, 2012: 159) (we discuss other educational programs designed to promote students' analysis of language and identity in Chapter 10).

It's not just that we have more than one identity and that different aspects of our identity are relevant in different contexts. Instead, our multiple identities interact with and impact each other. The importance of attending to these interactions is reflected in the term **intersectionality**, an analytic approach usually credited to Crenshaw (1989). Crenshaw argued that it is impossible to understand the experience of being a Black woman by considering the experience of being Black and the experience of being a woman separately. Thus, we cannot understand the discrimination faced by Black women if we look only at racism or sexism. Instead, it is crucial to look at the way different identities, and different forms of discrimination, intersect and interact. Similarly, we cannot discuss one aspect of identity (e.g. race) without also addressing other aspects (e.g. gender). In the case of Latinxs and Spanish-speakers in the US, it's crucial to take into account how class, race, national origin, immigration status and gender identities, for example, intersect with ethnolinguistic identities.

Immigration status

Another relevant identity category is immigration and/or citizenship status, as is apparent in De Fina's (2018) analysis of 15 narratives by Dreamers. *Dreamers* are people who were brought as children to the US but who do not have authorization to live and work in the US (because they either entered without authorization or overstayed their visas). They are called *Dreamers* as a reference to the DREAM (Development, Relief, and Education for Alien Minors) Act, which was introduced in 2001 to allow these US residents a path to citizenship, but which has failed to pass (see http://unitedwedream.org for current information). The name of the proposed law, and the identity category, references the idea of the American Dream, and it was purposefully chosen to frame these individuals as part of a longstanding American tradition. In so doing, it indexes qualities associated with a 'good immigrant' identity, such as being hardworking and upwardly mobile. In the narratives analyzed by De Fina, the speakers positioned themselves with regard to their national and ethnic backgrounds, but also in many other ways. One salient finding is that through the stories of their challenges and achievements, Dreamers constructed themselves as desirable citizens and also as social activists. This emphasis on Dreamers' work ethic, educational achievement and professional success is also apparent in mobilizations to provide permanent residency or a path to citizenship, which may have the unintended consequence of constructing other unauthorized immigrants, such as those who are less educated, as less 'deserving.'

Mangual Figueroa (2012) examined the treatment of differences in immigration status and citizenship in her research with a mixed-status Mexican family. The parents' descriptors of their children included such things as *'el que nació en México'* ('the one born in Mexico') or, for the children who were born in the US, *'los americanos'* ('the Americans'). This distinction determined some important aspects of the lives of the children and was part of their everyday constructions of identity within the family, thus underscoring the impact of institutions and governments on identities, even within the family.

In her research in Arizona, Ullman (2015) showed how unauthorized Mexican migrants strategically used language and other symbolic resources to avoid being apprehended by the Border Patrol. Specifically, one male participant used colloquial English ('s'up') and affected an appearance that he felt identified him as a *'cholo'* ('Chicanx gang-affiliated man') – shaved head, Dodgers baseball cap, sunglasses, oversized Chicago Bulls t-shirt, long shorts and high-top sneakers. While this was not his preferred manner of dress, he used it to index someone born in the US. In contrast, a female participant in the study strategically hid her English proficiency in order to conceal the fact that she lived in the US. Instead, she affected what she described as a 'Mexican' appearance, including not just Mexican-bought clothing, but also shampoo and other grooming products from Mexico, in order to perform a *'super Mexicana'* identity and give the impression that she had just crossed the border to go shopping, like many middle- and upper-class Mexicans do. Strikingly, when deployed in combination with other symbolic resources (such as clothing), both Spanish and English could serve as a way to perform authorization to be in the US. These examples show that national identity performances can be very gender specific; the *'cholo'* and *'super Mexicana'* identities might have female and male counterparts, respectively, but in Ullman's research they were intertwined with ideas about how men and women of these national/ethnic backgrounds behave. In the next section, we will look at more research on gender identities relevant to speaking Spanish in the US.

Gender

Other research has examined how gender identities – that is, socially constructed aspects of identity linked to ideas about the categories of male/female/non-binary and masculinity/femininity – are intertwined with Latinx identities. In Meador's (2005) study of a high school in the rural Southwest, 'good student' identities were linked to English proficiency and participation in competitive sports. Because Mexican immigrant girls were assumed not to be jocks or fluent English-speakers, they were precluded from being seen as 'good students,' limiting the identities available to them. Cuero (2009) discusses a similar situation with a Latinx boy who was positioned as not being a 'good student' because his behavior did not conform to school expectations, although his grades and test scores were equivalent to those of other students who were. Here, we also see that the identity of 'good student' relies on a constellation of characteristics, beyond doing well on school assignments. On the other hand, Cammarota (2004) also shows how academic achievement can be used by girls to resist gender discrimination; when they did well in school and went on to college, they became exposed to gender politics which empowered them.

Thus far, we have made several references to the use of **African American English** (AAE) by Latinx adolescents. Such usage is sometimes gendered, such as in Dunstan's (2010) research with Latinx and African American students in two North Carolina high schools, one in the city of Durham and the other in a rural community. She found that the Latinx participants in the more urban environment used AAE features at higher rates, in some cases even more than their African American peers. Gender and gang affiliation were also shown to be significant factors, suggesting that in this context AAE features were a linguistic resource used to perform not only ethnoracial identities but also masculine urban gang member identities. This analysis is consistent with Bucholtz's (1999) research, in which a White adolescent used AAE in order to portray himself as tough, a portrayal that both reflected and simultaneously reproduced racist notions regarding Black masculinity. These findings are echoed in a study by Carter (2013), also in North Carolina, who found that male Latinx students used core features of AAE far more than female students (and the girls in his study used more Spanish than English), and in his analysis of one Latinx gang-affiliated youth's frequent use of AAE features to index a particular type of masculine toughness. In addition, Carter suggests that the youth's use of AAE challenged the Black–White racial dichotomy; by using AAE differently from his African American peers he constructed a Latinx identity distinct from both Anglos and African Americans. Below, we will focus on how such racializations intersect with social class identities.

Sexuality

Although sexuality is often intertwined with gender, sexual identities have to do with social categories linked to sexual practices. Thus, for instance, a performance of a masculine persona (gender identity) simultaneously might be the performance of a homosexual persona (sexuality). Sexual identities also intersect with other aspects of identity. Woolley (2016) looks at discourses of ethnicity and sexuality in a northern Californian urban high school, using the concept of 'enoughness': what behavior is necessary to be considered sufficiently gay, or Latinx? In addition to discussions about who is or is not gay, and what criteria are used to determine this (i.e. gradations of being 'out'), the research participants also categorized their classmates in terms of performances of ethnicity. If you recall the example given above, one classmate was said not to 'count' as Latinx or Asian because she hung out with White kids. In other conversations, similar remarks were made about the uncertainty of the sexuality of a classmate, indicating that both ethnicity and sexuality are socially constructed and thus individuals must construct authentic identities in order to belong in ethnic or sexuality groups. Further, this research underscores that just because ethnic identities are salient in a given context, there are also other categories that have social meaning.

Cashman (2017) addresses how queer Latinxs use language to construct intersectional ethnic and sexual identities, challenging the idea that these operate independently. The participants in her research had a wide range of ideas about the importance of speaking Spanish; while some asserted that Spanish proficiency was not essential for Latinx identity, the link between language and identity was clearly part of the discourse of Latinidad for many. One interesting aspect of Cashman's research is the application of the concept of 'coming out' to both sexuality and language proficiency. That is, participants in her research often told stories about how they exposed or acknowledged their inability to speak Spanish which paralleled narratives about revealing their sexuality to family or friends. In both cases, there was an aspect of their identity that they felt was hidden because straight and/or Spanish-speaking identities were assumed and assigned to them by default. Thus, to be true to their own sense of their identities, they had to correct these false assumptions and run the risk of a homophobic reaction or of being judged not authentically Latinx.

In examining the intersections of queer, Latinx and bilingual identities and how these intersections played out in their everyday interactions, Cashman reports that many of her research participants encountered racism and **xenophobia** in queer communities, as well as homophobia and heterosexism in their Latinx communities. Thus, their sense of themselves as both queer and Latinx was often mitigated by roadblocks to acceptance. This intersectional discrimination is one focus of Jotería Studies, which addresses the concerns of queer people of Chicanx/Mexicanx/Latinx background. The word *jotería* derives from originally derogatory Mexican terms for people who do not fit binary, heteronormative sexuality categories. Among some Latinxs and Latin Americans, the words *joto* and *jota* have been reclaimed and are now used as terms of proud self-identification, much like the term *queer* (see Cashman, 2017, for discussion; see http://dreamersadrift.com/newest-vid/behind-the-image-quiero-que-me-llames-joto-with-yosimar-reyes for a poem and video in Spanish on the topic). Within Jotería Studies, there is an emphasis on both recognizing intersectionality and abandoning traditional hierarchies of identity categories (e.g. heterosexist structures which privilege straight lifestyles) (Bañales, 2014; Hames-Garcia, 2011). The overlaps between Queer Theory, Jotería Studies and the broader social constructionist approaches to identity are also exemplified in Carrillo and Fontdevila's (2014) research on gay Mexican immigrant men. Carrillo and Fontedevila emphasize the multiple understandings of sexual practices and the categories of 'gay' and 'homosexual' on both side of the Mexico–US border, arguing against monolithic understandings of national, gender, and sexual identities and demonstrating how these identities intersect.

Focusing more specifically on language in the discussion of the fluidity of identity categories, Rodríguez (2003) discusses how the **grammatical gender** marking in Spanish lends itself to queering language and, with it, traditional understandings of gender and sexuality. For example, she notes the use of *vestida* ('dressed') with the meaning 'in drag,' as well as the use of *buchota*, a borrowing of the English word *butch* (Rodríguez, 2003: 26). As we move on to discuss social class and race in the next section, we maintain this perspective of questioning monolithic social categorization.

Social class

Another aspect of identity that is often linked to ways of speaking is social class. Many studies in sociolinguistics include the variable of social class and examine how it is linked to linguistic features, but in keeping with what we said in the last section, and with the broader social constructionist approach, it is important to ask just what this category entails. What does it mean, for example, to be 'middle class'? Although one can use definitions based on factors such as income and education, we support a constructionist perspective; social class identities, like all other aspects of identity, are not limited to objective characteristics. Further, they are something we do and not something we have. One way that people enact middle- or upper-class identities is through the use of normative language practices. Fuller (2012) looks at children in German–English and Spanish–English bilingual education in Germany and the US, respectively, and shows how participants in elite bilingual education in Germany used less bilingual discourse than the Spanish-speakers in the US who were immigrant bilinguals. She argues that the middle-class German–English bilinguals have much to lose by not speaking the monoglot standard, and bilingual discourse is relatively infrequent and often marked with laughter, correction or commentary. The Spanish–English bilinguals in this study were all children of agricultural migrant workers and, in terms of rungs on the social hierarchy, they had little to lose as they were already low status in their communities. Although in the global context Spanish is an important language, in the rural US context of this study it was not valued beyond the ethnic community, and often framed as a disadvantage in schooling. Many of the children, unlike their elite bilingual counterparts in Germany, mixed languages freely in their ingroup interactions, using far more mixed utterances than the children in the German–English bilingual context, and without marking it as unusual speech. Some of these speakers did of course also conform to ideals of monolingual language production, but in general they appeared far less susceptible to the ideological pressure to maintain separate codes in conversation, perhaps because of their already racialized status. Thus, social class, intertwined with other aspects of their identities, played a role in the language patterns found in these bilingual classrooms. This study points to the impact of language ideologies, and of racialization, on multilingual practices.

Mock Spanish

In this section we examine Mock Spanish, another type of racializing discourse. Although somewhat difficult to define, Mock Spanish involves saying things that sound like Spanish but with no real attempt to actually speak Spanish. Hill's original examples include signs (e.g. '¡Adios, Cucaracha!' on an ad for a bug exterminator company), greeting cards ('Fleas Navidad' as the text in a Christmas card), and popular expressions such as 'no problemo' or 'hasta la vista, baby' (Hill, 1995, 2005). Mock Spanish is used by people who don't normally speak Spanish in order to portray Spanish-speakers (and people associated with Spanish) negatively while simultaneously positioning themselves positively.

Hill's analysis of Mock Spanish relies on two levels of indexicality, one for the speaker (*direct indexicality*) and another for Spanish-speakers or Latinxs (*indirect indexicality*). The direct indexicality of Mock Spanish allows the speaker/author to take a jovial stance, while the indirect indexicality relies on (and reinforces) negative ideas about Spanish-speakers. As Hill (2005: 113) writes: 'Mock Spanish keys an easygoing, humorous, yet cosmopolitan persona and positioning. Mock Spanish also reproduces racist stereotypes of Spanish speakers.' For instance, Hill (2005) discusses how the supposedly playful use of the word *mañana* to mean 'never' reinforces the stereotype of Latinxs (and particularly Mexicans) as lazy, putting off until tomorrow what they should do today. Similarly, the use of *comprende?* builds on the stereotype of Spanish-speakers being unable to understand English. Because Mock Spanish does not overtly express these racist stereotypes, but rather indexes them indirectly, Hill calls Mock Spanish a 'covert racist discourse.'

Hill (1995) outlines four strategies used in Mock Spanish. The first is semantic degradation, in which a neutral word in Spanish is given a negative connotation. Examples include the exterminator's advertisement cited above (i.e. '¡Adios, Cucaracha!'), as well as a farewell greeting card that on the outside says '*adiós*' and on the inside, 'That's Spanish for, sure, go ahead and leave your friends, the only people who really care about you, the ones who would loan you their last thin dime, give you the shirts of their backs, sure, just take off!' These usages of *adiós* are not neutral, but instead express negative aspects of goodbyes – getting rid of (and killing) cockroaches and abandoning friends. The use of Spanish to index negative meanings was crystal clear in then-candidate Donald Trump's use of 'bad hombres' when describing immigrants as drug-dealers; rather than a neutral word for 'men,' the Spanish word *hombres* indexes racist stereotypes of criminality and violence (Schwartz, 2016).

The second Mock Spanish strategy is euphemism, in which Spanish is used for taboo or potentially offensive expressions, for example *caca de toro* (literally, poopoo of bull, 'bullshit') on a coffee mug. Affixation of Spanish grammatical elements to English words is the third strategy. This most commonly consists of affixing a final *-o* to English words, as in *no problemo, el cheapo* or *indeed-o.* Such usages again directly index a fun-loving and playful nature for the (Anglo) speaker, but indirectly index denigration of Spanish and/or Spanish-speakers by implying that Spanish is not a fully-fledged or 'real' language. As Lippi-Green (2012) argues, trivialization is part of the process of language subordination.

Finally, the fourth strategy consists of using an exaggerated 'American' accent, which Hill calls 'hyperanglicization and bold mispronunciation' in order to indicate that this is not simply a case of struggling to pronounce Spanish correctly. Hill (1995) provides several examples from greeting cards: a thank-you card on which *gracias* is jokingly rendered as 'grassy ass' and accompanied by a drawing of buttocks covered in grass, and a Christmas card that wishes the recipient 'Fleas Navidad', which draws on the phonological similarity between Spanish *feliz* ('happy') and English *fleas.* In addition to referencing hyperanglicized pronunciation, these puns use words with silly or negative connotations, permitting the speaker (card purchaser) to perform a jovial persona who appreciates a good play on words, but they simultaneously denigrate Spanish.

Many users of Mock Spanish insist that they are just being playful and are not trying to make fun of Spanish or Spanish-speakers. Nonetheless, regardless of their intentions, Mock Spanish reproduces negative ideologies surrounding Spanish and Spanish-speakers. Further, many Spanish-speakers and Latinxs perceive it as trivializing or ridiculing them. In her research on the interpretation of Mock Spanish, Callahan (2010) found that the overwhelming majority of the 147 mostly non-Latinx participants understood examples of Mock Spanish as 'making fun.' Not all the participants found all the examples offensive, but they definitely saw the 'fun' of Mock Spanish as coming at someone's expense. Further, they viewed Anglos' use of Mock Spanish with Latinx **interlocutors** as less acceptable, and also considered Mock Spanish potentially less offensive when used by Latinx speakers than Anglos. The different levels of acceptability according to speaker and interlocutor confirm that the use of Mock Spanish is not neutral. Relatedly, Potowski (2011) interviewed 30 bilingual Latinxs about their reactions to 17 greeting cards combining English and Spanish. She found that participants more favorably evaluated the cards that combined English and Spanish in ways that sounded more 'authentic,' or like ways that bilinguals might actually use the languages together. In contrast, some participants felt the 'inauthentic' combinations sounded like people making fun of Spanish and Spanish-speakers while showing off that they knew a few words of Spanish, thus lending empirical support to Hill's analysis.

Not all uses of Spanish by Anglos (and other non-Latinxs) should be considered Mock Spanish. Further, speaking Spanish can be an act of solidarity. For this reason, we want to stress that Mock Spanish is not an attempt to speak 'real' Spanish or to align oneself with Spanish-speakers. Instead, Mock Spanish is self-consciously fake and, as Hill (1995) explains, it 'expresses iconically the extreme social distance of the speaker, and of Mock Spanish itself, from actual Spanish and any possible negative contamination that a speaker might acquire by being erroneously heard as a real speaker of Spanish.' Thus, Mock Spanish can be used as an index of Anglo identity (Barrett, 2006). Further, it not only devalues Spanish, but also constructs Whiteness as normative (Hill, 1995, 2005, 2008). Building on this work, Schwartz (2011) argues that Mock Spanish plays the same role as negative cultural stereotypes in Othering Spanish and Latinxs and reproducing Anglo dominance – a larger cultural practice he refers to as 'gringoism.'

Hill (1998, 2008) and others have also contrasted the functions and indexical meanings of Anglos' use of Mock Spanish with Latinxs' uses of Spanish. When used by members of the White anglophone majority, Mock Spanish and the mixing of English and Spanish index 'multicultural "with-it-ness"' (Zentella, 2003: 53). In contrast, when spoken by Latinxs, Spanish is racialized and considered out of place, while Spanish–English mixing is seen as a deficiency in need of correction and control (Hill, 1995, 1998, 2008; Zentella, 2003). Even when it does not involve racist intent, the **appropriation** of Spanish by White English-speakers who benefit (by appearing playful, funny, streetwise and/or hip) without incurring any of the discrimination or negative consequences faced by Spanish-speakers can play a role in the reproduction of social hierarchies and racial inequality.

Barrett (2006) further demonstrates that Mock Spanish is not neutral in the study he conducted in a Mexican restaurant in Arizona (mentioned above). There was a clear divide between the Latinx Spanish-speaking kitchen staff and the White anglophone servers and managers, and this divide was intensified through the use of Mock Spanish by some of the Anglo employees. Many of his examples show not just the lack of an attempt to really speak Spanish, but also a belittling attitude about the Spanish language (e.g. the use of 'ice-o' for 'ice'). Further, Anglos' use of Mock Spanish often impeded communication; in many cases, speaking English slowly and clearly might have cleared up any misunderstanding, whereas Mock Spanish increased confusion. Inevitably the Spanish speakers were blamed for the miscommunication, and they were often portrayed as unwilling as well as unable to understand. In this case, the burden of comprehension was placed completely on the hearer, even when the speaker produced purposely incomprehensible input.

Examples of Mock Spanish can be found in a children's book called *Skippyjon Jones* (Schachner, 2003). Although there are some real Spanish sentences in the text (e.g. '*Yo quiero frijoles*' 'I love beans', '*Buenas noches*' 'Good night', '*mis amigos*' 'my friends'), most of what appears is definitively Mock Spanish: Skippyjon calls himself 'El Skippito' and makes exclamations likes 'holy guacamole' and 'holy jalapeño,' and the text features rhymes created by adding *-o* or *-ito* to the ends of English words in time-tested Mock Spanish style: 'indeed-o, eato, birdito, snap-ito.' This negative trivialized depiction of Spanish and Spanish-speakers (Martínez-Roldán, 2013) is accompanied by a barrage of stereotypes and clichés: fiestas, siestas, castanets, burritos, banditos and piñatas. There are also a couple of examples of Spanish-accented English represented through the use of 'ee' in English words such as *is* and *big*, e.g. 'My ears are too beeg for my head' or 'It ees I, El Skippito Friskito' (Schachner, 2003). This is hardcore Mock Spanish, with all of the negative social meanings discussed by Hill, Barrett and Zentella, but it is being presented to small children as something that is playful. Despite the author's dedication of 'special thanks' and 'much love' to the '*muchachas hispanas*' ('Hispanic girls') who helped her learn Spanish, the book participates fully in the trivialization and racialization of Spanish.

Mock Spanish versus Spanglish

While we have not yet spent much time discussing Spanglish (see Chapter 10), we want to stress that Mock Spanish and Spanglish are different phenomena and should not be conflated. As we have just seen, Mock Spanish is a kind of 'fake' Spanish that Anglos use to distance themselves from Spanish-speakers. In contrast, Spanglish refers to the linguistic features and practices of Spanish–English bilinguals who may use them, as well as the term itself, in the construction and performance of ingroup identities. While there may be some linguistic overlap between Mock Spanish and Spanglish (i.e. the use of actual Spanish words and/or the linguistic integration of English words into Spanish), the faux Hispanification of English words is clearly Mock Spanish. Examples such as 'indeed-o' or 'ice-o' are not Spanglish, nor are the phrases which make jokes based on the pronunciation of Spanish words, such as 'Fleas Navidad' as discussed in Hill (1995), or 'holy frijoles' uttered by Skippyjon (Schachner, 2003). These examples are clearly not attempts to speak Spanish.

The mocking of Spanish accents

As we saw above, Skippyjon Jones also has examples of the mocking of Spanish-accented English, which is a related but different phenomenon from Mock Spanish. Márquez (2018) analyzes the mocking of accents in the context of a highway stop with restaurants and shops called South of the Border. This highway stop and tourist attraction lies just over the border between South and North Carolina, but the border referenced is the US–Mexico border and the theme is what might be called Mock Mexican. A key aspect of this theme is the construction of the character Pedro, who is voiced in a column in the local newspaper, such as in the following:

> Thees South of the Border, she grow an' grow & grow. ... So beeg pedro hisself have hard time keep opp weeth everytheeng goin' on. ... (Márquez, 2018: 12)

In addition to language, the stereotypical Mexican theme is also indexed by a huge statue of a man with a moustache in a sombrero (apparently Pedro himself), as well as smaller statues of men in serapes, also with moustaches and sombreros, and staff who also dress in this manner and feign Spanish accents in English. However, the form of 'playing Mexican,' as Márquez calls it, is also given a Southern flavor, with advertising including such gems as 'Pedro got all kinds of year 'roun' sports. ... Y'all come!' and the 'SPESHUL THEES WEEK: CONFEDERATE FRIED CHICKEN complete with all the trimmin's and REBEL FLAG' (Márquez, 2018: 16–17). Linguistically, this is a blend of stereotypes of a Spanish accent and stereotypes of Southern speech, allowing Pedro to maintain his Otherness while also being comfortably local; as a marketing ploy, this works well to attract both Northerners fascinated by the South and Southerners anxious about maintaining their Southern identity, which is constructed via the Confederacy. As a representation of Latinx identity, South of the Border contributes to the racialization of Spanish-speakers and discrimination against their supposed ways of speaking.

More mocking

Linguistic practices that involve mocking certain ways of speaking, as noted above, extend beyond Mock Spanish to other varieties associated with non-dominant groups, such as Mock AAE (Ronkin & Karn, 1999; Smokoski, 2016), Mock Asian (Chun, 2004, 2009, 2016; Reyes, 2016), Mock non-Standard Englishes (Fuller, 2009; Márquez, 2018) and Mock White Girl (Slobe, 2018). There is also sometimes mocking of dominant groups' language. For example, Carris (2011) discusses *'la voz gringa'* ('Gringa voice'), which involves mocking Anglo pronunciation of Spanish words. Given that Anglos are dominant and English normative, mocking Anglicized pronunciation doesn't have the same power to reproduce inequality as Mock Spanish does. Instead, such performances suggest resistance to the hegemonic sociolinguistic hierarchy concerning Spanish and English. However, we should not ignore the fact that *la voz gringa* involves gendered features of language and in this way continues the theme of mocking non-dominant groups, in this case women and girls. In the data discussed by Carris, the stereotypical pronunciation and lexicon used to mock an Anglo speaking Spanish are the same features Slobe (2018) reports in Mock White Girl, i.e. intonation and pitch reminiscent of Valley Girl speech. Thus, while challenging one sort of hegemony, the male Latinxs in Carris's study simultaneously reproduced gender hierarchies and hegemonic masculinity.

Rosa (2016c) discusses what he calls 'inverted Spanglish,' essentially a mocking of Mock Spanish by Latinxs. While using many of the same features as Mock Spanish, inverted Spanglish serves to show that the speaker is proficient in both English and Spanish, but it is also a parody of non-Spanish speakers and/or Mock Spanish speakers. Thus, such usages can be an important index of Latinx ingroup identity and bilingualism, while also indexing the speakers' critical stance toward assimilationist attitudes and the racialization of Latinxs.

Conclusions and Connections

Identity construction, and performances as enacted through language is an integral part of many other topics discussed in this book. We have noted that many different ways of speaking are used in the service of the construction of various aspects of identity. However, it is important to note that the relationships between linguistic form and social meaning used to construct the identities of individuals are rooted in language ideologies circulating in the wider society (as discussed in Chapter 4), and this in turn plays a role in patterns of maintenance and shift (see Chapter 2). Further, we have noted that speakers construct more than their own identities – they also construct social categories, such as Latinx or Gringa, through language use and specific references to the characteristics of group members as well as talk about who belongs and who does not. As we've seen, this is intertwined with the construction of race and ethnicity we presented in the last chapter.

Ideas about identity construction will continue to be of importance in the next chapters. In our discussion of Spanish in the media (Chapter 7), we will see that media representations play a salient role in the reproduction of identity categories and their social meaning. We will also see connections between social identities and language policy, which will be discussed further in Chapter 8; regulations about who has the right to speak what language and in what context are dependent on linkages between different kinds of speakers and specific forms of talk. Positioning English as the only legitimate language necessarily positions Spanish as the language of the disenfranchised, and this relationship is iterative. These societal ideologies surrounding Spanish, as we have seen, can play a role in individual language use. In Chapter 9 on Spanish and Spanish-speakers in education, we see that the identities of students, including how they are constructed by the students themselves and by educators and institutional structures, have an important impact in schooling. Finally, in Chapter 10 our discussion of the structural aspects of speaking Spanish in the US reiterates the fact that particular ways of using language are acts of identity.

Discussion Questions and Activities for Chapter 6

(1) What cultural behaviors aside from language are part of the construction of ethnic identities? Think about clothing and other ways of adorning the body, hair (on the head, face and body), ways of walking, sitting, standing or gesturing, and interests or activities. In what ways are there intersectional identities constructed through these cultural behaviors, such as ethnicity and gender?

(2) Throughout this chapter we have repeatedly stressed that the indexical and symbolic meanings of language and language varieties are content-dependent. How do the symbolic meanings and identity functions of AAE differ in: (a) Bailey's research; and (b) Carter's (2013) and Dunstan's (2010) research? What are some of the different indexical meanings of speaking Spanish? What factors contribute to the different meanings?

(3) Watch the video, *If Latinos said the stuff White people say* (https://www.buzzfeed.com/abefg/if-latinos-said-the-stuff-white-people-say). This video 'flips the script' in an attempt to humorously expose the assumptions underlying the things White people say to Latinxs. But are these situations really equivalent? In what ways do they differ? (Think about power differentials as well as differences in what dominant and non-dominant groups know about each other and why.) In any case, what ideas about the categories of Latinx and White are represented in the 'stuff people say' and how are they challenged in this video?

(4) What linguistic and interactional factors influence whether utterances that include actual Spanish (such as *¿qué pasa?* or *amigo*) should be considered Mock Spanish or simply Spanish? What identities do these usages construct for the speaker, and what language ideologies and social categories are reproduced (or challenged) by their use? In what contexts does the use of Spanish by non-Latinxs convey symbolic meanings other than mocking?

(5) Read the following essay by a Puerto Rican origin man who travels to Argentina on a Fulbright scholarship to teach English. Discuss the different claims to Latinx authenticity the author mentions, as well as what others expect of him and why. See https://www.washingtonpost.com/news/post-nation/wp/2017/08/31/i-dont-speak-spanish-does-that-make-me-less-latinx/?utm_term=.8d13a892c3c9.

Further Reading and Resources

Aldama, A.J., Sandoval, C. and García, P.J. (eds) (2012) *Performing the US Latina and Latino Borderlands.* Bloomington, IN: Indiana University Press.

Bucholtz, M. (2016) On being called out of one's name: Indexical bleaching as a technique of de-racialization. In J.R. Rickford (2016) *Raciolinguistics: How Language Shapes our Ideas about Race* (pp. 273–289). New York: Oxford University Press.

Hurtado, A. and Cantú, N.E. (eds) (2020) *MeXicana Fashions: Politics, Self-adornment, and Identity Construction.* Austin, TX: University of Texas Press.

Mendoza-Denton, N. (2008) *Homegirls: Language and Cultural Practice among Latina Youth Gangs.* Malden, MA: Blackwell.

Parra, M.L. (2016) Understanding identity among Spanish heritage learners: An interdisciplinary endeavor. In D. Pascual y Cabo (ed.) *Advances in Spanish as a Heritage Language* (pp. 177–204). Amsterdam: John Benjamins.

Rodríguez, J.M. (2003) *Queer Latinidad: Identity Practices, Discursive Spaces.* New York: New York University Press.

Walker, A., García, C., Cortés, Y. and Campbell-Kibler, K. (2014) Comparing social meanings across listener and speaker groups: The indexical field of Spanish/s. *Language Variation and Change* 26 (2), 169–189.

Chapter 7

Spanish and Spanish-speakers in US Media

Objectives

To discuss portrayals of Latinxs in the media, examine the role of language in such portrayals, analyze the relationship between language ideologies and media representations of Latinxs and their language use and encourage critical consumption of these media portrayals.

Introduction

In the previous chapters, we addressed the history of Spanish and Spanish-speakers in the US, examined language ideologies and policies and analyzed the role of language in societal understandings and individual performances of **Latinidad** and other identities. In our discussions of how Spanish and multilingualism are framed in US society, we noted various competing and sometimes contradictory discourses, including some that value and foster Spanish-language use and maintenance and others that constrain them, as well as racializing ideologies that stigmatize Latinxs and their language varieties and practices. In this chapter we examine the role of the media in the reproduction of these **hegemonic ideologies** about language and identities, as well as consider how it also sometimes challenges them. We also explore the ways in which representations influence viewers' attitudes toward Latinxs (Tukachinsky *et al.*, 2017).

After a discussion of the history of the portrayal of Latinxs in US media, the rest of the chapter focuses on recent media. First, we examine mainstream English-language television and film and discuss how Latinxs and speaking Spanish are portrayed in these venues, with a subsequent section looking at representations in the news. We then focus more specifically on the role of language in such representations. Building on this, we provide an overview of Spanish-language media, with a primary focus on television and how the target audience (including its linguistic repertoire) is constructed in these productions. Finally, we look at research and empirical data on Spanish in public signs and advertising in the US and the built environment.

An underlying issue in the discussion of *how* Latinxs are portrayed is the extent to which Latinxs appear in mainstream media at all. Smith *et al.* (2019), in an analysis of 1200 popular films from between 2007 and 2018, show that only 5.3% of the characters were Latinx, with 47 films having no Latinx speaking characters at all. Negrón-Muntaner (2014) found that while the Latinx population rose 43% between 2000 and 2010, the portrayal of Latinxs in English-language media remained quantitatively the same. She calls this 'the Latino media gap,' noting that 'as Latino consumer power grows, relative Latino media presence shrinks' (Negrón-Muntaner, 2014). The lack of Latinx representation in mainstream media can have an important affective and ideological impact on Latinx and non-Latinx viewers alike by sending implicit messages about social belonging and subtly reinforcing the idea of the US as a White English-speaking society.

Lichter and Amundson (1997) trace the history of Latinxs in television, noting not only that **ethnoracial** minorities were vastly underrepresented, but also that until the 1960s the few exceptions to an essentially all-White world were very stereotypical portrayals, such as Blacks as railroad porters and Latinxs as bandits. During the 1960s, the number, range and quality of ethnoracial minority characters slowly began to increase, with some programs self-consciously portraying diversity by including characters with a careful selection of ethnoracial and gender identities (e.g. *The Mod Squad*, which featured a White male, a Black male and a White woman in lead roles). It is only since the 1990s that Latinxs have routinely been included in these formulaic attempts to show diversity. More recently, Asian characters have also been added to the mix.

Thus, when not a complete **erasure**, the historical representation of Latinxs can largely be described as tokenism in terms of quantity, and stereotypes in terms of quality. In the next section, we focus on this latter aspect, and discuss the framing of Latinidad in both Spanish- and English-language media in detail. We also address how language, including varieties of both Spanish and English, is used as a symbolic resource in constructing these representations.

Stereotypical Portrayals of Latinxs

There are a number of stereotypes about Latinxs that appear over and over again in films and television portrayals, as well as in news coverage (see Serna, 2017, for a comprehensive discussion of Latinx participation in the film industry). In particular, Ramírez Berg (2002) identifies six recurring stereotypical Latinx roles or stock characters that are part of film storytelling convention (Ramírez Berg, 2002: 68). These roles, all of which tend to be presented in contrast to an **Anglo** (White) male hero or protagonist, are: *El Bandido, The*

Male Buffon, The Latin Lover, The Harlot, The Female Clown and *The Dark Lady*. All of these roles can be traced back to the early days of film; in addition to providing some historical examples of each, we also present more contemporary examples illustrating how these stereotypes have endured in today's media.

El Bandido is the Mexican bandit, a portrayal that goes back to silent films such as *Broncho Billy and the Greaser* produced in 1914 (yes, that's right, the Latinx character was actually referred to as a 'greaser' in the title). Mexican bandits were also the back-up bad guys in Westerns (following Indians, the staple bad guys); the heroes were rarely Latinx (Chávez, 2003: 96). The Bandido role continues today in various permutations: the Latin American gangster/drug runner and the Latinx inner city gang member are the more contemporary versions of the same Latinx villain (Ramírez Berg, 2002: 68–69). Other male stereotypical characters include The Male Buffoon, a character who provides comic relief by offering someone to laugh at; a classic example of this is Ricky Ricardo in *I Love Lucy*.

The Latin Lover, arguably the most prominent stereotype, is the erotic Latinx, often dangerous and violent but filled with sexual promise and prowess. In early examples, there was often a disconnect between the Latinx characters and the European actors who played them. This tendency can be traced back to Rudolph Valentino, an Italian immigrant who played various 'exotic' roles calling for a dark-haired and dark-eyed sex symbol, such as an Arabian sheik, an Indian rajah or a Spanish bullfighter. The Latin Lover characters were rarely, if ever, played by Mestizo, Indigenous or Afro-Latinx actors; through much of the 20th century even putatively Spanish characters were often played by Anglos, such as Douglas Fairbanks in *The Mark of Zorro* (1920). More recently, this role was reprised by the Spanish actor Antonio Banderas in *Zorro* (1998). Nonetheless, even as more Latinx actors have been cast in Latinx roles, Rodríguez (1997) notes that there are physical differences between Latin Lover types and Bandidos with '... the Latino villains being poorer and darker in coloration and the Latin lovers being upper class and conforming physically to European prototypes' (Rodríguez, 1997: 81). Thus, cinematic representations of Latinx continue to link Whiteness to moral good as well as to sexual and/or romantic desirability. This both reflects and reproduces the racism and colorism that we discussed in Chapter 4.

There are also female versions and variations of these male stereotypes. In particular, The Harlot is a lusty, hot-tempered woman, a temptress and a nymphomaniac, such as Katy Jurado in *High Noon* (1952), while The Female Clown is a Latina who is portrayed as silly, usually in addition to being sexually promiscuous, e.g. Lupe Vélez in *Mexican Spitfire* (1940). Both of these types have characteristics that make them undesirable to the White Anglo male hero, whom they inevitably lust after. In contrast, The Dark Lady is cool and classy; she is exemplified by Dolores del Río in *Flying Down to Rio* (1933) (Ramírez Berg, 2002: 76). Again, this character's portrayal largely revolves around lust; the difference is that The Dark Lady inspires lust in others whereas The Harlot and The Female Clown display passions of their own. Rodríguez (1997: 80) conflates these three categories into two, what she calls 'señoritas' (wealthy and virtuous women) and 'spitfires' (poorer women portrayed as sexually 'easy').

Latinxs and Spanish-speakers in English Language Media

Cortés (1997:131) notes that Chicanas began to be portrayed as 'real people' in the mid-1940s; in the 1970s the ethnic stereotyping decreased. However, one consequence of this was that since then, 'movies have littered the screen with Latinas who come off as little more than Spanish-surnamed Anglas' (Cortés, 1997: 134). In other words, because films only represented Latina identity through stereotypes, the elimination of the stereotypes meant that many representations of Latinxs lost all culturally specific characteristics. One exception to this erasure of Latinx identity even within films that have Latinx roles is what Cortés calls 'urban violence films,' which he argues was the main film genre representing Latinx experiences as such. However, this depiction of Latinxs as members of street gangs built on the Bandido stereotype by portraying gangs as central to the life of urban Latinxs (Ramírez Berg, 2002). Thus, it is rooted in a racist ideology in which Latinx men are constructed as violent and uneducated and part of the worst of US society.

Another common portrayal centers on the difficulties of Latinx and immigrant life, including the depiction of noble attempts to transcend poverty and other social problems through hard work and perhaps even a bit of talent or intellect. Ramírez Berg (2002:111–112) argues that 'the Chicano social problem film' often overlaps with a broader narrative pattern focusing on assimilation. There are multiple versions of this assimilation narrative, all of which involve Latinxs striving to achieve the so-called American Dream. In one version of the narrative discussed by Ramírez Berg, Latinx characters realize that success is incompatible with their core cultural values, including honesty, loyalty, commitment to family and a strong work ethic. At the same time, traditionally mythologized 'American' values such as ambition, competitiveness and shrewdness are portrayed as problematic, at least when adopted by Latinxs. Thus, in Ramírez Berg's reading, even though Latinx culture is portrayed in a positive light, Latinx characters ultimately must choose between remaining marginalized in ethnic enclaves or betraying their heritage and risking their morality. This genre includes *Bordertown* (2006), *Real Women Have Curves* (2002) and *Spanglish* (2004), and TV shows *Ugly Betty* (2004–2010) and *American Family* (2002–2004). The portrayal of Latinxs struggling to integrate into the middle class may be an attempt to represent authentic Latinidad (Sowards & Pineda, 2011: 137), but at the same time it serves to reinforce the stereotype of Latinxs as poor, uneducated immigrants, with success stories largely portrayed as exceptions to the rule. Further, in many cases, linguistic and cultural assimilation is portrayed as the key to success.

Recently, we find more nuanced representations in the critically acclaimed *One Day at a Time* (2017–present), which portrays a three-generation Cuban American family. The show, a remake of a 1970s sitcom, explores not only cultural and linguistic diversity, assimilation and citizenship, but also a wide range of issues related to the femininities, masculinities and sexualities of the characters, which go beyond the stereotypes of Latin Lovers and Dark Ladies. In this show, the Cuban-born grandmother, played by Rita Moreno, is something of a 'spitfire' in a somewhat more stereotypical portrayal. Nonetheless, the main characters also include Penelope, her US-born adult daughter who served in the US military, as well as her feminist, academically successful granddaughter Elena, who comes out as a lesbian in Season 1. News that Netflix was cancelling the show after the third season due to insufficient viewership was met with dismay and various social media campaigns to reverse the decision or to convince another network to pick up the show, showing how much Latinx audiences value representation. Ultimately, it was picked up by PopTV and a fourth season is scheduled to air in 2020.

Guzmán and Valdivia (2004: 208) describe the dominant discourses about Latinxs as portraying them as 'ethnically homogenous, racially non-White, Spanish-dominant, socio-economically poor and most often of Mexican origin,' but some marketing professionals seem to be working to change this stereotypical representation. Tukachinsky *et al.* (2017) note that most of the worst stereotypes, which portray Latinxs as stupid and lazy, sexually promiscuous, of lower socio-economic status and primarily in the roles of 'cops and crooks' (Tukachinsky *et al.*, 2017: 541), are becoming less frequent. Further, Negrón-Muntaner (2014) observes an increase in Afro-Latinx actors, for instance, although they are still underrepresented. Changing demographics in the US have influenced media representations of Latinxs in several ways, but one of the main influences is that film producers do not want to offend the potentially lucrative Latinx market (Chávez, 2003: 96). In recent years Latinx audiences and activists have demanded improvement, for example through social media and other fora.

Negrón-Muntaner (2014: 2) notes that in the 2010–2013 period she studied, there were no Latinx leads in the top ten films and TV shows, and 67% of the Latinx supporting characters in mainstream television were women. But how are these women portrayed? Guzmán and Valdivia (2004: 217) argue that the Latin Lover and Dark Lady stereotypes evolved to survive in films of the 21st century but they did not go away. In other words, although media representations of Latinxs have become a bit more varied and complex as time goes on, they often still portray Latinxs as embodying an exotic sensuality. According to Guzmán and Valdivia, representations of Latinas continue to 'build on a tradition of exoticization, racialization and sexualization, a tradition that serves to position Latinas as continual foreigners and a cultural threat.' Bush (2015) suggests that the representation of Latinxs as highly sexualized and passionate is part of their broader portrayal as hot-tempered and with a propensity for violence. An interesting twist on the topic of Latina sexuality is found in the recent series *Jane the Virgin* (2014–present), in which the main character, a young Venezuelan American women, aims to remain a virgin until she is married, but is accidentally artificially inseminated and becomes an unwed mother. While Jane's sweet and submissive grandmother and her fiery mother in some ways represent the two extremes in television portrayals of Latinas, the show also challenges those stereotypes by presenting them as more complex characters (Martinez, 2015).

As part of the analysis of Latinx representation in popular film, media scholars have gone beyond looking at the characteristics and narrative arc of Latinx roles to also consider the ways in which Latina bodies are portrayed. For example, a great deal of popular and scholarly attention has been paid to actress and pop icon Jennifer Lopez's buttocks, to the media fetishization of her posterior, and to her own expressed satisfaction with her body (Beltran,

2002). Mendible (2010), in her analysis of the Latina body in popular film, suggests that the frequent focus on large buttocks could potentially be inclusive of diverse body types and standards of beauty, but instead it usually serves to further exoticize other Latina women. Further, her analysis reveals that positive evaluation of voluptuous derrieres (in addition to the obvious objectifying nature of this focus) coexists with, and leaves intact, hegemonic standards of beauty that favor Whiteness and skinniness. This finding is echoed by Molina-Guzmán (2010), who also examines the portrayal of Latina bodies in the media and concludes that ethnic women in general continue to be sexualized and constrained in the ways they are portrayed, thus highlighting the **intersectionality** of ethnoracial and gender identities.

According to some media scholars, the stereotypical portrayal of the exotic Latina is often found in films with just one or two Latinx characters, rather than those depicting Latinx communities or comprising multiple Latinx roles. In other words, the Latin Lover and Dark Lady roles are most likely to appear in movies comprised largely of White characters in which the Latinx character is uniquely dark and mysterious or a sensual outsider. This can be said to apply in the case of Gloria in the sitcom *Modern Family*, played by Colombian American actress Sofia Vergara, in which her voluptuousness, emotional volatility and hardscrabble impoverished background stand out in comparison with the affluence and more restrained behavior of Gloria's Anglo husband and his family. In contrast with the portrayal of Gloria, Baez (2007) found that three Latina-centric movies that she examines – *Selena* (1997), *Girlfight* (2000) and *Real Women Have Curves* (2002) – presented more nuanced depictions of Latinas and thus challenged some of the dominant stereotypes about gender and ethnicity. Nonetheless, as we saw, much of the research on Latinxs in mainstream media suggests that the stereotypes live on. In addition, even while at some level the films analyzed by Baez challenge stereotypical representations of Latina women, they can simultaneously reinforce tired notions about the importance of traditional gender roles in Latinx families, or about Latinxs as poor, uneducated immigrants. Similarly, the television series *Orange is the New Black* moves beyond the tokenism of earlier representations of Latinas, while also including a diversity of **phenotypes** as well as language proficiencies and practices (including Spanish dominance, Spanish–English bilingualism and English monolingualism), but it nonetheless can be seen as reproducing the same old tropes of Latinx criminality and poverty.

In addition to criminal behavior and sexuality, Latinx representation in the media often touches on issues of immigration status and integration into US society. Speaking Spanish is often a key element in the portrayal of the undocumented, the unintegrated and the unlawful (we'll return to this topic in the section on the language of Latinxs in the media). Here too, there is often a fine line between exploring social issues and reproducing stereotypes. For example, in their analysis of *Ugly Betty*, Sowards and Pineda (2011) interpret the portrayal of Betty's father's difficulties as an undocumented immigrant as part of an authentic portrayal, but what seems 'authentic' to some audiences may seem formulaic or clichéd to others. In particular, Amaya (2010) argues that *Ugly Betty* reproduces stereotypes about Latinx citizenship status and employment patterns. Further, Betty's mistreatment in the workplace is framed as a natural or normal part of her job experience that she must get through in order to advance – just another obstacle to overcome on the road to success – rather than illegal discrimination that she should complain about or report, thus naturalizing exploitative labor conditions. Also touching on issues of immigration is an episode of *Jane the Virgin* in which Jane's undocumented grandmother is admitted to a hospital but threatened with deportation on her release. A message flashed on the screen, 'Yes, this really happens. Look it up. #immigrationreform,' suggests that the show's producers hadn't included the grandmother's immigration status as a formulaic way of constructing her character, but because they saw the show as a site of education and/or political activism, rather than 'simply' entertainment (Martinez, 2015).

Beyond the depiction of Latinxs as potentially undocumented, *Ugly Betty* also addresses the issue of integration, and especially the tension between ethnic Otherness and cultural assimilation (Avila-Saavedra, 2011). On one hand, the difference between the Latinx and non-Latinx characters is often highlighted, and Betty's more assimilated behavior (such as not speaking Spanish) is tacitly endorsed. On the other hand, Betty and her family's Latinidad is positioned as part of, and compatible with, mainstream US culture; they celebrate Halloween and Thanksgiving, pay their taxes and watch Oprah just like everyone else. Avila-Saavedra argues that this portrayal simultaneously provides Latinx viewers with a model of US Latinx identity construction and educates non-Latinx viewers about an important sub-group in US society.

Avila-Saavedra (2011) also examines how Latinx comedians – George Lopez, Carlos Mencía and Freddie Prinze Jr. – explore themes of Latinx belonging. The basis of much of the humor is the recognizable distinctiveness of Latinxs, but at the same time it often reproduces familiar US ideologies about individuality and achievement. Specifically, these comedians suggest that they have reached their places in life through getting an education and, especially, hard work, just like other US Americans. Thus, like in *Ugly Betty*, assimilation is rewarded and portrayed as an improvement upon the unintegrated immigrant experience, which is associated with poverty and discrimination.

This section examined how Latinxs are portrayed in fictitious storylines in mainstream English-language media. As we saw, representations have improved in both quantity and quality since the early days, but Latinx characters and actors are still underrepresented and stereotypes still abound. In some cases, the specific portrayals might seem less problematic if there was more Latinx representation overall, which would allow for greater diversity of roles; when there are so few Latinx roles and stories, each one takes on heightened symbolic meaning. In addition, we have shown that representations can simultaneously reinforce and challenge dominant ideologies about Latinxs in the US, and that not all viewers or critics interpret them in the same way. In the following sections, we look at representations in English-language news, and then turn to Spanish-language media. As we will see, many of the same themes can be found in these other types of media portrayals of Latinx, although different foci also emerge.

Latinxs in English Language News

In a masterful understatement, Valdeón (2013: 440) notes that 'The relationship between the Hispanic population of the USA and its anglophone media cannot be described as a happy one.' As is the case in television programs and movies, research on news coverage of Latinxs uniformly shows that they are underrepresented in the news; Latinxs appear in less than 1% of news stories, and the coverage tends to be negative (Negrón-Muntaner, 2014; Santa Ana, 2013). Stereotypes of the family-oriented yet overly sexualized Latina so common in films also appear in news coverage (Bush, 2015; Correa, 2010), but the main stereotype in news reports is of unauthorized Latinx immigrants who do not learn English (Markert, 2010) and commit crimes (Beck, 2010; Chiricos & Eschholz, 2002) (see our discussion of these stereotypes, and their inaccuracy, in Chapters 2 and 4). Research that compares the relative representation in news coverage of Blacks, Latinxs and Whites to their proportion in crime reports has found that Latinxs are underrepresented while Blacks are overrepresented and portrayed as particularly ruthless (Dixon & Azocar, 2006) (see our discussion of **racialization** in Chapter 5). This finding offers an important reminder that 'visibility' is not always positive, and that media coverage of Latinxs should be looked at as part of a larger racialization and negative stereotyping of people of color.

In his research on the representation of Latinxs in news, Santa Ana (2002) analyzed the metaphors used to discuss immigrants and immigration in a year's worth of newspaper articles. His analysis reveals that the most common metaphors represented immigrants as 'animals' or 'invaders,' thus portraying them as subhuman, undeserving of rights or protection, and intent on hurting the nation. Santa Ana found that the most common metaphor for immigration was 'dangerous waters,' such as in talk of 'waves' of immigration 'flooding' the nation, which represents immigrants as an undifferentiated mass (rather than individual people) that is likely to cause damage. Similarly, a recent analysis of coverage of immigration-related issues found that many US news outlets use terms like 'illegal alien' and/or reproduce anti-immigrant discourses of extremist groups, in contradiction to the Society for Professional Journalism's policy against dehumanizing language (Ndulue *et al.*, 2019) (we discussed the problems with this term in Chapter 3).

Rosa (2016a) notes that in much coverage of immigration, speaking English is portrayed as the key to success and the solution to the challenges of the immigrant experience. Strikingly, this is the case in both positive and negative discourses, including 'Latino spin' (Dávila, 2008), which represents Latinx as model immigrants, and 'Latino threat' discourse (Chavez, 2013), which represents Latinxs as a problem population that is dangerous for US national culture and identity. Further, Rosa argues, even when the media portray Spanish positively, the focus tends to be on the future, such as in claims that Spanish is on the rise and will one day become a valuable resource. However, these predictions have been around for years, and the imagined future, in which Spanish is appreciated and acquisition of English leads to acceptance and economic success, never seems to arrive. In addition, this emphasis on the future importance of Spanish relies on erasure of the role of Spanish and Latinxs in the history and present of the US; as we have discussed, Spanish-speakers have been in what is now US territory for over 500 years, longer than many other ethnolinguistic groups who are considered part of the mainstream, and the language is already important and valuable. Moreover, the portrayal of English as the key to success reproduces the inaccurate notion that the problems faced by Latinxs are based on their lack of English, rather than structural inequality. According to Lippi-Green (2012: 70), this type of discourse – in which 'promises are made' to speakers of minority languages and 'non-standard' varieties that success will follow assimilation to the dominant language or variety – is part of a broader process of linguistic subordination. Further, it portrays language as the cause of marginalization, rather than the mechanism (see Chapter 4). As we will see in the next section, language use is intertwined with all of the negative and stereotypical portrayals of Latinx in both popular television and film and news sources.

Representing Latinx Language Use: Monolingual Norms and Deviant Behavior

This section examines representations of Latinxs' language use in Hollywood films and on TV, as well as portrayals and discourses about Latinxs' language use in newspapers and television news programs. As has been discussed in earlier chapters, certain ways of speaking can index particular identities and this indexicality is also used in the portrayal of fictional characters. Thus, just as Spanish is constructed as an inherent aspect of Latinx identity and a prerequisite for Latinx authenticity in 'real life,' this is also the case regarding fictional Latinx characters. In other words, Spanish is one way to show that a character is authentically Latinx. Nonetheless, in media portrayals, Spanish also tends to index specific character traits, rather than just ethnoracial identity. For example, Bush (2015), in his study of Latinx characters in daytime soap operas, notes that Spanish is often used to mark scenes in which the speaker is particularly emotional (that hot-blooded Latin character!) or for 'secret conversations' (Bush, 2015: 1159) which mark them as **Other**. In this section we emphasize the ways in which media portrayals of Spanish reflect and reproduce dominant discourses surrounding Spanish and Spanish-speakers.

In Chapter 3 we discussed the ideology that monolingualism is the natural state of affairs for individuals and societies, and its **hegemony** in the US. Petrucci (2008) shows how the representations of languages other than English in the US media presuppose and reinforce **normative monolingualism**. Looking at ten films involving supposed Spanish-speakers produced between 2000 and 2004, he identified three strategies used to signal that characters were speaking Spanish. None of the films simply had actors speak Spanish for key dialogue that was supposed to be in Spanish (perhaps with subtitles for an anglophone audience). Instead, one strategy was to make Spanish audible in the background, even as all dialogue important to the plot took place in English. With this strategy, Spanish didn't convey actual information but instead created ambience, almost like set design. Another strategy was for actors to speak Spanish-accented English. The third, related strategy was for actors to speak English but to incorporate emblematic uses of Spanish: terms of endearment, profanity and easily recognizable **cognates** likely to be understood by anglophones; many people recognize things such as '*mi amor*' or '*hijo de puta*' even if they do not speak Spanish, and most can also make sense of such things as '*¡Viva el presidente!*' (Petrucci, 2008: 411). And even if the semantic content of these phrases were not understood, it would not prevent the viewer from following the plot of the movie.

In addition to these strategies, as Bürki (2008: 12) points out, in some films and programs when the characters say something in Spanish, they immediately translate into English, such as when a character on *Miami Vice* stated 'On the other hand, if what you wish is *el plomo*, the lead, than do that.'

Petrucci argues that although the motivation for emblematic and ambient uses of Spanish seems to be primarily pragmatic – after all, the target audience is largely English-speaking – the consequence is the representation of the world as normatively anglophone. Specifically, the use of accented English to signal that the characters are speaking in Spanish, while still allowing monolingual English-speakers to understand (without having to read subtitles), reinforces the notion that English-speakers should be able to understand everything without having to learn another language. Further, it bolsters the common idea that it is 'rude' or 'inappropriate' for Spanish-speakers to speak Spanish in the presence of English monolinguals, even when they are not part of the conversation. The belief that minority language speakers should always accommodate English-speakers is reflected in casual situations and in the attacks on Spanish-speakers in public spaces (such as those discussed in Chapter 4), and they are also the basis of many workplace English-only policies (see Chapter 8). A focus group study in Ohio (https://mershoncenter.osu.edu/research-project-directory/immigrants-assimilation-and-cultural-threat-political-exploration) (http://mershoncenter.osu.edu/expertise/ideas/immigrants.htm) shows that although such opinions are not universal, they are not uncommon. In addition, portraying the speaking of Spanish via accented English reinforces the notion that proficiency in Spanish interferes with English, and that Spanish-speakers never speak English natively (which, as we discussed in Chapter 2, is inaccurate). The emblematic use of cognates for 'flavor' also constructs Spanish as somewhat less than a real language, one that consists primarily of English words with a Spanish accent (like in **Mock Spanish**, which we discussed in the previous chapter).

Some Spanish-dominant immigrants in the US do speak English at home some or even all of the time, as do many US-born Latinxs. Some of them do so because they want their children to have the benefit of learning the dominant language when they are young or because they are advised by teachers that speaking Spanish to their children will confuse them or delay their linguistic development and school progress (see Chapter 9). As we discussed in depth in Chapter 2, immigrants face considerable challenges in the effort to pass Spanish on to their children. These portrayals on the big screen, or even the smaller television screen, of Latin American immigrants all speaking English normalize this behavior and make Spanish seem expendable.

Another problem worth noting with these portrayals of accented speech is that they conflate three different linguistic situations: (1) dialogue that, according to the plot, is in Spanish; (2) the speech of people who learned English as a second language and have a 'foreign' accent; and (3) the speech of people who speak Latinx English natively and may or may not speak Spanish (see the section on Latinx Englishes in Chapter 10 for a fuller discussion). In some ways it doesn't matter that these things are conflated; perhaps a bigger concern is that accented English is often used to show Spanish-speakers and Latinxs in a decidedly negative light. In this regard, Lippi-Green (2012) has shown that the accents used for certain characters rely on social stereotypes about members of particular social and ethnic groups and are a means of reinforcing prejudice against linguistic minorities. This is clearly the case when accented English and Latinx English are represented as non-standard and problematic, and linked to negative and stereotypical characteristics such as poverty, lack of assimilation, traditional gender roles, etc. On one hand, accents are used to index Latinidad in general, but accents are also used to distinguish among 'positive' and 'negative' characters along moral, intellectual and class lines. For example, Betty from *Ugly Betty* speaks standard English whereas her sister Hilda has a marked accent. Although Hilda is not an unsympathetic character, she is less educated and less intelligent than Betty and we are also given the impression that she is sexually promiscuous. This linking of Latinx English or accented English (it's not clear which) to characters who have socially undesirable traits reinforces stereotypes of ethnic varieties as inferior to standard English because the speakers are uneducated, have loose morals, and so forth.

Sofia Vergara's rendering of Gloria, discussed earlier in this chapter, is another example where accented English is a key element in her portrayal as a sensual Female Clown, with numerous jokes based on her English-language mispronunciations and misunderstandings. Casillas *et al.* (2018) show that Gloria's language use is part of the racialized portrayal of her character, noting the frequent jokes about her English pronunciation and grammar. This representation serves to reinforce stereotypes of Latinxs as unintegrated Others. Further, Casillas *et al.* argue that, while other characters on the show develop nuanced personalities throughout the episodes, Gloria remains a caricature of a highly sexualized and linguistically incompetent Latina. The impact of this character in a long-running and widely viewed television series is the reinforcement of racial and linguistic hierarchies, giving viewers a license to mock accented speech and dismiss language-based discrimination as comical.

In some cases, the line between actors and the characters they play is a blurry one. This is the case with Sofia Vergara and Gloria, both of whom are portrayed as highly sexualized, with accented English being one part of that portrayal. (The fact that the degree of Vergara's accent varies suggests her own agency in such portrayals and constitutes an example of using language to perform identity and index particular characteristics, as discussed in Chapter 6.) Hinojos (2019) draws attention to the long history of using accented English to portray actors, as well as characters, as racialized Others by analyzing the depiction of the speech of the Mexican actor Lupe Vélez in fan magazines from the first half of the 20th century. In this written medium, Vélez' accent was portrayed through spellings such as *Meestar* for 'Mister' and *wan'* or *han'* for 'want' or 'hand.' It's worth stressing that while these non-standard spellings might capture Vélez' speech, similar informal transcriptions are rarely, if ever, used to capture the wide range of accents used by native speakers. Instead, they are used only to draw attention to and caricature 'foreign' accents and 'non-standard' varieties. These portrayals and the prejudice against particular accents has, of course, consequences for actors. For example, Beltran (2007) explains that during the transition from silent film to 'talkies' in the later 1920s, actors with Spanish-inflected accents were sidelined to minor, racialized roles. This was part of the construction of 'authentic' US identity as non-Latinx, the centering of Whiteness and the marginalization of Latinxs.

In addition to the use of accented English to signal Spanish and/or negatively characterize Latinx characters, another common type of language use in media portrayals of Latinx is non-convergent or asymmetrical bilingual discourse, in which different characters speak different languages to each other (Bürki, 2012). This portrayal usually involves members of different generations; the parents and/or grandparents speak Spanish and the younger generation answer in English or a combination of English and Spanish. A prototypical example of this is in *¿Qué pasa U.S.A.?*, a sitcom that aired on public television from 1975 to 1980 (most of the episodes are available on YouTube). Funded by a Department of Education grant program designed to help school districts overcome the educational disadvantages, prejudice and isolation faced by minority children (see Chapters 8 and 9), the program focused on a three-generation Cuban American family living in Miami. It's worth emphasizing the central role of the Cuban-born producers, writers, directors and actors in *¿Qué pasa U.S.A.?*, as well as the fact that the primary intended audience was Cuban American, although it also garnered critical acclaim and viewership among Anglo and monolingual English-speaking audiences (Rivero, 2012). The storylines explore various cultural challenges faced by the three generations, with questions of language often playing a prominent role. For example, in one episode from the first season, 'We speak Spanish' (https://www.youtube.com/watch?v=Em4KBzIo3fk), addresses the monolingual Spanish-speaking grandparents' complaints about their grandchildren's English-inflected Spanish, as well as the shame that some children feel regarding their parents' accented English. The two teenagers borrow English words into Spanish and make numerous, creative, cross-linguistic jokes and puns (for example, Joe refers to Mrs. Peabody as *la señora cuerpo de chícaro*, literally 'Mrs. pea body'). Further, the show includes extended dialogue in Spanish as well as non-converging bilingual discourse, without subtitles (in some cases, characters paraphrase in English what others said in Spanish). Thus, the show is often referred to as the first bilingual sitcom on US television (Rivero, 2012), but to our knowledge no other show has come close to including anywhere near as much bilingual discourse. Like the centrality of Latinxs and Spanish-speakers in both the production and the reception of *¿Qué pasa U.S.A?*, the amount of untranslated Spanish and the degree of bilingualism distinguish it from the English-language shows discussed in this section. Nonetheless, we include it here because it aired on a network that broadcasts almost exclusively in English (i.e. PBS) and reached a general audience.

More recently, non-converging bilingual discourse has also been noted by Androutsopoulos (2007: 220) and is utilized in *One Day at a Time*, discussed earlier. We also see this in *Jane the Virgin*, where Jane's grandmother speaks Spanish. There is a certain realism to this portrayal; such intergenerational patterns of asymmetrical codeswitching are well-documented (Boeschoten, 1990; Fuller, 1997) and the portrayal reflects the three-generation shift to English discussed in Chapter 2. However, in many cases Spanish also indexes negative social characteristics; it tends to be older, poor, uneducated and socially backward (e.g. sexist) characters that speak Spanish while the younger, more likeable and smarter characters answer in English. This representation positions Spanish in the past, framing it as incompatible with modernity as well as an encumbrance to achieving social power, rather than a positive part of the Latinx experience. Thus, these portrayals may reinforce the notion of assimilation to English as a moral as well as a social good.

A very different portrayal of Spanish can be found in programming aimed at children; in children's shows, the use of Spanish often has a pedagogical aim (Moran, 2007). For example, *Sesame Street* has a Spanish word of the day and programs such as *Dora the Explorer* and the spinoff *Go, Diego, Go!* feature the use of Spanish as part of the repertoires of the main characters, but with certain phrases explained or used repetitively to foster language learning. These shows also focus on multiculturalism and appreciation of diversity (De Casanova, 2007). Although similar to shows for adults in that Spanish is associated with ethnoracial identity, they differ in that Spanish is rarely stigmatized. On the contrary, in the animated *Dora the Explorer*, for example, the protagonist is a smart, young, bilingual Latina girl who uses both Spanish and English to complete her adventures. (In the 2019 live action movie, *Dora and the Lost City of Gold*, set in Peru, teenage Dora's linguistic repertoire also includes Quechua, part of the producers' concerted efforts to accurately represent the diversity of Latin American language and culture; Llamoca, 2019.) Knowledge of Spanish is portrayed in a positive light, rather than as a barrier to English, and Dora switches effortlessly between Spanish and English depending on the linguistic abilities of her **interlocutors**. Thus, the disdain for Spanish that occurs in the adult world, discussed further in the next sub-section, is replaced with a pluralist ideology for young viewers. Still, despite the television show's linking of Spanish to the protagonist's Latina identity, Spanish is framed as a resource available for all children; Spanish-speaking children often engage in teaching Spanish to non-Latinxs and the pedagogical emphasis is clearly on the learning of Spanish by non-Latinx children, rather than Spanish maintenance or development among children who already speak Spanish. (For an in-depth discussion of the history of *Dora*, including the visual representation of her pan-Latina identity, listen to the episode of NPR's Latino USA podcast on the show's legacy: https://www.latinousa.org/2019/08/14/doratheexplorer/.)

Decisions about which languages are heard as well as how they are heard – that is, if they are portrayed as part of everyday life or highlighted as 'foreign' or 'exotic' – participate in the construction of linguistic diversity as either normal or deviant. While in many cases the representation of Spanish in the media reflects and reinforces dominant ideologies, Kelly-Homes and Milani (2011) show that media representations of multilingualism can also challenge existing stereotypes and present multilingualism as a natural part of everyday life. In contrast with the earlier techniques used to represent Spanish described by Petruccio (2008) and discussed above, this approach does not present accented English as if it were Spanish, but instead simply uses Spanish to represent characters speaking Spanish. In some cases, English subtitles are provided (e.g. *Quinceañera* (2006), *Orange is the New Black* (2013–2019)), but in others, such as *One Day at a Time* (discussed earlier in this chapter), viewers who do not speak Spanish simply do not have access to those parts of the dialogue, but they can still follow the show since the key content is offered in English. Such portrayals offer a counterpoint to the erasure of Spanish and constitute a more realistic portrayal of multilingualism, in the sense that people who are supposedly speaking Spanish actually do so, while they also acknowledge and provide access to non-Spanish speaking audiences. The Netflix series *Narcos* (2015–) has received a great deal of attention for its combined use of English and Spanish in a program heavily marketed to (and viewed by) English-speaking audiences in the US. Here too, characters actually speak in Spanish when they are portrayed as doing so, but rather than limiting the Spanish dialogue to things that won't interfere with the plot if they are not understood, English-language subtitles are provided. Both of these bilingual story-telling techniques are also used in *Orange Is the New Black* and FX's *The Bridge* (2013–2015). In addition to offering a more realistic representation of bilingualism, the increased inclusion of Spanish in (predominantly) English-language programming also reflects a greater recognition on the part of producers and advertisers of Spanish–English bilinguals as potential audiences and consumers. We return to this topic below.

Constructing the Latinx Audience: Spanish Language Media and Beyond

Spanish-language media has become increasingly available in the US over the last decades, with the Spanish-language networks Univisión and Telemundo being widely accessible, along with Spanish-language cable channels, streaming services and online media. Millions of viewers in the US still tune in daily to watch a wide variety of programming, including news, sports and variety and talk shows, as well as telenovelas and other series such as *Color de la Pasion*, Univisión's most watched program in 2017 (https://www.statista.com/statistics/497739/spanish-tv-programs-usa/). There has also been tremendous growth in Spanish-language streaming services such as Netflix, including original Spanish-language programming as well as Spanish dubbing and subtitling for programs produced in English and other languages.

A key focus in the investigation of Spanish-language media is how languages, language varieties and ways of using language are used to frame the audience members in particular ways while also reproducing particular ideologies about language such as Spanish's role in Latinx identity. In her research, Dávila (2012) examines how Spanish-language advertising and media produce an image of what she describes as a homogenous Latinidad that speaks only or mostly Spanish. Culturally, this group is portrayed as family-oriented and traditional, with a collective identity that contrasts with the highly individualistic mainstream US culture.

Dávila's findings are echoed by Fullerton and Kendrick (2000), who show that in Spanish-language television commercials, women are largely portrayed as homemakers, as well as by Rivadeneyra (2011), whose analysis of telenovelas finds a parallel trend of depicting women primarily in the role of caretakers and men primarily as workers. While a dichotomy persists between portrayals of women as either overly sexualized or modest and traditional (Dávila, 2012), much of the programming on Spanish-language television is family-oriented and does not present overly sexualized female characters. Correa (2010), in her work on portrayals of Latinx women, notes that in the Spanish-language version of the *Miami Herald*, *El Nuevo Herald*, women's actions were often framed as family-oriented and self-sacrificing, in contrast with the English-language version of the newspaper, which focused on the achievements of successful Latinas bringing credit to their communities but also creating a new market. Correa analyzes these differences in terms of hegemonic ideologies that see Latinx culture as collectivist and US mainstream or Anglo culture as individualistic. These representational tendencies can have the impact of constructing Spanish as inherently linked to 'traditional' cultural values.

In terms of ethnoracial representation in Spanish-language programming and advertising in the US, Dávila (2012) maintains that most characters and actors on Spanish-language television in the US have a generic 'Latin look' consisting of olive skin and dark hair, and thus do not reflect the phenotypical diversity of the US Latinx population. As Spanish-language media production and consumption has become increasingly transnational, with television shows produced in Miami broadcast throughout Latin America (and vice versa) or streamed via international services like Netflix, programming seen in the US was often designed for Spanish-speaking multiple markets. In this context, the 'Latin look' is used to signal a Latinx identity to US viewers (and advertisers), while the lack of Indigenous and Afro-Latino representation aligns with the norms and the racial bias of Latin American media and societies. In contrast with the Whiteness of actors playing central characters, Rivadeneyra (2011) argues that darker skinned actors primarily appear in stereotypical roles, often as villains or characters with questionable morality. However, while Alford (2018) continues to lament the lack of Afro-Latinxs in mainstream media, she notes that new media sources such as Instagram provide more opportunities for greater inclusivity.

Rivadeneyra's research on the views of Latinx adolescents about Spanish-language television demonstrates that they perceive it as less stereotypical than mainstream English-language programming. In addition, news programs on Spanish-language networks such as Univisión and Telemundo include more coverage of Latin America as well as issues impacting US Latinxs than do English-language networks. Along these lines, Emmy-winning Univisión news anchor Jorge Ramos has become well known for his frequent questioning of President Trump's rhetoric and policies toward immigrants and Latinxs. Strom (2015), in her analysis of Spanish-language news articles and pictures in Minnesota press, finds a strong presence of what she terms 'transformative texts,' that is, representations of Latinxs standing up to discrimination through activism. Although the Pew Research Center reports that more and more Latinxs are getting their news in English (Lopez & Gonzalez-Barrera, 2013), this does not always mean that Latinx audiences are ignored. For example, in Moran's (2015) study of LatiNation, an English-language TV news show aimed at US-born Latinxs, participants who strongly identified as Latinx saw themselves as the target audience and found the coverage inspirational, underscoring the symbolic importance of seeing oneself represented and 'spoken to,' regardless of the language in which that happens.

In addition to the generic 'Latin look,' Spanish-language media often presents a homogenized view of US Latinxs' language, through the use of Spanish and the specific types of Spanish used. In the mid-20th century, when Spanish-language radio and television were produced for regional or local audiences, the specific varieties used tended to reflect the make-up of the local Spanish-speaking population (Dávila, 2012). For example, Mexican varieties were typical in commercials and programs produced and broadcast in the Southwest, while Caribbean varieties were more frequent in the Northeast.

Nowadays, the linguistic influence of local demographics is perhaps most noticeable in commercials for local businesses, while national programming and advertising campaigns tend to minimize linguistic variation. The focus on a generic, non-regional Spanish reflects the standard language ideology, while the fact that the putative generic is closest to Mexican Spanish reflects linguistic hierarchies about the relative value of different varieties (see Chapter 3). Even Fox News picked up on this and presented a segment which addresses linguistic biases and the idea of Mexican varieties as 'neutral' in the US (https://www.foxnews.com/lifestyle/not-all-accents-are-equal-in-spanish-language-media). The standard language ideology has also been documented in Spanish-language radio by De Fina (2013), who reports that Spanish-dominant hosts sometimes make fun of other hosts' accents and correct their Spanish.

Dávila (2012) argues that presenting Latinxs as a culturally homogenous Spanish-speaking group is primarily the result of advertising agencies trying to capitalize on the Latinx market by convincing advertisers of the distinct cultural values and language practices of Latinxs, and thus creating a need for distinct Spanish-language advertising campaigns. Nonetheless, because this commodification of language and culture includes the construction of Latinxs as a distinct social group in the US, it plays an important role in reproducing the notion of a pan-Latinx identity. One way in which this happens is through the use of *nosotros* ('we') in Spanish-language media in implicit reference to all Latinxs or Spanish-speakers, which discursively unifies various national origin groups (Dávila, 2012). Research on Spanish-language radio programming also reflects this unifying tendency; De Fina (2013) documents the use of the terms *la raza* and *nuestra comunidad* in addition to explicit self-identification as 'Latinxs' as linguistic strategies for the construction of pan-Latinx unity, together with a focus on news from Latin American countries or Latin American residents in the area of the broadcast. Strom (2015) notes additional symbolic meanings of the use of the first person plural pronoun (*nosotros* 'we'), arguing that it can index activism and can also be inclusive not only of Latinxs but also of non-Latinxs who want to stand up to discrimination.

Despite the portrayal of Latinxs as a homogenous group and the use of 'generic' Spanish, there is some linguistic variation represented in the Spanish-language media in the US. This includes the local programming with regional variation that we mentioned above, as well as other cases of 'non-generic' accents in national programming. One particularly salient example is Andrés Cantor, the Univisión commentator famous to both English-speaking and Spanish-speaking audiences for his signature drawn-out bellowing of 'gooooooooool!' during World Cup soccer matches. Cantor reports never having played down his Argentine accent (García, 2018). Of course, it should be noted that within the ideological hierarchies of national varieties of Spanish, Argentinean accents are often judged more favorably than varieties associated with racialized groups (Alfaraz, 2002, 2014; Valdés *et al.*, 2003) (see Chapter 10). Further, recent research has found that Spanish networks such as Univisión have begun to show more linguistic variation, including Spanish-Caribbean accents as well as English and Spanish–English bilingual programming (Avilés-Santiago & Báez, 2019; Beltran, 2016; Piñón & Rojas, 2011). Avilés-Santiago and Báez (2019) see this as a strategy to target *billennials* (i.e. bicultural and bilingual millennials) with linguistically more varied and inclusive presentations of

Latinidad. Still, the inclusion of linguistic variation and translanguaging challenges the idea that linguistic homogeneity and a 'neutral' standard variety are the basis for defining Latinx culture and identity. Instead, it brings into focus not only linguistic variation, but also the diversity of Latinx cultures, backgrounds and experiences.

The increase in advertising and material created for a bilingual, bicultural Latinx population (Baez & Avilés-Santiago, 2016; Chávez, 2015) reflects the growing percentage of Latinxs who are English-dominant and who prefer English-language programming (Lopez & Gonzales-Barrera, 2013), together with advertisers' attempts to capture this growing market. For example, see the discussion of Target's bilingual advertisements at https://thinknowresearch.com/blog/targets-bilingual-ads-are-on-target/. In fact, some Spanish-language advertising campaigns, such as the Target ads mentioned above, geared specifically to the US market include a mix of English and Spanish and sometimes also make explicit reference to language mixing, as a way to speak – and sell – to bilingual Latinxs.

A related trend is the production of two versions of an advertisement targeted toward Latinxs, one in English and one in Spanish. Sometimes these ads are completely in one language or the other, while at other times both versions include the two languages, although to differing degrees. One example of this is a pair of 2015 Honda ads staring Latinx comedian Felipe Esparza and a young Latinx couple (both versions are available at https://www.ispot.tv/topic/comedian/LQC/felipe-esparza). The ads begin with Esparza describing young Latinxs as 'so versatile,' like the Honda Fit, a car model marketed to younger consumers. According to Sebreros (2014, cited in Betti, 2015), bicultural Latinxs 'seek out brands that treat them as unique, not as stereotypes,' and this ad seems to do that by making fun of clichés about both Latinxs and millennials. For example, Esparza expresses surprise that the couple are on their way to the movies rather than a party, and that they value the spacious trunk for transporting groceries, rather than fixie bicycles. Later, the professionally dressed Latina leaves for work and Esparza comments 'always defying expectations,' presumably in reference both to young Latinxs and to the Honda Fit. Both ads include the tag line '*Un buen Fit*' (literally, 'a good Fit') as well as the English word 'party.' While one ad is almost all in Spanish and the other mostly in English, both versions use Spanish–English bilingualism to index Latinx identity, while the existence of two versions also reflects awareness that not all Latinxs use both languages to the same degree. The recognition of bilingualism, the inclusion of translanguaging and the parody of generalizations in these ads are a welcome challenge to normative monolingualism as well as stereotypes, although of course the primary motivation is to attract Latinxs as consumers.

While language purists may object to this linguistic hybridity or see it as contributing to the erosion of Spanish among US Latinxs, others view it as a reflection of varied cultural and linguistic practices and part of the natural process of language change (Amaya, 2013). Further, bilingualism and translanguaging have become common strategies both for indexing and speaking to bicultural Latinxs, as well as a topic of interest to them. Indeed, there are numerous websites and YouTube channels (such as Flama, Mitú and Pero Like) oriented toward bilingual or English-dominant Latinxs where issues of Spanish proficiency and language mixing are frequently the focus of humorous videos.

The differences between monolingual Spanish-language programming and bilingual Spanish–English programming isn't just linguistic; the content of programming also varies according to the target audience. For example, Gonzalez Tosat (2017) finds that while the majority of Spanish-language radio stations have religious programs, those with bilingual programming tend to be less religious, illustrating that the Spanish and bilingual audiences are constructed as having some different values and practices. Betti's (2015) work on advertisements echoes this, describing the use of Spanish, English and Spanglish as targeted to people with different identities. In other words, the greater inclusion of bilingualism corresponds to a broader strategy designed to reach the growing market of bilingual consumers. Of course, broadcasters' and advertisers' choice of language(s) and content responds in part to the identities, practices and preferences of this growing audience, but it also plays a role in constructing that audience and shaping those identities, practices and preferences.

Spanish in Linguistic Landscapes

The term *linguistic landscape* refers to the use of language in the built environment, including signs, business names, window displays, advertisements and graffiti – in short, all public, visible use of language (Landry & Bourhis, 1997). Early work on linguistic landscape tended to see the use of particular language as a reflection of **ethnolinguistic vitality**, but more recently researchers have stressed that linguistic landscapes do not necessarily reflect actual language use in the community; instead they are influenced by the social status and perceived value of particular ways of using language (Ben-Rafael *et al.*, 2010; Gorter, 2013; Helôt *et al.*, 2012; Leeman & Modan, 2010; Stroud & Mpendukana, 2009). Further, linguistic landscapes, like other representations of language, including the language use in television, film and newspapers we have discussed in this chapter, rely on and reproduce ideologies about language(s) and their speakers.

In some cases, the use of a minority language is targeted at speakers of that language, as shown in Berry's (2004) study of Latinx-owned businesses in Reno. In this case, the customers were all Spanish-speaking and Spanish was deemed the best language to attract their business. So too, Hepford (2017) discusses the language policies and packaging and signing practices of Lowe's Home Improvement Store, noting that the use of Spanish is explicitly a means to target the growing population of Latinx homeowners. However, as Leeman and Modan (2010: 191) argue, language is a 'readily identifiable index of ethnicity and cultural authenticity' and it is often commodified as such. Thus, businesses sometimes employ minority languages to make a place seem more 'authentic' or 'exotic' in order to attract customers who are not speakers of that language. Further, in their research on Washington, DC's Chinatown, Leeman and Modan found that Chinese writing was often used more as a decorative element for branding the neighborhood than for linguistic communication. They stress that languages in the built environment can have multiple symbolic meanings and they also play a role in constructing public space in particular ways.

Research by Fuller (2016) on the use of Spanish in Chicago has shown that although Spanish is clearly used to target Spanish-speaking buyers, the goods and services that it is used to sell also construct a particular image of Spanish-speakers. Food is the most common product advertised with Spanish, and Spanish serves to both target Spanish-speakers and construct the product as authentic. However, other services offered in Spanish indicate the kind of needs some members of a Spanish-speaking community might have: the signs with translation into Spanish offered immigration lawyers, check cashing, government-subsidized daycare programs and jobs as dishwashers. All of these serve to construct the Spanish-speaking community as a population of poor immigrants. In some cases this is made explicit – such as the radio station that says its programming is '*Mexicano como tú*' ('Mexican like you') and the bank that says it accepts identification cards '*de tu país*' ('from your country') – and clearly that country is not the US.

The visibility of Spanish, and thus of the Latinx population, in these linguistic landscapes is sometimes perceived as a threat by non-Spanish speakers, as was argued in a study done in a Pittsburgh neighborhood (Mitchell *et al.*, 2010). These findings show that although only 5% of the population was Latinx, there was nonetheless newspaper coverage about the fear of the growing Latinx population. On the other hand, the absence of Spanish signage can imply disregard for Spanish-speakers and trigger negative emotions; Martínez (2014) found that the Spanish-speaking youth in Hidalgo County, Texas, expressed disapproval about the English dominance in signs in healthcare facilities, and they interpreted this as an indication that they were not as appreciated as English-speakers. Other work on Spanish in the linguistic landscape in the US notes that the use of English on signs in bilingual San Antonio reinforces English hegemony (Hult, 2014); similarly, English in a historically Latinx neighborhood in Chicago has been shown to be connected to frames referencing 'hipster' identity, while Spanish indexed the family-oriented migrant background of the local Latinx population (Lyons & Rodríguez-Ordóñez, 2015).

While in some cases Spanish in the linguistic landscape frames Latinxs as impoverished immigrants, some bilingual signs position Spanish-speakers as belonging in US society and as members of the middle class. In Fuller's (2016) research in Chicago, signs aimed at a more middle-class and established population tend not to simply translate all information but to use Spanish more emblematically. The American Family Insurance Company proclaims that it offers discounts up to 65% in both English and Spanish, which includes Spanish-speakers as members of American families (see Figure 7.1). The furniture store Mi Casa Furniture gives most of the information about what they offer in English (living rooms, bedrooms, etc., layaway, credit), but also uses a Spanish slogan which is not translated, '*Reventando precios*' *...!* ('smashing prices ...!'). The name of the store, 'Mi Casa Furniture', although (partly) in Spanish, uses a phrase that many non-Spanish speakers know, as it is part of the clichéd phrase for hospitality often used by anglophone Americans, *mi casa es su casa* ('my home is your home').

Such uses of Spanish move away from practices that fix Spanish-speakers in the linguistic landscape as monolingual and foreign. Other such signs include bilingual puns (a t-shirt shop named *Es-tee-lo*, which references *estilo*, the Spanish word for 'style') but may also rely on stereotypes of Spanish-speakers. For example, the sexualized image

Figure 7.1 Sign in Little Village, Chicago: 'American Family Insurance'

of a Latina is referenced in the Puerto Rican restaurant named Ay! Mami which uses the slogan '*una cocina caliente*' ('a hot cuisine'), with *hot* having the same potentially sexual meaning as in English; see Figure 7.2). Thus, in many cases, such uses could be considered examples of Mock Spanish, a covert racializing discourse that reproduces stereotypes about Latinxs.

Spanish as part of the mainstream can be seen more clearly when we venture away from these local linguistic landscapes into national advertising campaigns. Spanish (and, alas, Mock Spanish) can be seen with increasing frequency. One example is of course Taco Bell, with its previous slogan of '*Yo quiero Taco Bell*' ('I love Taco Bell'), uttered by a Chihuahua,

Figure 7.2 Sign in Humboldt Park, Chicago: *'Ay! Mamai "Una cocina caliente"'*

and the more recent uses of *más* ('more') with various English verbs – 'Live más' (the Taco Bell foundation also offers a scholarship with this name) and a former slogan used to advertise job openings, 'Want más?' (followed by 'Experience Taco Bell. Apply today.'). There are differences of opinion regarding whether these slogans should be considered Mock Spanish, but it is uncontroversial to claim that the target audience for the ads for Taco Bell food, employment or scholarships, and for the Spanish contained in them, is not just Spanish-speakers or Latinxs, but the general population. Thus, these uses of Spanish should not be considered as an index of the ethnolinguistic vitality of Spanish, but rather as a way of indexing Latinidad and/or Mexicanidad for the sake of selling tacos. Further, we offer a cautionary note about interpreting the use of Spanish (and other minority languages) in the public sphere as an acceptance of multilingualism; depending on how Spanish is used, the line between multilingual playfulness and Mock Spanish is very thin. While not all instances of playful bilingualism are mockery (see Chapter 6), they also do not necessarily reflect a pluralist ideology. Crucially, we must also be aware that the use of a language in the linguistic landscape (and elsewhere) is not always a reflection of that language's vitality (Leeman & Modan, 2010) and can serve to reproduce particular ideologies.

Conclusions and Connections

Media representations of Spanish and Spanish-speakers play a part in the reproduction of stereotypes and the positioning of Spanish as the language of the poor, criminal and foreign. Unsurprisingly, the hegemonic language ideologies we discussed in Chapter 4 are also often reproduced in the media, with negative attitudes about non-standard varieties and language mixing being particular common. However, as more Latinxs are involved in media production, we see more nuanced depictions of the Latinx experience and more pluralist language ideologies. We also see Spanish as increasingly not only an index of Latinidad, but also becoming part of the mainstream media. As discussed in the last chapter on identities, this sometimes involves mockery and appropriation.

However, Spanish-language media are also an important resource in the maintenance of Spanish in the US, and its history, as discussed in Chapter 3, has contributed to its unique position in the US linguistic landscape; it is both a means to reach target consumers who speak Spanish and an emblematic resource for bilinguals and even those who know little more than *adiós* and *nada*.

As we will see in the coming chapters, the role of Spanish in society and the underlying ideologies – the development of which is strongly influenced by the media – is part of the context in which language and educational policies are developed (as discussed in Chapters 8 and 9, respectively) and multilingual practices emerge (as will be discussed in Chapter 10). We invite you to keep in mind, as you continue reading, how depictions in the traditional media such as film and television, as well as contemporary virtual communities and communication, are part of speaking Spanish in the US.

Discussion Questions and Activities for Chapter 7

(1) Are there recent movies or television shows you have seen that depict Latinxs? How is language used in these shows? Discuss the use of Spanish, standard English and 'accented' English and the identities of the characters.

(2) Analyze the linguistic landscape of a particular area or building. What languages other than English appear in the built environment and how are they used? Among other issues, consider: (a) the formal aspects of language, including spelling, regional features and translanguaging; (b) who the non-English languages are directed toward (i.e. speakers of that language or English-speakers); (c) any differences in the information available in the different languages; and (d) the symbolic and ideological meaning or ideological impact of the linguistic landscape you have analyzed.

(3) How much of your media consumption is in the more traditional venues of TV and film, and how much is on new media platforms such as Instagram, Twitter, etc.? Do you note differences in representation, as discussed by Alford (2018; see https://www.nytimes.com/2018/07/28/opinion/sunday/race-black-latina-identity.html)?

(4) What is the difference between use of a language and appropriation of it? How would you characterize Taco Bell's use of Spanish words in the advertisements discussed in this chapter (or others you find online)? What does such usage index? Would you classify it as Mock Spanish? Why or why not?

(5) Watch the ad for Toyota Camry Hybrid that aired during the 2006 Super Bowl (see https://adage.com/videos/toyota-hybrid/617) in which a father and son speak to each other in a mix of English and Spanish. How does this ad represent their language use and its relationship to identities? How does it portray English and Spanish? In addition to the topics discussed in this chapter, you may wish to refer to the chapters on identities and ideologies.

Further Reading and Resources

Casillas, D.I. (2014) *Sounds of Belonging: US Spanish-language Radio and Public Advocacy*. New York: New York University Press.

Cepeda, M.E. (ed.) (2016) *The Routledge Companion to Latina/o Media*. New York: Routledge.

Dávila, A. (2012) *Latinos, Inc.: The Marketing and Making of a People*. Berkeley, CA: University of California Press.

Dávila, A. and Rivero, Y.M. (eds) (2014) *Contemporary Latina/o Media: Production, Circulation, Politics*. New York: New York University Press.

Dixon, T.L. (2017) Good guys are still always in white? Positive change and continued misrepresentation of race and crime on local television news. *Communication Research* 44 (6), 775–792.

Salzman, R. (2014) News or noticias: A social identity approach to understanding Latinos' preferred language for news consumption in the United States. *Mass Communication and Society* 17 (1), 54–73.

Vidal-Ortiz, S. (2016) Sofía Vergara: On media representations of Latinidad. In J.A. Smith and B.K. Thakore (eds) *Race and Contention in Twenty-first Century US Media* (pp. 93–107). New York: Routledge.

Chapter 8

Language Policy and Spanish in the US

Objectives

To provide an understanding of language planning and policy, the specifics of historical and current language policies in the US and Puerto Rico, and the ways in which language policies interact with language ideologies.

Introduction

In Chapter 4, we introduced the language ideologies framework and explained some of the ways in which language ideologies are expressed and reproduced in discourse and social practices. In this chapter we focus on one of the key manifestations of language ideologies: language policy. We begin by defining **language planning and policy** (LPP) as well as presenting the main types of LPP. From there, we move on to a consideration of Ruíz's 'orientations' framework, and the ways in which language ideologies are embodied in language policies. After providing these conceptual tools with which to analyze language policy, we focus on language policy in the US, beginning with a historical overview and then examining primary aspects of policy including language-in-education, language rights, language-based discrimination and Official English. Finally, we discuss language policy in Puerto Rico. Throughout the chapter, we stress the interaction of language policies with other kinds of social and political concerns.

Language Planning and Policy

Let us begin by saying that although some scholars distinguish between *language planning* and *language policy*, others see them as roughly synonymous (e.g. García, 2015). Schiffman (1996) offers one of the simplest and most straightforward definitions of *language policy*: 'decision-making about language,' while Cooper (1989: 45) defines *language planning* as an attempt to manage other people's language behavior: 'Language planning refers to deliberate efforts to influence the behavior of others with respect to the acquisition, structure, or functional allocation of their language codes.' In addition, some scholars combine the two terms as *language planning and policy* (e.g. Ricento & Hornberger, 1996). For the sake of convenience, in this book we do not distinguish between the three terms. Because there are myriad ways to influence people's language use, LPP encompasses a vast array of public and private efforts.

Early LPP research focused primarily on the overt policies of national governments regarding linguistic diversity or newly recognized languages in postcolonial societies. These include the development of standard varieties and spelling conventions, as well as decisions about the official status of different languages, language use in schools and the language rights available to speakers of non-official languages, among other issues. Subsequent LPP scholarship has stressed that policies include implicit, covert or tacit rules that influence language use as well as official laws and explicit regulations (Schiffmann, 1996; Shohamy, 2006; Wiley & García, 2016). There are also language policies that operate on a smaller scale, such as in a specific workplace or school (Ricento & Hornberger, 1996; Shohamy, 2006), and recent research has examined language policies within households and families (King *et al.*, 2008).

Language policies reflect particular language ideologies. For example, a policy that makes one language the official language of a country embodies the **one nation-one language** ideology, ideas about the importance of that language, and notions about national identity and belonging. Further, such policies don't just reflect language ideologies, they officialize and disseminate them. Thus, LPP plays a role in reproducing social and political hierarchies and power (Johnson & Ricento, 2013; Tollefson, 1991, 2006). As Tollefson puts it:

> language planning-policy means the institutionalization of language as a basis for distinctions among social groups (classes). That is, language policy is one mechanism for locating language within social structure so that language determines who has access to political power and economic resources. Language policy is one mechanism by which dominant groups establish hegemony in language use. (Tollefson, 1991: 16)

However, language policies can serve inclusionary as well as exclusionary goals, such as when institutions like government agencies provide services and materials in multiple languages (Leeman, 2018c). In addition, language ideologies can also limit the extent to which official policies are implemented (Hornberger, 2005; Hornberger & Johnson, 2007; Leeman, 2018c).

Types of language planning

Early work on language planning focused on two types of planning: *status planning* and *corpus planning* (Kloss, 1968). Status planning primarily involves assigning particular functions and uses to particular languages. For example, are there any official languages in a given country or region? What language(s) will schools operate in? Do people have the right to interact with government agencies in their preferred language? In some cases, status planning is promotion-oriented and seeks to elevate the prestige of a language (such as in language revitalization efforts), while in other cases it is restriction- or repression-oriented and is designed to reduce or eliminate the use of disfavored languages (Wiley, 2004).

Corpus planning involves decisions about the formal properties of the language, such as through the development of spelling systems, the standardization of grammar and the creation of new vocabulary items. As we discussed in Chapter 4, Spain's government-funded language academy, the *Real Academia Española* (RAE), defines the standard in Spain, and it also plays a central role in establishing a 'pan-Hispanic' norm. The US does not have any official language academies. In the case of English, status planning is carried out unofficially through decentralized methods such as dictionaries, grammar books and style guides, as well as education and mass media. In the case of Spanish, the *Academia Norteamericana de la Lengua Española* (ANLE), which defines its mission in part as the establishment of norms or standards for Spanish in the US, is a non-profit institution without any US government support or status. As a member of the international *Asociación de Academias de la Lengua Española*, it collaborates with other Spanish language academies around the world.

While the field of LPP has traditionally framed status planning as the determination of the functions and prestige of languages and language varieties, corpus planning can also play a role. Specifically, because the codification of a standard variety implies that other varieties are non-standard or incorrect, it shapes attitudes toward different varieties including which ones are considered acceptable for various societal functions and uses. In this regard, the ANLE has shown itself to be hostile to words and language practices (such as **codeswitching** or **translanguaging**) that exhibit any influence from English. The ANLE goes as far as to link Spanglish to 'alingualism, ghetto status, and marginalization' and to call it 'damaging to its speakers' (Zentella, 2017a: 31). In so doing, the ANLE's standardization efforts relegate US varieties of Spanish and their speakers to subordinate status.

In addition to corpus and status planning, a third type of language planning typically discussed in the literature is *acquisition planning*, which consists of decisions about which language(s) people will learn, as well as where and how they will learn them (Wiley & García, 2016). The primary focus of acquisition planning is educational policy regarding the language(s) used as the **medium of instruction** (i.e. in which languages are classes taught), which additional languages (if any) will be taught, and whether language study is optional or required. In the US case, acquisition planning encompasses policies regarding how to teach English to people who don't speak it, whether to offer bilingual education, and whether students should be taught 'foreign' languages and, if so, which ones and when (see Chapter 9). Acquisition planning can also include offering language courses for adults, such as immigrants who want to learn English. Acquisition planning is intertwined with, and dependent on, corpus and status planning, as the planned status of a language has implications for educational policy, and decisions about the language standards impact which varieties are taught in schools.

In recent years there has been a growing interest in **family language policy**, which centers on decisions (typically by parents or other caretakers, but also by children) about which language(s) will be used in the household. This relatively new area of research incorporates insights from the study of language acquisition, language socialization and language policy, while also contributing to these fields (King *et al.*, 2008). Examinations of family language policy, and the correlation of different policies with different linguistic outcomes, can help shed light on **ethnolinguistic vitality** and broader patterns of language maintenance and/or shift (see Chapter 2). Research on family language policy has shown particular interest in the interaction of societal and familial language ideologies, as well as their impact on household language use. For example, if parents take up societal ideologies that frame Spanish maintenance as interfering with English acquisition or assimilation to a new cultural identity, or that portray English as the key to success, they may be less likely to speak Spanish to their children (Schwartz, 2010). Although it is common to think of parents and caretakers as the ones who set the rules regarding household language use, children also play a role in shaping family language policy, such as by refusing to speak Spanish, which may lead adults to switch to English (Ager, 2001). Although family language policy can reflect dominant ideologies, it can also be a means to resist the societal subordination of Spanish, such as when parents make active efforts to transmit Spanish to their children, provide literacy training in Spanish or encourage children to speak Spanish in the home (Schecter & Bayley, 2002; Schwartz, 2010; Velázquez, 2014, 2018). Researchers have also examined the relationship of family language policy to multilingual families' use of linguistic resources in the construction and negotiation of familial identities (King, 2016).

Orientations to Language in Planning and Policy

One of the most influential analytical tools in the field of LPP is Ruíz's (1984) concept of 'orientation' to language. Ruíz defined an orientation as 'a complex of dispositions toward language and its role, and toward languages and their role in society' (Ruíz , 1984: 16). He argued that orientations 'delimit the ways we talk about language and language issues, they determine the basic questions we ask, the conclusions we draw from the data, and even the data themselves' (Ruíz , 1984: 16). Clearly then, orientations to language constrain what is 'thinkable about language and society' (Ruíz, 1984: 16), and they are similar to language ideologies and discourses. Ruíz was most interested in exploring how societal attitudes, values and orientations shape LPP, which is why we present his work here rather than in the chapter on ideologies.

Ruíz's primary scholarly focus was language-in-education policy for minority language children. More than just developing a theoretical model, he wanted to draw attention to – and challenge – negative conceptions of individual and societal multilingualism, as well as to offer a better alternative (Hult & Hornberger, 2016). In other words. Ruiz's critical analysis of LPP was part of his commitment to social justice. Although he also gave examples of other orientations toward language, Ruíz's primary focus was on the three orientations that he thought most relevant for the US case: language-as-problem, language-as-right and language-as-resource.

Language as problem

As Ruíz explains, early work in LPP largely framed language issues as 'problems' that could be solved by policy or 'treatment' (Ruíz, 1984: 10). For example, Ruiz's analysis of policy documents and newspaper reporting in the US shows how minority languages were often represented as roughly akin to poverty and substandard housing. The language-as-problem orientation was not just discursive but was also reflected in US language-in-education policy. Specifically, federal support for bilingual education was first provided only for children living in poverty, and even after the scope was broadened, it was designed to transition children to English, thus solving the 'problem' of their home language by gradually eliminating it from schools and perhaps beyond.

Language as right

Ruíz's second orientation conceptualizes language within a legal framework that encompasses the right not to be discriminated against based on language (known as **negative language rights**), as well as the right to use one's language (called **affirmative language rights**). Language rights are constructed differently in different policy frameworks, but they are typically linked to broader protections of minority or **minoritized** groups, such as the right to participate in representational democracy, to obtain education and/or to maintain and develop one's cultural identity. Official recognition of minority rights (including language rights) by national governments as well as international institutions such as the United Nations has proliferated since the mid-20th century.

Within the international human rights legal framework, language is often framed as necessary for the maintenance and development of cultural identity, and thus the protection of minority groups' rights is seen as requiring the protection of minority languages (Gilman, 2011; Skutnabb-Kangas, 2013). More than just protection, according to Gilman (2011: 12), language rights are intended to 'guarantee diversity and promotion of multiple cultural identities in a society.' This framework is exemplified in the following two excerpts from the UN Declaration on the Rights of Persons Belonging to National or Ethnic, Religious and Linguistic Minorities (https://www.ohchr.org/en/professionalinterest/pages/minorities.aspx), which was adopted by the UN General Assembly in 1992:

> **Article 1**
> States shall protect the existence and the national or ethnic, cultural, religious and linguistic identity of minorities within their respective territories, and shall encourage conditions for the promotion of that identity. [...]

> **Article 2**
> 1. Persons belonging to national or ethnic, religious and linguistic minorities [...] have the right to enjoy their own culture, to profess and practice their own religion, and to use their own language, in private and in public, freely and without interference or any form of discrimination. [...]

According to the UN, countries shouldn't just protect minority languages and identities; they should 'encourage the conditions' for them to flourish. In other words, it's not enough to allow speakers of minority or minoritized languages to use those languages without being discriminated against; instead governments should facilitate language maintenance, intergenerational transmission and/or revitalization. As we will discuss in more detail below, language rights in the US are far more limited than how they are envisioned in the UN declaration.

For Ruíz (1984), one problem with the language-as-right orientation is that it relies on and promotes legalistic discourse, which in his view is unlikely to lead to support for minority languages among majority language groups. Further, according to Ruíz, the language-as-right orientation is inherently adversarial because, he argues, a claim to something for one group always means a claim against another group. For these reasons, Ruíz's original work expressed skepticism that the language-as-right orientation could result in public support for minority languages. While we agree that a regime of language rights does not always rest on or lead to widespread support for linguistic pluralism or minority languages (see Leeman, 2018c), we reject the premise that gains for one group necessarily mean a loss for another group. In fact, that sounds a little like the zero-sum ideology we discussed in Chapter 4. Nonetheless, Ruíz clearly believed that support for minority languages was in everyone's best interest, as do we.

Language as resource

In order to garner public support for educational policies fostering minority languages, Ruíz championed what he called a 'language-as-resource' orientation, which envisions languages as valuable not just for their speakers but for society as a whole. In this regard, Ruíz mentions the importance of languages for international diplomacy, national security and commercial concerns and laments the destruction of the nation's existing language resources as well as the poor job the US does of teaching additional languages to English monolinguals. In his proposed language-as-resource orientation, languages would be seen as a something to be managed, conserved and developed, akin to natural resources, rather than simply tolerated.

Some scholars have critiqued the language-as-resource orientation as favoring market-based and national security-focused approaches to languages that benefit the state, rather than minority language speakers themselves (Petrovic, 2005; Ricento, 2005). These critiques argue that such an approach might lead to short-term policy improvements promoting specific **commodified** languages but would not challenge the broader societal ideology of **normative monolingualism**. Recognizing this concern, Ruíz (2010) called for a broader (non-economic) understanding of the instrumental value of languages which would foster appreciation of multilingualism in schools, the media and throughout society. Ruíz saw the language-as-resource orientation as the most promising for a multilingual, pluralist language policy regime.

Ruíz's research on orientations toward language provide a useful way for thinking about the ways in which language ideologies undergird and constrain language policy, and thus it's worth keeping them in mind as you read about language policy in the US, which is the focus of the remainder of this chapter. We now look at the history of language policy in the US, a topic we touched on in Chapter 3.

Historical Perspectives on Language Policy in the US

As we saw in Chapter 4, dominant language ideologies portray the US as if it were currently, and always had been, an English-speaking country. This portrayal not only misrepresents the current situation, but it also **erases** the linguistic diversity and multilingualism that have been present throughout US history. In fact, this multilingual history begins long before the formation of the US; at least 375 distinct, mutually unintelligible languages were spoken in what is now the continental US before the arrival of Europeans (Mithun, 2001; Taylor, 2002).

Beginning in the 16th century, as colonizers and settlers arrived from Spain, England, France, Portugal, Russia and the Netherlands, they added various European languages to the mix. So too, the enslaved peoples brought from Africa were linguistically as well as culturally diverse. Of the 12 million Africans enslaved in the Americas, 2–3 million were Muslim, some small percentage of whom were literate in Arabic, even when this was not their primary language (Lepore, 2002; Wiley, 2010). Of course, other European languages were the primary languages of government and public life in the territories that would later be incorporated into the US; Spanish was the **hegemonic** language of Florida, the Southwest, Louisiana (which was under Spanish rule from 1763 to 1803) and Puerto Rico (see Chapter 3).

During the British colonial period there was a great deal of linguistic tolerance and a laissez-faire policy toward European languages (Wiley & García, 2016). Thus, schools operated in the languages of the local community, including French, German and Spanish (see Chapter 9), and newspapers and religious services were available in a panoply of languages (Schmid, 2001). Government documents were often available in multiple languages (King & Ennser-Kananen, 2013) and even the First Continental Congress, which met for the first time in 1774 to discuss responses to unpopular British policies, published some of their materials in French and German (Crawford, 1990).

The presence, and acceptance, of European languages continued long after independence. German was particularly well represented, especially but not only in Pennsylvania, and it was used in churches, schools and many areas of government into the 20th century. Many states required that certain legislative sessions and notices be translated into various European languages. Nonetheless, this tolerance of linguistic diversity was not officialized in the US Constitution, nor was there was explicit recognition of language rights anywhere else in federal policy. Although courts have interpreted the First Amendment to the Constitution, which establishes freedom of speech, as protecting language choice, this is not mentioned explicitly in the text itself. As we will discuss later in this chapter, courts have also interpreted other Constitutional amendments as conferring certain linguistic rights.

The lack of explicit language rights reflects a lack of salience of language as a marker of social difference in the period following US independence, when race and social class were far more important categories (Leeman, 2004). And as we noted in Chapter 4, English was not yet a defining element of national identity. Even Noah Webster (of *Webster's Dictionary* fame), who sought to promote nationalism and unity following US independence via the establishment of an American language academy and a new US orthography distinct from British spelling conventions, was more interested in eliminating variation within English than in restricting other languages (Lepore, 2002). In any case, Webster was unsuccessful in his efforts and no language academy was established. Nor was an official language declared. However, it may be that since English was the de facto national language, making it official did not seem necessary (Wiley & Wright, 2004). To this day, the US does not have an official language at the federal level.

In contrast to the tolerance of European languages, colonial laws and practices restricted African and Native languages, and used this language restriction as a tool of subordination. It was common practice to mix enslaved Africans of different language backgrounds so that they could not communicate with each other, and enslaved people were forbidden from speaking their native languages or teaching them to their children (García, 2009; Wiley, 1998). Other language policies were made explicit in the **slave codes**, which in many Southern states made it illegal for enslaved people to learn to read or write in English (Wiley & García, 2016). These early language policies make it abundantly clear that language can be a tool of power and that language policies are often about social control rather than language per se: the repression of African languages and the restrictions on literacy were designed in part to make it harder for enslaved people to rebel (Wiley, 2014).

Language policies were also used as a way to subjugate Native peoples. Although literacy in Cherokee and other Native languages was promoted into the 19th century, the primary goal was to facilitate conversion to Christianity and promote the acquisition of English (Wiley, 1998). As Wiley (1998) explains, the ultimate motivation of this forced assimilation was the 'pacification' of Indigenous peoples. As White settlers encroached on more and more Native land, the policy of deculturation gave way to expulsion and forced migration; in 1830 President Andrew Jackson signed the Indian Removal Act, forcing the Cherokee, Chickasaw, Choctaw, Creek and Seminole peoples to give up their lands and relocate west of the Mississippi River.

Following the Civil War, the policy of coercive assimilation and Native language eradication was escalated. The US government established English-only boarding schools for Native American children, who were forcibly removed from their families and required to attend schools where they were severely punished if they spoke their first languages (García, 2009). Children of different language backgrounds were purposely mixed at the schools, in order to prevent language maintenance (Wiley, 1998; Wiley & García, 2016). The policy of sending Native children to off-reservation boarding schools remained the dominant model until the 1975 passage of the Indian Self-Determination and Education Assistance Act, which gave federally recognized tribes greater control over education.

As you likely recall from Chapter 3, at the end of the Mexican-American War in 1848 Mexico ceded 525,000 square miles of land to the US. On paper, the Treaty of Guadalupe Hidalgo granted US citizenship to the approximately 56,000 Mexican citizens living in the annexed territories unless they explicitly chose to refuse it, but in practice Indigenous peoples (such as the Pueblos) were excluded (Lozano, 2018). At the time, because only Whites were eligible to become naturalized citizens, the treaty's granting of citizenship to Mexicans (many of who were Mestizo) was subsequently interpreted by courts as meaning that they were officially White (Gross, 2008). However, despite this 'legal Whiteness,' in practice Mexicans and Mexican Americans were racialized as non-White and subjected to exclusion and segregation in many aspects of life including housing, schools and public facilities (Gómez, 2007). Hostility and racism toward Mexicans were sometimes expressed or carried out with reference to Spanish language, as they still are today.

Nonetheless, despite the subordination of Spanish-speakers and **treaty citizens** to **Anglos**, Spanish was a language of governance and education (Lozano, 2018). Lozano explains that this was largely a matter of convenience or necessity while the population was predominantly Spanish-speaking, rather than a matter of principle. There were also geographic differences in the treatment of Spanish and Spanish-speakers, which were tied in part to demographic differences. Specifically, areas where Spanish-speakers constituted a majority tended to offer more protections, whereas areas with a higher ratio of Anglos tended to offer only limited or temporary support. For example, in New Mexico, where the majority of the population was Spanish-speaking, Spanish was widely used by politicians and received greater legal protection than in other states (Lozano, 2018). So too, in California the 1849 constitution required that all state laws, regulations and decrees be printed in Spanish as well as English. Using the terminology of the ethnolinguistic vitality model we presented in Chapter 2, we might say that greater density was associated with greater institutional support. However, when the Gold Rush brought an influx of Anglos to California, transforming the state's demographics and making Spanish-speakers a minority, the revised 1879 constitution restricted official proceedings to English (Crawford, 1992). The new policy not only reflected demographic changes; by making knowledge of English a gatekeeping mechanism for full civic and economic participation, it conferred greater social status and political power on Anglos.

The period leading up to the turn of the 20th century brought a growing suspicion of, and hostility toward, all non-English languages and their speakers. This ideological shift came in response to an increase in overall immigration as well as in the proportion of immigrants from southern and eastern Europe compared to those from northern and western Europe who had made up a larger share of earlier immigrants (Bonfiglio, 2002; Wiley, 2000). Anti-immigration activists saw the newer immigrants as changing both the linguistic and the racial make-up of the country, and 'foreign languages' were often equated with 'foreign races' (Bonfiglio, 2002; Leeman, 2013). The intensifying racism of this period was not focused solely on immigrants; African Americans were a primary target, and Jim Crow laws expanded throughout the South. Readers likely know that Jim Crow consisted of laws and rules imposing racial segregation and discrimination on most aspects of public life. Everything from schools, public transportation and theaters to restaurants and drinking fountains were often designated as 'Whites only,' and when separate 'Colored' facilities were available, they were of inferior quality. In contrast, there is less public awareness that in the Southwest, Mexican Americans and Native Americans were also subjected to segregation and exclusion from facilities reserved for Whites. An example of this racist treatment is the sign the Lonestar Restaurant Association in Dallas distributed to its members to hang in their windows, which read 'NO DOGS, NEGROES, MEXICANS' (http://www.loc.gov/exhibits/civil-rights-act/segregation-era.html#obj024, accessed 1 October 2018).

With **nativism** and racism on the upswing, immigration from China and Japan was banned outright, and new restrictions were placed on immigration from Europe. In addition, new language policies put increased emphasis on English, both for immigrants and for the US-born. For example, the Naturalization Act of 1906 (signed into law by President Theodore Roosevelt, whose derogatory reference to the 'polyglot boarding house' you may remember from Chapter 4) for the first time made knowledge of English a requirement for immigrants who wanted to become US citizens. In 1917 an English language literacy requirement was also added. As **xenophobia** increased in the lead-up to World War I, widespread restrictions were enacted on the teaching of 'foreign' languages as well as on the mailing of newspapers and magazines in languages other than English (Wiley, 2000; Wiley & García, 2016). Some states went as far as to ban German language use in religious services, on the phone and in the street (Crawford, 1990). Just as 21st century language ideologies intertwine language, race and US national identity, early 20th century language policies were inseparable from anti-immigrant sentiment and anxiety about the ethnoracial make-up of the country (Leeman, 2013, 2018c).

Anti-immigrant and racist sentiment eventually led Congress to pass new immigration restrictions and national origin quotas in 1921 and 1924 which were explicitly designed to return the ethnic and racial make-up of the US population to how it had been in 1910. Although the quotas, and the exclusion of Asians, underwent some modifications in subsequent decades, they remained largely in place until the Immigration and Nationality Act of 1965. Mexicans were not included in the national origin quotas of the 1920s but they were nonetheless subjected to intense scrutiny and arbitrary exclusion at the border (Hernandez, 2017; Ngai, 2004). Further, as we discussed in Chapter 4, during the Great Depression and even as late as the 1950s, hundreds of thousands of Mexicans and Mexican Americans, more than half of whom were US citizens, were deported to Mexico (Balderrama & Rodriguez, 2006; Malavé & Giordani, 2015; Zayas, 2015).

In this climate of institutionalized racism, nativism and English-only sentiment, official uses of Spanish were restricted and protections for Spanish-speakers were eliminated. For example, the 1910 federal law establishing the process for Arizona and New Mexico to become states required that their new constitutions: (1) create a public school system taught exclusively in English; and (2) make knowledge of English a requirement for all state officials (Crawford, 1992; Lozano, 2018). It's important to remember that these language policies were not just about the languages that people should speak or about how new citizens should be assimilated. Instead, they were also about the distribution of political power within those states (Lozano, 2018). This was also the case when, after becoming a state in 1912, Arizona implemented English literacy requirements for voting; the new requirements disenfranchised monolingual Spanish-speakers even though the Treaty of Guadalupe had promised them full citizenship rights. In New Mexico the state constitution offered only temporary protections for Spanish, including a plan to hire bilingual teachers in order to help Spanish-speaking children to learn English, and a requirement that laws be printed in Spanish for 20 years.

English-only policies also became the norm in schools, as did the segregation of Mexican and Mexican American children on the basis of language or linguistic identity. By the 1930s, more than 85% of Mexican-origin children in the Southwest attended substandard segregated schools that were taught only in English (Lozano, 2018). School districts often used children's use of Spanish as a justification for segregation and assignment to inferior 'Mexican schools', saying that they couldn't keep up with English-medium schooling, but in reality many Mexican American children were English-dominant or even monolingual in English (San Miguel, 2001). Of course, knowledge of Spanish didn't mean that the children didn't also know English (see the discussion of the **zero-sum ideology** in Chapter 4), and this treatment is yet another example of the **racialization** of Spanish (see Chapter 5), as well as the use of language policy for social exclusion.

In this review of language policies from the colonial period through the mid-20th century, we hope to have provided some insights into the historical foundation of current ideologies and policies as well as to have shown how language policies are largely about non-linguistic issues and are inseparable from politics and power. Indeed, early language policies focused on the restriction and/or eradication of Native American and African languages as a mechanism of control and domination. In contrast, European languages were at first largely tolerated in US public life and in schools, with local governments providing some materials in multiple languages. However, around the turn of the 20th century, all non-English languages came under suspicion as indicators either of potential loyalty to foreign powers or of 'undesirable' ethnoracial identities. As a result, language policies became increasingly restrictive, as did immigration policies. Still, linguistic assimilation was a means by which European immigrants already in the country could Americanize and become part of the 'melting pot' – an option that was not available to Native Americans, Africans or Asians who were racialized as unassimilable Others (Leeman, 2004; Schmidt, 2002; Wiley, 2000). Nor were assimilation and incorporation options for the majority of people living in the Southwestern territories at the time of annexation, or for the subsequent immigrants who arrived from Mexico and Puerto Rico. Although there were some early protections for Spanish, these were limited and mostly temporary, and there a lack of services and education in Spanish. Language was only one aspect of subordination; Latinxs were also subjected to segregated and/or substandard housing and schools, as well as discrimination in employment and public accommodations.

Language and Civil Rights in the US

In the 1950s and 1960s, African Americans, Latinxs, Asian Americans and Native Americans organized to demand equal rights, equitable working conditions, better schools and an end to discrimination. Two groups founded in the 1960s were especially influential: the Young Lords and MEChA (*Movimiento Estudiantil Chicano de Aztlán* 'Chicano Student Movement of Aztlán'). The boycotts, walkouts, political organization and lawsuits of these Latinx activists resulted in significant legal and political achievements.

Two Supreme Court cases were crucial in ending school segregation: *Méndez v. Westminster* (1947) and *Brown v. Board of Education* (1954). In the first, *Méndez v. Westminster*, five Mexican American families challenged Orange County, California's policy of school segregation which, based on Spanish surnames and skin complexion, assigned some 5000 children to 'schools for Mexicans' (Macías, 2014). The Supreme Court found in favor of the families but did not go as far as to find segregation unconstitutional. Still, the ruling led California to prohibit school segregation within that state. A few years later, in the more well-known case of *Brown v. Board of Education*, the Supreme Court found that the exclusion of African American children from White schools was a violation of the Fourteenth Amendment, which guarantees equal protection to all citizens.

The Supreme Court rulings against segregated schools were then expanded upon in two key pieces of federal legislation. First, the Civil Rights Act (1964) outlawed discrimination based on race, color, religion, sex or national origin in voting and also prohibited racial segregation in schools, employment and public accommodations. Second, the Voting Rights Act (1965) contained multiple provisions designed to eliminate discrimination in voting, including the prohibition of literacy tests and other mechanisms used to disenfranchise racial minorities, as well as a requirement that districts with a history of discrimination get advance approval before making any changes to voting procedures.

These landmark civil rights laws have been tremendously important in the fight against racial discrimination. However, in the US, language rights are not recognized directly, nor are minority languages protected or promoted.[1] Indeed, just as the Constitution does not explicitly establish language rights, neither do the Civil Rights Act nor the Voting Rights Act explicitly prohibit discrimination based on language. Instead, to the extent that there are language rights in the US, they derive from other explicitly named rights. Specifically, the prohibition of national origin discrimination and the constitutional rights to equal protection, due process and a fair trial have been interpreted by the courts to confer some minority language rights, as we discuss in the following sections. Ideologies that link citizenship and national belonging, and hostility toward Latinxs and other ethnoracial minorities, have meant that such rights are frequent targets of attack and they are not always respected.

Language and national origin discrimination in schools

One focus of MEChA's activities was to increase Chicanx representation and inclusion at colleges, in part through the creation of ethnic studies programs. MEChA activism extended beyond the university, however, and students also worked with community activists for improvements in K-12 schools; as we saw earlier, many Latinx and Spanish-speaking children were routinely relegated to low-quality segregated schools. (Low-quality schools, as well as the racialization of Latinx children in educational policy and practice, are a continuing problem and the ongoing focus of protest and social justice advocacy, as we discuss in Chapter 9.)

As part of the push for better schools and more inclusive educational content and practices, together with a desire to value and maintain Spanish, many Latinx parents also called for bilingual education. This led to Congress passing the 1968 Bilingual Education Act, which made some competitive funding available for low-income districts to implement bilingual education programs for children aged three to nine. This was a far cry from ensuring that all minority language children received education in their home languages, both because school districts' participation was voluntary, and because only a tiny fraction of children were served. Further, as we mentioned earlier, Congress seemed to adopt a language-as-problem orientation in its linking of bilingualism to childhood poverty (Ruíz, 1984). Nonetheless, the Bilingual Education Act brought national attention to bilingual education and the need for educational support for minority language children.

In 1974, the Supreme Court case of *Lau v. Nichols* led to federal policy for the first time requiring school districts to provide educational support for children with limited English-speaking ability. Kinney Kinmon Lau was a monolingual Chinese-speaking boy who attended public school in San Francisco. The case centered on whether the school's English-only instruction constituted educational discrimination against Kinney and his Chinese-speaking classmates with limited knowledge of English. As we noted above, the *Brown* decision and the Civil Rights Act had prohibited educational discrimination and segregation, but it wasn't completely clear how far that prohibition went (Moran, 2009). There was no question that schools were not allowed to purposefully segregate or discriminate by race. But what about exclusionary educational practices that might not be intentionally discriminatory but that had the same effect? Was the educational neglect of minority language children also illegal? In the *Lau* case, the Supreme Court ruled that teaching exclusively in a language that the children didn't know, without any additional support or assistance, excluded them from participation and meaningful access to education (Moran, 2009). Because this exclusion was based on language, and language was linked to race, ethnicity or national origin, the Supreme Court ruled that San Francisco's treatment of Kinney and the other children constituted a violation of the Civil Rights Act.

We want to emphasize a few crucial points about the *Lau* ruling and its implications. First, the Supreme Court did *not* rule that schools had to provide education in students' home languages (although this was what many parents and children's advocates wanted). Instead, it only required schools to make some kind of accommodation for students who didn't speak English (Crawford, 2008; Moran, 2009). While the ruling set the stage for subsequent federal policy to increase funding and expand bilingual education throughout the country, the Supreme Court had not determined that education in children's home language was *required* by the Constitution or the Civil Rights act. This meant that Congress, states and local districts were free to eliminate bilingual education when the political winds shifted in the 1980s. And, in fact, this is pretty much what happened (see Chapter 9 for further discussion).

A second, related, point is that the *Lau* case only applied to children with limited English ability, rather than all children who spoke minority languages. As we will see, this is consistent with the overall US approach to language policy and rights. It is also the reason why the Census Bureau's language questions focus on English-speaking ability (Leeman, 2018c), as we discussed in Chapter 2. In contrast with the affirmative, promotion-oriented rights of the international human rights framework we presented earlier in the chapter, language policies in the US focus on helping people who don't speak English to gain access to education and other public services. Although this sometimes involves providing services in minority languages, the goal is not to encourage or promote the use and development of minority languages. Instead, providing some services in minority languages is a way of managing the 'problem' of not speaking English (Gilman, 2011; Leeman, 2018c). This is evident in the wording of the Equal Educational Opportunity Act 1974, which was passed in the wake of the *Lau* ruling.

> No state shall deny equal educational opportunities to an individual on account of his or her race, color, sex, or national origin by the failure of an educational agency to take appropriate action to overcome language barriers that impede equal participation by its students in its instructional programs. (Equal Educational Opportunity Act 1974, Sec. 204 [f])

As we discuss in Chapter 9, the vast majority of bilingual education programs implemented in the wake of *Lau* were designed to transition children to English-only education, rather than to promote first language maintenance, development or literacy.

A third aspect of the *Lau* ruling that is worth emphasizing is that it established a legal precedent recognizing language as a protected category when it is used as a proxy for ethnicity, race or national origin, which has had an important impact well beyond the context of education. In the *Lau* case, the Supreme Court ruled that the plaintiffs' lack of English proficiency was linked to their Chinese ancestry and thus that it was illegal to discriminate against them on this basis. As we will discuss below, this reasoning also established the legal precedent for the prohibition of accent-based discrimination. Even as recent years have seen a series of court decisions curtailing *Lau v. Nichols* (for example, by limiting the extent to which policies that negatively impact only certain groups are considered discriminatory even if there was no discriminatory intent), the recognition of language-based discrimination as a type of national origin discrimination remains intact (Moran, 2015).

Language and the Voting Rights Act

Although the Fourteenth and Fifteenth Amendments banned racial discrimination in voting, Southern states used poll taxes, English literacy tests, property-ownership requirements and other exclusionary mechanisms to discriminate against African Americans and keep them from exercising the right to vote. In addition to prohibiting these barriers, The Voting Rights Act (1965) sought to ensure that states and local governments with a history of racial discrimination didn't just come up with new ways to disenfranchise minority voters. For this reason, it also required districts with a documented history of electoral discrimination to get pre-approval before making any changes to electoral procedures.[2]

The 1965 version of the Voting Rights Act focused only on racial minorities, but after courts found discriminatory practices against Puerto Ricans living in Northeastern states, in 1974 Congress added protections for 'language minorities' (Culliton-Gonzalez, 2008). As part of this expansion, districts with (1) a sufficient proportion of historically discriminated-against language minorities (at least 5%) and (2) literacy rates below the national average were required to provide voting materials in those languages. Interestingly, there wasn't any reference to limited English-speaking ability, meaning that counts of language minorities also included bilinguals. In any case, by adding these provisions Congress recognized not only that language could serve as a proxy for ethnoracial identity, but also that linguistic discrimination was a means by which ethnoracial discrimination could be enacted. In other words, it officially recognized that language was sometimes used as a gatekeeping mechanism for exercising one's rights, and as a tool with which to exclude some groups from power.

In 1982 the reauthorization of the Voting Rights Act brought it more in line with the rest of federal language policy by focusing on people who were 'unable to speak or understand English adequately enough to participate in the electoral process,' rather than all minority language speakers. In this way, the Voting Rights Act offers no specific protections or language rights to English-proficient (i.e. bilingual) minority-language speakers. On the contrary, it focuses on overcoming language barriers or 'compensating' for individuals' linguistic deficiency in English (Gilman, 2011; Leeman, 2018c; Skutnabb-Kangas, 2013). Of course, if a district is required to produce materials in Spanish (or another language), anyone is allowed to use them.

The provision of voter registration and voting materials in Spanish is especially salient for Puerto Ricans who, as American citizens, have the right to move anywhere in the country and to participate in elections wherever they live. In 2018, civil rights organizations sued the state of Florida, where tens of thousands of Puerto Ricans settled after being displaced by Hurricane María, for failing to provide voter services in Spanish (Hernández, 2018). After a judge ordered 32 Florida counties to provide Spanish-language ballots, in 2019 the governor issued regulations that would require them state-wide, beginning in 2020 (Kam, 2019).

Language access and Executive Order 13166

As a result of an uptick in immigration in the 1980s and 1990s, the share of the population with limited English proficiency also went up. This also brought a growing awareness of language barriers that impede access to public services well beyond education and voting. Not being able to communicate with government agencies isn't simply an inconvenience; it can have serious, life-altering and even life-threatening consequences. Think, for example, of dialing 911 in an emergency and the operator not understanding what you are saying; imagine attending a parent–teacher conference and the school personnel being unable to tell you how your child is doing in school; and consider what it would be like to go the hospital and have the doctor be unable to understand what you say or explain your medical instructions.

In order to reduce some of these language barriers, President Clinton issued Executive Order 13166, 'Improving Access to Services for Persons with Limited English Proficiency.' Signed in the year 2000, EO 13166 requires all federal agencies and programs to take 'reasonable steps' to ensure 'meaningful access' by Limited English Proficient (LEP) persons. Like the policies described above, EO 13166 is rooted in the Constitution's and the Civil Rights Acts' protections against discrimination based on race, ethnicity and national origin. And like these other policies, it focuses on providing access for LEP individuals, rather than on promoting the use of minority languages or even on allowing bilinguals to interact with the government in their preferred language.

EO 13166 is an important element of federal language policy because it requires all federally funded programs to make plans for language access. Nonetheless, it doesn't actually require that services for all LEP individuals be provided – only that 'reasonable efforts' be made. Thus, while EO 13166 has definitely had a positive impact, the availability of minority language materials varies greatly, depending to some extent on the willingness of the agencies and service providers in question. To give just one highly visible example, the Obama administration maintained a Spanish-language version of the White House website (the archived version is available at https://obamawhitehouse.archives.gov/espanol), but the Trump administration removed it shortly after taking office in January 2017. Still, other federal agencies such as the Social Security Administration continue to offer Spanish language sites (https://www.ssa.gov/espanol/).

It is not only in such highly visible and symbolic contexts (like the White House website) where language access services can be limited by the attitudes or ideologies of the service provider. In his research in a hospital near the US-Mexico border, Martínez (2008, 2009) interviewed patients and healthcare providers about Spanish language interpretation and services. Martínez found that many healthcare providers believed that everyone in the US had a moral obligation to learn English, and this made them less likely to prioritize language access for Spanish-speaking patients or comply with federal guidelines. Further, there were few Spanish-speaking doctors, and interpreting was often done in an ad hoc way, such as by receptionists rather than trained interpreters or healthcare professionals. Patients also reported being treated with a lack of respect or being required to repeatedly request Spanish-language information. The impact of such neglect significantly impacts quality of care and patient outcomes and can be catastrophic (Martínez, 2010). Indeed, the literature on language barriers in healthcare provides numerous heart-wrenching accounts of how a lack of interpreters led to miscommunication between patients and doctors and ultimately resulted in patient death (Flores, 2006).

In 2010 the Affordable Care Act (colloquially known as *Obamacare*) strengthened the regulations requiring the provision of interpreting services in federally funded and federally facilitated health-related services. The guidelines stipulate that interpreters must be 'qualified,' but in practice this is not always the case, and there is no requirement that medical interpreters be licensed or certified (Jacobs *et al.*, 2018). Serious medical errors are more common with unqualified or ad hoc interpreters – such as children, friends or random strangers – than when professional interpreters are used (Flores *et al.*, 2012). Having children do the interpreting introduces more risk because it is unlikely that they are familiar with medical terminology in two languages (or even one).

In addition to considering the risks for patients, we must not lose sight of the implications for the child interpreters themselves, for whom it can be traumatic to be involved in such impactful medical discussions. Even outside of medical contexts, children who serve as language brokers must navigate various linguistic and social borders, including child/adult and English/Spanish but also client/provider and in some cases citizen/non-citizen and insider/outsider (Orellana, 2009; Reynolds & Orellana, 2009). Children are put in the position of speaking for powerful institutions while simultaneously representing their families to those institutions, a high-stakes anxiety-producing task, and they are subjected to evaluations from both sides (Reynolds & Orellana, 2009). It should be noted that, in doing so, they often develop an impressive range of linguistic and sociolinguistic resources and strategies (Orellana, 2009).

As mentioned above, EO 13166 requires federal agencies and federally funded programs to make a reasonable effort to provide language access. It does not apply to other kinds of governments, such as states or cities. However, there are also language access policies that have been implemented at those levels. For example, the states of Florida, Maryland and Massachusetts, among others, have policies requiring that at least some translations and minority language services be provided. Cities with comprehensive language access policies include New York, Oakland (California), San Francisco and Washington, DC, which require many or most city agencies to provide translations or interpreters (for more information on DC's language access program see https://ohr.dc.gov/page/LAportal/public). Language access is an example of inclusionary language policy, designed to facilitate equal opportunity and protection.

The right to an interpreter in court

Another context in which federal policy offers some language rights is in the court system. In addition to the Fourteenth Amendment and Civil Rights Act protections against racial, ethnic and national origin discrimination, the Fifth and Sixth Amendments also provide a legal argument for language rights for LEP individuals. This is because the rights of criminal defendants to due process, a fair trial, effective counsel and the opportunity to confront witnesses are largely meaningless if the proceedings are all carried out in a language that the defendant doesn't understand. However, the Supreme Court has not specifically recognized minority language speakers' general right to an interpreter, but instead leaves the appointment of an interpreter to the discretion of the court (Dasevich, 2012). Thus, regardless of whether it is the defendant that requests an interpreter or there is another reason to think that the defendant might not be able to understand the proceedings, it is up to the judge in the case to decide whether or not to appoint one. Further, there is no standard measure of English ability and no requirement for a professional linguistic evaluation. Speaking a language well enough for everyday activities and having the linguistic proficiency to participate in court proceedings are very different things, and people who can get by in English may struggle to understand what's going on in court. Nonetheless, they don't have the right to an interpreter if the judge feels that their English is good enough. Here too, US language policy focuses on minority language services as a means to overcome the 'deficiency' of being LEP, rather than to allow citizens to interact with the legal system in their preferred language (Gilman, 2011; Haviland, 2003; Leeman, 2018c). Another concern is that in most court systems, court-appointed interpreters are provided only during in-court proceedings, but not pre-trial meetings or other contexts, leaving LEP defendants to rely on 'inadequate substitutes' such as random bystanders, police employees and co-defendants (Rahel, 2014).

Language-based discrimination

In the previous sections we saw that in the US there are some limited rights to use Spanish (and other minority languages) when voting, interacting with the government, defending oneself in court or interacting with federally supported programs. But what about the right not to be discriminated against based on language? For example, is it legal to refuse to hire Spanish-speakers? What about people who speak English with an accent? Can employers implement English-only policies at work? Even without explicit constitutional protections or legislation forbidding it, discrimination based on language characteristics such as accent or language variety is generally illegal, since language can be a proxy of race, ethnicity or national origin. However, there is less societal awareness of the illegality of language discrimination (in comparison with ethnic and racial discrimination), and ideologies about the normalcy of English in the US and the existence of 'good' vs. 'bad' language are often taken for granted, not just by employers but also by judges and juries (Lippi-Green, 1994, 2012).

One example of language-based discrimination that is rooted in ethnic, racial or national origin discrimination is **linguistic profiling**, in which someone recognizes the ethnic or racial identity of another person just by hearing them talk, and then discriminates against them based on this identity. Much of the research on linguistic profiling has looked at racial discrimination carried out over the phone, when the perpetrator cannot see the victim or identify them based on physical appearance. Particularly well-known is Baugh's research on linguistic profiling and housing discrimination. Baugh (2003, 2017) found that individuals who called landlords in response to a housing ad were more likely to be told that nothing was available when they spoke with an African American or Latinx accent than when they spoke with a 'standard' (White) accent. (You can see how this happens in the Department of Housing and Urban Development's public service announcement, 'Accents,' at http://www.youtube.com/watch?v=HAZMIC_OwTw, accessed 22 October 2018). In these cases of linguistic profiling, language is the covert means by which the landlords identify the ethnic or racial identity of the caller. Federal guidelines make it clear that denying housing based on language spoken, accent or limited English proficiency is illegal (Misra, 2016).

In other cases, language discrimination is more overt or explicit. In fact, many people are comfortable saying that they won't hire someone based on the way they speak, even if they wouldn't publicly admit to discriminating by race. However, as is explained in the federal Equal Employment Opportunity Commission (EEOC) guidelines (https://www.eeoc.gov/

laws/guidance/national-origin-guidance.cfm#_Toc451518801, accessed 15 October 2018), unless there is a specific job-related reason, it is illegal to make employment decisions based on accent or knowledge of English, because these are tied to protected categories. Therefore, as illustrated in examples on the EEOC website, it would be illegal to assign an experienced job applicant who speaks Spanish-accented English to a position as a dishwasher if you assign similarly experienced non-Latinxs to the higher paid position of server. In contrast, if there is an aspect of the job that requires spoken or written communication in English (such as taking customer orders), then it would be legal to exclude job candidates with only limited proficiency, because there is a specific job-related activity that they are unable to complete. Importantly, the EEOC guidelines make it clear that 'customer preference' is not a legitimate reason for employers to discriminate. Nonetheless, despite these federal rules, courts rarely find in favor of people who have been discriminated against based on accent (Lippi-Green, 1994, 2012). One likely reason is that judges may also adhere to the standard language ideology, which portrays particular ways of speaking as objectively superior (as discussed in Chapter 4). When someone takes for granted that only standard 'unaccented' English is 'correct,' it's easy to assume that people who speak in other ways are uneducated or less competent, especially in educational contexts (Leeman, 2012a). It's also worth noting that the EEOC guidelines only discuss 'foreign' languages and accents, and there is no mention of 'non-standard' varieties of English such as **African American English** (AAE).

Linguistic discrimination in the workplace can also take the form of English-only policies that forbid employees from speaking other languages (sometimes even going as far as to ban other languages during breaks). In some cases, even bilingual employees who are hired in part for their ability to communicate with Spanish-speaking customers are then fired for speaking Spanish when other customers or co-workers complain (Zentella, 2014). But are such practices legal? According to the EEOC guidelines, 'blanket rules requiring employees to speak English (or another language) at all times are presumptively unlawful.' In contrast, however, English-only policies *are* permissible when there is a legitimate business reason (i.e. 'to promote safe and efficient job performance or business operations'), when they are limited to certain times or places, and when they are applied equally to all speakers of all languages.

These English-only rules, and the court cases that have upheld them, reflect a misunderstanding of multilingualism and the mistaken notion that mandating the use of English doesn't impose any burden on people who know how to speak it; since they are capable of speaking English, the thinking goes, they can easily comply with the policy (Del Valle, 2003; Gilman, 2011). This overlooks the differential proficiency speakers may have, as well as the role of language choice in social interaction and identity performance. Strikingly, in the *Garcia v. Spun Steak* case (1993), the court dismissed the idea that being allowed to speak Spanish was part of the right of cultural expression, thus taking a very narrow view of the relationship of language to ethnicity and national origin (Del Valle, 2003; Gilman, 2011). In sum, then, a monolingual Spanish-speaker can't be excluded from a job based on a lack of English ability (assuming the job doesn't require knowledge of English), but a bilingual can be told not to speak Spanish in certain contexts. Thus, as Gilman (2011) explains, even though language discrimination in employment is illegal, there is no right of bilinguals to speak in their preferred language at work.

Thus far we have focused on the way in which minority language speakers' rights to be free of discrimination (i.e. negative language rights) are conceptualized in US language policy. As we saw, even when anti-discrimination policies exist on paper, they are not always enforced or upheld. Similarly, even though legal scholars and policy makers generally agree that the government cannot prohibit the private use of Spanish (or any other language), there have been some cases where judges have demanded that parents speak English to their children or risk having them taken away (Barry, 2005; Verhovek, 1995). And in a recent incident captured on a cellphone video, a Border Patrol agent detained two women at a Montana gas station, explaining that he was suspicious of them based on the fact that they were speaking Spanish (watch the video at https://www.nbcnews.com/news/latino/border-patrol-agent-detains-women-speaking-spanish-montana-gas-station-n876096, accessed 22 October 2018). The American Civil Liberties Union, which has filed suit on behalf of the women, argues that it was unconstitutional to question the women based on their language or accent, as these were used as a proxy for ethnoracial identity (Stack, 2019). In addition to language restrictions and discrimination carried out by employers or the government, there have been numerous cases of private citizens confronting people for speaking Spanish on the street, in stores or while dining out, as we have discussed in previous chapters. As hurtful and disturbing as it is to be insulted and told to speak English or 'go back' to another country, the Supreme Court affirmed in *Matal v. Tam* (2017) that hate speech is constitutionally protected by the First Amendment.

Official English

Many people seem to assume that English has official status in the US, and this is sometimes the 'justification' for demands to speak English and calls to end all government services in other languages. But as we noted earlier, even though English is the de facto national language, the US has never had an official language. Since the 1980s, however, there has been a move to change this, first via a 1981 proposal to amend the Constitution. After the failure of that amendment, various bills have been introduced and passed in either the House or the Senate, but none has made it through both chambers of Congress. In contrast with the failure of such efforts at the national level, 31 states as well as various counties and cities have passed laws or (state) constitutional amendments making English their official language (Grovum, 2014). The states where English has official status include Hawaii, where Hawaiian has also been an official language since 1978, and Alaska, where the state's Indigenous languages were also granted official status in 2014 (Canfield, 2014), as well as four states (New Mexico, Oregon, Rhode Island and Washington) that have passed official resolutions in support of language diversity (Fuller & Torres, 2018).

The details of just what it means to make English an official language are sometimes a bit murky, and the specific provisions of the various bills and constitutional amendments range from vague statements about preserving English to more specific regulations regarding language use in government business (Liu *et al.*, 2014). Further, as we explained earlier, some minority language services (such as electoral materials) are directly linked to federal civil rights and constitutional protections, and thus are required regardless of the status of English at the state or local level. Nonetheless, supporters of granting English official status are united in their goal to reduce or eliminate governmental support for minority languages, such as bilingual education, language access services and ballots (Schmidt, 2007). At the state level, efforts to ban bilingual education have often been carried out separately from attempts to declare English the official language, but they can be considered part of the same political movement (we'll discuss bilingual education in more depth in Chapter 9). An additional area of state-level policy efforts has sought to eliminate driver license tests in languages other than English. Clearly, the focus of granting English official status is on reducing or eliminating minority language services for LEP individuals as well as any other policies perceived as supporting minority language maintenance, rather than 'foreign language' programs benefiting English-speakers or international diplomacy (Schmidt, 2007). In most cases, making English the official language would ban certain government activities in languages other than English, and thus Official English movements are sometimes referred to by opponents as 'English-Only.' However, the two most prominent Official English organizations, US English and ProEnglish, reject the *English-Only* label, arguing that they aren't trying to ban the private use of minority languages, but rather government support for minority languages as well as their use in government.

Why do some people want to give English official status? Let us consider the arguments put forward by supporters, as well as the assumptions reflected in those arguments, and the connection of these movements to language ideologies. Most obviously, the Official English movement is tied up with the one nation-one language ideology discussed in Chapter 4 which sees the use of a single language as promoting unity and the common good. Advocates of Official English view English as an essential element of US national identity, while other languages are seen as divisive and a threat to mainstream culture and tradition. Further, the thinking goes, people who speak minority languages are immigrants who voluntarily chose to come to the US, and as such they have a moral obligation to learn the language of their new country (Schmidt, 2007). In any case, Official English supporters argue, English is needed for socio-economic advancement, so everyone benefits from learning it. A related argument is that bilingual education and minority language services impede English acquisition, so offering them hurts minority language speakers and fosters division. If English isn't made official, and minority language services and bilingual education aren't eliminated, the argument continues, immigrants and their offspring will be isolated in ethnolinguistic enclaves. Finally, supporters of Official English suggest that limiting the government to a single language is fair, because it treats everyone equally (Schmidt, 2002).

Now let us take a closer look and evaluate the stated motivations for Official English. Many of the arguments put forth by supporters rest on the premise that immigrants aren't learning English (or are doing so at a slower rate than previous immigrants), together with the idea that official status will make them do so more quickly, so let's start there. This premise is simply wrong. First, previous immigrants didn't learn English anywhere near as quickly as the dominant narrative would have us believe (Wiley, 2000; Wilkerson & Salmons, 2008). Secondly, while the English ability of immigrants is largely dependent on age of arrival and length of time in the US, essentially all US-born individuals learn and master English (see

Chapter 2). The three-generation pattern of language shift remains largely intact, and it's not English but Spanish (and other minority languages) that are at risk of being lost. We also want to point out that the ideology of **normative monolingualism** that sees languages as existing in a **zero-sum** relationship (discussed in Chapter 4) leads some people to assume that if an individual speaks a minority language, then they don't speak English. In fact, as we saw in Chapter 2, the vast majority of speakers of Spanish in the US also speak English well or very well (this is also the case for other minority or minoritized languages).

But what about those immigrants that have arrived more recently or that struggle with English because they were first exposed to it later in life, or perhaps because they find language learning difficult? (Maybe you have studied another language and can relate to how difficult it can be, and how long it can take to become fluent.) Advocates of Official English sometimes refer to minority language services as a 'crutch,' but it's hard to imagine that simply declaring English the official language or refusing to provide services in minority languages would make anyone learn English overnight. In fact, bilingual education has been shown to be more effective for teaching English literacy, as we'll discuss in the next chapter. And there is also a moral question: Should people be denied access to medical care, emergency services or the right to interact with the government as 'punishment' for not having learned English fast enough? Moreover, the idea that it is somehow more 'fair' for everyone to use the same language (i.e. English) ignores the fact that this would mean that some people receive services in their native language while others don't. This is roughly akin to representing 'standard' varieties as universal and equally accessible to all, when in fact the standard is closely allied with dominant groups (see Chapter 4). In other words, treating everyone equally does not necessarily mean treating everyone equitably.

In the previous paragraph, we talked about the language abilities of immigrants and their descendants, and in doing so we left unchallenged a false premise of the Official English movement. So let us address that now. As we explored in depth in Chapter 3 as well as in the section on historical perspectives on language policy, and as Schmidt (2002, 2007) also points out, people who speak minority languages are not necessarily immigrants, or the descendants of immigrants, who have chosen to come to the US, nor is the US an inherently monolingual English-speaking country. Instead, the multilingual history of the US also includes Native peoples who lived in what is now the US before the arrival of Europeans, people who were brought to the US as slaves, residents of territories conquered and annexed by the US, and refugees (Schmidt, 2002; Wiley, 2000). The impression that multilingualism is something new is not based on objective reality but rather on the hegemony and naturalization of English in the US, as well as the erasure of linguistic diversity (Schmidt, 2007).

Even more importantly, framing the US as a historically English-speaking nation and minority language speakers as immigrants also erases the historical and contemporary use of language as way to marginalize racialized Others. As we saw, language has been a mechanism for the subordination of Latinxs and other groups, and for the privileging of English and Whiteness. Minority languages, and especially Spanish, serve as indexes of those racialized identities, and in many cases anxiety about the supposed displacement of English really reflects anxiety about the displacement of Whites by non-Whites (Schmidt, 2007). Indeed, as Zentella (1997b) notes, the Official English movement has, since its founding, been imbued with a deep-seated 'Hispanophobia.'

The underlying racial animus of Official English and English-Only movements is important to keep in mind when assessing the claim that giving English official status would help speakers of Spanish and other minority languages to achieve the 'American Dream.' On one hand, yes, it's true that it is extremely difficult to succeed in the US without knowing English. But speaking English is not the magic solution that allows racialized groups to overcome racism, just as speaking 'standard' language varieties does not magically free other racialized groups from systemic discrimination (Leeman, 2005, 2018c; Lippi-Green, 2012; Macedo, 1997; Villa, 2002). In fact, not only are such promises often broken, but they are one step in what Lippi-Green (2012) calls 'the language subordination model,' which devalues disfavored languages and language varieties, and pressures speakers to abandon them. Further, declaring English the official language sends a powerful symbolic message about who counts as a 'real' American and contributes to the **Othering** of minority language speakers. The impact of defining US national identity through English is particularly harmful for Latinxs, who dominant ideologies link to Spanish regardless of the language(s) they speak (Leeman, 2013).

Before leaving this topic, we want to stress that opponents of making English the official language don't think that people shouldn't learn English. Sometimes referred to as *pluralists* (Schmidt, 2002), opponents of the English-Only movement support inclusionary policies that recognize and value language diversity and multilingualism. Further, they generally support policy approaches that foster English acquisition while also supporting the maintenance and development of minority languages by native speakers as well as others who might wish to learn them. This position is sometimes referred to as *English Plus*, a name that highlights the goal of supporting bilingualism in English and another language (or multilingualism in English and several additional languages). As we noted earlier, four states have pushed back against the English-Only movement while still acknowledging the centrality of English in US life by passing resolutions in favor of linguistic diversity, and two states have made Indigenous languages and English official. In addition, of the states that had banned bilingual education, all but one (Arizona) have now subsequently overturned them (see Chapter 9).

In this section, we have seen that despite claims that Official English is a common-sense effort to promote national unity while also helping immigrants achieve the American Dream, the reality is quite different. Not only are Official English policies unnecessary, they have negative symbolic and material consequences. Rather than preventing division, they contribute to it via exclusion and racialization. The case of Official English highlights the intertwining of various language ideologies both with each other and with language policies, as well as the ways in which policies reflect and reproduce ideologies.

Language Policy in Puerto Rico

As a condition of the treaty that ended the Spanish-American War in 1898, Spain ceded its colony of Puerto Rico to the US. Like in the continental US, the emphasis of language policy in Puerto Rico was the 'Americanization' of the local population, especially via education. Puerto Rico's Official Languages Act (1902) made both Spanish and English official languages and permitted the use of both in government transactions. Nonetheless, and despite some support for using Spanish to 'Americanize' the local population, language-in-education policy imposed English as the primary medium of instruction (although in some years Spanish was used in lower grades, with students transitioning to English in high school) (Pomada, 2008; Rodriguez-Arroyo, 2013). This policy proved highly problematic for students and teachers alike because many had only limited, if any, proficiency in English. Like the residents of the annexed territories in the Southwest, when Puerto Ricans were made citizens of the US in 1917, they were not required to demonstrate knowledge of English.

In the first half of the 20th century, governors of Puerto Rico were appointed by the US president, but since 1948 Puerto Ricans have been allowed to elect their own governor. The administration of the first elected governor implemented a policy of Spanish-medium instruction for public schools shortly after taking office in 1949, a policy that has remained in effect. As for official languages, in 1991 the Official Languages Act was revoked, and Spanish was declared the sole official language of Puerto Rico. Some saw this as a political ploy by the pro-Commonwealth party to gain votes (Pomada, 2008), in part by demonstrating a commitment to a Puerto Rican identity distinct from the US, while others saw it as an attempt to stymie statehood campaigns (Crawford, 1997). And in fact, when the pro-statehood party returned to power in 1993, Governor Pedro Rosselló revoked the Spanish-only policy and reinstated official bilingualism (Pomada, 2008).

In recent years, there has been a move to promote students' development of English proficiency through various means, including bilingual education. Supporters stress the instrumental value of English, including perceived economic advantages as well as greater political integration with the US (and possible statehood) (Rodriguez-Arroyo, 2013). Detractors see it as a rehash of Americanization policies that subordinate Puerto Rican culture and reproduce inequality based on access to English. The fact that the push for bilingual education has coincided with increased privatization and the closing of schools, especially following the devastation of Hurricane María, has only increased suspicions.

Conclusions and Connections

In this chapter we have seen that the US has had a variety of language policies throughout its history. These policies are tied up with the language ideologies we discussed in Chapter 4, but they are also shaped by other political and ideological concerns. Language policies determine who can become a citizen, who can vote and who has access to education; they influence people's access to jobs and housing and they can have life-or-death consequences in healthcare and emergency services. And of course, language-in-education policies are key in shaping the future of Spanish and other minority languages, as we discuss in Chapter 9. At various historical moments, language policies in the US have been used to repress and dominate, to limit access to political and social power and to define national belonging and identity. Importantly, however, language policies have also been used to combat discrimination and to promote inclusion and equity.

Although English is not the official language of the US, and the US has always been a multilingual nation, one historical trend has been the growing hegemony of English. This hegemony was reflected and reproduced in early 20th century English-only policies in schools and government (including the 1906 introduction of an English language requirement for citizenship) as well as the more recent movement to make English the official language. These exclusionary policies have played a role in the racialization of Spanish and Latinxs discussed in Chapter 5. However, this trend has also been broken by inclusionary policies that have made space for minority languages in the public realm. Recent years have seen a growing incidence, awareness and appreciation of multilingualism, at least among some segments of the population, which has led to more pluralist language policies, including language access and innovative bilingual education programs and certifications (as we'll discuss in the next chapter). At the same time, there have been ongoing efforts to grant English official status, as well as proposals to require applicants for visas to demonstrate knowledge of English prior to arrival. Of course, it's up to people who care about these issues to get involved in the political process and advocate for the policies at the local and national levels, as well as share what they know about these issues with friends and family. Moreover, it's important to remember that policies operate at multiple levels, and individuals can sometimes promote or implement pluralist or inclusionary policies at the local or micro level (such as in individual cities, schools or even classrooms), even in the face of exclusionary policies at the national level (Hornberger, 2005).

Discussion Questions and Activities for Chapter 8

(1) Our discussion of language access and Spanish-language services focused on government entities and government-funded programs, such as in voting and healthcare. While we noted that language-based discrimination is illegal in employment, housing and public accommodations, we didn't discuss the use of Spanish by private companies, such as by telephone customer service representatives or store salespeople. Compare the use of Spanish by governmental and private entities in terms of language policies and the ideologies that govern them.

(2) One frequent target of Official English supporters is the ubiquitous 'press one for English', and there is even a song by the Rivoli Revue about it. Watch the video (https://www.youtube.com/watch?v=sEJfS1v-fU0) and analyze the statements and myths it contains as well as the language ideologies it reflects. You may also wish to comment on the images. Next, consider the language policies the authors might propose to solve the 'problem' they identify. Use what you have learned in this chapter to evaluate the legality of those policy proposals.

(3) Discuss the orientations to language reflected in some of the US language policies discussed in this chapter. Is there ever more than one orientation reflected in a single policy? Do you think it is ever possible to change orientations to language by enacting new language policies, or are language policies always a reflection of orientations? Give examples to support your position(s).

(4) Ask a few friends or family members about the status of English in the US as well as in your state. Find out what they know about the status, whether they think English should be official, and what their rationale is either way. Ask them about which kinds of services they think should or shouldn't be provided in languages other than English and why. Analyze their responses in light of the information provided in this chapter. You may also wish to consult Ronald Schmidt's article (listed in further readings) or James Crawford's (2006) congressional testimony, available at http://www.ailadownloads.org/advo/Crawford-CrawfordTestimony.pdf.

Notes

(1) The one partial exception is reflected in the 1990 Native American Languages Act, which declares that it is US policy to 'preserve, protect, and promote the rights and freedom of Native Americans to use, practice, and develop Native American languages.' However, this policy has never been fully funded or implemented, and it applies only to Native American languages, which are defined as having a unique 'special status.'

(2) In 2013 the Supreme Court overturned the pre-approval provision in a 5–4 decision that relied on voter registration data supposedly showing that the difference in registration rates between Blacks and Whites had been reduced dramatically since 1965. However, Hispanic/Latino origin was not taken into account, nor were the differential citizenship rates among groups (Gabrielson, 2017). The fact that 'Whites' included Latinxs (including non-citizens) had the effect of making White registration rates appear lower than they otherwise would have done, underscoring that official ethnoracial classification, and the construction of **Latinidad** as an ethnic rather than a racial category, can have a wide-ranging impact (see Chapter 5). Since the 2013 decision, numerous states have implemented more restrictive voting procedures that have disproportionately disenfranchised ethnoracial minority voters.

Further Reading and Resources

Lozano, R. (2018) *An American Language: The History of Spanish in the United States.* Berkeley, CA: University of California Press.

Martínez, G. (2010) Language and power in healthcare: Towards a theory of language barriers among linguistic minorities in the United States. In J. Watzke, P. Chamness and M. Mantero (eds) *Readings in Language Studies: Language and Power, Vol. 2* (pp. 59–74). Lakewood, FL: International Society for Language Studies.

Schmidt, Sr., R. (2002) Racialization and language policy: The case of the USA. *Multilingua* 21 (2–3), 141–162.

Skutnabb-Kangas, T. (2012) Role of linguistic human rights in language policy and planning. In C.A. Chapelle (ed.) *The Encyclopedia of Applied Linguistics*. https://doi.org/10.1002/9781405198431.wbeal1026

Zentella, A.C. (2014) TWB (Talking While Bilingual): Linguistic profiling of Latina/os, and other linguistic torquemadas. *Latino Studies* 12 (4), 620–635.

Chapter 9

Spanish in US Schools

> **Objectives**
>
> To review language-in-education policy regarding Spanish in the US, to explain the most common educational program types for English language learners, Spanish/English bilinguals, learners of Spanish as a second language and heritage speakers of Spanish, as well as to analyze how language ideologies both influence educational policies and are reproduced by schooling practices.

Introduction

As sizeable Latinx communities have become established in more areas of the US, there are both more Latinx children in schools and more schools with significant numbers of Latinx children (Lopez *et al.*, 2018). In 2015, 26% of the 50.4 million K-12 students in the US were Latinx (de Brey *et al.*, 2019). As we have stressed in previous chapters, Latinxs in the US come from many different backgrounds and have very diverse life experiences. So too, Latinx students are linguistically diverse, and some don't speak Spanish. While there are many important non-linguistic issues related to the schooling of Latinx children (see Gándara & Contreras, 2009, for discussion), in this chapter we concentrate on issues related to language and language education. Our primary focus is on educational policies and programs for Spanish-speakers, including English language learners (ELLs), Spanish/English bilinguals and **heritage speakers** of Spanish, although we also discuss the teaching of Spanish as a second or additional language.

According to the Census Bureau, 16% of people living in the US aged 5–17 years speak Spanish at home (ACS 2017 Five-year estimates). Children and adolescents who speak Spanish at home encompass a wide array of linguistic profiles and abilities, including children who are more proficient in Spanish, children who are more proficient in English and children who are highly proficient in both languages. In some ways, ELLs and heritage speakers represent opposite ends of a continuum of language experiences and linguistic profiles that are closely tied to family and immigration history; recent immigrants from Latin America tend to be ELLs, whereas their children and grandchildren tend to be dominant in English with more limited ability in Spanish (see discussion of language maintenance and shift in Chapter 2). However, as we discussed in Chapter 2, a wide array of factors shape individuals' language maintenance or loss.

While our primary focus is on language, we want to stress that the question of which language(s) to teach or use in the classroom is not simply a practical issue concerned with the effectiveness of instruction. Instead, the treatment of language by schools and educational policies is intimately tied up with broader questions of educational equity including, but not limited to, the role of schools in reproducing social hierarchies and societal ideologies. Because schools are places where children not only learn 'things,' but where they also learn which 'things' are worth knowing, it is crucial that we ask ourselves which cultures, practices and values are reflected in, and promoted by, educational policies and teaching practices. And at the same time, we need to think about which cultures and peoples are either omitted from the curriculum or presented as 'problematic' or 'wrong', as well as consider the implications of this symbolic **erasure** and racialization. Typically, schools elevate the culture – including the ways of speaking – of the 'mainstream' White middle class and present these as both the key to success and the model to which all students should aspire. This unitary focus and elevation of White middle-class cultures and knowledges is especially problematic for children who speak other languages, as well as for children who speak non-standard varieties of English. As we will address in the following sections, these ideologies and the practices that grow out of them shape the experiences of Latinxs and how they use their languages in the educational context and beyond.

A Short History of Minority Language Schooling in the US

It is a common perception that education in the US has always been in English, but this is actually far from the truth. At least since the time of US independence, children were educated in many different immigrant languages (e.g. German, Italian, Polish) in their local communities; bilingual education programs as well as schools that taught largely or completely in non-English languages were fairly common through the latter half of the 19th century (Baker, 2011: 184; García, 2009a: 163; Ramsey, 2010: 12). In the Southwestern territories annexed from Mexico, Catholic parochial schools were taught in Spanish, which represented one way in which local populations sought to maintain their language (Dubord, 2010). In some rural parts of the Southwest, it took 100 years after annexation for public instruction to be offered in English (Lozano, 2018). In fact, it was not until the turn of the 20th century that public education became widespread in the US, as did laws requiring children to attend school. For instance, by 1900, 33 states had passed compulsory attendance laws (Lozano, 2018).

The establishment of compulsory education coincided with the growing prominence of English in the construction of US national identity as well as anxiety regarding the cultural and linguistic assimilation of immigrants and Spanish-speaking people living in the newly annexed territories (see discussion in Chapters 3, 4 and 8). Further, the growth of public education, together with the trend toward diminishing local control of schools, also contributed to a greater emphasis on English (Ramsey, 2010). These trends, and the understanding of schools as a site for the 'Americanization' of minority language children, were also reflected in educational policy and practice. As we saw in Chapter 3, the 1910 law that allowed New Mexico and Arizona to become states also required that public schools be taught exclusively in English (Lozano, 2018; Wiley, 2000). Similarly, Puerto Rico's language-in-education policy prioritized English as the **medium of instruction** until the 1940s (Rodriguez-Arroyo, 2013). In 1919 the Americanization Department of the US Bureau of Education adopted a resolution recommending (but not requiring) that all US schools be conducted exclusively in English (Baker, 2011: 184). Although the federal government didn't end up adopting that policy, some states did prohibit teaching in languages other than English, and Nebraska even banned 'foreign' language instruction in private schools. In the 1919 case of *Nebraska v. Myers* the Supreme Court ruled that it was unconstitutional for states to ban teaching in other languages, but many public school systems, which were playing a bigger and bigger role in the education of the nation's young, simply decided not to offer any, which did not violate the ruling (Fouka, 2016; Pavlenko, 2003). Since that time, English-only education has been the norm throughout the country.

Through at least the first half of the 20th century, the majority of Mexican American children in the Southwest attended English-only segregated schools (Gándara, 2012; Lozano, 2018). Moreover, many teachers forbade the use of Spanish, even on the playground, and severely punished children for speaking Spanish (MacGregor-Mendoza, 2000). Although New Mexico required that Spanish be taught in Grades 5–8, it was targeted toward second language learners and framed Spanish as a 'foreign' rather than a 'local' language (Lozano, 2018). To be clear, Spanish was not the medium of instruction but was instead an add-on subject. Similarly, Texas allowed Spanish to be taught as a subject, but bilingual education was illegal in the state until the 1960s (Lozano, 2018). In addition to the repression of Spanish, the history of Latinx education is characterized by segregation and schooling inferior to that provided for non-Latinx White children (Gándara, 2012; Lozano, 2018).

The 1960s saw growing activism for minority rights around the world. One aspect of such struggles was a quest for educational equity, including schooling in minority languages. In the US, the Chicanx and Puerto Rican Civil Rights movements included calls for the elimination of segregated schools, access to quality education, an end to racial discrimination in the hiring of teachers, and bilingual education, among other issues (Flores & Garcia, 2017). This activism led to the passage of the 1967 Bilingual Education Act, which sought to address the high dropout rates of Latinx students by providing federal funds for school districts that wanted to offer bilingual education or other programs for students with limited English-speaking ability (García, 2009a: 169). Thus, the origins of federal support for bilingual education were linked to efforts to address educational inequality and close the 'achievement gap.' As Ruíz (1984) pointed out, the discourse surrounding this policy, as well as the policy itself, reflected the **language-as-problem orientation** toward language that we discussed in the last chapter.

As we discussed in greater detail in the last chapter, the 1974 Supreme Court decision in *Lau v. Nichols* found that the San Francisco school district's failure to offer educational accommodations for Chinese-speaking children who didn't speak English constituted national origin discrimination, which had been outlawed by the Civil Rights Act (1965). That decision led to new legislation significantly expanding bilingual education for limited English-speaking children from other language backgrounds, especially Spanish. Although some early programs sought to maintain and develop children's first language, in the vast majority of cases the educational objective was to use the minority language only temporarily while English was being acquired, and then to transition to English-only schooling as quickly as possible.

Contrary to popular belief, the *Lau* decision didn't require bilingual education, or even education in children's native language(s) – only some sort of accommodation for children who didn't speak English, as we explained in the last chapter. This made it possible for the Reagan administration (1981–1989), which was largely hostile to bilingual education and minority language rights more broadly, to drastically reduce bilingual programs (Baker, 2011: 187–188). There has also been significant action against bilingual education at the state level, often in the form of referendums. In 1998 California voters passed Proposition 227 mandating that 'all children in California public schools shall be taught English by being taught in English' (Proposition 227, 1998). Similar propositions were passed in Arizona in 2000 and in Massachusetts in 2002, although a similar constitutional amendment was voted down in Colorado (Escamilla *et al.*, 2003) and the Massachusetts and California propositions have since been repealed. These ballot initiatives can be considered part of the broader English-Only movement (see Chapter 3).

Federal 'accountability' measures have also hindered bilingual models of language education for minority language learners. In 2002 the federal No Child Left Behind Act instituted mandatory English-language testing in core subjects for all children (including ELLs), thus intensifying the focus on English acquisition and effectively reducing support for bilingual education (Menken & Solorza, 2014). In 2015 the Every Student Succeeds Act, which replaced the No Child Left Behind Act, further increased accountability requirements for the development of English language proficiency among ELLs. Although the new law gives states increased funding for ELLs and allows more flexibility on the specific accountability measures employed, the focus remains on the development of English rather than the support of students' home languages (Fránquiz & Ortiz, 2016). Furthermore, the testing and accountability regimes that reward schools and teachers for high test scores (and punish them for low ones) don't include 'foreign' languages as a core subject. This means that the incentives that motivate schools' investment in subjects such as math or English reading don't exist for courses that promote students' Spanish-language development, and thus they are often deprioritized and underfunded if they exist at all (Pomerantz & Huguet, 2013). In sum, although bilingual education programs found some federal support in the 1970s, in the 1980s federal language-in-education policy in the US became increasingly English-only.

Yet despite a history of a lack of federal and state support for or approval of bilingual education, there is a parallel history of dual language programs started through grassroots movements which in large part grew out of the activism of parents and communities that wanted to maintain and value Spanish as a cultural resource. This latter history begins with the establishment of the Spanish–English bilingual program at the Coral Way School, a public school in Dade County, Miami, in 1963 (Ovando, 2003). The Coral Way program and many others that followed were the result of local organization and activism, not state or federal programs, and the local involvement in the development of the programs may have been key to their success (Thomas & Collier, 2002). Such efforts, as well as a growing recognition of the value of multilingualism for majority as well as minority language children, have led to recent pushback against English-only schooling. Indeed, in 2016 California voters approved the repeal of Proposition 227 by a wide margin, thus giving more flexibility (but not state funding) to local districts to implement bilingual programs.

Further evidence of a growing appreciation of bilingualism is the creation of the **Seal of Biliteracy**. This certificate recognizing a student's attainment of proficiency in two (or more) languages is affixed to the student's high school diploma. A growing number of school districts and states participate in this program, now approved or under consideration in at least 38 states (see https://sealofbiliteracy.org/ for an up-to date list). In the next section we explore how both this appreciation of bilingualism and **monoglossic** ideologies influence instructional programs for ELLs.

Educating English Language Learners: Program Types

This section focuses on the education of children who come from homes in which Spanish is spoken, with particular attention to the medium of instruction. Educational models range from placing students in English-medium classrooms (i.e. taught in English) with little or no additional support, to fully bilingual programs that are taught in both English and Spanish. When comparing and contrasting the different program types, we are interested in two central questions. First, is the aim to foster bilingualism, or rather to transition children to speaking English, with little or no concern for Spanish language maintenance? In other words, are these programs oriented toward **additive bilingualism** or **subtractive bilingualism** (Lambert, 1975)? Secondly, is there attention to, and support for, students' learning of 'content' (such as math or social studies) while they are learning English? We address these questions for the five program types that have been the focus of most recent research (Kim *et al.*, 2015): (1) mainstreaming; (2) English as a second language instruction; (3) transitional bilingual education; (4) maintenance bilingual education; and (5) two-way immersion (TWI).

English immersion/mainstreaming

In this model, ELLs are placed in mainstream classrooms and given the same instruction as native English speaking students. There is very little or no special programming for teaching English, and there is no Spanish-medium instruction. Further, there is normally little or no support to help students develop and maintain grade-level content knowledge in core subjects while they learn English. For this reason, although school administrators are more likely to refer to this curricular model as *English immersion* or *mainstreaming*, many education scholars use the term *submersion* (Baker, 2011) to reflect what can happen to ELLs enrolled in English-medium education without any academic or linguistic support. Not surprisingly, most research has found that this model does not help ELLs to catch up with their English-speaking peers either in terms of English proficiency or in content knowledge (Kim *et al.*, 2015).

You may be wondering how mainstreaming is legal given the Supreme Court's ruling in *Lau* that a lack of accommodation for children who don't speak English constitutes national origin discrimination. As we noted in the last chapter, the legal reasoning undergirding that case has been increasingly challenged, with several courts rejecting the argument that policies that impact different groups differently (e.g. English-only education) are discriminatory if there is no malicious intent (Moran, 2015). Further, even when state or local policies require some accommodation for ELLs, enforcement is often lax.

English as a second language (ESL) instruction

In contrast with the sink-or-swim philosophy of mainstreaming, some schools provide ELLs with instruction aimed at English acquisition. The specifics of ESL instruction vary from program to program, but one common model is 'pull out' instruction, meaning that ELLs are taken out of the regular classroom activities for ESL. This is common in elementary education, when students in the US typically spend the entire day with one teacher in the same classroom. In middle school and high school, where students usually have different class periods with different teachers, ESL instruction is often offered during one or more periods, and ELLs attend the rest of their classes with mainstream students (Kim *et al.*, 2015).

ESL instruction, in contrast to submersion, recognizes ELLs' need for support in the acquisition of English while also learning other subjects, and the ESL lessons sometimes specifically focus on assignments for those other subjects. Depending on the students' English proficiency level, it can still be a challenge for them to keep up in mainstream content courses. Further, being pulled out of regular instruction for ESL can mean that they miss key parts of core content lessons, as well as opportunities to benefit from peer interaction (Serafini *et al.*, 2018). Some school systems have attempted to remedy this gap by offering sheltered English immersion, or classes that combine ESL instruction with subject matter content designed specifically for ELLs. However, too often, sheltered English immersion programs keep ELLS in classrooms for years, effectively blocking their access to more academically rigorous content. This has led some educational experts to compare such programs to the historical segregation of Mexican and Mexican American children in substandard schools discussed earlier (Gándara, 2012).

Transitional bilingual education

Although transitional programs are bilingual, in that they are taught in two languages, the primary aim is English language learning and linguistic assimilation rather than the maintenance or development of bilingual abilities. Thus, like ESL instruction, transitional bilingual programs are intended only for ELLs. In these programs, some core content is taught in Spanish as a way to let students cover grade-level content until they have learned English. Typically, transitional bilingual programs gradually increase the amount of English used (such as with Spanish-to-English ratios of 90–10 in the first year, 70–30 in the second and 50–50 in the third). In *early-exit bilingual programs*, children stay in these programs for one to three years and are then placed in mainstream, monolingual classrooms. In *late-exit bilingual programs*, students spend about four to six years before moving to English-only classes. Because transitional programs gradually replace the home language (in this case, Spanish) with the majority language, they are seen as promoting subtractive bilingualism. In general, these programs seem to foster greater academic success than simply ESL instruction because students learn subject matter in their native language (Kim *et al.*, 2015).

Maintenance bilingual programs

In contrast with transitional programs, maintenance bilingual programs are designed to foster maintenance and development of the minority language (Spanish) while also promoting the acquisition or further development of English. Maintenance bilingual programs designed primarily for minority language speakers are rare in the US. The most well-known examples are schools in Hawaiian and Native American languages, for which revitalization efforts receive some limited federal support, in accordance with the Native American Languages Act discussed in Note 1 in the last chapter (McCarty & Lee, 2014; Yamauchi *et al.*, 2000). In the next section we discuss a particular kind of maintenance program that serves both minority and majority language students.

Two-way immersion (TWI)

The most common type of maintenance bilingual programs in the US are two-way immersion (TWI) programs, also sometimes referred to as *dual language* or *dual immersion* programs. Whatever the term used, these programs aim to enroll both minority language students and majority language students, with the goal being for all students to become bilingual and biliterate. Because they seek to promote additive bilingualism among ELLs, TWI programs can be considered a type of educational and linguistic enrichment for English-speaking children. In the US, the most common dual immersion programs are Spanish–English and they typically try to have a balance of students dominant in each language. Some programs conduct half of the school day in English and half in Spanish, while others switch languages each day, and still others designate certain subjects to be taught in English and certain subjects in Spanish. In most cases, TWI programs are offered only in elementary school (kindergarten through fifth or sixth grade), although some programs continue through middle school (which typically goes through eighth or ninth grade).

Although exact statistics are difficult to find, the number of TWI programs seems to be increasing, based on government reports (McKay-Wilson, 2011) and the directory provided by the Center for Applied Linguistics (http://www.cal.org/twi/directory/). However, they are disproportionately available to students of higher socio-economic status (Flores & García, 2017; Pomerantz & Huguet, 2013). As mentioned above, although these programs were originally designed to serve ELLs, many seem to focus more on serving the interests of the mainstream population (Delavan *et al.*, 2017). We discuss this further in the language commodification section below.

Effectiveness of Bilingual and Dual Language Education Programs

Assessing whether bilingual education is the most effective or best way to educate children is not a straightforward matter. One of the first questions to consider is: What counts as achievement or learning? What is it that we want students to learn? Next, what is an appropriate way to measure student achievement? In the US today, quantitative measures of student learning, teacher performance and school quality reign supreme. Thus, learning outcomes are often measured with standardized tests, typically in reading and math, although other subjects may also be tested, especially in higher grades. Standardized tests are always given in English, so there is a built-in bias against ELLs who must complete tests in their second (or third) language. Further, reading ability in Spanish is not recognized or included in most standardized achievement measures. The Language Assessment Scales for Spanish (see http://ericae.net/eac/eac0131.htm) are used in some districts, but they are not part of the universal testing regime in the US.

A related methodological problem with some studies attempting to compare educational approaches is the timeframe in which learning outcomes are compared; while mainstreamed children may at first show higher levels of English development than children in dual language programs, this apparent advantage can disappear or reverse itself over time. According to Thomas and Collier (2002: 319), a child needs at least four years to attain academic proficiency in a second language, making it crucial to consider long-term, rather than short-term, outcomes.

Further, as we saw earlier, there are multiple models of bilingual education, and they are not necessarily equally effective. However, some studies lump transitional and TWI programs in a single catchall category which they then compare to mainstreaming and ESL. Similarly, it's important to be careful with comparison or control groups; some reports about the 'positive impact' of California's Proposition 227 on ELLs' test scores failed to note that similar gains were found for all students (including English monolinguals), suggesting that gains by ELLS were part of a larger trend rather than due to the elimination of bilingual education (Butler *et al.*, 2000; Garcia & Curry-Rodríguez, 2000). Finally, there are many other variables that influence how well children do in school, such as socio-economic class, the educational level of parents and caretakers and the age of arrival of immigrant children; these need to be controlled for in comparative studies.

Despite all the complicating factors in assessing program effectiveness, there are some clear findings. In fact, *all* of the comprehensive studies done by qualified researchers have found that the children in maintenance programs do better in the long run (Collier & Thomas, 2017; Lindholm-Leary, 2001, 2014; Lindholm-Leary & Hernandez, 2011; Ramirez *et al.*, 1991; Serafini *et al.*, 2018; Thomas & Collier, 1997, 2002). For example, the studies by Thomas and Collier compared students in eight different types of programs in a range of rural and urban districts around the country. Their most recent research included 7.5 million student records from 36 school districts in 16 states! Thomas and Collier found that the longer children received instruction in Spanish, the better they tended to do in both English and core content, although these advantages only showed up after a minimum of three years. Other recent research, including studies that randomly assigned students to different educational programs (a key aspect of good methodological design), has also found that students in dual language programs do better on reading tests than those in English-only instruction (and just as well in math and science) (see Serafini *et al.*, 2018, for a review of this research). The reasons for the superior outcomes in dual language programs are clear: it is easier to learn to read in a language you know, and literacy skills transfer from one language to another. As Serafini *et al.* (2018) put it in their overview of long-term outcomes, 'the evidence suggests that [...] children's first language appears to play a facilitative role in acquiring the second language, English, and in promoting academic achievement over the long-term.'

We want to focus for a moment on the fact that dual language programs promote proficiency in *two* languages, rather than one, in marked contrast with mainstreaming, ESL and transitional bilingual programs. While this might seem obvious, it is largely overlooked or ignored in early (and even some recent) studies evaluating student outcomes in English, reading and math. Students' development in Spanish wasn't considered an important goal or achievement, and the focus of research on bilingual education was to investigate whether the use of Spanish slowed down or impeded English acquisition or academic performance. You may wish to take a moment to reflect on the language ideologies underlying these assumptions. Not surprisingly, students who receive instruction in Spanish are more likely to develop Spanish literacy skills, and children who learn to read in their home language are more likely to maintain that language, and this is another important advantage of TWI programs (Lindholm-Leary, 2014, 2016).

In addition, research attests to the effectiveness of bilingual education for social development. Not surprisingly, children flourish when their home experiences (i.e. language and cultural practices) are recognized, respected and valued. For example, Collins *et al.* (2011), in a study of 228 Latinx kindergarten children, found that dual language competence correlated with higher emotional and behavioral wellbeing. Further, numerous studies have documented that the loss of Spanish is associated with lower levels of motivation, self-esteem and overall language skills (e.g. Beck & Allexsaht-Snider, 2002; Quiroz, 2001; Weisman, 2001). Indeed, in her research in a Texas school, Valenzuela (1999) found that, together with inadequate funding and an overall lack of caring for and about Mexican American students, the 'subtractive schooling' oriented toward English acquisition and acculturation stripped students of their native culture and language without preparing them to succeed in the mainstream. Thus, there is a growing call for teaching practices that incorporate and sustain students' cultures (and language practices) as a means to both improving student outcomes and promoting greater equity (e.g. Gándara, 2012; Macedo, 1997; Nieto, 2010; Paris, 2012; Valenzuela, 1999).

Moreover, the development of bilingualism and the appreciation of linguistic and cultural pluralism among *majority* language children is also valuable for their intellectual and social development, as well as their future academic and professional endeavors. Further, studies have shown that learning academic content, as measured by tests taken in English, is not hindered – and they learn a second language (see for example Potowski, 2007 for a description of their Spanish use). Thus, TWI programs not only serve minority language children, but they are enriching for mainstream students as well. For this reason, many educational experts advocate 'bilingualism for all' policies, such as those that exist in many developed nations around the world.

Why, you may well ask, if studies consistently show that maintenance and TWI bilingual education are effective, are such programs not supported by federal and state policies and funding? This is a complex issue, with multiple factors likely playing a part. However, language ideologies play a key role, especially the **one nation-one language ideology**, the related normative monolingualism which imagines that maintenance of minority languages and cultures interferes with acquisition of English, and the racializing discourse that sees minority languages, and multilingualism, as having little value. Another contributing factor is the view that Spanish-speakers' interests and needs are not as legitimate as those of other groups or that bilingual education provides them with unfair 'special' treatment. (Of course, 'bilingualism for all' could definitively invalidate both these notions.)

Additional objections include the cost, as well as the straw man argument that, given the diversity of minority languages in the US, it would be impossible to offer bilingual education in all of them (which no-one was advocating). Of course, bilingual education does involve certain costs in time and money, as does all education. In our view, a commitment to funding high-quality public education is essential for a democratic society in which all children are valued and prepared for meaningful participation. TWI programs are one proven means of creating an environment that values pluralism and benefits children from both minority and majority language backgrounds, as well as promoting academic achievement for all.

Spanish as a Second or Additional Language

Thus far we have focused on pedagogical models and program types for ELLs, although, as we noted, TWI programs also enroll English-speaking children. Much of that discussion focused on the medium of instruction. At this point we turn our attention to the teaching of Spanish as a subject, or what is sometimes referred to as *Spanish as a foreign language*. Given all that we have said thus far, and especially in Chapter 3, you are probably are not surprised to hear that we reject the notion that Spanish is 'foreign' to the US; hence the scare quotes and our preference for the terms *Spanish as a second language* and *Spanish as an additional language*. Nonetheless, in some ways the *foreign* moniker is actually an accurate reflection of the way in which Spanish has traditionally been taught in this country, with the classroom focus being primarily on the Spanish spoken outside the US borders.

In any case, Spanish is by far the most commonly taught non-English language in the US at the elementary and secondary levels (ACIE, 2017). However, it is only a small minority of students in the US who study any 'foreign' language at all: only approximately 20%, according to ACIE (2017). Further, language instruction is concentrated at the middle and high school levels, and generally consists of only a few hours a week. The picture is similar at the post-secondary level, where in 2016 'foreign' languages were only 7.5% of college enrollments, and enrollments in Spanish were roughly equivalent to all other languages combined (Looney & Lusin, 2018). These percentages reflect a significant and consistent decline over the past decade, despite widespread internationalization efforts on the part of universities, as well as educational and public discourse touting the benefits of multilingualism for individuals and for the country.

Spanish for Heritage Speakers

Spanish language instruction in the US has traditionally been designed for monolingual English-speaking students whose only, or primary, exposure to Spanish is in the classroom. As such, it often fails to meet the needs of heritage language speakers – students with a personal or cultural connection to Spanish who have had exposure to Spanish in a naturalistic (versus instructional) setting (Fairclough & Beaudrie, 2016: 2). There has been some discussion and debate about exactly who should be considered a heritage language speaker and various definitions have been proposed (Hornberger & Wang, 2008; Leeman, 2015; Van Deusen-Scholl, 2003; Zyzik, 2016). For some scholars, the label should be used only for people with some productive ability in Spanish, while for others a cultural connection is sufficient (Valdés, 2005). In any case, heritage language speakers are a heterogeneous group in terms of linguistic experiences and abilities; it includes everyone from Spanish-dominant immigrants with years of academic preparation in Spanish to third-generation immigrants with limited speaking ability.

Despite the diversity of heritage speakers of Spanish, there are some common patterns. As a result of dominant language ideologies, and because the most common educational model is English-only schooling, many heritage language speakers have not had the opportunity to develop Spanish literacy, and they may have far greater comprehension skills than productive ability (Beaudrie *et al.*, 2014; Carreira & Valdés, 2012; Leeman & King, 2015). Further, heritage language learners may speak varieties of Spanish that differ from those typically taught in 'foreign' language classes, and since they are usually bilingual their language practices may include **codeswitching** or **translanguaging**.

Beginning in the 1960s, educators have developed Spanish teaching materials, pedagogical approaches and curricula specifically for heritage language speakers. Now typically referred to as *Spanish for heritage learners* or *Spanish as a heritage language*, these programs were originally referred to as *Spanish for bilingual speakers* (García, 2005; Valdés, 2005). They are also sometimes called *Spanish for fluent speakers* or *Spanish for native speakers*. Such programs reflect a growing recognition of the need for supporting Spanish proficiency among heritage speakers, but the percentages of schools where they are offered are still quite low. Rhodes and Pufahl (2014) report that in 2008 only 7% of elementary schools and 8% of high schools offered such classes. At the college level such classes are more common, at least in the some areas of the country and in universities with high Latinx enrollment; Beaudrie (2011) found that almost 40% of universities in the Southwest where Latinxs made up at least 5% of the student body offered Spanish as a heritage language programs. Nonetheless, in most colleges across the country, there are no programs or courses specifically for heritage speakers, and thus they have no option but to enroll in traditional 'foreign' language classes (Carreira & Chik, 2018).

Much research on Spanish heritage language education has sought to describe the characteristics of heritage speakers of Spanish and to develop appropriate pedagogical techniques. In addition, researchers have examined how particular teaching approaches reproduce language ideologies, which we discuss in the next section. One key concern in both lines of scholarship has been the treatment of linguistic variation, especially so-called non-standard and/or contact varieties of Spanish. Early approaches focused on the acquisition of 'standard Spanish,' and sought to eradicate students' 'non-standard' language practices (Valdés, 1995). With the development of the field of sociolinguistics in the 1970s, and the recognition of the legitimacy of all language varieties, more inclusive approaches have been put forward. These programs and pedagogies represent an important effort to better meet the educational and affective needs of heritage language learners enrolled in Spanish classes, but in many cases classroom practices reinforce the standard language ideology. In addition, Spanish for heritage learners programs take place within the limited context of 'foreign' language education, rather than using Spanish as the medium of instruction for other subjects. Thus, they do not challenge the overall model of English-medium instruction for the vast majority of the school day (Leeman & King, 2015). Still, Spanish for heritage learners provides another educational context in which to recognize students' knowledge and identities as Spanish-speakers and to promote their development of the critical analytical and linguistic skills needed to challenge the societal subordination of Spanish (Leeman & Serafini, 2016).

Language Ideologies in Education

In Chapter 4 we outlined the language ideologies framework, presented some language ideologies surrounding Spanish in the US and showed how these ideologies impact the everyday experiences of Latinxs. In this section we focus more narrowly on language ideologies in educational contexts. Our interrelated goals are: (1) to explore how particular ways of thinking about language influence the educational opportunities and outcomes for speakers of Spanish; and (2) to provide insights into the ways in which schools play a role in reproducing or challenging language ideologies.

English hegemony

It should be fairly obvious that the dominant English-only educational model reflects and promotes a belief in the supreme importance of English. This framing of English as a valuable good and the key to success is evident in the names of the Arizona and California initiatives eliminating bilingual education: 'English for the Children.' But current policy doesn't just frame English as necessary for success in US society (Fitzsimmons-Doolan *et al.*, 2017); other languages are largely ignored and constructed as unworthy of maintaining or learning, as is reflected in their exclusion from the curriculum and accountability measures. In some cases, speaking a language other than English is seen not just as unimportant, but as a hindrance to academic achievement. This view is inseparable from the indexical value of Spanish as a marker of **Latinidad**. Moreover, schools that put the utmost priority on English acquisition, while ignoring students' advances in subject matter learning, sacrifice those students' academic achievement and compromise their subsequent opportunities (Gándara, 2012). Thus, English-only policies are both a reflection of racialization and a mechanism of the racialization process. Minority language speakers are further racialized by the way in which some schools treat ESL as a type of remedial education, which frames ELLs as intellectually challenged or deficient, rather than recognizing their existing linguistic repertoires and seeing them as active learners engaged in the complex process of acquiring a new language.

Outside forces also shape what happens within classrooms and schools. For example, when special subjects are taught in English and English is the dominant language in children's lives outside of school, this both reflects the **hegemony** of English and contributes to its elevation in school, including its use by children as the primary language in the playground (Fuller, 2007, 2009; Fuller *et al.*, 2007; Nuñez & Palmer, 2017; Pease-Alvarez & Winsler, 1994; Potowski, 2004, 2007). The hegemony of English can also encroach onto the bilingual domain of dual language programs. It is striking to note that even in Spanish–English bilingual programs which explicitly aim to foster bilingualism, there is more opportunity for language development in English than in Spanish (Nuñez & Palmer, 2017). In some cases, curricular constraints, such as a focus on standardized testing, contribute to emphasis on English, despite bilingualism being the stated aim of the program and/or teachers (Henderson, 2017; Martínez-Roldán, 2015). For example, in a study in an afterschool program designed to support Spanish use, Martínez-Roldán (2015) found that some of the bilingual teacher candidates working with the children nonetheless pushed students to read in English, despite their preference for Spanish.

However, some studies have also documented awareness and resistance to the hegemony of English. For example, DePalma (2010) describes the conscious efforts of one kindergarten teacher to combat the privileging of English by constructing Spanish as a 'power language' and incorporating it into a broader array of activities than was dictated by the curriculum, although this was ultimately perceived as taking time away from achieving academic goals. So too, Lopez (2012) describes how the teacher in the classroom she studied promoted Spanish as a language which belonged in the US and especially in the classroom, referring to it as 'our language' – meaning the language of all children in the bilingual classroom, not only Latinxs. Freeman (2000) documents a dual immersion program in Washington DC that explicitly sought to counter English dominance not only in the curriculum and classroom practices, but also in parent–teacher nights and community events. In those contexts, everything was done bilingually and Spanish was often the first language, before a translation into English. These practices were part of the school's broader project to promote linguistic and cultural pluralism and social justice. Together, such programs, as well as the efforts of individual teachers, make it clear that it is possible to implement inclusive and pluralist language-in-education policies at the local or classroom level, even within the broader context of English hegemony, an issue we return to later in this chapter.

Normative monolingualism and monoglossic ideologies

Clearly, the assumption of monolingualism as the norm is reflected in education that emphasizes the teaching of just one language as well as in the lack of federal and state support for 'foreign' language education. Think for a moment of the contrast with educational policies that teach children two or more languages from earliest childhood, such as the European Union's 'mother tongue plus two.' However, monoglossic ideologies are also reflected in the idea that even when two or more languages are taught, they should be kept strictly separate, resulting in what can be called **dual monolingualism**. Many bilingual programs are structured in this way, dictating that certain subjects or certain times of the day are for speaking one language or the other (Fitts, 2006; Henderson, 2017). While some educational experts have called for translanguaging pedagogies (e.g. García, 2009b), this is not the general norm, and many schools dictate a portion of the day that should be taught in one language or another, which reinforces dominant ideas about the separation of language.

Normative monolingualism and monoglossic language ideologies are also reflected in Spanish language classes. For one, the assumption tends to be that the 'default' student is a White second language learner raised in a monolingual English-speaking home (Leeman & Serafini, 2020; Schwartz, 2018). This ignores and erases the growing percentage of heritage language speakers or treats them as something unusual or outside the norm (Leeman, 2010; Leeman & King, 2015; Pomerantz & Schwartz, 2011). Further, Spanish language teaching often reinforces the idea that Spanish is a 'foreign' language by focusing almost exclusively on Spain and Latin America and not Spanish in the US (Alvarez, 2013; García, 1993). Relatedly, multilingualism in those contexts also often goes unmentioned, and most students of Spanish never learn anything about Indigenous and minority languages, some of which have co-official status (Leeman, 2014). In addition to content, classroom practices and rules also reflect monolingual ideologies; many Spanish as a second language and Spanish as heritage language classes forbid the use of English and translanguaging, and treat any bilingual discourse as a form of linguistic contamination or corruption (Leeman, 2018b; Loza, 2017; Showstack, 2015; Villa, 2002).

Zero-sum ideologies of language and culture

One aspect of monolingual ideologies is the notion that languages are in a constant state of competition, at both the societal and the individual levels, which we call the **zero-sum ideology**. As we discussed in Chapter 4, the one nation–one language ideology entails seeing multilingualism as a threat to the integrity or unity of the nation. At the individual level, zero-sum ideologies similarly see any cognitive or emotional 'space' used for one language or culture as leaving less cognitive space available for other languages and cultures. Thus, the zero-sum ideology undergirds opposition to bilingual education by positioning languages as competing with each other. In this way, it undermines any efforts to maintain minority languages, which are seen as putting English at risk and impeding immigrant assimilation and acquisition of English. Indeed, the zero-sum ideology is embodied in policies oriented toward subtractive bilingualism (i.e. ESL programs and transitional bilingual education), subtractive acculturation and 'subtractive schooling' (Valenzuela, 1999) more broadly. We also see this in the labeling of the policy eliminating bilingual education as 'English for the Children,' as if the only way to promote English acquisition were to do away with Spanish-medium schooling.

The standard language ideology

The standard language ideology impacts both English and Spanish language contexts. As we discussed in Chapter 4, linguistic hierarchies construct the varieties of English spoken by, or associated with, racialized groups and speakers of lower socio-economic status as 'incorrect' or 'bad.' The standard language ideology also establishes hierarchies among different varieties of Spanish. As is the case in English, in Spanish it is also the varieties of the upper middle class that are held up as the model of 'educated,' 'correct' and/or 'good' language. In both English and Spanish, the 'standard' varieties are portrayed as objectively superior, and 'non-standard' varieties are portrayed as not just linguistically but also morally or intellectually deficient (Lippi-Green, 2012; Milroy, 2007). Obviously, when standardized tests and school practices only recognize one particular way of speaking, this disadvantages speakers of other varieties, and thus the standard language ideology contributes to academic and societal inequality.

Spanish language education in the US historically favored the varieties of Spanish spoken in Spain (Ducar, 2009; García, 1993; Herman, 2007; Leeman, 2012b). Although there is now greater inclusion of Latin American national and regional varieties, not all such varieties are portrayed as having the same prestige or legitimacy, based in large part on the perceived characteristics of the speakers. For example, Caribbean varieties are often subordinated to other varieties, in part due to racialized perceptions of the speakers as well as a sense that these varieties deviate from written norms (Alfaraz, 2002; Dávila, 2012; Valdés *et al.*, 2003). Further, even when different national and regional varieties are accepted (or even celebrated), social varieties often are not (Leeman, 2018b; Leeman & Serafini, 2016). In the context of Spanish language education, heritage speakers whose home varieties are seen as rural or associated with lower socio-economic status may be judged negatively, even in classes designed specifically for these learners. In fact, some heritage language educators see their role as that of replacing (or 'fixing') their students' bad (or 'broken') language with the standard variety (Leeman, 2005; Martínez, 2003; Valdés, 1981, 1995; Villa, 2002).

A correlate of the standard language ideology is linguistic purism, which sees language change as deterioration and external linguistic influences as contamination. Together with monoglossic ideologies, then, the standard language ideology sees any influence of English on Spanish as problematic, despite the normalness of such influence in language contact situations. In the next chapter we offer a more thorough discussion of language contact phenomena, and we present research demonstrating that codeswitching or translanguaging should be considered a linguistic resource or skill, rather than a sign of linguistic deficiency; for now we want to note that the field of Spanish teaching often insists on maintaining complete separation between languages. Monoglossic ideologies are enacted through classroom Spanish-only policies that punish practices that are completely normal in bilingual communities. The common but inaccurate notion that codeswitching is primarily the result of gaps in the speakers' linguistic knowledge, rather than an act of identity or a conversational strategy, is reflected in the definition provided on the American Council on the Teaching of Foreign Language (ACTFL) website: 'Switching from one language to another to complete an idea, thought, or sentence, often when one lacks the word or phrase in the language one started off in' (https://www.actfl.org/publications/guidelines-and-manuals/actfl-proficiency-guidelines-2012/glossary#code-switching, accessed 1 May 2019)

An example of the role of standard language ideology in the disparagement and marginalization of lower socio-economic status speakers can be seen in the work of Allard *et al.* (2014) in a high school in an East Coast suburban setting that is part of the New Latinx Diaspora, i.e. a region where the Latinx population has grown recently. They found that not only were the Latinx students positioned as poor students because they were ELLs, but a parallel discourse also positioned them as deficient Spanish-speakers. Even monolingual English-speakers passed judgment on native Spanish-speaking students while stereotyping their parents as illiterate and unable to teach their children either English or Spanish. This disparagement echoes the racializing discourses that portray bilingual students as 'languageless' or 'alingual' (Rosa, 2016b) that we discussed earlier. Comments about the Spanish spoken by the children referred to it as 'kitchen Spanish' and 'hillbilly Spanish,' both terms that link deficiency to lower socio-economic class status.

In Chapter 4 we discussed the role of the standard language ideology in professional contexts, including resistance on the part of employers to hiring speakers of non-standard varieties. For that reason, we want to point out that the standard language ideology doesn't only impact students; it can also have negative consequences for teachers perceived as speaking in a non-standard way. The standard language ideology plays a role, for example, when the state of Arizona sought to fire English teachers who spoke 'with an accent' (Leeman, 2012a), and when US Latinxs are not seen as speaking 'the right kind' of Spanish for teaching (Bustamante & Novella, 2019; Valdés *et al.*, 2003; Villa, 2002; Zentella, 2017).

Language commodification

In contrast with the negative portrayal of minority languages and bilingualism tied to monoglossic ideologies and the language-as-problem orientation toward language, the language-as-resource orientation sees bilingualism as something to be valued and supported (Ruiz, 1984). Rather than focusing on the cultural, social or social justice motivations for sustaining minority languages and cultures, the ideological process of language **commodification** focuses on the economic value of linguistic knowledge. One example of this is that language and language skills are seen as assets that can help individuals in the job market. Similarly, linguistic knowledge can be portrayed as a national resource that makes countries more competitive globally. Further, the teaching of Spanish as a second language has become a huge industry, especially in Spain where the large numbers of international students on study-abroad programs has led this sector of the economy to be dubbed *language tourism* (Bruzos Moro, 2017). Through the *Instituto Cervantes*, the Spanish government has sought both to promote the study of Spanish around the world and to maintain Spain's status as its symbolic 'owner,' thus benefiting Spanish economic interests (Mar-Molinero & Paffey, 2011; Villa & Del Valle, 2014).

While not commodification, in that the focus is not on financial concerns, another instrumentalist discourse portrays the maintenance of minority languages as useful for national security reasons (Bale, 2014; Ricento, 2009). The emphasis on the practical and economic value of languages in general, and Spanish in particular, is part and parcel of a broader trend in which the primary objective of higher education is increasingly seen as the acquisition of job skills and professional training (Leeman, 2007).

In some cases, advocates of language study adopt commodifying discourses as a way to convince students, parents and policy makers that multilingualism is worth the time, effort and cost required. This can be an effective strategy in some cases, such as for getting parents to enroll their children in dual language programs or for encouraging college students to take classes in their heritage language. Recent analyses of the discourses surrounding dual language education found this kind of commodification and the 'gentrification' of such programs, meaning that they are more often available and/or designed for elite and middle-class populations (Delavan *et al.*, 2017; Valdez *et al.*, 2016a, 2016b). As we discussed earlier in the chapter, TWI programs are beneficial for Spanish-speakers, but even when such programs exist, they are not equally accessible for students of all backgrounds.

These commodifying ideologies are, we argue, problematic for many reasons; in addition to potentially promoting inequalities, a focus only on economic and job-market concerns ignores the significance of language for cultural identity and the importance of cultural identity in educational settings (Leeman & Martínez, 2007; Weisman, 2001). Further, while the framing of certain languages as valuable commodities may benefit languages seen as professionally useful, such as Spanish and Mandarin, it inadvertently weakens arguments for preserving 'less useful' languages (Leeman & Martínez, 2007). In other words, if the main reason to learn or maintain a language is to get a better job, maybe there isn't any reason to preserve Navajo, Mixtec or Finnish, etc. (To be clear, we reject that argument!) Moreover, the promised job-related benefits don't always pan out (Subtirelu, 2017).

What often seems to be missing from much educational discourse about the value of Spanish (as well as other minority languages) is that it is valuable for the emotional, social and cognitive development of Spanish-speakers and thus its preservation is tied to broader issues of social justice. Further, for second language speakers, Spanish is also a cultural resource and language learning can be an essential tool in fostering pluralist ideologies.

Differential bilingualism

As we discussed above, monoglossic and zero-sum ideologies frame minority language maintenance by immigrants and their children as problematic both for the children themselves and for society. These ideologies contribute to the racialization of Spanish-speakers; speaking Spanish within this mindset makes a person racially Other and language is framed as the cause of social inequality, rather than a mechanism through which discrimination is carried out. (In some cases there are different expectations for people who 'look Latinx' – not only that they speak Spanish, but also that they have limited English skills and that they come from low-income backgrounds or live in immigrant neighborhoods, for instance.)

Further, such ideologies are the foundation of subtractive bilingualism. In contrast with the negative portrayal of the **circumstantial bilingualism** of Latinx children who grow up speaking Spanish at home, the **elective bilingualism** of Anglophones who choose to learn Spanish is framed positively. This distinction is sometimes referred to as **differential bilingualism** (Aparicio, 1998) and reflects a double standard. Latinxs' bilingualism is 'bad' and reflects an unwillingness to assimilate, but elite elective bilingualism is 'good.' Rather than an unwillingness to participate in mainstream culture, quite the contrary, elective bilingualism is seen to be a ticket to success. Thus, learning Spanish when you already speak English is intended to be additive bilingualism. In contrast, those who speak Spanish before learning English should undergo subtractive bilingualism because maintaining Spanish is seen as detrimental to English proficiency, academic achievement and social belonging. These ideologies are also tied up with the 'gentrification' of bilingual education discussed in the previous section.

Pluralist and heteroglossic ideologies

Earlier we have examined monolingual and monoglossic ideologies underlying language-in-education policies and circulating in educational contexts. Despite the strength of these ideologies, there are also some bright spots. Indeed, the growth of dual language education, even in cases where English hegemony continues, is evidence that this hegemony is not complete. Further, schools don't always mirror the broader society and, as we noted, there are cases of schools, programs and classrooms where linguistic and cultural pluralism is valued, and bilingual discourse is seen as a legitimate and effective means of communication (Brunn, 1999; Jacobson, 1998; Shannon, 1999). In another example, García and her associates (García, 2009a, 2009b; García *et al.*, 2017) have documented the classroom use of translanguaging, which they define as '*multiple discursive practices* in which bilinguals engage in order to *make sense of their bilingual worlds*' (García, 2009a: 45, italics in original). Rather than being required to conform to a monoglossic standard imposed by teachers, students made use of all of their linguistic resources to complete academic tasks. Similarly, in a case study of two teachers (Henderson, 2017), teachers fluidly shifted between languages and opened up opportunities for students to use bilingual discourse.

As we discussed in Chapter 4, contradictory ideologies sometimes compete within a single context, and in some cases **heteroglossic ideologies** and approaches have been found to coexist with standard language ideologies and/or the elevation of English. For example, in the after-school program she studied, Martínez-Roldán (2015) documented both productive translanguaging practices and the promotion of English. Similarly, Martínez et al. (2015) observed translanguaging in a dual language program even though the teachers in this program also often espoused purist ideologies about language separation. Along the same lines, in her research in a college-level Spanish for heritage speakers program, Showstack (2015, 2017) found that the instructor and students took up different discourses at different moments, sometimes echoing institutional discourses about 'academic Spanish' but at other times celebrating local practices that draw from both English and Spanish. Importantly, all of this research highlights that multiple competing ideologies can coexist and circulate in the same educational spaces, and with them practices that fall somewhere between the strict policing of language choice and the defense of translanguaging practices.

What many of these studies bring out is the importance of individual teachers' agency in creating an environment that is encouraging of bilingualism. While official and unofficial policies certainly constrain what happens in the classroom (Hornberger, 2005), educators can play a key role in pushing against those constraints or challenging them outright (Palmer, 2007). For example, Gort and Sembiante (2015) report on classroom teachers' use of flexible bilingual practices to counter the language separation ideology of their school. These practices included codeswitching, translation, bilingual recasting and language brokering, which drew on the children's repertoires and experiences. In the next section we present a few examples of educational programs and approaches designed specifically to counter hegemonic ideologies in English-medium and Spanish language instruction.

Critical Pedagogical Approaches to Language Education

As we have seen, the failure to recognize and value the experiences of Spanish-speaking students not only contributes to language loss and shift to English, but it also negatively impacts educational achievement and social wellbeing. Further, when schools reinforce monoglossic and standard language ideologies, they contribute to social inequality and undermine democratic ideals. Still, as we discussed in Chapter 4, people who are negatively impacted by language ideologies sometimes take up those same ideologies. **Critical pedagogy** seeks to promote social justice by helping students critically analyze and challenge structural inequalities and hegemonic ideologies (Burbules & Berk, 1999; Freire, 1970). In this section we present just a few examples of critical pedagogical programs designed to make language education more representative and inclusionary, to promote students' understanding of the role of language in social and political life and to help students develop the analytic tools to resist dominant language ideologies.

One innovative program is the School Kids Investigating Language in Life and Society (SKILLS) program, originally developed at the University of California Santa Barbara in 2010 and which has been taught in a variety of educational contexts, mostly for secondary school students. The aim of the course is to offer students an opportunity to learn to talk about language in society with a focus on social justice, racism and activism. The program is taught mainly in English, but addresses issues in multilingualism. While the majority of the student participants are Latinx, and a main focus is the experience of students of color, students of a variety of other backgrounds have also completed this course. Bucholtz *et al.* (2018) discuss how SKILLS is designed to draw on the knowledge and proficiencies of the students, and to help Latinx youth to recognize the process of racialization and the reproduction of inequalities that they experience as well as to position themselves as activists in the fight against discrimination.

Within the context of Spanish language education (and university Spanish programs), there have been numerous calls to expand the focus beyond Spain and Latin America by incorporating the linguistic varieties and practices, as well as the literatures and cultures, of US Latinxs (e.g. Alonso, 2006; Alvarez, 2013). Educators have also called for attention to sociolinguistics and language variation as well as discussions about the legitimacy of all varieties of Spanish, and a consideration of the 'normalness' of language contact phenomena like translanguaging and borrowing. In many cases these calls have focused on Spanish for heritage language speakers programs (e.g. Beaudrie *et al.*, 2014; Leeman, 2005; Valdés, 1995), but there have also been calls to include such discussions throughout the Spanish curriculum, including for second language learners (e.g. Leeman & Serafini, 2016; Pascual y Cabo & Prada, 2018). Those taking a critical pedagogical approach don't just seek to incorporate more varieties in the classroom, they strive for students to understand how language variation works, and how language is tied up with social and political issues including identity, inequality and race (e.g. Holguín Mendoza, 2018a; Leeman, 2005, 2018b; Martínez, 2003; Potowski & Shin, 2018). Recent proposals also recommend that the study of Spanish should include discussions of multilingualism, language ideologies and language policy (e.g. Leeman, 2018b; Leeman & Serafini, 2016), similar to what we are doing in this book! The fact that an increasing number of Spanish departments across the country are now offering courses on Spanish in the US (something quite rare just 20 years ago) shows a growing recognition of the presence and importance of Spanish in the US.

We also want to highlight the growing number of college Spanish service-learning programs that engage students in critical discussions of language ideologies and policies, as well as of their role in structural inequality, and then provide supported opportunities for students to work in local communities (e.g. Holguín Mendoza, 2018a; Leeman *et al.*, 2011; Lowther-Pereira, 2015; Martínez & Schwartz, 2012; Pascual y Cabo *et al.*, 2017). By working as translators and interpreters in local clinics or by leading an after-school Spanish as a heritage language program, participants in these programs develop identities as language experts but also as agents of social change working to challenge dominant language ideologies and the inequities that they sustain.

Educating Diverse Populations: Beyond Language Differences

In this chapter we have focused on Spanish in education and we have suggested that language-in-education policies play an important role in reproducing language ideologies and societal patterns of language shift to English, as well as shaping the experiences of Latinxs in schools. Of course, other factors such as socio-economic status and racism also play an important role. In a report for the National Research Center for Hispanic Children and Families, the authors note that 61% of Latinx children live in low-income households (Wildsmith *et al.*, 2016: 2). Gándara and Mordechay (2017: 149) discussed the effect of poverty on educational success, noting that in addition to influencing the resources children have outside of school (including nutrition and healthcare), it also determines 'where children will go to school, with whom, and by whom they will be taught.' As we discussed above, program types, classmates and teachers are critical influences on educational success, and high-quality educational programs are less available for children living in poor neighborhoods and school districts. Certainly, educational policies that make public school funding contingent on local tax revenues, thus allocating more money to affluent areas, have an impact on academic outcomes and the experiences children have in school, which in turn influence their place in society as they grow older. Nationally, only 75% of Latinxs complete high school, whereas 87% of non-Latinx Whites and 89% of Asian Americans do (Gándara & Mordechay, 2017: 148–149); these figures reflect schools' failure to serve Latinx students.

As we have touched on throughout this chapter, racialization is a key issue that impacts Spanish-speaking children and Latinxs of all linguistic backgrounds. Research has addressed the negative impact of racialization on the social and emotional wellbeing as well as the academic performance of Latinx students in school (Garcia, 2015). Studies have shown that the discourse of deficit is still prevalent in the devaluing of the knowledge and backgrounds of Latinx and other racialized students (Espinoza-Herold & González-Carriedo, 2017; Fernández, 2002; Flores & Rosa, 2015; Vega *et al.*, 2015; Villenas, 2012). As we have stressed, language ideologies such as normative monolingualism, the standard language ideology, the hegemony of English and the subordination of Spanish, as well as the educational policies and practices that reproduce them, play a key role in the racialization of Latinxs. This racialization, together with the concomitant devaluing of Latinxs' linguistic and cultural knowledge, can lead to Latinx students being denied access to opportunities and encouragement, as well as to their exclusion from accelerated courses and gifted tracks that lead to college. Given the impact of educational classification, tracking and the racialized expectations of students, Achinstein *et al.* (2015) advocate for a 're-labelling' process which seeks to challenge how minority students are categorized in order to position them as potentially college-bound and promote their academic achievement.

As we have seen, structural racism, racialization and language ideologies have an impact throughout the educational system. At the societal level, socio-economic inequality and language ideologies influence not only the availability of quality schools but also programmatic concerns such as whether students have access to bilingual education, Spanish language education or ESL, and also the goals of such programs and the outcomes they promote. At the school and classroom level, attitudes and behaviors that systematically position Latinxs as racially, culturally, academically and/or linguistically inferior also shape outcomes. For this reason, Latinx advocates and activists have sought to expand the curriculum to recognize and value Latinx histories, experiences and cultures, such as through the inclusion of ethnic studies programs as well as through the recognition and valuing of Spanish.

While not the only challenge facing minority language and other racialized students, language-in-education policies and teaching approaches that recognize, value and sustain students' cultural and linguistic backgrounds are clearly relevant for creating positive learning environments and fostering student agency and academic success for all students (Giroux, 1991; Leeman, 2005, 2014; Nieto, 2010; Paris, 2012; Valenzuela, 1999). To cite just one example of the impact that Spanish language education can have on students' academic achievement, graduation rates among Latinx students at Roosevelt High School in Minneapolis went up by 15 percentage points following the creation of a Spanish as a heritage language program with a curriculum focusing on both language and identity (Hinrichs, 2016). This example shows a clear correlation between academic success and attention to and validation of students' language backgrounds.

Conclusions and Connections

In this chapter we have seen how various topics covered in this book are all relevant for the analysis of language-in-education policies for Latinx education. Hegemonic ideologies that devalue bilingualism, promote subtractive acculturation and equate Whiteness with high status are both reflected and reinforced within the English-only educational models that predominate within the US, despite the overwhelming research demonstrating the advantages of additive bilingual programs. These ideologies and policies, together with the broader racialization of Latinx children, perpetuate inequality. Moreover, monolingual ideologies also have a negative impact on majority language children, as they have only limited opportunities to learn an additional language. Even in the context of Spanish language education, the standard language ideology and differential bilingualism favor second language learners and subordinate heritage language learners.

The hope for educational improvement lies in consciousness-raising and activism – among teacher trainers, researchers, educators and parents as well as students and communities – about: language ideologies; critical analysis of discourses about race, ethnicity, social class and minority languages and their speakers; and the promotion of alternative visions of multilingualism and linguistic diversity. Language ideologies are directly related to what happens in schools in terms of programs and policies (i.e. making space for Spanish maintenance and learning) as well as in terms of everyday practices (valuing diversity in language and culture). We advocate actively addressing what are often implicit ideas (and biases) about Spanish, and its speakers, in the US. Through such engagement, we can create better opportunities for education in the US for all children, including both those who speak Spanish and those who don't.

Discussion Questions and Activities for Chapter 9

(1) Is it the job of students to adapt to educational practices in order to be successful, or is it the job of educational systems to figure out how best to serve local populations in order to help them achieve success? What are the implications, in terms of curriculum and classroom practices, for each of these options?

(2) What are some of the historical reasons for, and goals of, public education? If you were running for office and arguing in favor of free public education, what would you say? Along the same lines, what do you think the purpose of higher education is or should be? How about Spanish language education (whether for second or heritage language speakers)?

(3) Do an internet search regarding the benefits of bilingualism. What kinds of benefits are mentioned (e.g. cognitive, social, economic, etc.)? Are there any assumptions about differences between circumstantial or elective bilingualism, or any other ideologies reflected in the discussion of benefits? Finally, do you think discussion of these benefits would be useful for changing school policy? Why or why not?

(4) If you have ever taken a language instruction course (especially but not limited to Spanish or ESL), reflect on your experience and analyze the language ideologies embodied in the course design, textbooks, teaching practices and learning activities. Which language varieties and cultures were included and/or taught? How was the 'value' of language learning portrayed?

(5) Listen to (at least) the first half of the 'The Breakdown: Battle Over MEChA' on National Public Radio's *Latino USA* podcast (https://www.latinousa.org/2019/04/16/mechabreakdown). What was the context and motivation for the founding of the group, and what were their goals? How did MEChA seek to promote educational success and how was this connected to other social and political concerns? Analyze the podcast with regard to these topics covered in other chapters: (1) the motivation for and indexical meanings of the identity labels; (2) Latinx ethnoracial identity; (3) gender-inclusive language; and (4) intersectionality.

Further Reading and Resources

Brooke-Garza, E. (2015) Two-way bilingual education and Latino students. *Educational Leadership and Administration: Teaching and Program Development* 26, 75–85.

Flores, N. and García, O. (2017) A critical review of bilingual education in the United States: From basements and pride to boutiques and profit. *Annual Review of Applied Linguistics* 37, 14–29.

Fránquiz, M.E., Leija, M.G. and Salinas, C.S. (2019) Challenging damaging ideologies: Are dual language education practices addressing learners' linguistic rights? *Theory Into Practice* 58 (2), 134–144.

Leeman, J. (2018b) Critical language awareness and Spanish as a heritage language: Challenging the linguistic subordination of US Latinxs. In K. Potowski (ed.) *Handbook of Spanish as a Minority/Heritage Language* (pp. 345–358). New York: Routledge.

Martínez, G. and Train, R. (2019) *Tension and Contention in Language Education for Latinxs in the United States: Experience and Ethics in Teaching and Learning*. New York: Routledge.

Valdés, G. (2015) Latin@s and the intergenerational continuity of Spanish: The challenges of curricularizing language. *International Multilingual Research Journal* 9 (4), 253–273.

Valenzuela, A. (1999) *Subtractive Schooling: U.S.–Mexican Youth and the Politics of Caring*. Albany, NY: SUNY Press.

Chapter 10

Structural Aspects of Speaking Spanish in the US

Objectives

To introduce readers to some linguistic features of the most common varieties of Spanish spoken in the US, Latinx Englishes and Spanish–English language contact, as well as to examine attitudes toward these varieties and practices.

Introduction

So far in this book we haven't spent much time talking about the formal linguistic characteristics of Spanish as it's spoken in the US. In part, that's because our focus is on the sociopolitical aspects of speaking Spanish, but it's also because there is a long scholarly tradition of dialectology (i.e. the study of geographic and regional variation), and thus there are a wealth of other publications examining the linguistic features of the varieties of Spanish in the US that interested readers can consult (e.g. Bills, 1997; Espinosa, 1911; Lipski, 1993, 2008; Otheguy & Zentella, 2011).

Nonetheless, a unitary focus on either linguistic form or the social aspects of language isn't really possible. For one thing, language variation and change are shaped by language-external social and political factors. And by this point in the book, it should be more than clear that linguistic form, and linguistic variation, are laden with social and symbolic meanings. In particular, speakers draw from the different varieties, registers, styles, pronunciations and words in their linguistic repertoires to construct and perform various kinds of identities. So too, listeners ascribe identities and make judgments about speakers based on the way they talk. And as we've seen, language varieties and linguistic features associated with specific national origins provide a wealth of resources for making meaning and expressing identity, as do language practices that combine Spanish and English. Further, people often have strong opinions and attitudes regarding particular varieties, languages and linguistic practices, even though there is nothing objectively better or worse about any of them. And as we've also seen, these attitudes and ideologies are used to justify a range of social and political practices.

In this chapter we examine the linguistic features of varieties of Spanish spoken in the US as well as the formal characteristics of language contact and multilingual discourse. From there, we will move on to address research on contact between different varieties of Spanish in the US. We also look at the other side of the language contact coin by examining some features of English varieties influenced by Spanish. In the final section, we address attitudes about these different linguistic structures and practices.

Varieties of Spanish in the US

The diverse national origins and histories of the people who speak Spanish in the US are reflected in the ways in which Spanish is spoken. When Spanish conquistadors and colonists began settling in the Americas at the end of the 15th century they brought with them the language varieties and linguistic resources that they had used before their arrival, and these obviously played a key role in shaping the sounds, structures and vocabulary of the Spanish first spoken in North America, just as the particular origins of British colonists and settlers influenced how English was spoken in the British colonies. For example, settlers from the Canary Islands were well represented among settlers in Louisiana as well as in the Caribbean. As a result, Isleño Spanish (the vestigial variety of Spanish that was spoken in southern Louisiana through the 20th century) as well as Cuban, Dominican and Puerto Rican varieties were all influenced by the Spanish of the Canaries (Lipski, 1993, 2008).

So too, Spanish-speaking immigrants and refugees who come to the US today arrive with specific **linguistic repertoires** and practices, and thus contemporary patterns of migration have an impact on the kinds of Spanish spoken in different parts of the US. For example, in New England, New York and Florida you are more likely to hear a variety of Caribbean Spanish; in Phoenix, Arizona, Mexican varieties are far more common; and in Northern Virginia there's a greater chance of hearing Salvadoran, Bolivian or Peruvian Spanish. Logically, changes in migratory flows can lead to changes in how Spanish is spoken. To be clear, the ways people speak change over time, and the longer someone is in the US, the more likely it is that their linguistic repertoire is different from the one with which they arrived, as we discuss in more depth later in this chapter.

It's important to remember that sending and receiving locations are not monolithic in terms of linguistic identities, varieties and practices. For example, not all Spanish-speakers in

Phoenix are Mexican or Mexican American, nor do all Mexicans speak the same anyway. In Chapter 4 we discussed the language ideology that imagines languages as distinct, bounded entities linked to nations (Anderson, 1991). Similarly, in Spanish dialectology there is a longstanding tradition of discussing language varieties as if the boundaries between them corresponded to the political boundaries between nations (Penny, 2000). However, just as languages are socially constructed, the delineation of language varieties along national borders is also based on ideologies and convenience as much as (or more than) linguistics. Still, there is something to be said for convenience, and we will largely follow this tradition in our discussion of the linguistic features spoken by different national origin groups.

Like most things, languages are not static entities but instead undergo constant change and evolution (Aitchison, 2001; Bybee, 2015), and this is also true for Spanish. There is nothing inherently good or bad about language change, but language purists often look down on change is if it reflected corruption, decay or decline. Nonetheless, despite these attitudes, many changes eventually come to be accepted and seen as normal. Think, for example, of the case of Latin. It is only through language change and deviations from the prescribed norm that we have the **Romance languages**, including Spanish, today. Similarly, language change has led to geographic variation within Spanish. This is because language change doesn't happen overnight, and it doesn't affect all words, all linguistic or social contexts or all speakers at the same time. Sometimes changes are eventually adopted by all speakers; in other cases they only reach some varieties, some communities or some subset of speakers. In cases where a variety retains an older form while other varieties adopt a change, the older form is referred to as an *archaism*. Some examples of archaisms in the US include the past tense forms *truje* (vs. *traje* 'I brought') and *asina* (vs. *así* 'thus'), both of which are found in the Southwest.

But what is the source of language change? Sometimes, change can be attributed to language-internal factors, or causes within the language itself. One such motivator of change is ease of articulation when a particular sound or combination of sounds is difficult to pronounce, such as in the case of the double N in the Latin word *alunnus* ('student'), which became 'mn' in the contemporary Spanish word *alumno*. Another type of change is simplification, in which linguistic contrasts are eliminated. For example, in most varieties of Spanish either *ser* or *estar* (both of which are verbs meaning 'to be') can be used with adjectives that describe age, size and physical appearance, depending on the intended meaning. For example, *el caballo es viejo* ('the horse is old') describes the horse as old (in contrast with other horses), while *el caballo está viejo* means the horse is or looks old (compared to how it used to be) (Falk, 1979). However, in some Mexican varieties this distinction is disappearing, and *estar* is consistently used with such adjectives (regardless of the meaning) (Silva-Corvalán, 1994). Silva-Corvalán found that in Los Angeles the extension of *estar* was most common among people who either were born in the US or immigrated at an early age. The lack of educational opportunities in Spanish led to greater propensity for language change among the second and subsequent generations.

In other cases, language change is prompted by language-external causes, such as when a language comes into prolonged contact with another language or another variety. Long-term, widespread bilingualism increases the likelihood of cross-linguistic influence. One common language contact phenomenon is **borrowing** – the incorporation in one language of words from another language. Historically, Spanish has incorporated borrowings from various languages, including Arabic (e.g. *almohada* 'pillow'), Nahuatl (e.g. *tomate* 'tomato') and English (*fútbol* 'football/soccer'), just as English has incorporated words from Spanish such as *alligator* (from *el largarto* 'lizard') and *ranch* (from *rancho*). We discuss additional features and consequences of language contact later in this chapter. As the percentage of Spanish-speakers who were born in the US rises (see Chapter 2), such contact may play a greater and greater role in shaping Spanish in the US.

Obviously, Spanish in the US has been in extensive contact with English, but it is also characterized by contact among different varieties of Spanish, as immigrants have arrived from many different places. In some cases, immigrants take up some features of Spanish as it is spoken in their new home, but they may also change the character of that Spanish if the ways in which they speak spread to other people. Recent arrivals may have an even stronger influence on the kind of Spanish one hears in the US due to the endurance of the three-generation pattern of language shift we discussed in Chapter 2. The children and grandchildren of immigrants are increasingly English-dominant, and thus they may only use Spanish in limited domains such as with parents and relatives, potentially limiting their contact with speakers of other varieties.

In the following sections we briefly present examples of lexical, phonetic and structural features that characterize the most numerous national origin groups in the US: Mexicans, Puerto Ricans, Cubans, Dominicans and Salvadorans. Our goal is not to provide a comprehensive overview of these varieties of Spanish, but rather to describe a few salient features in a way that is accessible to readers without training in linguistics.

Lexical variation

Differences in the lexicon, or vocabulary, among varieties of Spanish are often the focus of casual conversations about variation in how Spanish-speakers talk (see, for example, the YouTube video about the different words for 't-shirt' at https://www.youtube.com/watch?v=LjaD_oFg90A, or the *Why not Spanish?* webpage which gives different words for 'hotdog' and 'drinking straw' at https://www.whynotspanish.com/lexical-variations-spanish-many-words/). Some lexical variation in Latin American Spanish is the result of language contact with various African and Indigenous languages, and in some cases the Spanish words used in different places reflect borrowings from different Indigenous languages. For example, the Nahuatl-origin *aguacate* ('avocado') is used throughout Mexico and Central America, while the Quechua word *palta* is used in much of South America.

Phonetic variation

One immediately noticeable aspect of linguistic variation is pronunciation. Sometimes a person just needs to say a word or two for her **interlocutors** to recognize a particular accent. Many of the sounds that distinguish varieties of Spanish found in the US occur at the ends of syllables. These include /s/,[1] which is sometimes aspirated (i.e. pronounced like the English letter *h*) or elided completely, such that the word *los* is pronounced 'loh' or 'lo'.

These pronunciations are typical of Caribbean and Central American varieties, as is the **velarization** of /n/, in which the back part of the tongue makes contact with the back part of the mouth, producing a sound similar to the last sound in the English words *going* or *walking*. Velarization of /n/ most often occurs at the end of an utterance (or before a pause). Two interrelated features of Caribbean Spanish that also impact sounds at the end of syllables are the **lateralization** of /r/ (i.e. pronounced 'l') and **rhotacization** of /l/ (i.e. pronounced 'r'). An example of lateralization is pronouncing the name *Marta* as 'malta'; and an example of rhotacization is pronouncing *Alba* as 'arba'. In some areas, either one or the other of these phenomena predominates, but in others they are both found.

Also typical of the Caribbean is the deletion of /d/ between vowels, such that words like *cortado* and *pensado* are pronounced as 'cortao' and 'pensao'. One other feature typical of Puerto Rican Spanish is the pronunciation of *rr* (and *r* at the beginning of a word) almost like the English letter *h*. This pronunciation together with the lateralization of /r/ (i.e. 'Puelto Hico') is emblematic of Puerto Rico, much in the same way as 'pahk the cah' is emblematic of Bostonian English.

In contrast, in Mexican Spanish syllable-final /s/ is typically retained. In addition, /n/ before a pause is pronounced with the tip of the tongue making contact in the front of the mouth, behind the teeth. One feature that is common to some Mexican and Puerto Rican varieties is the pronunciation of *ch* like *sh* (such that words like *muchacho* are pronounced as 'mushasho') (Lipski, 2008). Finally, one of the more salient phonetic features found in Mexico (as well as in the Andes), but not the Caribbean or Central America, is the reduction of unstressed vowels, especially next to /s/, such that *mestizo* might be pronounced more like 'mstizo' and *pues* like 'ps'.

In addition to syllable-final aspiration of /s/, many Salvadoran-speakers aspirate syllable-initial /s/ and pronounce it with the tip of the tongue between the front teeth, such that it sounds almost like English *th*. For example, *sí* ('yes') sounds almost like the beginning of the English word *theater*.

Structural variation

As we mentioned in Chapter 6, one characteristic associated with Central American Spanish is *voseo*. Voseo consists of the use of *vos* to mean 'you' (i.e. as the second person singular pronoun), as well as the corresponding verb forms which typically have stress on the final syllable (*vos hablás* vs. *tú hablas*). In some places such as Argentina, Honduras and Uruguay, *vos* is equivalent to *tú*. In other places, including El Salvador, *vos* is part of a three-tiered pronominal system in which *vos, tú* and *usted* are used to express different social meanings, with *vos* being used for the most intimate relationships, *usted* to express the most social distance and *tú* falling somewhere in between (Rivera-Mills, 2011).

Another example of variation related to pronoun use is whether the pronouns are expressed overtly or 'dropped.' In contrast with English, in which pronouns are generally required, in Spanish they are not, so the English phrase *I speak Spanish* could be expressed either as *Yo hablo español* or simply *Hablo español*. In Caribbean varieties, overt subject pronouns are more commonly used than in other varieties (we discuss this in more detail below, in the context of contact among varieties of Spanish). Another feature of Caribbean varieties of Spanish is that personal pronouns can occur as the subject of infinitives, such as in the examples provided by Lipski (2008: 125): *para yo hacer eso* ('for me to do that'); *antes de tú venir aquí* ('before you came here'), which in other varieties of Spanish might be rendered as *para que yo haga eso* and *antes de que vinieras aquí.* A third feature of Caribbean Spanish is the non-inversion of questions, such as in the example cited by Bullock and Toribio (2014: 156): *¿Cuánto un medico gana?* ('How much does a doctor earn?'), which in non-Caribbean varieties would likely be expressed with normative subject-verb inversion: *¿Cuánto gana un medico?*

In addition to the features of varieties of Spanish associated with the national origins of Spanish-speakers in the US, contact with English is a key factor shaping Spanish in the US. In the next section we examine the varied phenomena associated with language contact, including cross-linguistic influences as well as multilingual practices and discourse.

Language Contact Phenomena

In various places in this book we have made reference to people combining Spanish and English in conversation, a phenomenon often referred to as **codeswitching**. In Chapter 4 we explained that some scholars taking a heteroglossic approach to multilingualism prefer the term **translanguaging** in order to emphasize that speakers' linguistic repertoires do not line up neatly with traditionally defined languages, and to focus more on language use rather than linguistic form (e.g. García, 2009b; García & Wei, 2014). However, even though languages are socially constructed, and the classification of particular ways of speaking as belonging to one language or another is ideological or political rather than linguistic (see Chapter 4), this doesn't mean that speakers don't *think* of different ways of speaking as belonging to different languages (Auer, forthcoming). In other words, different languages (and language varieties) exist in the sense that they have cognitive and social meaning for speakers, and the large body of research on language contact focusing on linguistic structure generally starts from the assumption that individual features can usually be identified as belonging to one language or another. This research focuses on the structural and cognitive interaction of language systems, such as which elements come from which linguistic systems, how they are combined in contact situations and what cognitive mechanisms are involved in switching. Some language contact scholars interested in the linguistic features and structure of bilingual language use argue that the translanguaging framework offers few insights in this regard (Bhatt & Bolonyai, 2019). The following discussion focuses on the body of literature on formal features of language contact.

We present definitions and examples of language contact phenomena in the next section, but first there are two important points to be made. First, it is natural and normal for all languages in extended contact to influence each other, and for speakers to use forms associated with different languages in their speech, whether through borrowing or codeswitching. Thus, the language contact phenomena associated with Spanish in the US are also found in many other linguistic contexts; languages in contact invariably influence each other, albeit often in asymmetrical ways (Fairclough, 2003; Lipski, 2007). Borrowing is a normal phenomenon and can occur even when there is already an existing word that means the same thing as the borrowed word. Similarly, codeswitching should not be assumed to be the result of linguistic gaps; bilinguals who know specific words in both languages may nonetheless codeswitch these words (Zentella, 1997a). Further, monolinguals also combine linguistic resources without regard to whether these are associated with different language varieties or styles. In other words, borrowing and codeswitching are common phenomena and they are not a sign of linguistic deficiency.

Secondly, despite the normality of language contact phenomena and multilingual discourse, **hegemonic ideologies** often view them negatively, especially in contexts where **normative monolingualism** and/or the **standard language ideology** are strong, as we have discussed repeatedly. Spanish that shows signs of contact with English is held up for ridicule, and multilingual discourse is often taken as a sign that a speaker cannot speak either language; that is, it is seen as a sign of linguistic deficiency (Myers-Scotton, 2006: 10). In many cases multilinguals themselves share these negative attitudes rooted in hegemonic ideologies, and they also believe that languages should remain 'pure' and linguistically distinct. As we have seen over and over again, ideologies about language are never just about language (Woolard, 1998); negative attitudes about Spanglish and language contact phenomena reflect the racialization of the people with whom they are associated. This is also the case for negative portrayals of translanguaging as well as broader framings of multilingualism as 'languagelessness' (Rosa, 2019: 128). But as we'll discuss below, nothing could be further from the truth; in fact, rather than a linguistic deficiency, the use of two languages in juxtaposition requires sophisticated structural knowledge of both of them (Toribio, 2000; Waltermire, 2014). Moreover, as we showed in Chapters 5 and 6, multilingual discourse is a powerful resource for performing identities and communicating other social and symbolic meanings. Further, many cases of codeswitching demonstrate an impressive linguistic creativity; for just a few published examples, see the children's books listed in the Further Reading for this chapter, the video linked in Discussion Question 2, the discussion of *¿Qué pasa USA?* in Chapter 7, and Tato Laviera's poem *Spanglish*, available at: https://www.poetryoutloud.org/poem/spanglish). Such creativity is also evident in conversational multilingual discourse.

Spanglish

Before continuing, the use of the term *Spanglish* should be problematized. One issue is that it's not completely clear exactly what it denotes; the term is perhaps most commonly used to mean the use of English and Spanish within a single utterance, but it is also sometimes used to refer to borrowings or Spanish constructions which have developed in a contact situation. We've also heard *Spanglish* used to refer to the language of non-native speakers of Spanish; although this last usage is less common, it is another case of the term being used to refer to incomplete knowledge of Spanish (in line with the ideology we discussed in the previous section).

As we have discussed, **monoglossic** and standard language ideologies see codeswitching as a sign of linguistic deficiency and some people use the term *Spanglish* as a pejorative way of describing multilingual discourse and other language contact phenomena. As Rodriguez (2007: 38) puts it, 'Spanglish's critics view Spanglish as a dirty dialect that threatens to pollute Spanish and English.' This usage, and the framing of cross-linguistic influence as corruption and contamination, can be seen, for example, in the *Real Academia Española's* (RAE) treatment of Spanglish (see Chapter 8). When the RAE decided to add *espanglish* to its famed dictionary, it proposed to define it as:

> *Modalidad del habla de algunos grupos hispanos de los Estados Unidos, en la que se mezclan, deformándolos, elementos léxicos y gramaticales del español y del inglés.*
>
> Manner of speaking of some Hispanic groups in the United States, in which lexical and grammatical elements of Spanish and English are mixed, deforming them.
>
> (RAE, 2014, cited in Zentella, 2017a: 32)

Following public and academic outcry, the RAE eventually eliminated the word *deformándolos* ('deforming them') from the definition, thus eliminating the explicit disparagement. Nonetheless, the definition still implies that Spanglish is limited to 'some Hispanic groups in the United States.' This is consistent with the RAE's broader portrayal of Spanglish as an aberration (Zentella, 2017a), and it provides a clear example of the role of dictionaries (and language academies) in reproducing the standard language ideology.

In contrast with the derogatory manner in which the term *Spanglish* is often used in the media and everyday conversations, it is used by many speakers of US Spanish with a positive connotation. In addition, there are various humorous books and 'dictionaries' about Spanglish that use the word in their titles, such as Cruz and Teck's (1998) *The Official Spanglish Dictionary: Un User's Guide to More Than 300 Words and Phrases That Aren't Exactly Español or Inglés* and Santiago's (2008) *Pardon my Spanglish.* There are also bumper stickers, t-shirts and other artifacts of popular culture where people refer to themselves as speakers of Spanglish, showing that the term is sometimes used to mark an ingroup way of speaking to celebrate the creativity of these linguistic practices. There are also novels and a growing collection of children's books celebrating Spanglish (see Further Reading and Resources below). Thus, non-linguists who use the term *Spanglish* include those who see this way of speaking as a creative variety or practice as well as a valued marker of US Latinx and/or Spanish-speaking identity.

Within academia the term *Spanglish* also has both supporters and detractors. For example, Otheguy and Stern (2010) reject the term, arguing that it is misleading because it portrays language contact between Spanish and English as something different from other cases of language contact and that it frames the Spanish spoken in the US as 'less than' Spanish. They state:

> We reject the use of the term Spanglish because there is no objective justification for the term, and because it expresses an ideology of exceptionalism and scorn that actually

> deprives the North American Latino community of a major resource in this globalized world: mastery of a world language. Thus on strictly objective technical grounds, as well as for reasons of personal and political development, the term Spanglish is to be discarded and replaced by the term Spanish or, if greater specificity is required, Spanish in the United States. (Otheguy & Stern, 2010: 85)

Otheguy and Stern's point is that Spanish spoken in the US is just like other varieties that have changed and adapted to new environments as a result of extended language contact; they see the term *Spanglish* as portraying natural language development as if it were something unusual or negative. On the other hand, for some people the term *Spanglish* does just the opposite – it indexes a celebration of the heteroglossic nature of linguistic performance and an attempt to normalize multilingualism (e.g. Cruz & Teck, 1998; Santiago, 2008; Stavans, 2003; Stavans & Albin, 2007). Further, Zentella (2017a) suggests that a focus on the term itself detracts from a more important battle: fighting the subordination of Spanish and Spanish-speakers in the US.

These debates about the term *Spanglish* serve to remind us that the meanings of words and labels are neither unitary, fixed nor neutral. Instead, words can have multiple meanings, according to the context, the speakers and the hearers, and they are sometimes hotly contested. Like the ethnoracial identity labels we discussed in Chapter 5, *Spanglish* can mean different things to different people, and these different meanings are tied up with ideologies about language and identity. Thus, these debates about whether or not to use *Spanglish* are about much more than a single word or what that word refers to. In the following discussion we will continue to use *Spanglish* when it is used by the authors whose work is being discussed, but as descriptive terms we will use *contact varieties of Spanish, language contact phenomena* and *multilingual discourse.*

Language Contact Phenomena Defined

As mentioned above, while scholars working within the translanguaging framework challenge the notion of languages as clearly delimited entities, much of the research on language contact phenomena is based on the idea of languages as distinct entities and seeks to determine how different languages influence each other. This research has had, and continues to have, an important place in the study of Spanish in the US and thus we present it here.

Borrowing

In Haugen's (1950) landmark work, he defines various types of influence of one language on another, many of which are relevant in the case of Spanish in the US. As we noted above, *borrowing* is the incorporation of a word from one language into another, with the incorporated word typically called a *loanword* or *loan*. The language that incorporates an element from another language is called the recipient language, and the language from which the element is taken is the donor language.

One way of knowing that a loanword has been fully incorporated in the recipient language is phonological integration. A word that is phonologically integrated is pronounced according to the normal pronunciation of the recipient language, rather than the donor language. Think, for example, of how the Spanish-to-English borrowings *patio* and *ranch* are pronounced; they sound like English rather than Spanish. Similarly, the more recent borrowing shown in Figure 10.1, this one from English to Spanish, has also been phonologically integrated. In this example, the English word *please* has been borrowed into Spanish, with the spelling *plis* indicative of phonological integration.

In contrast, if the pronunciation from the donor language is preserved, the word is not considered to have been incorporated in the recipient language. Thus, a phonologically unintegrated word can be seen as part of the donor language (and thus a case of codeswitching), while a phonologically integrated word can be seen as having become part of the recipient language vocabulary. Nonetheless, despite this cut-and-dried-sounding criterion, phonological integration is not easily determined. One of the issues is the sound correspondences between the two languages; if the languages have similar phonological systems, integration is easier but also less detectable. However, phonological integration also depends on the level of bilingualism of the individual speakers (especially in terms of phonology, or what is commonly thought of as 'accent'). That is, if someone speaks Spanish with an American accent, it may be difficult to know if that person is codeswitching (between English and English-accented Spanish) or if a Spanish word has been phonologically integrated into English. And of course, these notions are predicated on the idea of distinct languages.

Some scholars distinguish between borrowings used exclusively by bilinguals (sometimes called *spontaneous* or *nonce borrowings*) and *established borrowings*, which are also used by monolinguals of the recipient language. This distinction highlights the way in which language contact can impact the speech of monolinguals in addition to bilinguals, and thus contribute to broader language change. The process is generally thought to be that bilinguals first use a word from language X in language Y; later, it spreads to monolingual discourse and becomes established more widely among bilinguals and monolinguals alike.

Figure 10.1 *Tacos plis!* Billboard outside Los Angeles, California (September 2018)

The underlying idea about the process of language contact and change is that what begin as innovations in the speech of bilinguals eventually become established in wider circles as these words or structures are taken up by other speakers. When new words or structures become widely used, they may eventually be validated by linguistic authorities (such as in the case of *patio* in English).

In other language contact phenomena, it is not the words themselves that are transferred from one language to the other, but the meanings of those words or the way they are used. This is the case for **syntactic calques**, also known as loan translations (Haugen, 1950: 214; Myers-Scotton, 2006: 218; Otheguy, 1993). Syntactic calques are literal translations, often idiomatic phrases or metaphors in which existing words in the recipient language are used with a structure from the donor language. Perhaps the best known calque in Spanish in the US is *llamar para atrás* for 'to call back' (standard Spanish employs *volver a llamar* or *devolver la llamada* 'to return the call') (Fernández, 1983: 19). Other examples of syntactic calques include *tuve un buen tiempo* (vs. *lo pasé bien* or *me divertí* 'I had a good time') and *John está supuesto a venir* (vs. *Se supone que John va a venir* 'John is supposed to come) (Lipski, 2003: 238).

A similar phenomenon is what Haugen calls *semantic loans* or *loanshifts* (Haugen, 1950: 214, 219; Myers-Scotton, 2006: 218). Also known as *semantic calques*, these are existing words that take on a new meaning, usually because of their phonological similarity to words from the donor language. For example, Smead (2000: 162) notes that in the US *colegio* has gained the new meaning 'college' (cf. 'school' or 'high school' in other Spanish varieties), and Ardilla (2005: 72) notes that the use of *ganga* ('sale' or 'bargain' in other varieties) has acquired the meaning 'gang' (which in other varieties is *pandilla* or *mara*). Other semantic calques common in the US are *introducir* (vs. *presentar*) when introducing someone to another person and *aplicar* (vs. *solicitar*), such as when applying for a job.

As mentioned above, language contact phenomena first appear in the speech of bilinguals in multilingual discourse, with individual speakers using their languages in new and creative ways that can eventually spread to monolinguals as well. We want to stress, however, that language contact is not the only cause of language change which, like variation, is inherent to all languages. In the next section we briefly review the underlying ideas about social motivations for multilingual discourse and then describe several key areas of research.

Multilingual discourse: Codeswitching or translanguaging

Multilingual discourse by any name – whether it is called codeswitching, translanguaging or Spanglish – is a dynamic form of communication which develops out of particular cultural contexts. There is a long history of its study; decades before the term *translanguaging* came into use, scholars studied the pervasive use of two or more languages in discourse. Auer (1984: 9) discusses 'the creation of a new code,' Myers-Scotton (1993a: 119) describes what she calls 'codeswitching as an unmarked code' and Gafaranga and Torras (2002: 11) refer to 'language alternation as the medium.' All of these terms refer to the use of elements of two (or more) languages as a frequent occurrence that is socially meaningful, with its own norms.

In this section we begin to show that multilingual discourse is not only a natural practice but also serves important social and conversational functions.

As discussed in Chapter 6, languages, varieties and linguistic styles are resources that speakers use in the construction and performance of their social identities, as well as to accommodate the preferences of their interlocutors (Zentella, 1997a). We noted that while languages may index particular ethnoracial or national identities, there is no one-to-one correspondence between, for example, speaking Spanish and Latinx identity. Further, it is not just speaking English or Spanish but also the specific features of whichever language is spoken that play a role in stance-taking and identity performance. Switching back and forth between languages across turns or within them and inserting words, phrases or clauses from one language into another can also be acts of identity. This understanding of the construction and performance of a bilingual self challenges the normative ideology that languages, and ethnolinguistic identities, are separate and distinct. For instance, Fuller (2012) discusses how the relatively restricted use of bilingual discourse – mostly just inserting nouns from one language into another – among German–English bilinguals contrasts with the much more elaborate types of bilingual discourse found among Spanish–English bilinguals in her data, which included switching of all types of words and phrases (see examples in Exercise 4 below). Her analysis shows that these differences can be explained by participants' different ideological stances with regard to multilingualism.

In addition to being a resource for identity work, research has shown that switching from one language to another can also be a conversational strategy or a contextualization cue to help **interlocutors** interpret what is being said. For example, codeswitching can be used to indicate a shift in topic, a change in stance or a move from one interactional role to another, such as recounting an event or quoting someone (see Auer, 1988, 1995; Cashman, 2005; Fuller *et al.*, 2007; Zentella, 1997a). In Fuller *et al.* (2007) an example of this is given which shows how a boy in a bilingual classroom uses Spanish – accompanied by loud volume – to attract attention to his contributions to the discussion. Because the lesson is in English, the switch to Spanish creates salience for his contributions to the conversation. (In this conversation, the three students, Miguel, Antonio and Dora, and the researcher, Janet, are discussing a multiple-choice worksheet related to a text they have read; thus the letters *C* and *A* refer to answers to the questions.)

Miguel: {reading} The main purpose of the expedition was to, to find out
Antonio: Oh! C! C! C!
Janet: Which was what?
Miguel: es ta bl, (frieded)
Antonio: C! *!La C!*
('The C!')
Janet: establish friendly relationships with the Indians. Is that what it says?
Miguel: Yeah.
Antonio: Yeah, and trade, uhm,
Miguel: Trade
Antonio: and ways and and trade with the Indians
Janet: Wait a second. It says here the main purpose of the expedition was to find a water route across the continent to the Pacific Ocean.

Antonio: Water route?
Janet: Is that one of 'em?
Miguel: No.
Dora: A
Miguel: Oh, yeah. They are all 'A's.
Janet: I know. That's funny.
Antonio: *Pero tambien la, la 'C' 'ta bien, ?verdad?*
('But also C is correct, right?')
Miguel: **Si:**
('Yes')
Janet: Is that also, is that also one of the answers?

(Adapted from Fuller *et al.*, 2007: 144–5)

In this example, it isn't Spanish per se that indexes a particular discursive element or social meaning, but rather the act of switching which, like the change in volume, provides contextualization cues for how to interpret the utterance.

Codeswitching constraints

Another major body of research on multilingual discourse focuses on grammatical patterns in the juxtaposing and combining of languages. This research has sought to determine where switches occur and whether there are constraints that limit where they can occur. In other words, are there any generalizations or patterns in the way that bilinguals codeswitch? Is it possible to switch at any point in a sentence and use any part of speech from either language, or are there some limits? In contrast with the disparaging views of codeswitching that portray it as a random mixing or a jumbled mess, a large body of research shows that there are consistent grammatical patterns and *codeswitching constraints* that limit where changes occur. In other words, bilinguals tend to switch languages between certain structures and to agree about which switches sound natural or possible, and which ones sound impossible or unnatural. For example, Toribio (2000) asked bilingual participants to read aloud fairy tales in which she had included various switches between Spanish and English. Participants showed significant consensus regarding which switches were easier and harder to read aloud, suggesting they shared intuitions about what kinds of switches are possible. According to most participants in Toribio's study, the examples in (1) are acceptable, while the examples in (2) are not (the asterisk is used in linguistics to indicate a structure is not grammatically acceptable).

(1)

a. *Al cumplir ella los veinte años, el rey invitó* many neighboring princes to a party.
'Upon her turning 20 years old, the king invited many neighboring princes to a party'

b. Since she was unmarried, he wanted her to choose *un buen esposo.*
'Since she was unmarried, he wanted her to choose a good husband'

c. Princess Grace was sweet y *cariñosa con todos.*
'Princess Grace was sweet y caring with everyone'

d. *Juro por Dios que te casaré con el primer hombre* that enters this room!
'I swear to God that I'll marry you to the first man that enters this room!'

e. At that exact moment, a beggar arrived *en el palacio.*
'At that exact moment, a beggar arrived in the palace'

(2)

a. * Very envious and evil, the *reina mandó a un criado que matara a la princesa.*
'Very envious and evil, the queen ordered a servant to kill the princess'

b. * *El criado la llevó al bosque* and out of compassion abandoned *la allí.*
'The servant took her to the woods and out of compassion he abandoned her there'

c. * *La reina le ofreció a Blancanieves una manzana que había* laced with poison.
'The queen offered Snow White an apple that she has laced with poison'

d. * *En la cabina vivían siete enanitos que* returned to find Snow White asleep.
'Seven little dwarves that lived in the cabin returned to find Snow White asleep'

e. * *Los enanitos intentaron pero no* succeeded in awakening Snow White from her sleep.
'The little dwarves tried but did not succeed in awakening Snow White from her sleep'

(Toribio 2000, 185; our translations)

You may be able to see some patterns in these examples; for instance, participants rejected switches when the resulting word order was acceptable in one language but not the other (as in 2a), between a verb and a direct object pronoun (as in 2b) and between a negative adverb and the verb it modifies (as in 2e). Further, in the second part of the study, participants were asked to retell a fairy tale using codeswitching, and they did not make switches in these kinds of grammatical contexts. Toribio's findings show the existence of implicit codeswitching constraints that limit where switches can occur.

Since the 1970s, a large body of research, the details of which we will not discuss here, has sought to determine exactly what the constraints are, using a wide array of theoretical frameworks and models (Bhatt & Bolonyai, 2011; MacSwan, 2014; Myers-Scotton, 1993b; Pfaff, 1979; Poplack, 1980). Such research can shed light on cognitive questions about how bilinguals store, process and access their two languages. But more important for our focus here is that, regardless of the framework, this research has consistently demonstrated that codeswitching is not a random hodgepodge or a sign of 'semilingualism.' On the contrary, it conforms to structural constraints and implicit rules, just like monolingual discourse does.

Convergence? Focus on Pronouns

As we've seen thus far, words from English and Spanish are often combined in multilingual discourse, and words (as well as word meanings) may be borrowed from one language into the other. But is there more going on below the surface? That is, are there other aspects of language – word order, tense marking or patterns of variation – that are also influenced by language contact? In this section we will address another language contact phenomenon called *convergence*. When bilingual speakers increasingly use linguistic structures that are possible in both languages, their linguistic systems or usage are said to converge. In our explanation, we focus on the use of subject pronouns, but extensive research has also been done on convergence with English in other aspects of the verbal system of Spanish in the US (Koontz-Garboden, 2004; Lipski, 1993; Lynch, 2000; Montoya, 2011; Montrul, 2007; Silva-Corvalán, 1994, 2004).

Multiple studies have examined the use of overt subject pronouns in US contact varieties of Spanish, focusing on one point of difference between Spanish and English structure. As we noted in our discussion of linguistic variation earlier in the chapter, Spanish does not require subject pronouns to be overtly expressed. Instead, because verb endings tell us a lot about who the subject is (e.g. whether it is first or second person and singular or plural), pronouns are largely redundant and can be 'dropped.' Although there is some variation, in many varieties of Spanish overt pronouns are used primarily for emphasis or contrast. For example, the unmarked or default way of saying 'I love you' in Spanish would be *te quiero* (without an overt pronoun). But if the speaker was responding to a person lamenting that no-one loved them, they might say *yo te quiero*, with an overt pronoun. The overt pronoun adds emphasis, which in English might be expressed through higher volume or stress ('*I* love you'). Similarly, if the speaker wanted to contrast themselves with someone else, they could do so by using explicit pronouns, such as in *yo te quiero pero ella no* ('I love you but she doesn't').

The point here is that the use of overt subject pronouns in Spanish depends on pragmatic issues, or what the speaker is trying to say in a given context. This is very different from English, in which overt pronouns are generally required (with a few exceptions). If Spanish were converging with English we would expect to see increased use of subject pronouns in US Spanish varieties in all contexts, even without contrast or emphasis. Several studies have investigated whether Spanish-speakers in the US use more subject pronouns due to influence from English. When reviewing this research, one critical question to ask is, more than whom? In other words, what is the relevant comparison group? This is a particularly important question because, as we noted, Caribbean varieties tend to have more overt pronoun use than other varieties. And if there is more use of subject pronouns, can we show that this is due to influence from English?

Silva-Corvalán (1994: 162f) noted that the bilingual speakers in her California study did not use more subject pronouns overall than monolingual Spanish-speakers. Similarly, Flores-Ferrán (2002, 2004) did not find higher rates of overt subject pronoun use among speakers of Puerto Rican Spanish in New York City, leading her to argue that contact with English does not lead to convergence in this regard. However, as we noted, Caribbean Spanish varieties have higher rates of overt subject pronoun use than other Latin American varieties of Spanish, so the baseline was already quite high. For this reason, research that compared across national origin groups can shed additional light on this issue. For example, in their research with Spanish-speakers in New York, Otheguy *et al.* (2007) and Erker and Otheguy (2016) found: (1) differences in pronoun use among newcomers (with

Caribbean speakers showing the highest rates of pronoun use); (2) an increase in subject pronoun use over generations among non-Caribbean speakers; and (3) a decrease in pronoun use among Caribbean-origin speakers. These results suggest that not only contact with English but also contact with other varieties of Spanish can influence language use (and that the latter is the explanation for decreased pronoun use among Caribbean speakers). This research underscores the challenges of identifying the causes of language change, especially in the context of Spanish in the US where there is simultaneous contact both with other languages and with other varieties. We return to the impact of contact between national and regional varieties of Spanish in the next section.

Rather than comparing across national origin groups or looking at different generations of speakers, some studies have focused on other speaker variables in comparisons of pronoun use. For example, Montrul (2004) found that a higher rate of pronoun use was correlated with lower Spanish proficiency, suggesting influence from English. Thus, she argues that a high rate of overt pronoun use was not a linguistic change or a feature of a particular variety, but rather convergence in the speech of particular English-influenced speakers. Cacoullos and Travis (2010) also looked at the influence of bilingual speech in their study of the first person singular pronoun *yo*. They found that while New Mexican Spanish-speakers did not produce more subject pronouns than speakers of non-contact varieties overall, there was a tendency for speakers to produce more overt pronouns in the presence of Spanish–English codeswitching. They explain these results by arguing that, rather than language contact leading to convergence within contact varieties in general, the influence of English appears only within the conversations where it appears. Similarly, Prada Pérez (2018) argue that when speakers are in a bilingual mode (Grosjean, 2001; Kroll & de Groot, 2005) they produce more subject pronouns than when they are in a monolingual Spanish mode. Martínez (2007) found that Spanish heritage language writers used more overt pronouns when they were writing a formal essay which they knew would be graded than when they did free writing as part of a brainstorming activity, indicating that in formal writing there may be transfer of literacy skills from English. All of these studies indicate that situational and interactional factors influence pronoun production and underscore the difficulty of determining the influence of contact with English.

Contact between Varieties of Spanish

As we've discussed previously, even though in some areas of the country one national origin is predominant among Latinxs, such as Mexicans and Mexican Americans in the Southwest, in other communities Latinxs of diverse national origins are in contact (see Chapter 2). Thus, although it may be to different degrees in different areas, Spanish in the US is characterized by language contact among different varieties of Spanish as well as between Spanish and English. In many cases, the features distinguishing different regional and national varieties, such as those we discussed earlier in the chapter, are salient to both the speakers themselves and their interlocutors, and thus are at a level where they can be intentionally manipulated by speakers. As discussed in Chapter 6, such features are a resource that can be used in the performance of different types of identities related to specific national origins, pan-Latinx identities or locally negotiated relationships.

Researchers have begun to examine the linguistic outcomes of extended contact among different varieties of Spanish. As we noted above, Erker and Otheguy (2016) found convergence among different varieties of Spanish regarding pronoun use in New York, and they documented similar patterns in the pronunciation of *s*, which is one feature distinguishing Caribbean from other varieties of Spanish, as we discussed earlier in this chapter. In their study of contact among different varieties of Spanish, Potowski and Torres (forthcoming) examined the pronunciation and lexicon (i.e. vocabulary) of Mexicans and Puerto Ricans in Chicago. They found that Puerto Ricans, who are outnumbered by Mexicans by about eight to one, were much more familiar with Mexican vocabulary than vice versa. In addition, Puerto Ricans were more likely to accommodate to speakers of Mexican Spanish in the pronunciation of *rr* but not *s*. Thus, this study offers some evidence that the smaller group (i.e. Puerto Ricans) accommodate more than the larger group, although other factors may also play a role such as the salience of certain features as well as their association with particular class or racial identities.

Potowski (2016) studied the speech of MexiRicans – people raised in a home with one Mexican-background and one Puerto Rican-background parent – living in Chicago. Her research found that most speakers (70%) used phonology and lexicon (i.e. vocabulary) that corresponded largely to one variety or the other, although there was individual variation in the features used. Further, some speakers used features from both varieties, in many cases depending on the addressee. These findings are consistent with our discussion in Chapter 6 of how speakers use features to perform identities: speakers can use different features to index different aspects of identity, or to convey social meanings to their interlocutors; the features they choose vary across interactional contexts.

Another particular feature of Spanish, already discussed in Chapter 6, is *voseo*, that is, the use of the second person singular pronoun *vos* and the corresponding verbs forms (Rivera Mills, 2011). In Rivera Mills' data from three generations of Honduran and Salvadoran background Spanish-speakers living in the US, the findings show a decrease in the use of *vos* over time, and also less productive use of the verb forms, indicating gradual linguistic assimilation and loss of voseo over time.

Beyond English and Spanish

Historically, as we have discussed, Spanish in North America has had extended contact with Native and African languages. Contemporary language contact among Latinxs in the US is not limited to just Spanish and English; in addition to languages spoken by other immigrant groups, Central and South American Indigenous languages are also part of the linguistic repertoires of some Spanish-speakers in the US. As we noted in Chapter 2, there is a growing percentage of immigrants from Latin America, and especially Central America, who speak Indigenous languages (such as K'iche,' Mixtec and Nahuatl) (Bazo

Vienrich, 2018). Further, some Spanish-speaking immigrants from South America, especially Bolivia and Perú, may also know Aymara or Quechua. Thus, the extended contact between Spanish and Indigenous languages that exists outside the US also continues within the US, but with English added to the mix.

The longstanding subordination of Indigenous languages to Spanish in Latin America extends into the US, where both are subordinated to English and Spanish. Indigenous languages are nonetheless an important part of the linguistic repertoires and identities of their speakers. Morales (2016) looks at the linguistic performances and language attitudes of Latinx children in a Spanish–English bilingual program in California, some of whom had Zapoteco as a heritage language. For the most part, they were in the program because their parents valued Spanish, which in some cases was also a heritage language and in all cases the language of communication with most other Mexican immigrants. However, this did not mean that Zapoteco ceased to be an important part of their identities and community repertoires.

Fuller (2012) opens her discussion of multilingualism in bilingual education programs with a discussion of how languages other than the languages of instruction – Spanish and English in the US and German and English in Germany – were treated by the children. In the German setting, the pluralist ideology was stronger in both the national context and the classroom studied, and this fostered appreciation of many of the home languages of the children, whether or not these languages were prestigious in the wider society. In the US program, the one child who was known to speak Purépecha, an Indigenous language spoken in Mexico, seemed embarrassed by any mention of it, and the other children occasionally mentioned this language with a laughing, mocking tone. The ideologies of both the US and Mexico, the monoglossic ideology and hegemony of English in the US and the racialization of and discrimination against Indigenous languages and their speakers in Mexico all worked against appreciation of his proficiency in a third language. However, such ideologies are not fixed, and the small, rural community where this study took place has seen changes in attitudes about Indigenous languages and identities. In recent years, the local community began sponsoring an annual Purépecha festival, with musicians from Mexico, traditional dances, and food from the Michoacan region. Still, Fuller spoke to a community leader at this event about the languages they used in the community, and he noted that little Purépecha was spoken; it is difficult enough to maintain two languages, he said, and Spanish and English took priority and were mastered by more people in the community.

Latinx Englishes

We use the umbrella term *Latinx Englishes* here to refer to varieties of English spoken in Latinx communities in the US. In multiple places in this book we have referred to **African American English** (AAE), and you are probably also familiar with other ethnoracial varieties of English and/or stereotypical depictions of them. For example, things such as *youse guys* and pronouncing *these* and *those* as 'dese' and 'dose' are salient elements of some Italian

American varieties of English and part of the stereotypical marking of someone as of Italian descent. (See the discussion of this from the video about linguistic diversity in the US, *American Tongues*, at https://www.youtube.com/watch?v=Kmum-eT4hzM.) Many or even most people who use Italian American English (including those in the video) don't speak Italian, since their families have been in the US for generations and have experienced language shift (see Chapter 2). Nonetheless, they speak a variety of English that has features that resulted from the English–Italian bilingualism of their ancestors.

Latinx Englishes are also the result of historical and ongoing contact situations. Although of course many children who grow up in Spanish-speaking families or local communities speak English like other members of the wider society in their locality or region, in some cases ethnic varieties develop. This inevitably has to do with identity; ethnic varieties are a way of marking ethnic group identity and they are often recognized by members of the group as well as by others. In a recent study on what she calls 'hispanicized English,' Callahan (2018) advocates an analytic approach focusing on linguistic repertoires and speaker agency. That is, speakers have a range of resources from which they can select features. As we discussed in depth in Chapter 6, it's not that people speak a particular way because of who they are, but rather that they use the resources in their repertoire to convey various social meanings or to construct themselves in particular ways.

It's not just (Latinx) speakers that associate certain elements of their linguistic repertoires with their ethnoracial identity; there is evidence that non-Latinxs also recognize certain types of speech as indicative of Latinx identity. In particular, in a study by Frazer (1996), non-Latinx college students could readily distinguish the speech of Hispanics (the term used in this study) from that of non-Hispanics. This indicates that certain ways of speaking would lead to a speaker being labeled as Hispanic by others, regardless of how s/he might self-identify. Significantly, the features of Latinx English that occurred in the speech of most of the 11 speakers in this study were related to intonation, which we will explain below.

Given the predominance of Mexicans and Mexican Americans among US Latinxs, most research on Latinx Englishes has focused on the varieties spoken in these communities, typically labeled Chicanx English, in order to emphasize that it is the English of US-born Mexican Americans. It is important to stress that Chicanx English and other Latinx Englishes do not consist of speaking English with a 'foreign' accent. Instead, Latinx Englishes are varieties in their own right. Certainly, as discussed by Callahan (2018), they are influenced by non-native speakers in their development, and these features of English are part of the repertoires in their communities. However, Latinx Englishes are often spoken by English monolinguals, just as Italian American varieties are spoken by people who don't know Italian (Bayley & Santa Ana, 2004; Fought, 2003; Metcalf, 1979; Ornstein-Galicia, 1984; Penfield & Ornstein-Galicia, 1985; Santa Ana, 1993; Santa Ana & Bayley, 2004).

Earlier research has tried to document features of Latinx Englishes: What makes them distinct from other American English varieties? In terms of grammatical structure, the literature indicates few features that are unique to Latinx Englishes (Bayley & Santa Ana, 2004; Fought, 2003; Penfield & Ornstein Galicia, 1985). However, the phonology is much more distinctive. Although earlier studies include many features (Penfield & Ornstein Galicia, 1985: 36), many of which could also be part of a 'Spanish accent,' or the speech of a

Spanish-speaking person learning English, the more recent work by Santa Ana and Bayley (2004) and Fought (2003) identified a much more streamlined list of features. Konopka and Pierrehumbert (2008) focus on the vowel system, while Bayley and Holland (2014) examine the pronunciation of the /s/ at the end of words as either 's' or 'z'. We will look here more closely at these studies.

For the most part, Santa Ana and Bayley (2004) say the vowels of Chicanx English are similar to the vowels of the local varieties of English, with some exceptions. One such feature is vowel reduction, which in most varieties of American English impacts vowels that are not in the stressed syllable, leading them to be pronounced 'uh'. In the word *because*, for instance, the first *e* is rarely pronounced 'e' in casual speech and the word sounds more like 'buh-cuz'. Speakers of Chicanx English tend to preserve the 'e' sound and pronounce this 'bee-cuz'. Another feature is the pronunciation of the vowel in *least*, which for most American English-speakers is pronounced as an 'e' followed by a 'y' sound. Speakers of Chicanx English often do not use this glide, and produce the 'e' sound without it (Fought, 2003: 64).

Generally speaking, the consonants of Latinx Englishes tend to mirror those of other American English varieties. One difference identified in Chicanx English is the final /z/ sound, which is often spelled with an *s*, such as in the words *boys* and *lives*. Bayley and Holland (2014) examined this feature in the speech of the Chicanxs in a public housing project in south Texas. They found that participants with a local orientation (i.e. having strong ties and the desire to stay in the community) more frequently used the 's' pronunciation, again highlighting the connection of language to social meanings and identities. In addition, because the 's' pronunciation did not correlate with first language (i.e. it was equally common among participants with English as a first language), this study also shows that this pronunciation is a feature of Chicanx English, rather than a 'foreign' accent.

What is arguably most noticeable about Latinx Englishes is intonation (Metcalf, 1979: 7, 10). Santa Ana and Bayley (2004) outline a number of intonational patterns that distinguish Chicanx English from other American English varieties, the most salient of which is final pitch contours. In other varieties of American English, there is a falling intonation at the end of statements and a rising intonation at the end of questions. (Try saying 'That sounds good' and 'Did she answer?' yourself to see if you can hear this.) In Chicanx English, on the other hand, both questions and statements tend to have rising and then falling intonation at the end (although the contour of the entire sentence is not the same, the end segments are). In particular, this contour in statements is something that is readily recognized as a marker of ethnoracial identity and is also incorporated into stereotypes of Mexicans. Santa Ana and Bayley note that Speedy Gonzales, a cartoon character, is in general a racist caricature of a Mexican and part of this depiction is his intonation. You may recognize this way of speaking as having the same intonation used to represent bandidos and peasants in Hollywood westerns (Santa Ana & Bayley, 2004: 429; see also discussion in Chapter 7).

It should be noted that most studies of Latinx Englishes looked at a single locality, a major exception being Metcalf (1979), which briefly compared research on Latinx Englishes in six different cities in California, Arizona and Las Vegas, as well as several towns in Texas. He found different phonological patterns in these different varieties, leading us to believe that however Latinx Englishes developed, they are highly localized. However, this study focused exclusively on the Southwest and is now 40 years old. Clearly, much work remains to be done on the different Latinx Englishes around the country.

Attitudes toward Varieties of Spanish and English

In this final section, we return to a more social aspect of language – the attitudes that speakers hold about varieties and particular language features. As we have noted throughout this book, language variation has social meaning; people associate different ways of speaking with different regional, social or ethnoracial groups. In this section we will look at studies that address the social meaning of different varieties of Spanish and of features of language contact we have discussed.

There are three main methodological approaches used in the language attitude research we will review. One is the use of interviews, questionnaires and/or surveys which ask directly how research participants feel about certain ways of speaking. The second, the *matched guise* technique, was developed to elicit attitudes indirectly (Lambert *et al.*, 1966). In this methodology, research participants hear the same people speaking in two different languages and rate them on various personal traits, normally using a seven-point scale. These traits typically include descriptors related to solidarity such as kindness and attractiveness, as well as characteristics related to prestige such as ambitiousness or intelligence. Participants are not informed that they are hearing the same people in two different recordings; the idea is that differences in ratings of people in the two languages reflect research participants' attitudes about the languages and the people who speak them. A variant of the matched guise, the *verbal guise*, uses different people for the different varieties. A third and increasingly frequently used method is called *perceptual dialectology* (Long & Preston, 2002; Preston, 1999). In this approach, research participants are typically asked to rate varieties for pleasantness and correctness (without listening to any recordings). In some perceptual dialectology studies, research participants are also asked to draw dialect regions on a map and label them, such that the varieties are ones that they name themselves, and the ways that they describe them come from the participants themselves.

These methodologies have been used in studies examining attitudes about different varieties of Spanish. Alfaraz (2002), in a perceptual dialectology study, shows that the Cubans in Miami she surveyed rated Peninsular Spanish (i.e. from Spain) as the most pleasant, followed by a preference for Spanish as spoken before the Revolution in Cuba (pre-1959). The preference for Peninsular Spanish fits with language ideologies discussed in Chapter 4, namely ideas about European varieties being superior, more 'standard' and more legitimate than the Spanish spoken in the former colonies. Further, the varieties of countries whose populations were perceived as poorer, more Indigenous or more Black were rated most negatively. So too, current Cuban Spanish was rated less favorably than post-Revolution Spanish (which was also associated with more recent Cuban immigrants).

The differences that Alfaraz found in attitudes toward pre- and post-Revolution Cuban Spanish were tied to the greater representation of Afro-Cubans among recent arrivals; as we discussed in Chapter 3, earlier Cuban immigrants tended be Whiter and wealthier. Specifically, participants explained their negative ratings for post-Revolution Cuban Spanish by saying that it was *anegrado* ('blackened'). Nonetheless, they ranked it higher than neighboring Dominican and Puerto Rican varieties.

In Alfaraz's study, the correlation of perceived race and poverty with ratings, together with the fact that there were clear differences in the ratings of varieties that are linguistically quite similar (i.e. Cuban, Dominican and Puerto Rican), underscores that language attitudes are not based on linguistic features themselves, but rather on attitudes and ideologies regarding the speakers. In a follow-up study, Alfaraz (2014) found that attitudes toward non-Cuban varieties had remained stable and continued to correlate with perceived racial make-up and relative poverty. In addition, participants rated the Spanish spoken in Cuba even more negatively than in the first study. As Alfaraz explains, these data revealed that attitudes are influenced by political ideology as well as beliefs about race and poverty.

A more recent study of language attitudes in Miami using the matched guise methodology (Carter & Callesano, 2018), which included the perceptions of Latinx youths of varied backgrounds, found a tendency for participants to make assumptions about non-linguistic traits linked to social class based on language. Carter and Callesano (2018) also found an ideology about the superiority of European language and culture, as did Montes-Alcalá (2011) in her survey-based study. In this study, 30 native Spanish-speakers of 11 different national origins who were living in the US completed a brief questionnaire about the country or countries with the best/worst Spanish, and the linguistic features they liked/didn't like. The best Spanish was most frequently said to be spoken in Spain (12/30 participants), although Colombia was also mentioned by 10 of the participants. For the worst Spanish, the top places listed were Puerto Rico, Mexico, the US and the Dominican Republic. In other words, the results show an overall favoring of peninsular Spanish and negative views of North American and Caribbean varieties.

Another study which looked at the values of Puerto Rican and Mexican varieties as evaluated by Mexican listeners found that these listeners rated their own variety more positively in general (Chappell, 2019). This analysis focused on one specific pronunciation feature – syllable-final /s/ – a salient difference between these dialects, as has been discussed above. In a relatively new methodology that is catching on in matched guise research, Chappell used computer technology to manipulate the pronunciation of recorded speech samples so that the /s/ sounded like either 's' or 'h'. Overall, participants judged speakers with the 'h' pronunciation more negatively (i.e. as less intelligent, hardworking and confident) than speakers with 's'. In addition, they judged Mexican Spanish speakers with 'h' much more harshly than they did speakers with the same pronunciation but who identified as Puerto Rican. In other words, not only did participants judge the Puerto Rican pronunciation more negatively in general, but Mexican Spanish speakers who used a feature associated with Puerto Rican Spanish were ascribed an even lower evaluation. There are several possible explanations for this including an ideology that people's speech should be true to their 'authentic' identity.

The stigmatization of US varieties in particular was found by Valdés *et al.* (2003), who looked at comments about linguistic varieties made in interviews with university Spanish instructors. The language of heritage speakers, in particular Chicanxs, was consistently described as incorrect and not up to academic standards – even, in some cases, by people who admitted that they knew little about it. This research underscores that it is racializing ideologies, rather than linguistic features, that shape perceptions of correctness (see Chapter 3), and that these ideologies impact how Latinx and other racialized students are treated in educational contexts, an issue which we discussed in the last chapter. Zentella (2007a) also analyzed interviews with Spanish-speakers of a variety of national backgrounds in New York City. Although the majority stated that 'we should not learn to speak like Spaniards' (Zentella, 2007a: 25), there were some interesting points of variation in this attitude. Few Cubans and Colombians felt that they should adhere to the peninsular norm, while more Dominicans and Puerto Ricans did, possibly because their varieties are generally less highly valued in pan-Latinx contexts. One linguistic feature cited by Zentella as a stigmatized marker is the deletion of syllable-final /s/ discussed earlier in this chapter.

Deletion of syllable-final /s/ is also mentioned in work by Rosa (2014), whose ethnographic work illuminates language attitudes among Puerto Rican and Mexican background youths in a high school in Chicago regarding different varieties of Spanish. The youths' comments revealed that ideas about pleasantness and correctness don't always coincide: varieties considered incorrect can have **covert prestige**; that is, they can be valued even if they are considered non-standard. In Rosa's study, members of both groups saw Mexican Spanish as 'correct (yet lame)' and Puerto Rican Spanish as 'cool (yet incorrect)' (Rosa, 2014: 50). In the words of one student of Puerto Rican background and another of Mexican background, respectively: 'Puerto Ricans got that shit in the bag ... they can knock out any Spanish thing, bro' (Rosa, 2014: 49); '[Puerto Ricans] don't say the words right ... they miss some words ... like sometimes they lose the 'r', sometimes they lose the 's' ... and it's really weird ... and with Mexicans, they know how to talk!' (Rosa, 2014: 49).

In many cases, language attitudes are shaped by identification with particular regional varieties, such as Puerto Rican or Mexican varieties. However, a study by Chappell (2018) shows that one linguistic feature, the pronunciation of the letter *v* as a 'v' sound, instead of a 'b' sound, was evaluated positively in the speech of women, but negatively in the speech of men. This finding suggests that there is more to language attitudes than regional associations, which should come as no surprise after our discussion of different aspects of identities in Chapter 6.

Researchers have also studied attitudes toward Latinx Englishes. In Dailey *et al.* (2005) a verbal guise methodology was used; instead of having the same speaker read a text in two different varieties, they had different speakers, whom they described as 'Anglo- and Hispanic-accented speakers,' read the same text, and they were rated by 190 students on a variety of personality traits. The Anglo-accented speakers were rated more positively in all categories, although the difference between Anglo- and Hispanic-accented speakers was less among raters who self-identified as Hispanic. This study also looked at the influence of the reported linguistic landscapes of the research participants. For Anglo respondents, whether they reported that there was a lot of Spanish in their surroundings or not made no difference. But for the Hispanic respondents, the more Spanish was reported to be in the local environment, the less favorably they rated the Anglo speakers. This study speaks to the impact of the visual as well as vocal environment on the shaping of language attitudes.

Some research has also been carried out on attitudes toward Spanish–English bilingual discourse. Montes-Alcalá (2000) looked at attitudes toward codeswitching and how they could be correlated with the patterns of language use of the research participants. She found 60% of those survey agreed that mixing of Spanish and English 'sounds pretty,' with only 40% saying this of written codeswitching. However, despite a somewhat positive view of language mixing, 80% disagreed with the statement that codeswitching earns respect, indicating a recognition of the stigmatization of language mixing. Interestingly enough, when the production of these same speakers was analyzed, it was found that those with negative attitudes had a higher percentage of intrasentential codeswitching in their speech. These findings reflect the commonplaceness of bilingual discourse; it is widely used despite a sense of it being stigmatized and also in cases where speakers, upon reflection, do not feel it is 'pretty.'

Anderson and Toribio (2007) looked in more detail at attitudes toward bilingual discourse, examining differences between attitudes toward monolingual Spanish, single-word insertions and codeswitching. Monolingual Spanish was rated most positively, with single-word insertions being preferred to more elaborate codeswitching patterns. The research participants in this study included both heritage speakers and second language learners of Spanish, and the findings show that those who were more fluent bilinguals rated all of the non-monolingual guises more favorably. Again, this study shows the acceptance of bilingual discourse as a natural part of the language of multilinguals. However, a more recent study carried out in two Texas border towns (Rangel *et al.*, 2015) had different findings. When asking research participants (bilingual students in Spanish classes at two universities) to rate (Standard Mexican) Spanish, English and codeswitching verbal guises, codeswitching received the lowest ratings for status, solidarity and personal appeal. Interestingly enough, Spanish and English in their monolingual guises were rated equally for status, with Spanish receiving higher ratings in the category of solidarity. So while some research may show more acceptance of bilingual discourse, we also see that even in contexts in which Spanish does not have lower social value, the hegemony of monoglot ideologies may be reflected in negative attitudes about language mixing.

Conclusions and Connections

This chapter has presented an overview of formal features of different varieties of Spanish as well as some linguistic analyses of the structural patterns resulting from language contact, including features of contact varieties of Spanish that are often called *Spanglish*. As we have discussed in previous chapters, such linguistic features are resources that speakers draw from in the performance of identities (see Chapter 6). In addition, not only is the combining of linguistic features from what are traditionally recognized as distinct languages commonplace among multilinguals, often playing a role in identity work, but it also serves as an interactional resource for the structuring of conversations. Nonetheless, despite clear evidence that multilingual discourse conforms to structural constraints, negative ideas about contact phenomena continue to circulate in US society and beyond. In this chapter we also saw that the language ideologies discussed in Chapter 4, especially monoglossic ideologies of language purity, can influence how speakers evaluate the use of Spanish and English as well as the people they associate with this linguistic practice.

Further, this chapter has made note of the historical development of different ways of speaking, from varieties of Spanish to borrowings across linguistic boundaries to the development of Latinx Englishes. Looking back at what was discussed in Chapter 2 about language maintenance and shift, we see that some of these linguistic developments (such as codeswitching or translanguaging) are clearly dependent on multilingualism, which in turn is embedded in complex societal norms and practices. In other cases, language contact features arise first in multilingual speakers, and then spread to monolinguals, such as in the case of African and Indigenous loanwords in Spanish and Spanish loanwords in English, and thus they can survive even when multilingualism doesn't. Whether we are looking at Spanish–English mixing, the influence of Spanish on English or the influence of English on Spanish, the language ideologies, social identities, policies and education of Latinxs in the US we have discussed in the previous chapters remain essential to our understanding of these structures.

Discussion Questions and Activities for Chapter 10

(1) Watch this 1954 clip from the English-language television series *I Love Lucy* in which the Cuban character Ricky Ricardo combines English and Spanish as he tells his infant son a bedtime story (https://www.youtube.com/watch?v=_9ivqXzmrZ0). Does this sound natural and why or why not? Can you identity specific language contact phenomena? What do you think about the inclusion of Spanish, and Spanglish, at a time in which it was extremely rare to hear either on national television? How does this portrayal fit with what was discussed in Chapter 7?

(2) Analyze the 2016 Xfinity advertisement 'Beautifully bilingual' (available online at http://creativecriminals.com/comcast/beautifully-bilingual-como-t). First, discuss the switches between Spanish and English with regard to the structural constraints and patterns discussed in this chapter (while also keeping in mind that this is the performance of a written text, rather than spontaneous oral language). Secondly, discuss how the cross-linguistic rhymes challenge purist notions about distinct languages with clear boundaries that must be maintained. Are there other elements in the ad that reinforce the idea of languages as distinct elements? Thirdly, what language ideologies are reflected in the ad? Fourthly, consider the ways in which the advertisement uses language (including but not only the combination of Spanish and English) to construct an identity and 'talk to' the viewer.

Why is Xfinity interested in portraying bilingualism in a positive light? In other words, is this a 'genuine' valuing of bilingualism or is it only about making more money, and does it matter?

(3) In part, debates about the term *Spanglish* parallel the controversies about the words once considered negative or derogatory such as *Chicano* or *queer* or that are now used for self-identification and have become normalized in academia (e.g. Queer Linguistics, Chicanx Studies), as well as broader public discourse (e.g. the inclusion of *Chicano* on the US census form). On one hand, such words have been used as insults and for that reason some people still reject them; on the other hand, there is power in reclaiming words and making them symbols of ingroup solidarity. In what ways is *Spanglish* similar to and different from reclaimed identity labels? Would you advocate the use or avoidance of the term? Why? You may also wish to consider the issue of whether the term represents Spanish–English contact in the US as exceptional, the argument made by Otheguy and Stern (2010).

(4) If you are a speaker of both English and Spanish, what do you think of the examples of codeswitching given below (from Fuller, 2005)? Are there some that sound better or worse than others? What might account for differences in opinion about judgments of these utterances, and how does that influence the study of structural constraints on language mixing?

(a) ***Porque*** they have a lot of ***protección***
('because they have a lot of protection')

(b) ***Estamos en*** page one-hundred and twenty-seven
('We are on page one-hundred and twenty-seven.')

(c) I'm gonna ***hacer todo los*** planets
('I'm gonna do all the planets')

(d) ***No, yo voy a*** do the Earth.
('No, I am going to do the Earth')

(e) For Mars draw a circle, then ***lo mides*** on the side
('For Mars draw a circle, then you measure it on the side')

Note

(1) In line with the convention in the field of linguistics, we use slashes to indicate phonemes, or the mental representation of sounds. But don't worry if you aren't familiar with this concept, as you'll still be able to understand. We use single quotes to indicate how something sounds, and italics for how it is spelled.

Further Reading and Resources

Braschi, G. (1998) *Yo-Yo Boing!* Pittsburgh, PA: Latin American Literary Review Press.

Elya, S.M. (2016) *La Madre Goose: Nursery Rhymes for los niños.* New York : G.P. Putnam.

Erker, D. (2017) The limits of named language varieties and the role of social salience in dialectal contact: The case of Spanish in the United States. *Language and Linguistics Compass* 11 (1), e12232.

Lipski, J.M. (2008) *Varieties of Spanish in the United States.* Washington, DC: Georgetown University Press.

Montes-Alcalá, C. (2015) Code-switching in US Latino literature: The role of biculturalism. *Language and Literature* 24 (3), 264–281.

Thomas, E.R. (2018) What a swarm of variables tells us about the formation of Mexican American English. In J. Reaser, E. Wilbanks, K. Wojik and W. Wolfram (eds) *Language Variety in the New South: Contemporary Perspectives on Change and Variation* (pp. 274–288). Chapel Hill, NC: University of North Carolina Press.

Toribio, A.J. (2011) Code-switching among US Latinos. In M. Díaz-Campos (ed.) *The Handbook of Hispanic Sociolinguistics* (pp. 530–552). Oxford: Wiley-Blackwell.

Chapter 11

The Future of Spanish in the US

> **Objectives**
>
> To reconsider some key points from each chapter, identify factors that will shape the future of Spanish in the US, and raise questions and issues that are expected to be of continued and/or growing interest and importance for Spanish-speakers in the US.

Introduction

From the outset, we have argued that language is inseparable from the people who speak it, their lived experiences and the sociohistorical and political context in which they live. For this reason, we have taken a sociopolitical approach to the analysis of speaking Spanish in the US in which we have drawn from multiple disciplines in addition to sociolinguistics. In this vein, we examined the history of Spanish in the US and showed how the earliest patterns of Spanish conquest and colonization, together with the subsequent annexation by the US of Florida, the Southwest, the West and Puerto Rico, set the stage for the contemporary **racialization** of Latinxs and Spanish-speakers, and the subordination of Spanish in the US. We also discussed how US labor needs, as well as economic, political and military involvement in Latin America, have influenced the patterns of migration of Spanish-speakers. In addition to deepening our understanding of Spanish-speakers in the US, knowledge of migration patterns also provides insights into the linguistic features and varieties of Spanish spoken in the US.

In our discussion about the history and present of Spanish in the US, we emphasized the role of language ideologies and their interaction with broader social and political forces. Some of the most powerful language ideologies are those that relate to various kinds of identity, such as the place of English and Spanish in the construction of US identity and national belonging, the necessity (or not) of Spanish for enacting 'authentic' **Latinidad**, and the social meanings associated with different language varieties, registers, styles and practices. We showed how such ideologies mediate between language and the social world: they not only shape how we think of and portray others based on their language, but they are also what allow language to serve as a resource for us to construct and perform our own identities. Ideologies also undergird **language planning and policy**, including efforts by the *Real Academia Española* (RAE) and the *Academia Norteamericana de la Lengua Española* (ANLE) to dictate language use, as well as decisions about which languages are used in government, in schools and even within families. As we have seen, this relationship is iterative in that these policies don't just reflect, but also reproduce language ideologies and linguistic hierarchies, and together they shape patterns of language use, including maintenance and/or shift. We've shown how language ideologies about Spanish, including its indexical meanings and perceived value, are also reflected and reproduced in official discourses and practices (such as the census) and English-language and Spanish-language media, as well as in everyday interaction and casual conversation.

As is evident even in the extremely brief summary given in the previous two paragraphs, and as we have pointed out throughout the book and especially in the concluding section of each chapter, the topics and issues covered in this book are interrelated and mutually influencing. While our primary focus has been on Spanish in the US, we have stressed that the relationship of language to social and political life is not limited to this particular case, and we hope to have provided the theoretical tools for examining these issues in other contexts. We hope that you will keep this interrelatedness in mind as you read this final chapter, in which we discuss the future of Spanish in the US. Each section in this concluding chapter corresponds to a chapter in the book and in each one we remind readers of key points from the corresponding chapter, while also highlighting particular issues and topics that we think will be particularly salient or influential in the future. Thus, we first consider issues related to demographics, with a focus on demographic tendencies and patterns of language maintenance and shift. Next, we discuss historical representation and some recent immigration policy proposals and trends, and the implications for Spanish in the US, before going on to consider evolving ideologies about Spanish, and so on, identifying some points for consideration related to each of the chapters in the book. We trust that despite our division of this chapter into sections, readers will see the threads weaving through them all. Our goal here is not to summarize each chapter, nor to offer concrete predictions for the future. Instead, we seek to identify a few key take-aways and to pinpoint a few factors that will shape the future of Spanish in the US, as well as to highlight topics and questions for readers to pay attention to in the days, months and years after this book goes to press.

Demographics, Maintenance and Shift

The growth of the Latinx and Spanish-speaking populations is a topic that is virtually unavoidable in discussions on a wide array of topics, everything from advertising (e.g.

Morse, 2018), religious outreach (e.g. Hodges, 2015) and the declining circulation rates of (English-language) newspapers (e.g. Ghoshal, 2014), to local and national politics. Indeed, political analysts continually point to the growing share of the electorate that identifies as Latinx, which has led to more and more political outreach and advertising in Spanish, including candidates saying a few things in Spanish during political debates or participating in campaign events on Spanish-language television channels such as Univisión. Some have celebrated this use of Spanish by non-Latinx as well as Latinx politicians as a welcome indication of increased ethnoracial and linguistic pluralism. Others have critiqued the **essentialist** and standard language ideologies that underlie demands for Latinx politicians to 'prove' their ethnoracial authenticity by speaking 'flawless' Spanish, even as non-Latinxs are lauded for speaking any Spanish at all (Rey Agudo, 2019; see Discussion Question 2 below). The greater visibility of Spanish has also been met with anti-immigrant and anti-Latinx sentiment as well as fears about the linguistic and ethnoracial make-up of the nation, fears which some politicians have sought to exploit and/or foment via racist rhetoric and nativist policies. Because so many people seem to think otherwise, we will repeat once again that English is not in any danger, and virtually all US-born Latinxs (like the children of other immigrant groups) speak English well, as do many immigrants themselves.

Many conversations about future trends include some discussion about the Census Bureau's projections of the number of Spanish-speakers in the US (e.g. Shin & Ortman, 2011). Based on the expected growth of the overall Latinx population and on recent trends in the ratio of Latinxs who speak Spanish, Census Bureau researchers projected that the Spanish-speaking population would continue to grow through 2020, but at a slower rate than the Latinx population (Shin & Ortman, 2011). We want to raise two concerns or uncertainties about the assumptions built into these projections. First, there is some reason to believe that the projected growth of the Latinx population may be too high (Lopez *et al.*, 2017). Specifically, it relied on the assumption that the descendants of Latin American immigrants would identify as Latinxs, but Lopez *et al.* (2017) have found that 'Hispanic identity fades across generations as immigrant connections fall away.' In other words, people with Latin American ancestry are less and less likely to self-identify as Hispanic or Latinx the more generations they are removed from immigration. Indeed, while 97% of immigrants born in Latin America or Spain self-identify as Hispanic or Latinx, only 92% of second generation (i.e. with at least one immigrant parent), 77% of the third generation and 50% of the fourth generation do. Moreover, Latinx rates of **exogamy** are increasing (Livingston & Brown, 2017), further reducing the chances that the grandchildren and great-grandchildren of today's immigrants will identify as Latinxs. Thus, the Latinx population might grow more slowly than projected.

The second uncertainty about the projected growth in the number of Spanish-speakers is related to the percentage of Latinxs who speak Spanish. As we've said time and again, not all Latinxs speak Spanish, and in fact the percentage of Latinxs that speak Spanish is gradually shrinking. Census Bureau researchers did take this this downward trend into account, but still their projection was based on just a few years of data, and thus doesn't reflect longer patterns. Nor does it go beyond 2020. Given increasing rates of exogamy, growing generational distance from immigration and continuing patterns of language shift to English, it's possible that the percentage of Latinxs who speak Spanish might decline even more quickly than assumed. This question will play a key role in the future of Spanish in the US.

These uncertainties raise the possibility that the Latinx and Spanish-speaking populations might grow more slowly than some people have assumed, but importantly they do *not* imply that there won't be any growth at all. Further, things could also go the other way. In other words, it's also possible that the increased number and proportion of Latinxs, and the greater visibility of Spanish, could slow language shift to English monolingualism. As we saw, demographic factors such as population size and density thus far have not stemmed the tide of language loss, even near the US–Mexico border, but perhaps the continued growth of the national Latinx population might reach a tipping point. If this were accompanied by greater awareness of the cognitive, emotional, social, cultural and economic value of Spanish, together with a recognition or celebration of ethnoracial and linguistic pluralism, this could lead to positive attitudes as well as institutional support for Spanish, two key factors for ethnolinguistic vitality.

Given the tremendous pressures favoring language shift to English, the future of Spanish in the US can't be taken for granted, and people who hope to maintain Spanish for themselves, their children, their friends and neighbors and/or society at large have their work cut out for them. Our discussion about research on patterns of language maintenance and shift in Chapter 2 made it clear that the survival of Spanish depends on two key factors – household language practices and language-in-education policy – both of which are strongly influenced by societal language ideologies such as **normative monolingualism**, English **hegemony** and the racialization of Spanish. Thus, efforts to preserve and maintain Spanish will need to be multifaceted and to address societal and structural issues as well as individual attitudes and choices.

History and Immigration

Of course, history itself doesn't change, so it might seem silly even to include it as a topic in a discussion about the future. However, while history itself might not change, understandings of history do evolve over time, as they are shaped not only by what has happened but also by current perspectives and interests. For example, scholars have increasingly examined the multilingual history of the US, acknowledged that US history did not begin in 1620 with the arrival of English settlers in Jamestown, and recognized that history is not made up solely of the stories of conquerors, colonists and those in power (Taylor, 2002). As the US becomes increasingly ethnoracially diverse and increasingly aware of both contemporary and historical ethnoracial diversity, we expect to see more and more incorporation of diverse histories, including those of Indigenous, African and other European peoples, as well as their cultures, languages, politics, alliances and conflicts, in the telling of the history of the US. Thus, we look forward to more re-examinations of dominant accounts of US history, such as Ramos' (2019) critical take on the way that the Battle of the Alamo and the annexation of Texas is portrayed in popular culture, political discourse and school curricula, as well as continued public debate about the commemoration of historical figures who played key roles in US expansion. So too, we look forward to continued questioning and destabilization of the hegemonic construction of American identity as inherently White and English-speaking. And this too may influence attitudes toward multilingualism and positively influence language maintenance.

As we have stressed, Spanish is not only an immigrant language in the US, given that Spanish was spoken in large parts of what is now the US long before the US existed. Over the years, as the population of the country has grown, and there has been continued immigration from Latin America (and other places), a smaller and smaller percentage of the Latinx and Spanish-speaking populations trace their roots back to the **treaty citizens** incorporated in 1848. Still, the patterns of racialization and discrimination established in that period have shaped, and continue to shape, the experiences of Latinx immigrants and their US-born descendants (Gomez, 2007; Vélez-Ibáñez, 2017). These patterns, together with the **erasure** of Indigenous and Mexican peoples as well as the role of slavery, in the history of US expansion in the Southwest, undergird both historical and current racialized understandings of what it means to be American, as well as the construction of Latinxs as inherently foreign (Ramos, 2019).

Perhaps one of the most quickly shifting topics that we have addressed in this book is immigration. In fact, fluctuating trends and new developments led us to revise and rewrite our coverage of immigration several times before the book went to press. One recent change is that for many years Latin American immigration in general, and apprehensions at the US–Mexico border in particular, had been on the decline. However, 2018 saw an increase in arrivals, especially from Central America, in unauthorized border crossings, and in the percentage of migrants made up of families with minor children. The Trump administration has adopted increasingly draconian policies of family separation, closing of border crossings, denials of asylum hearings and warehousing of migrants in inhumane conditions in tent cities, even as it proposes to cut the foreign aid to Central American countries, which will likely lead to more migration. Another issue predicted to contribute to increased migration is climate change, which the US Agency for International Development reports is contributing to prolonged drought in Central America and making it more difficult to grow crops (Markham, 2019).

As we explained in Chapter 3, immigration is impacted by both push and pull factors and thus conditions in both Latin America and the US will shape the future of immigration, which also makes predictions difficult. In the US there are several immigration- and asylum-related court cases currently under consideration. Although it's impossible to know how the rulings will go, increasingly conservative courts have allowed many restrictions to stand, so elected officials will play a key role in determining what happens next. Republican candidates largely support the building of a border wall and less foreign aid, and Democrats largely support a more human rights oriented approach that includes foreign aid, granting asylum for those whose lives are in at danger at home and providing a path to citizenship for Dreamers (the unauthorized immigrants who came to the US as children). Thus, the future of immigration policy, as well as the status of asylum seekers and Dreamers, is heavily dependent on the outcome of Congressional as well as presidential elections.

Language Ideologies

In addition to the fact that ideas about language are never just about language itself, another key take-away from Chapter 4 is that the social meanings of particular languages and linguistic features are not natural or inherent. On the contrary, symbolic and indexical meanings are socially constructed and mediated by ideology. Thus the symbolic meaning of Spanish – what it implies about the speaker, how it is perceived by society – depends on who is speaking it, who they are speaking it to, where and when they are speaking it and how they are speaking it. These factors influence whether Spanish is seen as a low-status language of poverty, such as is too often the case when spoken by Latinxs, or as a language of economic opportunity and cosmopolitanism as well as cognitive enrichment when spoken by upper middle-class Whites (Bruzos Moro, 2016). We have discussed this **differential bilingualism** and the contrasting representations of bilingualism in several places in the book. Will the positive cognitive, economic and social aspects of bilingualism continue to be seen as accruing only to mostly White elites, with Spanish still deployed as a mechanism of subordination when it comes to working- and middle-class Latinxs? Or might the positive, instrumentalist but largely **commodified** framings of bilingualism eventually spread? Or perhaps commodifying discourses about Spanish will lose ground, if job-seekers find that their linguistic skills are not actually rewarded?

Commodifying discourses don't seem likely to fade, in the short term anyway, since the emphasis on the economic value of Spanish is supported by a range of powerful institutions. In particular, it is linked to efforts by the Spanish government and Spanish corporations to maintain influence across the Americas as well as prominence on the world stage (Bruzos Moro, 2017; Villa & Del Valle, 2014). As a result, commodifying discourses are intertwined with triumphalist discourses celebrating both the large number of Spanish-speakers around the world and the US' rise in rankings of the countries with the most Spanish-speakers, which implicitly reconfigure the US as a 'Spanish-speaking country' (erasing Spanish's status as a minoritized language). As we saw in Chapter 2, the Census Bureau's questions on language don't include any questions about proficiency in the non-English language, itself a result of the hegemonic status of English (Leeman, 2018b). Thus, given what we know about patterns of language shift, the official statistics on the number of Spanish-speakers in the US seem to paint an overly rosy picture of the vitality of Spanish in the US.

Nonetheless, other ideologies about the value of Spanish, and of multilingualism in general, could gain prominence, either in place of or together with commodifying discourses. In the previous section we mentioned the possibility of new ways of understanding American national identity and belonging. With regard to language more specifically, might more widespread multilingualism lead not only to greater appreciation, but also a broader understanding of language's non-economic value? Could a critical mass of Spanish-speakers and other multilinguals who conceptualize their language abilities differently bring about such a change? And of course, one doesn't need to be multilingual oneself to recognize and appreciate multilingualism, so people who don't speak other languages could also contribute to new ways of thinking about Spanish in the US. One thing that is clear from our analysis of evolving constructions of American identity and shifting understandings of the role of English is that language ideologies change over time. Our hope is that the future will bring more positive societal perceptions of Spanish, as well as of stigmatized language varieties and multilingual practices such as **translanguaging**.

One goal of this book has been to promote readers' critical awareness of these issues, in the hopes that they might resist and challenge hegemonic ideologies regarding the relative worth of different languages, varieties and linguistic practices, and promote a more socially just and inclusive approach to language variation and multilingualism.

Race and Ethnicity

In Chapter 5 we saw that social constructions of ethnoracial identity – including how categories are defined, the labels used and their social meaning – differ across Latin American and US societies. The various ways of understanding social difference, and of imagining difference as linked to physical characteristics, are reflected in everyday interactions, in the identities and labels that people claim and ascribe to others and in official classifications such as the census. As such, scholars and policy makers have dedicated considerable efforts to investigating not only the ethnoracial identity of Latinxs themselves, but also the potential impact of the growing Latinx population on broader societal understandings of race. One area of particular interest in this regard has been the census classification. After a fairly extensive testing process, Census Bureau researchers advocated that the 2020 census use a combined race and ethnicity question that would include Hispanic/Latino origin as a response option, together with the officially recognized race categories. This suggestion was not taken up by the Office of Management and Budget (OMB), and two separate questions, one for Hispanic/Latino origin and one for race, were maintained. The question of whether Hispanic/Latino should be considered a race or an ethnicity will surely continue to be a topic of heated debate well into the future.

Another focus of heated discussion touching on Latinx ethnoracial identity is whether the US population will cease to be majority White, and if so, when this will happen. Based on immigration, birth and mortality rates, the Census Bureau has projected that the US will become 'minority White' in 2042 (Alba, 2016; Vespa *et al.*, 2018). However, this projection, as well as similar ones by the Pew Center placing the date a few years later, are controversial and have provoked significant debate (Frey, 2018; Myers & Levy, 2018; Tavernise, 2018). For one thing, although news coverage reported predictions about the 'White' population, the Census projections are actually about the 'non-Hispanic White' population. This is a clear example of what we said earlier: even though 'Hispanic or Latino' is officially an ethnicity it is often treated like a racial identity, even by the Census Bureau. In addition, projections about the relative size of the White population are based on a narrow definition of Whiteness – one that excludes Latinxs – together with assumptions about the racial identity of people of 'mixed' parentage. Specifically, the projected size of the White population excludes multi-race people (e.g. people with one White parent and one non-White parent, who might check the White box and another race category). Critics argue that this definition of Whiteness replicates the **one-drop rule** of racial classification and fails to take into account the fluidity of racial identity and classification (e.g. Alba, 2016; Frey, 2018). Further, the projections of a non-Hispanic White minority assume that descendants of Latin American immigrants will identify as Hispanic or Latino across generations, which, as we discussed above, is not necessarily accurate. Alternative projections have used broader definitions of Whiteness that included Hispanic or Latino Whites as well as people who choose White together with one or more other races. With this broader definition of Whiteness, the White population is projected to remain at 70% into the foreseeable future (Myers & Levy, 2018). Thus, projections about the relative size of the White population depend on how Whiteness is defined and how people self-identify, both of which are subject to shifting social norms and ideologies.

Which projection makes more sense and why does it matter? Some scholars argue that the idea that Whites will no longer constitute the majority group contributes to racial anxiety, racism and a political backlash among Whites (e.g. Alba, 2016; Myers & Levy, 2018). For example, in their empirical research with White Americans, Myers and Levy (2018) found that study participants who read simulated news stories about a White minority were more likely to express hostility to immigrants than did participants who read stories about increased diversity. Thus, supporters of using the broader definition of Whiteness that includes anyone who checks the White box, whether or not they also check additional boxes, argue that doing so leaves open the possibility of new understandings of ethnoracial identity and also has advantages in terms of social wellbeing. Scholars on the other side of the debate (e.g. Mora & Rodríguez-Muñiz, 2017) maintain that including Latinxs and 'mixed race' individuals within the counts of the White population would essentially erase their racialized status. Indeed, as we saw in Chapter 5, even people who choose the White category on the census don't necessarily identify as White nor are they necessarily treated as such in their daily lives (Dowling, 2014; Vargas, 2015). These debates underscore the far-reaching impact of census classifications and ethnoracial identity labels. Given the salience of ethnoracial identity in US society, as well the role of census statistics in public policy and politics, we have no doubt that these issues will be the focus of much future research and debate.

Identity

A theme that has come up repeatedly in this book (and even in this chapter) is the relationship of Spanish to Latinx identity. In particular, we have examined essentialist ideologies that imagine all Latinxs to be Spanish-speaking while also framing those Latinxs who don't speak Spanish as less authentic. We have also discussed racializing portrayals of this relationship, which frame Spanish as a quasi-biological feature of all Latinxs (even those who don't speak Spanish), and as a language that is inherently foreign and unwelcome in the US (Leeman, 2013). And as we noted, these ideologies and portrayals are relevant for the performance and negotiation of identity in everyday talk, in official classifications and in all sorts of policy realms. Still, demographic trends show that a growing percentage of Latinxs don't speak Spanish at home (although this statistic doesn't mean that they don't speak it at all). Further, many English-speaking Latinxs challenge the notion that they are less authentic than their Spanish-speaking counterparts (Shenk, 2007; for a comedic take on this issue, watch the Flama video 'Things non-Spanish-speaking Latinos are sick of hearing,' available at: https://www.youtube.com/watch?v=VKJe4BTC1Vg, accessed 17 April 2019). How will the relationship of Spanish to Latinx identity play out in the future? Will the rising percentage of English-dominant (and English monolingual) Latinxs loosen this connection? Or might language retention efforts, together with a broader pluralist push to value linguistic diversity and multilingualism, quell the decline in the percentage of Latinxs who speak Spanish?

If multilingualism is valued, this doesn't necessarily mean that Spanish would continue to index Latinx identity. In fact, broad societal appreciation of multilingualism, together with increased commodification of languages, could potentially lead to a symbolic decoupling of language from ethnic identity. This seems partially to have happened with French in Canada, where until the 1960s it was spoken primarily by people of Franco Canadian ethnic identity and was considered a marker of that identity. However, once Canadian national identity was reimagined as bilingual, and political rights and commercial interests heightened the value of French on the job market, French was reconfigured as a job skill, one also available to Anglophones (Heller, 2002, 2003; Roy, 2005). As we have seen, commodifying discourses also circulate in the US with regard to Spanish, perhaps nowhere more than in educational contexts (Bruzos Moro, 2016; Leeman & Martínez, 2007). Could a (partial) decoupling of Spanish and Latinx identity be underway in the US? Spanish is certainly available to non-Latinxs in order to access job opportunities (Subtirelu, 2017), but Spanish–English bilingualism is far from being considered an integral part of US national identity, and Spanish is still used in the discursive racialization of Latinxs, a process that relies on the symbolic link of Spanish to Latinx identity.

For these reasons, we see the commodified discourses surrounding Spanish, and the availability of Spanish as a resource for non-Latinxs, not as a decoupling of language and identity but rather as a case of contradictory ideologies and of multiple and shifting indexicalities, as well as differential bilingualism. Because there is no fixed social meaning for a particular language or a particular way of speaking, the symbolic meaning of Spanish depends on the context and the speakers. It is also for this reason that Latinxs and non-Latinxs alike can use Spanish to enact a wide array of identity categories and stances. For example, whether or not elite L2 speakers of Spanish are financially rewarded for their Spanish knowledge, they are sometimes able to use Spanish to present themselves as professionally minded forward-thinking job seekers (Pomerantz, 2002). In other contexts, Latinxs (as well as some Anglos) use Spanish to signal solidarity and/or ingroup status (Barrett, 2006). And as we saw, the use of Spanish, and even just the Spanish pronunciation of one's own name, can also be used to index Latinx pride and/or an unwillingness to give up all traces of one's ethnoracial identity. In this way, speaking Spanish or using Spanish pronunciation can be an act of resistance both to English hegemony and to assimilationist ideologies. In addition, research on **Mock Spanish** has shown that elements of Spanish can be used to enact a White identity or to perform a jovial, laid-back persona, even as it reproduces racist ideologies about Latinxs (Barrett, 2006; Hill, 2005; Schwartz, 2011, 2016). As recent years have seen increased use of and attention to Spanish in the public sphere, including in advertising and entertainment, and by politicians as well as by everyday folks, it will be worth paying attention to the ideologies and indexicalities surrounding its use, as well as to the identities that people use it to claim and ascribe to others.

As this discussion highlights, ethnoracial identity is not the only identity category relevant for Latinxs. Thus, we expect ongoing conversations about a wide range of micro- and macro-level and intersectional Latinx identities, as well as the ways they are expressed in language. So too, debates about the value and limitations of gender-inclusive terminology are sure to continue well into the future. Of many topics related to gender-inclusive language, we will be paying particular attention to whether the gender-neutral ending *-x* (such as in *Latinx*) is replaced by newer, more pronounceable forms. Zentella (2017) has proposed the use of *-u* (e.g. *Latinu*), while in Argentina and Chile the *-e* (e.g. *Latine*) seems to have become the gender-inclusive norm (López, 2018). In addition, we are curious to see whether individuals use these non-binary forms regardless of the sexual identity of the specific individuals referenced, or if they develop as a third option, used in addition to words with *-a* and *-o* endings.

Media

The last few decades have seen major changes in the representation of Latinxs, Spanish-speakers and Spanish, due not only to the growing Latinx population, but also to broader trends in the production and distribution of entertainment and news. In particular, whereas early Spanish-language programming in the US consisted of local Spanish-language media outlets, including both radio and television, often with low-budget advertising, these were gradually subsumed within, and sometimes replaced by, national Spanish-language networks running nationwide or international advertising campaigns (Dávila, 2012). Recent years have seen tremendous growth in the number of media outlets, with more and more radio and television stations and networks, but also online websites and channels, streaming services and satellite services.

This media fragmentation and diversification undergirds several important developments. For one, it has facilitated niche marketing and programming. At the same time as the politics of representation has gained societal prominence, media companies and advertisers have become acutely aware of the increased buying power of the Latinx population. This has led to an uptick in the number of Latinx characters in 'mainstream' English-language media (although stereotypes and erasures still abound), as well as more programming and advertising targeted specifically at US Latinx consumers. Further, whereas Latinx-oriented media was once almost exclusively in Spanish, more recent productions seek to appeal to the growing percentage of US-born Latinxs by incorporating and/or celebrating bilingualism and translanguaging, such as in the advertisements we included in the activities for Chapter 10, as well as through programming and advertising completely in

English. Online programming and web channels such as Mitú and PeroLike also produce content for and about Latinxs, often using a combination of English and Spanish.

Somewhat paradoxically, a second development is the increased internationalization and transnationalism of 'Latinx media' in the US. In the early years of US Spanish-language television, transnationalism primarily consisted of the importation of material originally intended for Latin American audiences (Dávila, 2014). However, even as the demographic, marketing and media trends discussed above have led to an increased media recognition of US Latinxs, Latin American and Spanish programs and movies are increasingly available to US audiences through subscription and on-demand services like HBO and Netflix. In addition, Netflix produces original Spanish-language programming, including series filmed in Argentina, Colombia, Mexico and Spain, for viewing around the world. These services also offer Spanish-language subtitling (and sometimes audio) for shows filmed in English, as well as English subtitles and audio for Spanish-language productions. As a result, the 'Latinx programming' in Spanish and English has expanded tremendously and it often has very little to do with US Latinxs per se. As for language, this increasing transnationalism also means that the language varieties and practices, as well as the related language ideologies, to which Latinxs are exposed may differ from those they encounter in their daily lives in the US. To take just one example, in the Netflix comedy *Club de Cuervos*, set in a fictitious town in Mexico, several characters frequently use English-language terms and expressions while speaking Spanish. Whereas in the US, English-influenced Spanish is sometimes seen as deficient, incorrect or uneducated and/or as an index of Latinx identity, on this show it is used to characterize, and caricaturize, wealthy, White Mexican businessmen as over-reliant on international 'management speak' and leadership training courses.

In Chapter 7 we noted that Spanish is increasingly heard in (predominantly) English-language movies and television shows, and we argued that this is a more realistic approach to language representation. It's not just in scripted programming that the presence of Spanish is increasing; in recent years advertisers have occasionally aired advertisements in Spanish (or partially in Spanish) during English-language programming. For example, during the 2019 Oscars, two of Verizon's six spots were in Spanish (Poggi, 2019), and Disney recently changed its rules to allow advertisers to more easily run Spanish-language ads (Steinberg, 2019). In addition, during the Oscars broadcast itself, several presenters and award winners spoke in Spanish (and translations into English were not provided in all cases). Several of the people who spoke in Spanish made it clear that doing so was intended as a revindication of immigrants, Latinxs and Spanish; in the words of actor Diego Luna: '*Ya se puede hablar español en los Oscars; ya nos abrieron la puerta y no nos vamos a ir*' ('One can speak Spanish at the Oscars now; they finally opened the door for us, and we're not going to leave').

In the past, public uses of Spanish in what had previously been constructed as English-only spaces were often met with pushback and complaints, and it will be interesting to see how this plays out in the future. We note that although media companies have slowly increased the use of Spanish within primarily English-language programming, much of the growth of Spanish-language media is far less visible to general audiences. In particular, technological advances have allowed media companies to offer optional subtitling, Spanish audio tracks and parallel Spanish-language websites, which may go largely unnoticed by anglophones. In this way, advertisers can have it all: they reach Spanish-speaking language audiences in their own language without the backlash from English-Only advocates who complain about being 'forced' to hear Spanish or press one for English. Still, the widespread availability of high-quality Spanish-language media (whether or not it is visible to everyone) constitutes an important type of institutional support for Spanish, as well as a symbolic recognition and a source of linguistic input, all of which may contribute to positive attitudes and language maintenance. So too, the increasing celebration of Spanish–English bilingualism in US-directed programming and advertising is a welcome celebration of the language and linguistic practices of Spanish-speakers in the US, one that can also shape perceptions.

Policy

In the US, the lack of an official language at the national level leads some people to think that there is no US language policy, but this is not the case. For one thing, 31 states have declared English to be their official language, albeit two of them in conjunction with Indigenous languages and four of them with resolutions supporting linguistic diversity. Still, there are numerous explicit language policies at the federal level, such as the English-language requirement for naturalization as a citizen, the provision of court interpreters to limited English proficient (LEP) defendants, and **Executive Order 13166**'s mandate that federal agencies make a reasonable effort to make their services available to LEP persons. As we saw, the language rights afforded by the latter two of these policies are based primarily on the right to be free of discrimination based on race, ethnicity and national origin.[1] In addition to these explicit policies, myriad implicit language policies also impact language use in government, in schools, in public spaces and within families. Both explicit and implicit policies shape and are shaped by language ideologies, and the broader sociopolitical context. Political movements to limit language access, such as prohibiting driver's license tests in languages other than English, have gone hand in hand with the rising incidence of xenophobic and anti-Latinx aggression of recent years. This may continue in the coming years, and if Republicans maintain control of the White House and the Senate and/or take control of the House, we expect to see an increased emphasis on English in federal policy, as well as a continued weakening of the Voting Rights Act. However, regardless of what happens at the federal level, we are also sure to see more of these language debates playing out at the state level.

Another issue to keep an eye on is how the RAE and the ANLE treat Spanish in the US, a topic that has already seen some debate. On one hand, these institutions have sought to maintain authority over and symbolic ownership of a 'standard' Spanish. In addition, Peninsular varieties are normalized as the default, with Latin American varieties accepted as long as they comply with the so-called pan-Hispanic norm, which continues to privilege the language practices of educated elites. In this framing, linguistic features and practices associated with language contact with English are seen as aberrations and scornfully referred to as *Spanglish*. On the other hand, as we noted above, these same institutions, together with the *Instituto Cervantes*, are very much invested in the promotion of Spanish as a world language, one worth knowing and studying. Their celebratory vision of the number of speakers around the world, as well as their continued acceptance and status as the ultimate linguistic arbitrators, relies in part on welcoming US Spanish-speakers within the fold. As the number of Latinxs in the US continues to increase, as more and more scholars and lay people are challenging the RAE and the ANLE's derogatory portrayal of US Spanish, and given the RAE's economic problems, it will be interesting to see how this ideological balancing act plays out. So too, we will be keeping a watchful eye on the academies' position on gender-inclusive language, which thus far has been unyielding despite increased activism from feminists and LGBTQ activists around the world. Still, the spread of innovative forms suggests not only recognition of the intertwining of social and political concerns but also of people's willingness to ignore the dictates of language authorities and give greater priority to inclusion than to language standards.

Education

Since the 1980s, Spanish language education and language education for Spanish-speakers in the US have been characterized by a series of policy paradoxes (King, 2009). In particular, Spanish-medium of instruction schooling and bilingual education for home-speakers of Spanish have seen significant declines, even as elementary Spanish as a second language programs gained popularity (King, 2009). Compounding this situation, the economic recession of 2008 and the disinvestment in public education, together with an increased emphasis on standardized testing, led to significant cuts even in 'foreign' language programs designed for second language learners (Pomerantz & Hueguet, 2013). Unfortunately, despite the economic recovery, public investment in education in general, and in language education in particular, has remained stagnant.

A more positive trend is the growth in two types of language education: **two-way immersion** (TWI) programs, primarily at the elementary school level, and Spanish for **heritage language speakers** (SHL), primarily offered at the high school and university level. As we discussed in Chapter 9, TWI programs are a type of maintenance bilingual education, and one of the most effective programs for English language learners in terms of overall academic achievement and their development of English literacy and language skills. They also offer the tremendous advantage of promoting additive bilingualism, in which students retain and develop their home language (in this case Spanish). In contrast with earlier models of maintenance bilingual education designed specifically for (Latinx) home-speakers of Spanish, which grew out of social justice movements and which received only limited public support, TWI programs are designed for home-speakers of both English and Spanish. Often linked to discourses about the need for global competencies, the TWI model has garnered greater public support and has become one of the fastest growing educational models (Flores & García, 2017; Varghese & Park, 2010).

To some extent, the popularity of TWI programs, as well as the increasing availability of the **Seal of Biliteracy**, reflects a more positive portrayal of multilingualism in general and of Spanish in particular. Nonetheless, TWI programs often embody and reproduce differential bilingualism in the ways in which they are described and promoted in policy documents, in classroom practices and in their greater availability to elite children (Flores & García, 2017; Palmer, 2009; Valdez *et al.*, 2016a). Similarly, Subtirelu *et al.*'s (2019) analysis of policy discourse surrounding Seal of Biliteracy programs raises significant concerns about the extent to which poor and racialized students will be able to participate, as well as about whether the program will recognize and validate the linguistic knowledge of home-speakers of Spanish, or instead reproduce inequities if official certifications of bilingualism end up going only to elite (White) L2 learners. This will be an important area of research, policy and advocacy in the coming years.

The other type of educational program that has seen tremendous growth in recent years is Spanish for **heritage language speakers** (SHL). The creation of SHL courses reflects a welcome recognition that traditional Spanish language education designed for L2 learners was not well suited for heritage language speakers, and did not take their linguistic characteristics and needs into account. Still, there is some concern that the creation of separate SHL tracks, and the continued construction of L2 education as the default, reproduces normative monolingualism and the notion that bilinguals and heritage speakers require separate and even remedial treatment (Leeman, 2010; Leeman & King, 2015).

While we're on the subject of educational discourses, we want to note that in some ways the development and discursive framing of SHL programs parallels that of bilingual education; specifically, the origins of SHL are also tied to the Chicanx and Puerto Rican civil rights and social justice movements, but like many TWI immersion programs, present-day SHL programs tend to emphasize a more instrumentalist approach to language, albeit in the case of SHL one oriented toward Latinxs and home-speakers of Spanish rather than (White) elites (Leeman, 2012b; Leeman & Martínez, 2007).

Nonetheless, in recent years, and co-occurring with commodifying discourses, there has also been a growing interest in critical pedagogical approaches to language education designed to promote students' appreciation and critical analysis of multilingualism and linguistic variation and their role in social and political life (e.g. Leeman, 2018b; Martínez, 2003). In addition, there has been a move to bring US varieties of Spanish to the center (e.g. Leeman, 2005; Torres *et al.*, 2018; Villa, 2002). Happily, these trends are not limited to SHL programs, but instead encompass: high school level college-preparatory instruction (e.g. Bucholtz *et al.*, 2017); upper-level literature and linguistics courses in the Spanish major (e.g. Leeman & Rabin, 2007; Leeman & Serafini, 2016; Rabin & Leeman, 2015); community-based service-learning programs (Leeman *et al.*, 2011; Lowther-Pereira, 2015; Martínez & Schwartz, 2012); and online education (e.g. Román-Mendoza, 2018). Such courses not only promote students' deeper understanding of language and sociolinguistics, as well as the world in which they live, but they also prepare students to recognize and resist dominant hegemonic ideologies, and thus are part of a broader push for anti-racist education and social justice. We are encouraged by the growth and diversity of such approaches to language education.

Linguistic Features

Although the focus of this book has been on social and political aspects of Spanish in the US, in Chapter 10 we provided an overview of some formal characteristics of different varieties of Spanish spoken in the US and some features that have been identified in Chicanx English, as well as a description of some language-contact phenomena. Key take-aways from this discussion, and the rest of the book, are related to: (1) the linguistic truism that language variation is inherent to all languages; (2) the principle that no language or language variety is better than any other; and (3) the fact that linguistic change is a given. Thus, attitudes and ideologies about the relative value of different varieties and practices, and whether a specific change is considered an innovation or a deterioration, are based primarily on non-linguistic concerns related to the people that they are associated with. Just like it always has everywhere it has been spoken, Spanish will continue to vary and change in the US.

Just as language variation and change are normal linguistic phenomena, we also saw that cross-linguistic influence and translanguaging are common practices in all multilingual situations. Actually, combining and shifting among varieties, registers and styles is also the norm in so-called monolingual speech. Not only do no two people share the exact same **linguistic repertoire**, but nobody speaks in exactly the same way all the time. Further, we saw that codeswitching or translanguaging is not a sign of linguistic deficiency. Instead, it requires sophisticated linguistic knowledge of multiple varieties or registers, and it conforms to implicit structural constraints. And in fact, codeswitching can also be used as a conversational strategy in the performance of identity. Recent years have seen a growing celebration (as well as a commodification) of translingual practices (such as in advertisements directed to English–Spanish bilinguals), despite the continued rejection by the RAE, the ANLE and other purists. As Spanish garners more and more attention, and there is greater and greater awareness of multilingualism, we will be interested to see how ideologies surrounding multilingual discourse evolve. We hope that there will be increased recognition of multilingual practices as not just as acceptable but as innovations expressive of identity and creativity.

Another topic that has already received some attention, and that we think will continue to be a focus of discussion and debate in the future, is whether it makes more sense to talk about *Spanish in the US* (*el español en los Estados Unidos*) or *US Spanish* (*el español de los Estados Unidos*) (e.g. Escobar & Potowski, 2015; Moreno Fernández, 2018; Otheguy, 2013; Torres Torres, 2010). In other words, does Spanish as it is spoken in the US constitute a specific national variety, along the same lines as 'Mexican Spanish' or 'Dominican Spanish'? In the case of varieties spoken in the former Spanish colonies like Louisiana and New Mexico and retained for many generations with limited impact from immigrant varieties, there is little controversy that these could be considered US varieties, as they have evolved over many generations. Thus, the debate centers on other ways of speaking Spanish, and whether they have 'enough' regionally specific features to be characterized as distinct US varieties of Spanish. Scholars who reject the *US Spanish* label typically argue that in most cases the Spanish spoken in the US reflects the origins of the speakers, rather than a local US variety. Further, because the people most likely to use Spanish outside the home are immigrants, and language shift to English typically takes place by the third generation, there is less opportunity for a local variety to develop than in areas where Spanish is the majority language and is reliably transmitted intergenerationally. On the other side of the debate, Escobar and Potowski (2015) argue that there are some linguistic forms that originated in the US, and these are recognized and labeled as *'estadounidismos'* by the RAE. They argue that this fact, together with the large number of Spanish-speakers in the US, the high percentage of whom were born in the US, and the extensive bilingualism among young Latinxs, are reasons to adopt the term *US Spanish*.

Rather than choosing sides in this debate, we are more interested in thinking about the reasons why there is a debate, as well as how the two positions interact with broader discourses. For one thing, as you likely realize, there is no straightforward answer to the question as to whether there are 'sufficient' features associated with Spanish as spoken in the US. Instead, as we have discussed repeatedly, the distinction between varieties, like the distinction between languages, is socially constructed rather than objectively defined (Otheguy, 2013; Penny, 2000). So why do some scholars prefer one label over the other? Does it matter which label is used? On one side, the move to claim *US Spanish* as a 'fully fledged' language variety represents an attempt both to legitimize the linguistic features and language practices of US Latinxs and to 'elevate' them to the status of a national variety, in part by garnering the power of ideologies that link nation to language. At the same time, it discursively reinforces the idea of the US as a 'Spanish-speaking country,' thus engaging the triumphalist and celebratory ideologies described above. On the other side, rejection of the *US Spanish* label and the underlying notion that Spanish in the US is significantly different from the varieties spoken elsewhere is a rejection of the idea of Spanglish or the development of a new language (e.g. Otheguy, 2013). Further, the term *Spanish <u>in</u> the US* implicitly rejects complacency about the status of Spanish and offers a subtle reminder of the possibility that its presence might be temporary and could be lost to language shift. Thus, yet again, non-linguistic and ideological concerns undergird debates that on the surface appear to be about language and labels. In the coming years, it will be interesting to pay attention to the formal features of Spanish in the US, in order to get a better sense of whether language contact with English, and among varieties of Spanish, is contributing to the development of a regional US variety. The debates about what to call the Spanish spoken in the US have already attracted the attention of the *Instituto Cervantes* (Moreno Fernández, 2018), and we'll be watching to see what position the RAE and the ANLE take in this regard, as well as how they navigate the tensions and inherent contradictions of validating *US Spanish* even as they denounce Spanglish.

Conclusions and Connections

In this book, we have seen how speaking Spanish in the US can have numerous, sometimes contradictory meanings and implications. To name just a few, it can be a performance of identity, an expression of solidarity, an act of resistance and/or a creative act. We hope that our interdisciplinary sociolinguistic approach has given you a sense of the myriad ways that we can think about what it means to speak Spanish in the US, while also demonstrating how analyzing the sociopolitics of language can give us a deeper understanding of Spanish-speakers, of Latinxs and of the nation itself. More broadly, we hope to have provided a greater appreciation of the role of language in social and political life, and we hope that you will think about the topics that we have covered here with regard to other languages, other people and other places.

As we have seen, the history of speaking Spanish in the US has not been an easy one and includes much suffering. But we have also seen tremendous advances in civil and human rights, and improvements in the situation of many Spanish-speakers and Latinxs. This is thanks to the efforts and activism of advocates, civil rights leaders, community organizers, students, politicians and everyday people. Still, there is much to be done. Thus, we ask you, the readers of the book, to think about what you hope the future of Spanish in the US will be and what you might do to make that hope become reality. The broad range of topics covered in this book underscores the multitude of issues that have an impact on Spanish and Spanish-speakers in the US. In turn, this highlights that there are a tremendous number of actions, big and small, in a vast range of contexts, in which it is possible to have a positive influence. There is not just one way to make a difference, and there is a need for advocacy and activism in all of the topics covered here. For example, you could get involved in political campaigns, do grass-roots organizing related to language policy or immigrant rights, work to create more inclusive media representations, become a teacher and promote critical language awareness, question monolingual assumptions, call out linguistic and other kinds of prejudice and discrimination, and/or make an effort to maintain Spanish and pass it on to your kids. Whatever you choose, and whether you speak Spanish yourself or not, we hope that you will make a positive contribution to the future of speaking Spanish in the US.

Discussion Questions and Activities for Chapter 11

(1) Skim through this book and reflect on what you have read. If someone asked you what the book is about and what the most important take-ways are, what would you say? What are the things that most interested, surprised or bothered you, and why?

(2) Read 'There is nothing wrong with Julián Castro's Spanish,' an op-ed about the criticism of the 2020 presidential candidate's Spanish (https://www.nytimes.com/2019/07/27/opinion/sunday/julian-castro-spanish.html) and discuss the issue in terms of the various language ideologies presented in this book. Next, analyze what the author says about some people questioning 'whether the label Latino applied to' Castro, and about the fuzzy meanings of the words *bilingual* and *fluent*. Can you use sociolinguistics to expand on what he says, both about the ethnoracial identity labels and the linguistic categories? Finally, analyze the apparent

contradiction between Castro's description of his Spanish ability and his observed linguistic practice. What explains the difference, and what ideologies are involved?

(3) Read 'Who changed the pronunciation of California cities? A story of assimilation and reclamation' (https://thebolditalic.com/who-changed-the-pronunciation-of-california-cities-505d1ef369b0) and analyze it using the material and topics covered in this book. Discuss how this issue reflects shifting perspectives on the history of Spanish in the US and analyze the different pronunciations in terms of: (1) indexicality, stance and identity; and (2) language contact and change. What attitudes and ideologies are represented in the arguments in favor of and against 'Spanish' pronunciation? How are these ideologies embedded in wider societal debates and discourses about Latinxs and diversity in general?

(4) Read the short essay, 'Growing up as a Japanese person in Peru,' by Shigueru Julio Tsuha, a Peruvian of Japanese descent who migrated to the US (http://www.discovernikkei.org/en/journal/2007/5/24/japanese-person-in-peru/). Discuss how the author's understanding of his youth changed as he gained a more critical understanding of language, ethnoracial identity and belonging. What does he suggest that the experiences of the Nikkei in Peru can tell us about the notion of assimilation? Drawing from topics covered in this book, discuss the role of names in identity as well as the multiple possible meanings of ethnoracial labels and slurs. Finally, you may wish to compare and contrast the situation of Nikkei in Peru to Latinxs in the US, and/or consider the layered and contradictory racializations that Nikkei Peruvians might experience when migrating to the US.

Note

(1) Court interpreters are provided based on the Constitutional right to participate in one's own trial.

Glossary

AAE: see **African American English.**

Additive bilingualism: Learning an additional language without losing one's first language(s); for example, learning English but also continuing to speak, read and/or write Spanish. Compare to **subtractive bilingualism.**

Affirmative language rights: The right to use a minority language, typically accompanied by protection and support for that language; compare to **negative language rights**.

African American English (AAE): A variety of English with origins in African American communities, sometimes popularly referred to as *Ebonics.*

Anglo: Adjective or noun used to refer to non-Latinx Whites. Sometimes used as a synonym of **Anglophone**.

Anglophone: Someone who speaks English as their dominant language or, more often, their only language.

Appropriation: The adoption or incorporation of cultural, linguistic or artistic practices associated with a minority or subordinated group by members of the dominant group, often without acknowledgement.

Binary race system: An ideological system in which there is a primary distinction between two race categories such as White and non-White.

Black Legend: The portrayal of Spanish colonial atrocities as more brutal than those committed by the British. Based largely on Spanish Friar Bartolomé de las Casas' 16th century accounts of the conquest and treatment of Native peoples, it was popularized by the British to justify their own imperialism in the Americas.

Borrowing: A word from one language that is used in another, also called a *loanword.* Examples of borrowings into Spanish include *fútbol* (from English) and *chocolate* (from Nahuatl). These are both established borrowings, used by monolingual Spanish-speakers around the world (and validated by language academies and in dictionaries). In contrast, borrowings such as *londri,* ('laundry') and *liquear* ('to leak') are found only in varieties where there has been more contact with English.

Calque, syntactic calque: The use of structures (often idiomatic phrases) from the donor language with words from the recipient language; also known as *loan translations.* One of the most commonly remarked upon calques from English to Spanish in the US involves the

English adverb *back* in expressions like *call back* or *give back* which are sometimes rendered as *llamar para atrás* or *dar para atrás*. Another documented calque from English to Spanish is 'How did you like' as *Cómo te gustó* in expressions such as *¿Cómo te gustó el libro?* ('How did you like the book'), vs. the normative *¿Qué te pareció el libro?* Like **borrowings**, calques are thought to begin with bilinguals but they may be taken up by monolinguals and eventually accepted by language authorities.

Casta: 'Mixed' race categories of the Spanish colonial period in the Americas that shaped social and political status.

Chicano/a/x: Mexican American. The term, widely believed to derive from *mexicano*, was often used with a pejorative meaning until it was reclaimed by Civil Rights activists in the 1960s and 1970s. For many, the adoption of the term signaled a rejection of *Mexican American*, which was seen as overly assimilationist. Thus, it indexes cultural pride and political activism. *Chicano* was added to the US census as an additional label for the Mexican or Mexican American category in 1990.

Chicanx English: A variety (or varieties) of English with origins in Mexican American communities. It is not learner English, but rather a native variety. Chicanx English is the most widely researched variety of Latinx Englishes.

Circumstantial bilingualism: Bilingualism which results either from migrating to a place where a different language is spoken, or from living in a society where the dominant language is different from one's home language (rather than a decision to acquire a 'foreign' language). Compare to **Elective bilingualism**.

Codeswitching: Combining languages, codes, speech styles or registers in a single utterance or conversation. Often, but not always, rests on the notion that languages and varieties are clearly definable entities. Compare to **translanguaging**.

Cognate: A word in one language that sounds like a word in another, with the same/similar meanings. For example, English *telephone* and Spanish *teléfono*.

Colorism: Prejudice, discrimination and/or inequality based on skin tone and **phenotype** including among people considered to be of the same race; social hierarchies privileging light skin and phenotypical characteristics associated with Whiteness.

Commodification, commodifying discourses: A way of thinking about and/or talking about cultural or linguistic practices that emphasizes their economic value for individual speakers, businesses and/or nations.

Covert prestige: The valuing of a language, variety or feature, not associated with elites, even if it is overtly disparaged. The association of subordinated and non-standard varieties and features with desirable traits.

Critical pedagogy: A variety of approaches to education that emphasize the role of traditional schooling in reproducing dominant ideologies and social inequality. Critical pedagogies seek to promote students' understanding of the relationship of everyday experiences and practices to broader social and political structures, in order to promote student agency and social justice.

Cyclical bilingualism: A term used to refer to the pattern of people learning Spanish (or another **minoritized** language) as children, undergoing shift to English (usually upon entering school), and then seeking to reacquire Spanish in adolescence or later. The term recognizes that people's bilingual competencies are not static over time, and that there is variability and change within 'generations.'

Differential bilingualism: The ideologies that racialize **circumstantial bilingualism** among Latinxs or portray it as a problem while seeing **elective and elite bilingualism** as an achievement and a cause for celebration.

Dual monolingualism (also: **double monolingualism**): A **monoglossic**, purist ideology about bilingualism that favors the complete separation of the two languages. In this ideology, bilinguals should speak each language like monolinguals do, without **translanguaging** or exhibiting signs of cross-linguistic influence.

Elective bilingualism: Bilingualism resulting from the active decision to acquire an additional language; typically used to refer to majority language speakers learning a 'foreign' language; compare to **circumstantial bilingualism** and **elite bilingualism**.

Elite bilingualism: Bilingualism among members of middle or higher socio-economic classes, which is often considered socially advantageous, especially in the case of prestigious languages; it is often **elective bilingualism**.

Endogamy: Marriage within an ethnoracial or linguistic group; contrast with **exogamy**.

English-only: Ideologies, policies or legislation that limit education or public services to English, or which discourage or forbid the use of other languages. Often used to describe Official English policies which make English the sole official language of either the US or a particular city or state.

Erasure: The phenomenon of ignoring or rendering invisible any practices or social groups that contradict the **hegemonic ideologies** or representations. For example, portraying US Latinxs as immigrants is an erasure of US-born Latinxs (who constitute the majority of Latinxs).

Essentialism/essentialist: The view that specific traits or characteristics are inherent to identity categories and the assumption that all members of the category share these characteristics. Essentialism sees identity as something that is internal to individuals, rather than socially constructed and negotiated. The notions that all Latinxs speak Spanish, or that women are inherently nurturing, are two examples of essentialism.

Ethnolinguistic vitality: A group's likelihood of maintaining a distinctive sense of identity. Because language is often constructed as an **essential** component of group identity, ethnolinguistic vitality is seen as influencing patterns of language maintenance and shift. Demographic factors, status factors and institutional support factors are the three kinds of factors hypothesized to play a role in ethnolinguistic vitality.

Ethnoracial: A term encompassing both ethnic and racial identity. Use of the term normally implies recognition that both ethnicity and race are social constructs, and that the consideration of a particular group identity as either one or the other is not straightforward. See Chapter 4 for a discussion of debates regarding whether 'Latinx' should be considered an ethnic or a racial identity.

Executive Order 13166: An executive order signed by President Bill Clinton in 2000 designed to improve language access services for people with limited English proficiency. It requires federal agencies and federally funded programs to examine the services they provide, to develop plans to provide 'meaningful access' and to take 'reasonable steps' to implement those plans.

Exogamy: Marriage outside of one's social group; contrast with **endogamy**.

Family language policy: Decisions and practices regarding the language(s) used in homes. Researchers originally stressed parents' decisions about language use but increasingly recognize that children also play a role in shaping household language practices.

First-generation Americans: The first members of a family to be born in the US, i.e. the children of immigrants. Compare with **first-generation immigrants** and **second-generation immigrants.**

First-generation immigrants: Immigrants, i.e. people who were born in one country but migrate to and live in another country. Compare with **generation 1.5**, **second generation immigrants** and **first-generation Americans**.

Generation 1.5: Term sometimes used to refer to people who immigrate as children, typically under the age of 10 or 12, in order to distinguish them from people who arrive as adolescents or adults; contrast with **first-generation immigrants** and **second-generation immigrants**.

Grammatical gender: Marking in a language of classes of nouns as male, female and sometimes neuter. In both English and Spanish, some nouns and pronouns referring to people and other animate beings are marked for gender (e.g. *daughter, son, him, her, hija, hijo, él, ella*). However, in Spanish as well as many other languages (but not English), all nouns have grammatical gender (e.g. *la mesa* 'the table' is feminine and *el libro* 'the book' is masculine). Gender for inanimate objects is purely grammatical; it doesn't have anything to do with the characteristics of the things themselves.

Hegemonic discourses and/or ideologies: Socially dominant ways of thinking or talking about something or someone that are often taken as common sense. See **hegemony**.

Hegemony: The dominance of one entity (especially a social group) over another. Dominance is often achieved not through force but by consensus that the dominant entity is deserving of that status. Can also refer to the dominance of a particular ideology or way of thinking.

Heritage language education: Language courses designed specifically for students who have had home exposure to the language.

Heritage (language) speakers: In the US, most often used to refer to people who were exposed to or learned to speak a minority language at home. May include people who are dominant in the heritage language as well as those who are dominant in the national language.

Heteroglossia: The co-existence of multiple language varieties, registers and styles within a named language. Scholars who take a heteroglossic approach to language stress that no two individuals use language in exactly the same way, and they generally see linguistic variation as a resource and/or something to be celebrated.

Heteroglossic ideology: The belief system that recognizes and embraces language variation within conventionally defined languages as well as the combining of different varieties and languages. The notion that there are a multitude of different ways of speaking a given language and speakers often switch fluidly among them; as a result, it is not possible to clearly delineate between languages. Contrast with **monoglossic ideologies**.

Iconicity: The ideological process in which a language or linguistic feature comes to be not only an index of a certain group, but an icon or symbol of the group; that is, it does not merely 'point to' the social group, but is assumed to be a representation of that group, sharing characteristics with it.

Index: To point to something or someone through speech, such as when the word *I* points to the person speaking. In this book we are most interested in the use of language to point to or signal social meanings, identities and the relationships between speakers. For example, speaking Spanish can index Latinx identity. A linguistic feature or behavior that points to a particular social category is called an *index* of that category.

Indexicality: The power of language to index social meanings and identities. See **index**.

Instrumentalist ideologies: Language ideologies that emphasize the usefulness of language for something else, such as the job market or national security. This contrasts with ideologies that stress the importance of language(s) for identity or cultural appreciation.

Interlocutors: A technical term for the people you talk to; conversation partners.

Intersectionality: The idea that different social categories (e.g. gender, social class, ethnicity, etc.) to which a person belongs are not simply additive or multiple; instead, they intersect and interact with each other. Thus it is not only that the experiences of a Latina woman are different from those of a Latino man, or that they can be understood in terms of her ethnoracial identity plus her gender. Instead, they are shaped by the interaction of the two categories. Most often used to draw attention to how two (or more) forms of discrimination (e.g. sexism and racism) interact to create new forms of oppression (e.g. the specific ways in which women of color are discriminated against) that are different from them both.

Language-as-problem orientation: A view of language reflected in language policies that portray multilingualism as a social or cognitive problem (Ruiz, 1984).

Language planning and policy (LPP): Specific attempts to shape language and language practices; may include a wide range of explicit and implicit policies in any kind of governmental, institutional or family context.

Language shift: The process of learning a new language and losing the first or heritage language. Usually used to refer to an intergenerational process in which children don't acquire or forget their parents' minoritized language and instead use only the majority language.

Lateralization (of /r/): The pronunciation of /r/ as 'l'; also known as 'lambdacism'. Characteristic of Caribbean varieties of Spanish, although also found in Southern Spain. Compare to **rhotacization**.

Latinidad: A Spanish-origin term meaning 'Latinx-ness'; used to express a pan-ethnic identity based on the idea that there are some shared cultural characteristics among Latinx peoples from different regional and **ethnoracial** backgrounds.

Linguistic profiling: Identifying or judging people's ethnoracial identity based on the way they talk, usually as part of **ethnoracial** discrimination.

Linguistic repertoire: The collection of linguistic resources, including language varieties, styles, accents and registers, etc., that a person knows. No two people have exactly the same linguistic repertoire.

Manifest Destiny: The mid- and late 19th century doctrine that US territorial expansion across North America was both inevitable and desirable. This doctrine was tied up with racism and religious intolerance as well as beliefs about the supposed superiority of US political institutions.

Medium of instruction: The language in which education takes place.

Mestizaje: The Spanish-language term for racial 'mixture,' especially between Indigenous and European peoples. This term also sometimes refers to the ideological representation of such 'mixture' as if it were evidence of a lack of racism. The term has been borrowed into English.

Mestizo/a/x: A Spanish-language term used to refer to people of mixed Native American and European ancestry that has been borrowed into English.

Minority or minoritized languages: Languages other than the national language or the language spoken by the dominant group (regardless of relative size); in the US, this means all languages other than English. Many scholars and activists prefer the term *minoritized* rather than *minority*, because it emphasizes the social and political processes that assign lower status to the language(s) of non-dominant groups.

Mock Spanish: The use of Spanish or elements of Spanish in an attempt to sound like one is speaking Spanish, without actually speaking Spanish, such as by adding an *-o* to words, or by using token Spanish lexical items, in many cases in ungrammatical ways. Examples include 'no problemo' and 'That's mucho bueno.' Mock Spanish implicitly portrays Spanish as linguistically inferior to English and reproduces negative ideologies and stereotypes about Spanish speakers, while allowing the speaker to portray themselves as laid back, savvy and/or jocular.

Monoglossic ideologies: The belief system that sees each language as consisting of a single linguistic system. As a result, one linguistic variety is generally considered superior to others, boundaries between languages are seen to be clearly defined, and **codeswitching** is frowned upon. See also **standard language ideology**; contrast with **heteroglossic ideologies**.

Mulato (Spanish), Mulatto (English): The terms used for the 'mixed' children of Black and White parents. At some historical moments in the US, it referred to a specific ratio (50%) of Black and White heritage, reflecting an ideology that imagines races as distinct physical categories that allow for the exact mathematical calculation of one's racial make-up.

Nativism, nativists: People who oppose immigration.

Naturalization/Naturalized: The treatment of an ideology or assumption as if it were 'common sense' or an objective fact, rather than a cultural construction.

Negative language rights: The right to be free from language-based discrimination. Compare with **Affirmative language rights**.

Normative monolingualism: An ideology that constructs monolingualism as the normal and preferred state for individuals as well as social and political entities, such as nation states. See also **zero-sum ideology** and **one nation-one language ideology**.

One-drop rule: The principle that all people with any sub-Saharan African ancestry (i.e. 'even one drop of Black blood') are considered Black. In the early 20th century this principle was enshrined in several US states' laws, which treated people of 'mixed' ancestry as legally Black and subjected them to segregation and discrimination, regardless of **phenotype** and social identity. While no longer a legal doctrine, in the US, multiracial people are often considered to belong to the non-White group. See also **Binary race system**.

One nation-one language ideology: The idea that each nation has or should have a single language to define it, and that the existence of multiple languages is inherently divisive. The one-to-one mapping of languages and nations is sometimes also used to argue that distinct ethnolinguistic groups should have political independence (such as in the case of Catalonia, for example). Both languages and nations are social constructions used to justify and reinforce each other.

Othering: The portrayal of a social group in such a way as to emphasize their difference from the dominant group in order to justify social or political exclusion.

Performance (of identity): Constructing and enacting identity through culturally meaningful behaviors. Performance perspectives see identity is enacted through actions and behaviors, rather than based on fixed category membership. Compare to **essentialism**.

Phenotype: Constellation of visible physical characteristics, such as eye color, hair type and skin color. These traits are often used in the **social construction** of race.

Pluricentric: Having several different geographic centers of prestige. Often, the most prestigious variety of a language is the one spoken by the elite in the political capital. The recognition of prestige norms in different national capitals purports to recognize linguistic variation, or at least regional variation.

Pull factors: Conditions in a receiving country that shape patterns of immigration. Pull factors that may attract immigrants include favorable economic, social or political conditions, as well as active recruiting or incentives on the part of businesses. Compare to **push factors**.

Push factors: Conditions in migrants' home countries that shape migration. Push factors that contribute to increased emigration include as gang violence, war, political or religious oppression, climate change and lack of economic opportunities. Compare to **pull factors**.

Racialization: The process by which people are grouped together and assigned to a shared identity category which represents them as essentially and/or biologically similar to each other as well as inferior to a dominant group. The racialization of cultural or linguistic characteristics or practices associated with specific social groups portrays those characteristics as inferior and as the cause of inequality.

Rhotacization, rhotacism (of /l/): The pronunciation of /l/ as 'r'; characteristic of Caribbean varieties of Spanish. Compare to **lambdacism**.

Romance languages: The languages derived from Latin, such as Catalan, French, Italian, Portuguese and Spanish, among others.

Seal of Biliteracy: An award or certification given by a school, district or state which recognizes that a student has attained proficiency in two or more languages. For more information, see https://sealofbiliteracy.org.

Second-generation immigrants: The children of **first-generation immigrants**; people whose parents immigrated. In some reporting, children of one US-born and one foreign-born parent are included in this category. Contrast with **first-generation Americans** and **generation 1.5**.

Slave codes: A series of 18th and 19th century state laws governing enslaved persons and their treatment. Among many other restrictions, slave codes often prohibited teaching enslaved people to read or write, and thus are some of the earliest explicit language policies in the US.

Social construct, social construction, social constructionism: An idea or category which is created within human culture through interaction and shared understanding, rather than an objective reality. Race is a social construct because although physical differences between groups of people exist, human variation does not neatly fit into biologically determined categories and racial identity cannot be determined biologically. Other social constructs include nation and language.

Social network theory: The study of how social relationships impact the production of knowledge, the transmission and spread of attitudes and behaviors, and the collective outcomes of groups. Within sociolinguistics, social network theory has been used to analyze the spread of language change as well as the maintenance or loss of minority languages.

Spanglish: A term used to describe language use which mixes Spanish and English; may include **borrowings**, **calques** and **codeswitching** or **translanguaging**. Some people use the term disparagingly and others use it positively to reference the creativity of these linguistic practices and their use to index ingroup identity.

Stance, stance-taking: Speakers' positioning of themselves within interaction, in relation to other speakers or to the topic at hand. Stance-taking is one way in which a speaker uses language to align or distance themselves from other speakers, ways of speaking and/or ideologies. Thus, stance-taking is a key aspect of the linguistic **performance of identity**.

Standard language ideology: The set of beliefs that are both possible and desirable to eliminate variation within language. Although no-one speaks the 'standard variety', ways of speaking that are *perceived* as standard are considered more 'correct.' In contrast, varieties perceived as 'non-standard' are considered intellectually and morally inferior. See also **Standard variety or language**.

Standard variety or language: A variety that is perceived as neutral and 'correct' which is generally the variety taught in school, used for national broadcasts and literature and associated with the middle and upper classes of society, often based on written norms. Because variation is inherent to all languages, it is impossible to define the standard variety, except for written language, and no-one actually speaks it. Thus standard languages are often referred to as idealized abstractions or ways of speaking that are perceived as standard and correct, rather than actual language varieties that anyone speaks. See also **Standard language ideology**.

Subtractive bilingualism: Learning a new language and giving up, or being forced to give up, one's first language. See also **zero-sum ideology**; compare to **additive bilingualism**.

Symbolic domination: Domination through the devaluing of subordinated social groups and convincing them that their place in the social hierarchy is justified; see also **hegemony**.

Translanguaging: Linguistic practices that combine elements from what have traditionally been considered different languages, as speakers fluidly draw from the full range of resources in their **linguistic repertoires**. The term is meant to recognize that languages and varieties are not bounded objects, but instead are socially and politically constructed. In contrast with **codeswitching**, it focuses on the social and symbolic aspects of language use, rather than the formal features.

Treaty citizens: The Mexican citizens who were granted US citizenship as part of the Treaty of Guadalupe Hidalgo (1848), which ended the US–Mexico war and transferred ownership of what is now the Southwestern US.

Two-way immersion (TWI) programs: Programs which offer bilingual education for both **minority language** and majority language students; together they learn both languages.

Velarization (of /n/): The raising of the back of the tongue (or *dorsum*) toward the back of the mouth (or *velum*) during the production of a sound. In all varieties of Spanish, the /n/ is velarized when it precedes a velar sound like /g/, such as in the phrase *un gato* ('a cat'). In some varieties of Spanish, /n/ is also velarized in other contexts, such as at the end of an utterance and/or before other consonants.

Xenophobia: Literally, fear of foreigners; also used to refer to hatred or racism toward migrants.

Zero-sum ideology: The notion that there is a fixed amount of 'space' for languages (in individuals as well as in society) and, as a result, languages are in competition with each other. In the case of individuals, **minority language** maintenance is (inaccurately) seen as impeding majority language acquisition. Similarly, within societies, minority languages are seen as threatening to majority languages.

References

AAA (American Anthropological Association) (n.d.) *AAA Statement on Race*. See https://www.americananthro.org/ConnectWithAAA/Content.aspx?ItemNumber=2583.

Achinstein, B., Curry, M.W. and Ogawa, R.T. (2015) (Re)labeling social status: Promises and tensions in developing a college-going culture for Latina/o youth in an urban high school. *American Journal of Education* 121 (3), 311–345.

ACIE (American Councils for International Education) (2017) *The National K-12 Foreign Language Enrollment Survey Report*. See https://www.americancouncils.org/language-research-fle-state-language-us.

ACS (American Community Survey) (2017) US Census Bureau. Accessible at https://www.census.gov/programs-surveys/acs

Acuña, R. (2015) *Occupied America* (8th edn). New York: Pearson Longman.

Ager, D.E. (2001) *Motivation in Language Planning and Language Policy*. Clevedon: Multilingual Matters.

Aitchison, J. (2001) *Language Change: Progress or Decay?* Cambridge: Cambridge University Press.

Alba, R. (2004) *Language Assimilation Today: Bilingualism Persists More Than in the Past, But English Still Dominates*. Albany, NY: Lewis Mumford Center for Comparative Urban and Regional Research, University at Albany. See http://mumford.albany.edu/children/reports/language_assimilation/language_assimilation01.htm.

Alba, R. (2016) The likely persistence of a White majority. *The American Prospect*, Winter. See https://prospect.org/article/likely-persistence-white-majority-0.

Alcoff, L.M. (2000) Is Latino/a a racial identity? In J. Gracia and P. De Greiff (eds) *Hispanics/Latinos in the United States: Ethnicity, Race, and Rights* (pp. 23–44). New York: Routledge.

Alcoff, L.M. (2015) Mapping the boundaries of race, ethnicity, and nationality. In I. Jaksic (ed.) *Debating Race, Ethnicity, and Latino Identity* (pp. 38–47). New York: Columbia University Press.

Alcorn, S. (2018) Oñate's foot. 99% *Invisible*, 4 December. See https://99percentinvisible.org/episode/onates-foot/.

Alfaraz, G.G. (2002) Miami Cuban perceptions of varieties of Spanish. In D. Long and D.R. Preston (eds) *Handbook of Perceptual Dialectology*, Vol. 2 (pp. 1–11). Philadelphia, PA: John Benjamins.

Alfaraz, G.G. (2014) Dialect perceptions in real time: A restudy of Miami-Cuban perceptions. *Journal of Linguistic Geography* 2 (2), 74–86.

Alford, N.S. (2018) Opinion: Overlooked by the media, women like me took to Instagram. *The New York Times Sunday Review*, 28 July. See https://www.nytimes.com/2018/07/28/opinion/sunday/race-black-latina-identity.html.

Allard, E., Mortimer, K., Gallo, S., Link, H. and Wortham, S. (2014) Immigrant Spanish as liability or asset? Generational diversity in language ideologies at school. *Journal of Language, Identity & Education* 13 (5), 335–353.

Almaguer, T. (2012) Race, racialization, and Latino populations in the United States. In D.M. HoSang, O. LaBennett and L. Pulido (eds) *Racial Formation in the Twenty-First Century* (pp. 143–161). Berkeley, CA: University of California Press.

Alonso, C.J. (2006) Spanish: The foreign national language. *ADFL Bulletin* 37 (2–3), 15–20.

Alvarez, S.M. (2013) Evaluating the role of the Spanish Department in the education of U.S. Latin@ students: Un testimonio. *Journal of Latinos and Education* 12 (2), 131–151.

Amaya, H. (2010) Citizenship, diversity, law and Ugly Betty. *Media, Culture & Society* 32 (5), 801–817.

Amaya, H. (2013) *Citizenship Excess: Latino/as, Media, and the Nation.* New York: NYU Press.

Anderson, B. (1991) *Imagined Communities: Reflections on the Origins and Spread of Nationalism* (revised edn). London: Verso.

Anderson, T.K. and Toribio, A.J. (2007) Attitudes towards lexical borrowing and intra-sentential code-switching among Spanish-English bilinguals. *Spanish in Context* 4 (2), 217–240.

Anderson-Mejias, P.L. (2005) Generation and Spanish language use in the Lower Rio Grande Valley of Texas. *Southwest Journal of Linguistics* 24, 1–12.

Andrews, G.R. (2004) *Afro-Latin America, 1800–2000.* New York: Oxford University Press.

Androutsopoulos, J. (2007) Bilingualism in the mass media and on the internet. In M. Heller (ed.) *Bilingualism: A Social Approach* (pp. 207–230). New York: Palgrave Macmillan.

Anzaldúa, G. (1987) *Borderlands/La Frontera.* San Francisco, CA: Aunt Lute Books.

Aparicio, F.R. (1998) Whose Spanish, whose language, whose power? An ethnographic inquiry into differential bilingualism. *Indiana Journal of Hispanic Literatures* 12, 5–26.

Ardila, A. (2005) Spanglish: An Anglicized Spanish dialect. *Hispanic Journal of Behavioral Sciences* 27 (1), 60–81.

Arriagada, P.A. (2005) Family context and Spanish-language use: A study of Latino children in the United States. *Social Science Quarterly* 86 (3), 599–619.

Auer, P. (1984) *Bilingual Conversation.* Amsterdam: John Benjamins.

Auer, P. (1988) A conversation analytic approach to code-switching and transfer. In M. Heller (ed.) *Codeswitching: Anthropological and Sociolinguistic Perspectives* (pp. 187–214). Berlin: Mouton de Gruyter.

Auer, P. (1995) The pragmatics of code-switching. In L. Milroy and P. Muysken (eds) *One Speaker, Two Languages: Cross-Disciplinary Perspectives on Code-switching* (pp. 115–135). Cambridge: Cambridge University Press.

Auer, P. (forthcoming) 'Translanguaging' or 'doing languages'? Multilingual practices and the notion of 'codes'. In J. MacSwan (ed.) *Language(s): Multilingualism and its Consequences.* Bristol: Multilingual Matters. See https://www.researchgate.net/publication/332593230_'Translanguaging'_or_'doing_languages'_Multilingual_practices_and_the_notion_of_'codes'.

Avila-Saavedra, G. (2011) Ethnic otherness versus cultural assimilation: US Latino comedians and the politics of identity. *Mass Communication and Society* 14 (3), 271–291.

Avilés-Santiago, M.G. and Báez, J.M. (2019) 'Targeting Billennials': Billenials, linguistic flexibility, and the new language politics of univision. *Communication Culture & Critique* 12 (1), 128–146.

Ayala, C.J. and Bernabe, R. (2009) *Puerto Rico in the American Century: A History since 1898*. Chapel Hill, NC: University of North Carolina Press.

Baez, J.M. (2007) Towards a latinidad feminista: The multiplicities of latinidad and feminism in contemporary cinema. *Popular Communication* 5 (2), 109–128.

Baez, J. And Avilés-Santiago, M. (2016) *Spanish Language Television*. Oxford Bibliographies in Cinema and Media Studies. Oxford: Oxford University Press.

Bailey, B. (2000a) Language and negotiation of racial/ethnic identity among Dominican Americans. *Language in Society* 29 (4), 555–582.

Bailey, B. (2000b) The language of multiple identities among Dominican Americans. *Journal of Linguistic Anthropology* 10 (2), 190–223.

Bailey, B. (2007) Heteroglossia and boundaries. In M. Heller (ed.) *Bilingualism: A Social Approach* (pp. 257–274). New York: Palgrave Macmillan.

Baker, C. (2011) *Foundations of Bilingual Education and Bilingualism* (5th edn). Bristol: Multilingual Matters.

Bakhtin, M. (1981) *The Dialogic Imagination* (M. Bakhtin, ed.; M. Holquist and C. Emerson, trans.). Austin, TX: University of Texas Press.

Balderrama, F.E. and Rodriguez, R. (2006) *Decade of Betrayal: Mexican Repatriation in the 1930s*. Albuquerque, NM: University of New Mexico.

Bale, J. (2014) Heritage language education and the 'national interest'. *Review of Research in Education* 38 (1), 166–188.

Bañales, X. (2014) Jotería: A decolonizing political project. *Aztlán: A Journal of Chicano Studies* 39 (1), 155–166.

Baptist, E.E. (2016) *The Half Has Never Been Told: Slavery and the Making of American Capitalism*. New York: Basic Books.

Barakos, E. and Selleck, C. (2019) Elite multilingualism: Discourses, practices, and debates. *Journal of Multilingual and Multicultural Development* 40 (5), 361–374. https://doi.org/10.1080/01434632.2018.154369

Baron, D.E. (1990) *The English-only Question: An Official Language for Americans?* New Haven, CT: Yale University Press.

Barrett, R. (2006) Language ideology and racial inequality: Competing functions of Spanish in an Anglo-owned Mexican restaurant. *Language in Society* 35 (2), 163–204.

Barry, E. (2005) Learn English, judge tells moms. *Los Angeles Times*, 14 February. See http://articles.latimes.com/2005/feb/14/nation/na-english14.

Bartolomé, L. and Macedo, D. (1999) (Mis)educating Mexican Americans through language. In T. Huebner and K.A. Davis (eds) *Sociopolitical Perspectives on Language Policy and Planning in the USA* (pp. 223–241). Philadelphia, PA: John Benjamins.

Batalova, J. and Zong, J. (2017) Cuban immigrants in the United States. *MPI Spotlight*, 9 November. See https://www.migrationpolicy.org/article/cuban-immigrants-united-states.

Batalova, J. and Zong, J. (2018) Mexican immigrants in the United States. *MPI Spotlight*, 11 October. https://www.migrationpolicy.org/article/mexican-immigrants-united-states.

Baugh, J. (2003) Linguistic profiling. In S. Makoni, G. Smitherman, A.F. Ball and A.K. Spears (eds) *Black Linguistics: Language, Society, and Politics in Africa and the Americas* (pp. 155–168). New York: Routledge.

Baugh, J. (2017) Linguistic profiling and discrimination. In O. García, N. Flores and M. Spotti (eds) *The Oxford Handbook of Language and Society* (pp. 349–368). Oxford: Oxford University Press.

Bayley, R. and Holland, C. (2014) Variation in Chicano English: The case of final (z) devoicing. *American Speech* 89 (4), 385–407.

Bayley, R. and Santa Ana, O. (2004) Chicano English: Morphology and syntax. In B. Kortmann, K. Burridge, R. Mesthrie, E.W. Schneider and C. Upton (eds) *A Handbook of Varieties of English, Vol. 2: Morphology and Syntax* (pp. 374– 390). Berlin: Mouton de Gruyter.

Bazo Vienrich, A. (2018) Indigenous immigrants from Latin America (IILA): Racial/ethnic identity in the U.S. *Sociology Compass* e12644.

Beaudrie, S.M. (2011) Spanish heritage language programs: A snapshot of current programs in the Southwestern United States. *Foreign Language Annals* 44 (2), 321–337.

Beaudrie, S. and Ducar, C. (2005) Beginning level university heritage programs: Creating a space for all heritage language learners. *Heritage Language Journal* 3 (1), 1–26.

Beaudrie, S. and Fairclough, M. (2012) *Spanish as a Heritage Language in the United States: The State of the Field*. Georgetown Studies in Spanish Linguistics. Washington, DC: Georgetown University Press.

Beaudrie, S.M., Ducar, C. and Potowski, K. (2014) *Heritage Language Teaching: Research and Practice*. Columbus, OH: McGraw-Hill.

Beck, S.A.L. and Allexsaht-Snider, M. (2002) Recent language minority education policy in Georgia: Appropriation, assimilation, and Americanization. In S. Wortham, E.G. Murillo Jr. and E.T. Hamann (eds) *Education in the New Latino Diaspora: Policy and the Politics of Identity* (pp. 37–66). Westport, CN: Ablex.

Beckert, S. and Rockman, S. (2016) *Slavery's Capitalism*. Philadelphia, PA: University of Pennsylvania Press.

Beckett, L. (2019) 'It can happen again': America's long history of attacks against Latinos. *The Guardian*, 15 August. See https://www.theguardian.com/us-news/2019/aug/14/it-can-happen-again-americas-long-history-of-attacks-against-latinos.

Beltran, M. (2002) The Hollywood Latina body as site of social struggle: Media constructions of stardom and Jennifer Lopez's 'cross-over butt'. *Quarterly Review of Film and* Video 19 (1), 71–86.

Beltrán, M. (2016) Latina/os on TV!: A proud (and ongoing) struggle over representation and authorship. In F.L. Aldema (ed.) *The Routledge Companion to Latina/o Popular Culture* (pp. 39–49). New York: Routledge.

Benner, A.D. and Graham, S. (2011) Latino adolescents' experiences of discrimination across the first 2 years of high school: Correlates and influences on educational outcomes. *Child Development* 82 (2), 508–519.

Ben-Rafael, E., Shohamy, E. and Barni, M. (2010) Introduction: An approach to an 'ordered disorder'. In E. Shohamy, E. Ben-Rafael and M. Barni (eds) *Linguistic Landscape in the City* (pp xi–xxvii). Bristol: Multilingual Matters.

Benwell, B. and Stokoe, E. (2006) *Discourse and Identity*. Edinburgh: Edinburgh University Press.

Berry, K.A. (2004) Latino commerce in northern Nevada. In D. Arreola (ed.) *Hispanic Spaces, Latino Places: Community and Cultural Diversity in Contemporary America*, (pp. 225–238). Austin: University of Texas Press.

Betti, S. (2015) La imagen de los hispanos en la publicidad de los Estados Unidos. *Informes del Observatorio*. Cambridge, MA: Observatory of the Spanish Language and Hispanic Cultures in the United States. See http://cervantesobservatorio.fas.harvard.edu/es/informes/informes-del-observatorio-observatorio-reports-009-032015sp-la-imagen-de-los-hispanos-en-la.

Bhabha, H. (1990) *The Location of Culture*. New York: Routledge.

Bhatt, R.M. (2008) In other words: Language mixing, identity representations, and third space. *Journal of Sociolinguistics* 12 (2), 177–200.

Bhatt, R.M. and Bolonyai, A. (2011) Code-switching and the optimal grammar of bilingual language use. *Bilingualism: Language and Cognition* 14 (4), 522–546.

Bhatt, R.M. and Bolonyai, A. (2015) On the theoretical and empirical bases of translanguaging. Paper presented at *International Symposium on Bilingualism* 10.

Bhatt, R.M. and Bolonyai, A. (2019) On the theoretical and empirical bases of translanguaging. *Working Papers in Urban Language and Literacies*, (254). Retrieved from https://www.academia.edu/39950581/WP254_Bhatt_and_Bolonyai_2019._On_the_theoretical_and_empirical_bases_of_translanguaging

Bialik, K. (2019) Border apprehensions increased in 2018 – especially for migrant families. *Fact Tank*, 16 January. Washington, DC: Pew Research Center. See http://www.pewresearch.org/fact-tank/2019/01/16/border-apprehensions-of-migrant-families-have-risen-substantially-so-far-in-2018/.

Bialystok, E. (2011) Reshaping the mind: The benefits of bilingualism. *Canadian Journal of Experimental Psychology/Revue Canadienne de Psychologie Experimentale* 65 (4), 229–235.

Billig, M. (1995) *Banal Nationalism*. London: Sage.

Bills, G. (1997) New Mexican Spanish: Demise of the earliest European variety in the United States. *American Speech* 72, 154–171.

Bills, G.D., Hudson, A. and Chávez, E.H. (1999) Spanish home language use and English proficiency as differential measures of language maintenance and shift. *Southwest Journal of Linguistics* 19 (1), 11–27.

Blatt, B. (2014) What language does your state speak? *Slate Magazine*, 13 May. See https://slate.com/culture/2014/05/language-map-whats-the-most-popular-language-in-your-state.html.

Blommaert, J. (2010) *The Sociolinguistics of Globalization*. Cambridge: Cambridge University Press.

Boeschoten, H. (1990) Asymmetrical code-switching in immigrant communities. In G. Lüdi (ed.) *Papers for the Workshop on Constraints, Conditions and Models* (pp. 85–100). Strasbourg: European Science Foundation Network on Codeswitching and Language Contact.

Bolnick, D.A., Fullwiley, D., Duster, T. *et al.* (2007) The science and business of genetic ancestry testing. *Science* 318 (5849), 399–400.

Bonfiglio, P.T. (2002) *Race and the Rise of Standard American*. Berlin: Mouton de Gruyter.

Bourdieu, P. (1991) *Language and Symbolic Power 1982* (J.B. Thompson, ed.; G. Raymond, trans.). Cambridge, MA: Harvard University Press.

Boyd, J.P. (1955) *The Papers of Thomas Jefferson*. Princeton, NJ: Princeton University Press.

Bristol, J.C. (2007) *Christians, Blasphemers, and Witches: Afro-Mexican Ritual Practice in the Seventeenth Century*. Albuquerque, NM: University of New Mexico Press.

Brooke, J. (1998) Conquistador statue stirs Hispanic pride and Indian rage. *The New York Times*, 9 February. See https://www.nytimes.com/1998/02/09/us/conquistador-statue-stirs-hispanic-pride-and-indian-rage.html.

Brunn, M. (1999) The absence of language policy and its effects on the education of Mexican migrant children. *Bilingual Research Journal* 23 (4), 319–344.

Bruzos Moro, A. (2016) El capital cultural del español y su enseñanza como lengua extranjera en Estados Unidos. *Hispania* 99 (1), 5–16.

Bruzos Moro, A. (2017) 'De camareros a profesores' de ELE: La mercantilización del español y de su enseñanza como lengua extranjera. *Spanish in Context* 14 (2), 230–249.

Bucholtz, M. (1999) You da man: Narrating the racial other in the production of white masculinity. *Journal of Sociolinguistics* 3 (4), 443–460.

Bucholtz, M. (2009) From stance to style: Gender, interaction, and indexicality in Mexican immigrant youth slang. In A. Jaffe (ed.) *Stance: Sociolinguistic Perspectives* (pp. 146–170). Oxford: Oxford University Press.

Bucholtz, M. (2016) On being called out of one's name: Indexical bleaching as a technique of deracialization. In H.S. Alim (ed.) *Raciolinguistics: How Language Shapes our Ideas about Race* (pp. 273–289). Oxford: Oxford University Press.

Bucholtz, M. and Hall, K. (2005) Identity and interaction: A sociocultural linguistic approach. *Discourse Studies* 7 (4–5), 585–614.

Bucholtz, M., Casillas, D.I. and Lee, J.S. (2017) Language and culture as sustenance. In D. Paris and H.S. Alim (eds) *Culturally Sustaining Pedagogies: Teaching and Learning for Justice in a Changing World* (pp. 43–60). New York: Teachers College Press.

Bucholtz, M., Casillas, D.I. and Lee, J.S. (2018) California Latinx youth as agents of sociolinguistic justice. In N. Avineri, L.R. Graham, E.J. Johnson, R.C. Riner and J. Rosa (eds) *Language and Social Justice in Practice* (pp. 166–175). New York: Routledge.

Bullock, B. and Toribio, A.J. (2014) Dominican Spanish. In M. Di Paolo and A.K. Spears (eds) *Languages and Dialects in the U.S.* (pp. 151–162). New York: Routledge.

Burbules, N.C. and Berk, R. (1999) Critical thinking and critical pedagogy: Relations, differences, and limits. In T.S. Popkewitz and L. Fender (eds) *Critical Theories in Education: Changing Terrains of Knowledge and Politics* (pp. 45–65). New York: Routledge.

Bürki, Y. (2008) El español en las películas estadounidenses: Aproximación discursiva. *Círculo de Lingüística Aplicada* 36, 3–25.

Bush, D.P. (2015) Syndicates, Spanish and slurs: Flexible latinidad on US daytime soap operas. *Journal of Popular Culture (Boston)* 48 (6), 1151–1170.

Bustamante, C. and Novella G.M.Á. (2019) When a heritage speaker wants to be a Spanish teacher: Educational experiences and challenges. *Foreign Language Annals* 52 (1), 184–198.

Butler, J. (1990) *Gender Trouble and the Subversion of Femininity.* New York: Routledge.

Butler, J. and Spivak, G.C. (2007) *Who Sings the Nation-State? Language, Politics, Belonging.* London: Seagull Books.

Butler, Y.G., Orr, J.E., Gutierrez, M.B. and Hakuta, K. (2000) Inadequate conclusions from an inadequate assessment: What can SAT-9 scores tell us about the impact of Proposition 227 in California? *Bilingual Research Journal* 24 (1–2), 141–154.

Bybee, J. (2015) *Language Change.* Cambridge: Cambridge University Press.

Cacoullos, R.T. and Travis, C.E. (2010) Variable yo expression in New Mexico: English influence. *Journal of the Rivera-Mills & Villa* 203, 185–206.

Callahan, L. (2010) Speaking with (dis)respect: A study of reactions to Mock Spanish. *Language and Intercultural Communication* 10 (4), 299–317.

Callahan, E. (2018) *Emerging Hispanicized English in the Nuevo New South: Language Variation in a Triethnic Community.* New York: Routledge.

Cameron, C.D.R. (1997) How the García cousins lost their accents: Understanding the language of Title VII decisions approving English-only rules as the product of racial dualism, Latino invisibility, and legal indeterminacy. *California Law Review* 85, 1347–1393.

Cammarota, J. (2004) The gendered and racialized paths of Latino and Latina youth: Different struggles, different resistances in the urban context. *Anthropology and Education Quarterly* 35 (1), 53–74.

Canfield, J. (2014) Once forbidden, Alaska's Native languages now official state languages. *KTOO Public Media*, 24 October. See https://www.ktoo.org/2014/10/24/forbidden-alaskas-native-languages-now-official-state-languages/.

Carreira, M. and Chik, C.H. (2018) Differentiated teaching: A primer for heritage and mixed classes. In K. Potowski (ed.) *The Routledge Handbook of Spanish as a Heritage Language.* New York: Routledge.

Carreira, M.M. and Valdés, G. (2012) Meeting the needs of heritage language learners: Approaches, strategies, and research. In S.M. Beaudrie and M.A. Fairclough (eds) *Spanish as a Heritage Language in the United States* (pp. 223–240). Washington, DC: Georgetown University Press.

Carrigan, W.D. and Webb, C. (2013) *Forgotten Dead: Mob Violence against Mexicans in the United States, 1848–1928.* Oxford: Oxford University Press.

Carrillo, H. and Fontdevila, J. (2014) Border crossings and shifting sexualities among Mexican gay immigrant men: Beyond monolithic conceptions. *Sexualities* 17 (8), 919–938.

Carris, L.M. (2011) La voz gringa: Latino stylization of linguistic (in)authenticity as social critique. *Discourse & Society* 22 (4), 474–490.

Carter, P.M. (2013) Shared spaces, shared structures: Latino social formation and African American English in the US South. *Journal of Sociolinguistics* 17 (1), 66–92.

Carter, P.M. and Callesano, S. (2018) The social meaning of Spanish in Miami: Dialect perceptions and implications for socioeconomic class, income, and employment. *Latino Studies* 16 (1), 65–90.

Carter, P.M. and Lynch, A. (2015) Multilingual Miami: Current trends in sociolinguistic research. *Language and Linguistics Compass* 9 (9), 369–385.

Carter, P.M., López, L. and Sims, N. (2014) A first look at Miami Latino English: Tracking Spanish substrate influence through prosodic and vocalic variation. Paper presented at *New Ways of Analyzing Variation (NWAV)* 43, Chicago, IL, 26 October.

Cashman, H. (2005) Identities at play: Language preference and group membership in bilingual talk in interaction. *Journal of Pragmatics* 37 (30), 1–15.

Cashman, H. (2017) *Queer, Latinx, and Bilingual: Narrative Resources in the Negotiation of Identities.* New York: Routledge.

Casillas, D.I., Ferrada, J.S. and Hinojos, S.V. (2018) The accent on Modern Family: Listening to representations of the Latina vocal body. *Aztlan: A Journal of Chicano Studies* 43 (1), 61–88.

Cenoz, J. and Gorter, D. (2006) Linguistic landscape and minority languages. *International Journal of Multilingualism* 3 (1), 67–80.

Cepeda, M.E. (2000) Mucho loco for Ricky Martin or the politics of chronology, crossover, and language within the Latin music 'boom'. *Popular Music and Society* 24 (3), 55–71.

Cepeda, M.E. (2010) Singing the 'Star-Spanglish Banner'. In G.M. Pérez, F.A. Guridy and A. Burgos (eds) *Beyond El Barrio: Everyday Life in Latina/o America* (pp. 27–43). New York: NYU Press.

Chappell, W. (2018) The sociophonetic perception of heritage Spanish speakers in the United States: Reactions to labiodentalized <v> in the speech of late immigrant and U.S.-born voices. Unpublished manuscript. See https://www.academia.edu/37264932/The_sociophonetic_perception_of_heritage_Spanish_speakers_in_the_United_States_Reactions_to_labiodentalized_v_in_the_speech_of_late_immigrant_and_U.S.-born_voices.

Chappell, W. (2019) Caribeño or mexicano, profesionista or albañil? *Sociolinguistics Studies* 12 (3–4), 367–393.

Chávez, C. (2015) *Reinventing the Latino Television Viewer: Language, Ideology, and Practice.* London: Lexington Books.

Chavez, L. (2013) *The Latino Threat: Constructing Immigrants, Citizens, and the Nation* (2nd edn). Palo Alto, CA: Stanford University Press.

Chavez, L.R., Campos, B., Corona, K., Sanchez, D. and Ruiz, C.B. (2019) Words hurt: Political rhetoric, emotions/affect, and psychological well-being among Mexican-origin youth. *Social Science & Medicine* 228, 240–251.

Chávez, R. (2003) Ethnic stereotypes: Hispanics and Mexican Americans. In P.M. Lester and S.D. Ross (eds) *Images That Injure: Pictorial Stereotypes in the Media* (2nd edn) (pp. 93–102). Westport, CN: Praeger.

Chiricos, T. and Eschholz, S. (2002) The racial and ethnic typification of crime and the criminal typification of race and ethnicity in local television news. *Journal of Research in Crime and Delinquency* 39 (4), 400–420.

Chun, E.W. (2004) Ideologies of legitimate mockery. *Pragmatics* 14 (2), 263–289.

Chun, E.W. (2009) Speaking like Asian immigrants. *Pragmatics* 19 (1), 17–38.

Chun, E.W. (2016) The meaning of *ching-chong:* Language, racism and new media. In H.S. Alim, J.R. Rickford and A.F. Ball (eds) *Raciolinguistics: How Language Shapes our Ideas about Race* (pp. 81–96). Oxford: Oxford University Press.

Chun, E.W. and Lo, A. (2016) Language and racialization. In N. Bonvillain (ed.) *The Routledge Handbook of Linguistic Anthropology* (pp. 220–233). New York: Routledge.

Collier, V.P. and Thomas, W.P. (2017) Validating the power of bilingual schooling: Thirty-two years of large-scale, longitudinal research. *Annual Review of Applied Linguistics* 37, 203–217.

Collins, B.A., Toppelberg, C.O., Suárez-Orozco, C., O'Connor, E. and Nieto-Castañon, A. (2011) Cross-sectional associations of Spanish and English competence and well-being in Latino children of immigrants in kindergarten. *International Journal of the Sociology of Language* 208, 5–23.

Commission on Language Learning (2017) *America's Languages: Investing in Language Education for the 21st Century*. See https://www.amacad.org/publication/americas-languages.

Compton, E., Bentley, M., Ennis, S. and Rastogi, S. (2013) *2010 Census Race and Hispanic Origin Alternative Questionnaire Experiment* (No. 2011, 2nd reissue). Washington, DC: US Census Bureau.

Cooper, R.L. (1989) *Language Planning and Social Change*. Cambridge: Cambridge University Press.

Correa, T. (2010) Framing Latinas: Hispanic women through the lenses of Spanish-language and English-language news media. *Journalism* 11 (4), 425–443.

Cortés, C.E. (1997) Chicanas in film: History of an image. In C.E. Rodriguez (ed.) *Latin Looks: Images of Latinas and Latinos in the U.S. Media* (pp. 121–141). Boulder, CO: Westview Press.

Coupland, N. (2003) Introduction: Sociolinguistics and globalisation. *Journal of Sociolinguistics* 7 (4), 465–472.

Crawford, J. (1990) Language freedom and restriction. In J. Reyhner (ed.) *Effective Language Education Practices and Native Language Survival* (pp. 9–22). Choctaw, OK: Native American Language Issues.

Crawford, J. (1992) *Language Loyalties: A Source Book on the Official English Controversy*. Chicago, IL: University of Chicago Press.

Crawford, J. (1997) *Language Policy – Puerto Rico and Official English*. See http://www.languagepolicy.net/archives/can-pr.htm.

Crawford, J. (2008) *Advocating for English Learners: Selected Essays*. Clevedon: Multilingual Matters.

Crenshaw, K. (1989) Demarginalizing the intersection of race and sex: A Black feminist critique of antidiscrimination doctrine, feminist theory and antiracist politics. *University of Chicago Legal Forum* 1. See https://chicagounbound.uchicago.edu/uclf/vol1989/iss1/8.

Cruz, G.J. (2017) The Insular Cases and the broken promise of equal citizenship: A critique of U.S. policy toward Puerto Rico. *Revista de Derecho Puertorriqueño* 57, 27–62.

Cruz, B. and Teck, B. (1998) *The Official Spanglish Dictionary: Un User's Guide to More Than 300 Words and Phrases That Aren't Exactly Español or Inglés*. New York: Fireside.

Cuero, K.K. (2009) Authoring multiple formas de ser: Three bilingual Latino/a fifth graders navigating school. *Journal of Latinos and Education* 8 (2), 141–160.

Culliton-Gonzalez, K. (2008) Time to revive Puerto Rican voting rights. *La Raza Law Journal* 19, 27–68.

Curtin, M. (2007) Differential bilingualism: Vergüenza and pride in a Spanish sociolinguistics class. In N.M. Antrim (ed.) *Seeking Identity: Language in Society* (pp. 10–31). Newcastle: Cambridge Scholars.

Dailey, R.M., Giles, H. and Jansma, L.L. (2005) Language attitudes in an Anglo-Hispanic context: The role of the linguistic landscape. *Language & Communication* 25 (1), 27–38.

Daniels, J.D. (1992) The Indian population of North America in 1492. *The William and Mary Quarterly* 49 (2), 298–320.

Dasevich, I. (2012) *The Right to an Interpreter for Criminal Defendants with Limited English*. See https://www.jurist.org/commentary/2012/04/iryna-dasevich-criminal-justice/.

Dávila, A. (2008) *Latino Spin: Public Image and the Whitewashing of Race*. New York: New York University Press.

Dávila, A. (2012) *Latinos, Inc.: The Marketing and Making of a People*. Berkeley, CA: University of California Press.

Dávila, A. (2014) Introduction. In A. Dávila and Y.M. Rivero (eds) *Contemporary Latina/o Media: Production, Circulation, Politics* (pp. 1–8). New York: New York University Press.

de Brey, C., Musu, L., McFarland, J., Wilkinson-Flicker, S., Diliberti, M., Zhang, A., Branstetter, C. and Wang, X. (2019) *Status and Trends in the Education of Racial and Ethnic Groups 2018* (NCES No. 2019-038; p. 228). See https://nces.ed.gov/pubsearch/pubsinfo.asp?pubid=2019038.

De Casanova, E.M. (2007) Spanish language and Latino ethnicity in children's television programs. *Latino Studies* 5, 455–477.

De Fina, A. (2013) Top-down and bottom-up strategies of identity construction in ethnic media. *Applied linguistics* 34 (5), 554–573.

De Fina, A. (2018) What is your dream? Fashioning the migrant self. *Language & Communication* 59, 42–52.

De Fina, A. and Perrino, S. (2013) Transnational identities. *Applied Linguistics* 34 (5), 509–515.

Delavan, M.G., Valdez, V.E. and Freire, J.A. (2017) Language as whose resource? When global economics usurp the local equity potentials of dual language education. *International Multilingual Research Journal* 11 (2), 86–100.

Del Valle, S. (2003) *Language Rights and the Law in the United States: Finding Our Voices*. Clevedon: Multilingual Matters.

DePalma, R. (2010) *Language Use in the Two-way Classroom: Lessons from a Spanish-English Bilingual Kindergarten*. Bristol: Multilingual Matters.

Dick, H.P. (2011) Making immigrants illegal in small-town USA. *Journal of Linguistic Anthropology* 21, E35–E55.

Dixon, T.L. and Azocar, C.L. (2006) The representation of juvenile offenders by race on Los Angeles area television news. *The Howard Journal of Communications* 17 (2), 143–161.

Dowling, J.A. (2014) *Mexican Americans and the Question of Race*. Austin, TX: University of Texas Press.

Duany, J. (2005) Neither White nor Black: The representation of racial identity among Puerto Ricans on the island and in the U.S. Mainland. In A. Dzidzienyo and S. Oboler (eds) *Neither Enemies nor Friends: Latinos, Blacks, Afro-Latinos* (pp. 173–188). New York: Palgrave Macmillan.

Duany, J. (2017) *Puerto Rico: What Everyone Needs to Know*. Oxford: Oxford University Press.

DuBord, E.M. (2010) Language policy and the drawing of social boundaries: Public and private schools in territorial Tucson. *Spanish in Context* 7 (1), 25–45.

DuBord, E.M. (2014) *Language, Immigration and Labor: Negotiating Work in the U.S.-Mexico Borderlands.* New York: Palgrave Macmillan.

DuBord, E.M. (2017) Bilingual tricksters: Conflicting perceptions of bilingualism in the informal labor economy. *Language & Communication* 58, 107–117.

Ducar, C. (2009) The sound of silence: Spanish heritage textbooks' treatment of language variation. In M. Lacorte and J. Leeman (eds) *Español en Estados Unidos y otros contextos de contacto: Sociolingüística, ideología y pedagogía* (pp. 347–367). Madrid: Iberoamericana.

Duchêne, A. (2019) Multilingualism: An insufficient answer to sociolinguistic inequalities. *Items: Insights from the Social Sciences,* 8 October. See https://items.ssrc.org/sociolinguistic-frontiers/multilingualism-an-insufficient-answer-to-sociolinguistic-inequalities/.

Duchêne, A. and Heller, M. (2011) *Language in Late Capitalism: Pride and Profit.* New York: Routledge.

Dunstan, S. (2010) Identities in transition: The use of AAVE grammatical features by Hispanic adolescents in two North Carolina communities. *American Speech* 85, 185–204.

Echenique, M. and Melgar, L. (2018, May 11) Watch the exodus and return of Puerto Rico's hurricane migrants. *CityLab,* 11 May. See https://www.citylab.com/environment/2018/05/watch-puerto-ricos-hurricane-migration-via-mobile-phone-data/559889/.

Eckert, P. (2012) Three waves of variation study: The emergence of meaning in the study of sociolinguistic variation. *Annual Review of Anthropology* 41, 87–100.

Erker, D. and Otheguy, R. (2016) Contact and coherence: Dialectal leveling and structural convergence in NYC Spanish. *Lingua* 172, 131–146.

Errington, J. (2000) Ideology. *Journal of Linguistic Anthropology* 9 (1–2), 115–117.

Escamilla, K., Shannon, S., Carlos, S. and García, J. (2003) Breaking the code: Colorado's defeat of the anti-bilingual education initiative (Amendment 31). *Bilingual Research Journal* 27 (3), 357–382.

Escobar, A.M. and Potowski, K. (2015) *El Español de los Estados Unidos.* Cambridge: Cambridge University Press.

Espinosa, A.M. (1911) *The Spanish Language in New Mexico and Southern Colorado.* Santa Fe, NM: New Mexican Printing Company.

Espinoza-Herold, M. and González-Carriedo, R. (2017) *Issues in Latino Education.* New York: Routledge.

Fairclough, M. (2003) El (denominado) Spanglish en Estados Unidos: Polémicas y realidades. *Revista internacional de lingüística iberoamericana* 1 (2), 185–204.

Fairclough, M. and Beaudrie, S. (eds) (2016) *Innovative Strategies for Heritage Language Teaching: A Practical Guide for the Classroom.* Washington, DC: Georgetown University Press.

Fairclough, N. (1992) The appropriacy of 'appropriateness'. In N. Fairclough (ed.) *Critical Language Awareness* (pp. 33–56). London: Longman.

Fairclough, N. (2001) *Language and Power* (2nd edn). London: Longman.

Falk, J. (1979) Visión de norma general versus visión de norma individual. *Studia Neophilologica* 51 (2), 275–293.

Farr, M. (2010) *Rancheros in Chicagoacán: Language and Identity in a Transnational Community.* Austin, TX: University of Texas Press.

Fears, D. (2003) The roots of 'Hispanic'. *The Washington Post*, 15 October. See https://www.washingtonpost.com/archive/politics/2003/10/15/the-roots-of-hispanic/3d914863-95bc-40f3-9950-ce0c25939046/.

Fernández, L. (2002) Telling stories about school: Using critical race and Latino critical theories to document Latina/Latino education and resistance. *Qualitative Inquiry* 8 (1), 45–65.

Fernández, R.G. (1983) English loanwords in Miami Cuban Spanish. *American Speech* 58 (1), 13–19.

Fishman, J. (1991) *Reversing Language Shift.* Clevedon: Multilingual Matters.

Fishman, J. (2001) 300-Plus years of heritage language education. In J.K. Peyton, D.A. Ranard and S. McGinnis (eds) *Heritage Languages in America: Preserving a National Resource* (pp. 87–97). Washington, DC: Center for Applied Linguistics.

Fitts, S. (2006) Reconstructing the status quo: Linguistic interaction in a dual language school. *Bilingual Research Journal* 29 (2), 337–365.

Fitzsimmons-Doolan, S., Palmer, D. and Henderson, K. (2017) Educator language ideologies and a top-down dual language program. *International Journal of Bilingual Education and Bilingualism* 20 (6), 704–721.

Flores, A. (2017) How the U.S. Hispanic population is changing. *Fact Tank*, 18 September. Washington, DC: Pew Research Center. See http://www.pewresearch.org/fact-tank/2017/09/18/how-the-u-s-hispanic-population-is-changing/.

Flores, G. (2006) Language barriers to health care in the United States. *New England Journal of Medicine* 355 (3), 229–231.

Flores, G., Abreu, M., Barone, C.P., Bachur, R. and Lin, H. (2012) Errors of medical interpretation and their potential clinical consequences: A comparison of professional versus ad hoc versus no interpreters. *Annals of Emergency Medicine* 60 (5), 545–553.

Flores, N. and García, O. (2017) A critical review of bilingual education in the United States: From basements and pride to boutiques and profit. *Annual Review of Applied Linguistics* 37, 14–29.

Flores, N. and Rosa, J.D. (2015) Undoing appropriateness: Raciolinguistic ideologies and language diversity in education. *Harvard Educational Review* 85 (2), 149–171.

Flores-Ferrán, N. (2002) *A Sociolinguistic Perspective on the Use of Subject Personal Pronouns in Spanish Narratives of Puerto Ricans in New York City.* Munich: Lincom-Europa.

Flores-Ferrán, N. (2004) Spanish subject personal pronoun use in New York City Puerto Ricans: Can we rest the case of English contact? *Language Variation and Change* 16, 49–73.

Flores-González, N. (2017) *Citizens but not Americans: Race and Belonging among Latino Millennials.* New York: New York University Press.

Fought, C. (2003) *Chicano English in Context.* New York: Palgrave Macmillan.

Fouka, V. (2016) Backlash: The unintended effects of language prohibition in US schools after World War I. Working Paper No. 591. King Center on Global Development, Stanford University, Stanford, CA.

Fránquiz, M.E. and Ortiz, A.A. (2016) Co-editors' introduction: Every Student Succeeds Act – a policy shift. *Bilingual Research Journal* 39 (1), 1–3.

Frazer, T. (1996) Chicano English and Spanish interference in the Midwestern United States. *American Speech* 71 (1), 72–85.

Freeman, R. (2000) Contextual challenge to a dual-language education: A case study of a developing middle school program. *Anthropology & Education Quarterly* 31 (2), 202–229.

Freire, P. (1970) *A Pedagogia do Oprimido*. Sao Paolo: Paz e Terra. See http://www.bibli.fae.unicamp.br/pub/pedoprim.pdf.

French, B.M. (2008) Maya ethnolinguistic identity: Violence, and cultural rights in bilingual Kaqchikel communities. In M. Niño-Murcia and J. Rothman (eds) *Bilingualism and Identity: Spanish at the Crossroads with Other Languages* (pp. 127–150). Amsterdam: John Benjamins.

Frey, W.H. (2018) The US will become 'minority White' in 2045, Census projects. *Brookings*, 14 March. See https://www.brookings.edu/blog/the-avenue/2018/03/14/the-us-will-become-minority-white-in-2045-census-projects/.

Fuller, J.M. (1997) Co-constructing bilingualism: Non-converging discourse as an unmarked choice. In A. Chu, A.-M.P. Guerra and C. Tetreault (eds) *SALSA (Symposium About Language in Society – Austin) IV Proceedings* (pp. 68–77). Austin, TX: University of Texas Linguistics Department.

Fuller, J.M. (2005) Unpublished corpus of Spanish-English language use in the classroom.

Fuller, J.M. (2007) Language choice as a means for shaping identity. *Journal of Linguistic Anthropology* 17 (1), 105–129.

Fuller, J.M. (2009) How bilingual children talk: Strategic codeswitching among children in dual language programs. In M. Turnbull and J. Dailey-O'Cain (eds) *First Language Use in Second and Foreign Language Learning* (pp. 115–130). Bristol: Multilingual Matters.

Fuller, J.M. (2010) Gendered choices: Codeswitching and collaboration in a bilingual classroom. *Gender and Language* 4 (1), 181–208.

Fuller, J.M. (2012) *Bilingual Pre-teens: Competing Ideologies and Multiple Identities in the US and Germany*. New York: Routledge.

Fuller, J.M. (2016) Minority languages in linguistic landscapes: Berlin and Chicago. Paper presented at the University of Illinois at Chicago Talks in Linguistics, 10 April.

Fuller, J.M. and Torres, J. (2018) Spanish in the United States. In C. Seals and S. Shah (eds) *Heritage Language Policies around the World* (pp. 13–29). New York: Routledge.

Fuller, J.M., Elsman, M. and Self, K. (2007) Addressing peers in a Spanish-English bilingual classroom. In K. Potowski and R. Cameron (eds) *Spanish in Contact: Educational, Social, and Linguistic Inquiries* (pp. 135–151). Amsterdam: John Benjamins.

Fullerton, J.A. and Kendrick, A. (2000) Portrayal of men and women in US Spanish-language television commercials. *Journalism & Mass Communication Quarterly* 77 (1), 128–142.

Gabrielson, R. (2017, October 17) It's a Fact: Supreme Court Errors Aren't Hard to Find. Retrieved from ProPublica website: https://www.propublica.org/article/supreme-court-errors-are-not-hard-to-find

Gafaranga, J. and Torras, M.-C. (2002) Interactional otherness: Towards a redefinition of codeswitching. *International Journal of Bilingualism* 6 (1), 1–22.

Gal, S. (1998) Multiplicity and contention among ideologies: A commentary. In B.B. Schiefflin, K.A. Woolard and P.V. Kroskrity (eds) *Language Ideologies: Practice and Theory* (pp. 317–331). Oxford: Oxford University Press.

Gándara, P. (2012) From González to Flores: A return to the Mexican room? In O. Santa Ana and C. Bustamante (eds) *Arizona Firestorm* (pp. 121–144). Lanham, MD: Rowman & Littlefield.

Gandara, P.C. and Contreras, F. (2009) *The Latino Education Crisis: The Consequences of Failed Social Policies.* Cambridge: Harvard University Press.

Gándara, P. and Mordechay, K. (2017) Demographic change and the new (and not so new) challenges for Latino education. *The Educational Forum,* 81 (2), 148–159.

Gannon, M. (2016) Race is a social construct, scientists argue. *Scientific American,* 5 February. See https://www.scientificamerican.com/article/race-is-a-social-construct-scientists-argue/.

García, A. and Gaddes, A. (2012) Weaving language and culture: Latina adolescent writers in an after-school writing project. *Reading & Writing Quarterly* 28 (2), 143–163.

Garcia, E.E. and Curry-Rodríguez, J.E. (2000) The education of limited English proficient students in California schools: An assessment of the influence of Proposition 227 in selected districts and schools. *Bilingual Research Journal* 24 (1–2), 15–35.

García, M. (2003) Recent research on language maintenance. *Annual Review of Applied Linguistics* 23, 22–43.

García, O. (1993) From Goya portraits to Goya beans: Elite traditions and popular streams in US Spanish language policy. *Southwest Journal of Linguistics* 12, 69–86.

García, O. (2005) Positioning heritage languages in the United States. *The Modern Language Journal* 89 (4), 601–605.

García, O. (2009a) *Bilingual Education in the 21st Century: A Global Perspective.* Malden, MA: John Wiley.

García, O. (2009b) Education, multilingualism and translanguaging in the 21st century. In T. Skutnabb-Kangas, R. Phillipson, A. Mohanty and M. Panda (eds) *Social Justice through Multilingual Education* (pp. 140–158). Bristol: Multilingual Matters.

García, O. (2015) Language policy. In *International Encyclopedia of the Social & Behavioral Sciences, Vol. 13* (2nd edn) (pp. 353–359). See https://ofeliagarciadotorg.files.wordpress.com/2011/02/languagepolicy.pdf.

García, O., Johnson, S.I., Seltzer, K. and Valdés, G. (2017) *The Translanguaging Classroom: Leveraging Student Bilingualism for Learning.* Philadelphia, PA: Caslon.

García, O. and Wei, L. (2014) *Translanguaging: Language, Bilingualism and Education.* New York: Palgrave Macmillan.

García, O., Morín, J.L. and Rivera, K. (2001) How threatened is the Spanish of New York Puerto Ricans? In J.A. Fishman (ed.) *Can Threatened Languages Be Saved?* (pp. 44–73). Clevedon: Multilingual Matters.

Garcia, S.E. (2018, July 6). Andrés Cantor thinks everything sounds better in Spanish (especially 'gooool'). *The New York Times.* Retrieved from https://www.nytimes.com/2018/07/04/sports/world-cup/andres-cantor-goooool.html

García Bedolla, L. (2003) The identity paradox: Latino language, politics and selective disassociation. *Latino Studies* 1 (2), 264–283.

Gelpí, H.G.A. (2011) The Insular Cases: A comparative historical study of Puerto Rico, Hawai'i, and the Philippines. *The Federal Lawyer* (March/April), 22–25, 74.

Ghoshal, D. (2014) Newspapers that aren't dying: Ethnic communities in NYC. *The Atlantic*, 26 June. See https://www.theatlantic.com/business/archive/2014/06/newspapers-that-arent-dying/373492/.

Giles, H., Bourhis, R.Y. and Taylor, D.M. (1977) Towards a theory of language in ethnic group relations. In H. Giles (ed.) *Language, Ethnicity and Intergroup Relations* (pp. 307–344). New York: Academic Press.

Gilman, D. (2011) A 'bilingual' approach to language rights: How dialogue between U.S. and international human rights law may improve the language rights framework. *Harvard Human Rights Journal* 24, 1–70.

Giroux, H.A. (1991) Series introduction: Rethinking the pedagogy of voice, difference, and cultural struggle. In C. Walsh (ed.) *Pedagogy and the Struggle for Voice: Issues of Language, Power and Schooling for Puerto Ricans* (pp. xv–xxvii). New York: Bergin & Garvey.

Goble, R.A. (2016) Linguistic insecurity and lack of entitlement to Spanish among third-generation Mexican American in narrative accounts. *Heritage Language Journal* 13 (1), 29–54.

Gómez, L.E. (2007) *Manifest Destinies: The Making of the Mexican American Race.* New York: New York University Press.

Gonzales-Berry, E. and Maciel, D.R. (2000) Introduction. In E. Gonzales-Berry and D.R. Maciel (eds) *The Contested Homeland: A Chicano History of New Mexico* (pp. 1–9). Albuquerque, NM: University of New Mexico Press.

González, C.M. (2018) The renaissance of a Native Caribbean People: Taíno Ethnogenesis. *Smithsonian Voices*, 3 October. See https://www.smithsonianmag.com/blogs/smithsonian-latino-center/2018/10/03/renaissance-native-caribbean-people-taino-ethnogenesis/.

Gonzalez, J. (2011) *Harvest of Empire: A History of Latinos in America* (2nd edn). New York: Penguin.

Gonzalez-Barrera, A. (2015) 'Mestizo' and 'mulatto': Mixed-race identities among U.S. Hispanics. *Fact Tank*, 10 July. Washington, DC: Pew Research Center. See http://www.pewresearch.org/fact-tank/2015/07/10/mestizo-and-mulatto-mixed-race-identities-unique-to-hispanics/.

Gonzalez-Barrera, A. and Krogstad, J.M. (2018) What we know about illegal immigration from Mexico. *Fact Tank*, 3 December. Washington, DC: Pew Research Center. See http://www.pewresearch.org/fact-tank/2018/12/03/what-we-know-about-illegal-immigration-from-mexico/.

González-Barrera, A. and Lopez, M.H. (2015) Is being Hispanic a matter of race, ethnicity or both? *Fact Tank*, 15 June. Washington, DC: Pew Research Center. See http://www.pewresearch.org/fact-tank/2015/06/15/is-being-hispanic-a-matter-of-race-ethnicity-or-both/.

González Tosat, C. (2017) La radio en español en los Estados Unidos. *Informes Del Observatorio/Observatorio Reports* 027-01/2017SP. https://doi.org/10.15427/OR027-01/2017SP

Gort, M. and Sembiante, S.F. (2015) Navigating hybridized language learning spaces through translanguaging pedagogy: Dual language preschool teachers' languaging practices in support of emergent bilingual children's performance of academic discourse. *International Multilingual Research Journal* 9 (1), 7–25.

Gorter, D. (2013) Linguistic landscapes in a multilingual world. *Annual Review of Applied Linguistics* 33, 190–212.

Gracia, J. (2000) *Hispanic/Latino Identity: A Philosophical Perspective.* Oxford: Blackwell.

Grosjean, F. (1982) *Life with Two Languages: An Introduction to Bilingualism.* Cambridge, MA: Harvard University Press.

Grosjean, F. (2001) The bilingual's language modes. In J. Nicol (ed.) *One Mind, Two Languages: Bilingual Language Processing* (pp. 1–22). Oxford: Blackwell.

Gross, A.J. (2008) *What Blood Won't Tell: A History of Race on Trial in America.* Cambridge, MA: Harvard University Press.

Grovum, J. (2014) A growing divide over official-English laws. *Stateline,* 8 August. Washington, DC: Pew Research Center. See http://pew.org/1akfU1z.

Guarnizo, L.E. (1994) Los Dominicanyorks: The making of a binational society. *Annals of the American Academy of Political and Social Science* 533, 70–86.

Guerra, G. and Orbea, G. (2015) The argument against the use of the term 'Latinx'. *The Phoenix,* 19 November. See http://swarthmorephoenix.com/2015/11/19/the-argument-against-the-use-of-the-term-latinx/.

Guzmán, I.M. and Validivia, A.N. (2004) Brain, brow, and booty: Latina iconicity in U.S. popular culture. *The Communication Review* 7, 205–221.

Hames-Garcia, M. (2011) Queer Theory Revisited. In M. Hames-Garcia and E.J. Martinez (eds) *Gay Latino Studies: A Critical Reader,* (pp. 19–45). Durham, NC: Duke University Press.

Harwood, J., Giles, H. and Bourhis, R.Y. (1994) The genesis of vitality theory: Historical patterns and discoursal dimensions. *International Journal of the Sociology of Language* 108 (1), 167–206.

Haugen, E. (1950) The analysis of linguistic borrowing. *Language* 26 (2), 210–231.

Haviland, J.B. (2003) Ideologies of language: Some reflections on language and U.S. Law. *American Anthropologist* 105 (4), 764–774.

Hedgpeth, D. (2019) Powhatan and his people: The 15,000 American Indians shoved aside by Jamestown's settlers. *The Washington Post,* 3 August. See https://www.washingtonpost.com/history/2019/08/03/powhatan-his-people-american-indians-that-jamestowns-settlers-shoved-aside/.

Heller, M. (1999) *Linguistic Minorities and Modernity.* London: Longman.

Heller, M. (2002) Globalization and the commodification of bilingualism in Canada. In D. Block and D. Cameron (eds) *Globalization and Language Teaching* (pp. 67–82). London: Routledge.

Heller, M. (2003) Globalization, the new economy, and the commodification of language and identity. *Journal of Sociolinguistics* 7, 473–493.

Heller, M. and Duchêne, A. (2007) Discourses of endangerment: Sociolinguistics, globalization. In A. Duchêne and M. Heller (eds) *Discourses of Endangerment: Ideology and Interest in the Defence of Languages* (pp. 1–13). New York: Continuum.

Helôt, C., Barni, M. and Janssens, R. (2012) Introduction. In C. Helôt, M. Barni and R. Janssens (eds) *Linguistic Landscapes, Multilingualism and Social Change* (pp. 17–26). Frankfurt am Main: Peter Lang.

Henderson, K.I. (2017) Teacher language ideologies mediating classroom-level language policy in the implementation of dual language bilingual education. *Linguistics and Education* 42, 21–33.

Hepford, E.A. (2017) Language for profit: Spanish–English bilingualism in Lowe's Home Improvement. *International Journal of Bilingual Education and Bilingualism* 20 (6), 652–666.

Herman, D.M. (2007) It's a small world after all: From stereotypes to invented worlds in secondary school Spanish textbooks. *Critical Inquiry in Language Studies* 4 (2–3), 117–150.

Hernández, A.R. (2018) Florida lawsuit seeks Spanish translation of ballots, alleges voting rights violations affecting Puerto Ricans. *The Washington Post,* 16 August. See https://www.washingtonpost.com/national/florida-lawsuit-seeks-spanish-translation-of-ballots-alleges-voting-rights-violations-affecting-puerto-ricans/2018/08/16/59f7776c-a171-11e8-93e3-24d1703d2a7a_story.html.

Hernandez, K.L. (2017) How crossing the US-Mexico border became a crime. *The Conversation,* 1 May. See http://theconversation.com/how-crossing-the-us-mexico-border-became-a-crime-74604.

Hernandez, T.K. (2002) Multiracial matrix: The role of race ideology in the enforcement of antidiscrimination laws, a United States-Latin America comparison. *Cornell Law Review* 87, 1093–1176.

Hill, J. (1995) Mock Spanish: The indexical reproduction of racism in American English. *Language & Culture,* 9 October. See http://language-culture.binghamton.edu/symposia/2/part1/index.html.

Hill, J.H. (1993) Hasta la vista, baby: Anglo Spanish in the American Southwest. *Critique of Anthropology* 13 (2), 145–176. https://doi.org/10.1177/0308275X9301300203

Hill, J.H. (1998) Language, race, and white public space. *American Anthropologist* 100 (3), 680–689.

Hill, J.H. (2005) Intertextuality as source and evidence for indirect indexical meanings. *Journal of Linguistic Anthropology* 15 (1), 113–124.

Hill, J.H. (2008) *The Everyday Language of White Racism.* Oxford: Blackwell.

Hill, J.H. and Hill, K.C. (1986) *Speaking Mexicano.* Tucson, AZ: University of Arizona Press.

Hinrichs, E. (2016) Spanish heritage program at Roosevelt High helps boost Latino graduation rates, students voice. *MinnPost,* 7 March. See https://www.minnpost.com/education/2016/03/spanish-heritage-program-roosevelt-high-helps-boost-latino-graduation-rates-studen/.

Hinojos, S.V. (2019) Lupe Vélez and her spicy visual "accent" in English-language print media. *Latino Studies* 17 (3), 338–361.

Hodges, S. (2015) Local pastors lead Hispanic outreach. *United Methodist News Service,* 1 October. See https://www.umnews.org:443/en/news/local-pastors-lead-hispanic-outreach.

Hoffman, A. (1974) *Unwanted Mexican Americans in the Great Depression: Repatriation Pressures, 1929–1939.* Tucson, AZ: University of Arizona Press.

Holguín Mendoza, C. (2018a) Critical language awareness (CLA) for Spanish Heritage language programs: Implementing a complete curriculum. *International Multilingual Research Journal* 12 (2), 65–79.

Holguín Mendoza, C. (2018b) Sociolinguistic capital and Fresa identity formations on the U.S.-Mexico border. *Frontera Norte* 60.

Hornberger, N.H. (2005) Opening and filling up implementational and ideological spaces in heritage language education. *The Modern Language Journal* 89 (4), 605–609.

Hornberger, N.H. and Johnson, D.C. (2007) Slicing the onion ethnographically: Layers and spaces in multilingual language education policy and practice. *TESOL Quarterly* 41 (3), 509–532.

Hornberger, N.H. and Wang, S.C. (2008) Who are our heritage language learners? Identity and biliteracy in heritage language education in the United States. In D. Brinton, O. Kagan and S. Bauckus (eds) *Heritage Language Education: A New Field Emerging* (pp. 3–35). New York: Routledge.

Horner, K. and Weber, J.-J. (2018) *Introducing Multilingualism A Social Approach* (2nd edn). New York: Routledge.

Horsman, R. (1981) *Race and Manifest Destiny*. Cambridge, MA: Harvard University Press.

Hult, F.M. (2014) Drive-thru linguistic landscaping: Constructing a linguistically dominant place in a bilingual space. *International Journal of Bilingualism* 18 (5), 507–523.

Hult, F.M. and Hornberger, N.H. (2016) Revisiting orientations in language planning: Problem, right, and resource as an analytical heuristic. *Bilingual Review/Revista Bilingüe* 33 (3), 30–49.

Hunt, K. (2007) Gingrich: Bilingual classes teach 'ghetto' language. *The Washington Post*, 1 April. See http://www.washingtonpost.com/wp-dyn/content/article/2007/03/31/AR2007033100992.html.

Hunter, M. (2016) Colorism in the classroom: How skin tone stratifies African American and Latina/o students. *Theory into Practice* 55 (1), 54–61.

Huntington, S.P. (2004) *Who Are We? The Challenges to America's National Identity*. New York: Simon & Schuster.

Husband, C. and Khan, V.S. (1982) The viability of ethnolinguistic vitality: Some creative doubts. *Journal of Multilingual and Multicultural Development* 3 (3), 193–205.

Ignatiev, N. (1995) *How the Irish Became White*. London: Routledge.

Inoue, M. (2006) *Vicarious Language: Gender and Linguistic Modernity in Japan*. Berkeley, CA: University of California Press.

Instituto Cervantes (2018) *El español, una lengua viva: Informe 2018*. Centro Virtual Cervantes. See https://cvc.cervantes.es/lengua/espanol_lengua_viva/.

Irvine, J.T. (1989) When talk isn't cheap: Language and political economy. *American Ethnologist* 16 (2), 248–267.

Irvine, J. and Gal, S. (2000) Language ideology and linguistic differentiation. In P. Kroskrity (ed.) *Regimes of Language: Ideologies, Polities, and Identities* (pp. 35–83). Santa Fe, NM: School of American Research Press.

Jacobs, B., Ryan, A.M., Henrichs, K.S. and Weiss, B.D. (2018) Medical interpreters in outpatient practice. *Annals of Family Medicine* 16 (1), 70–76.

Jacobson, M.F. (1998) *Whiteness of a Different Color: European Immigrants and the Alchemy of Race*. Cambridge, MA: Harvard University Press.

Jaffe, A. (ed.) (2009) *Stance: Sociolinguistic Perspectives*. New York: Oxford University Press.

Jenkins, D. (2018) Spanish language use, maintenance, and shift in the United States. In K. Potowski (ed.) *The Routledge Handbook of Spanish as a Heritage Language* (pp. 53–65). New York: Routledge.

Jobling, M.A., Rasteiro, R. and Wetton, J.H. (2016) In the blood: The myth and reality of genetic markers of identity. *Ethnic and Racial Studies* 39 (2), 142–161.

Johnson, D.C. and Ricento, T. (2013) Conceptual and theoretical perspectives in language planning and policy: Situating the ethnography of language policy. *International Journal of the Sociology of Language* 219, 7–21.

Johnstone, B. (2009) Stance, style, and the linguistic individual. In A. Jaffe (ed.) *Stance: Sociolinguistic Perspectives* (pp. 29–52). Oxford: Oxford University Press.

Johnstone, B. (2010) Indexing the local. In N. Coupland (ed.) *Handbook of Language and Globalization* (pp. 386–405). Malden, MA: Wiley-Blackwell.

June-Friesen, K. (2005) Recasting New Mexico history. *Alibi*, 20 October. See https://alibi.com/feature/13065/Recasting-New-Mexico-History.html.

Kam, D. (2019) State advances plan for Spanish-language ballots. *News Service of Florida*, 24 July. See https://news.wjct.org/post/state-advances-plan-spanish-language-ballots.

Kamen, H. (2008) The myth of a universal language. In H. Kamen, *Imagining Spain* (pp. 150–171). New Haven, CT: Yale University Press.

Katzew, I. (2005) *Casta Painting: Images of Race in Eighteenth-century Mexico*. New Haven, CT: Yale University Press.

Kelly-Holmes, H. and Milani, T.M. (2011) Thematising multilingualism in the media. *Journal of Language and Politics* 10 (4), 467–489.

Kim, Y.K., Hutchison, L.A. and Winsler, A. (2015) Bilingual education in the United States: An historical overview and examination of two-way immersion. *Educational Review* 67 (2), 236–252.

King, K.A. (2009) Spanish language education policy in the US: Paradoxes, pitfalls and promises. In M. Lacorte and J. Leeman (eds) *Español en Estados Unidos y otros contextos de contacto: Sociolingüística, ideología y pedagogía* (pp. 303–323). Madrid: Iberoamericana.

King, K.A. (2016) Language policy, multilingual encounters, and transnational families. *Journal of Multilingual and Multicultural Development* 37 (7), 726–733.

King, K.A. and Ennser-Kananen, J. (2013) Heritage languages and language policy. In C.A. Chapelle (ed.) *The Encyclopedia of Applied Linguistics*. See http://onlinelibrary.wiley.com/doi/10.1002/9781405198431.wbeal0500/full.

King, K.A. and Fogle, L. (2006) Bilingual parenting as good parenting: Parents' perspectives on family language policy for additive bilingualism. *International Journal of Bilingual Education and Bilingualism* 9 (6), 695–712.

King, K.A., Fogle, L. and Logan-Terry, A. (2008) Family language policy. *Language and Linguistics Compass* 2 (5), 907–922.

Kloss, H. (1968) Notes concerning a language-nation typology. *Language Problems of Developing Nations* (pp. 69–85). Malden, MA: John Wiley.

Kloss, H. (1977) *The American Bilingual Tradition.* Rowley, MA: Newbury House.

Knafo, S. (2013) When it comes to illegal drug use, White America does the crime, Black America gets the Time. *Huffington Post,* 17 September. See https://www.huffingtonpost.com/2013/09/17/racial-disparity-drug-use_n_3941346.html.

Koc-Menard, N. (2017) Processes of racialization after political violence: The discourse of marginality in the community of Chapi, Ayacucho. In M. Back and V. Zavala (eds), *Racialization and language: Interdisciplinary perspectives from Peru* (pp. 66–91). New York: Routledge.

Konopka, K. and Pierrehumbert, J. (2008) Vowels in contact: Mexican heritage English in Chicago. *Texas Linguistic Forum* 52, 94–103.

Koontz-Garboden, A. (2004) Language contact and Spanish aspectual expression: A formal analysis. *Lingua* 114, 1291–1330

Kroll J.F. and De Groot, A.M.B. (2005) *Handbook of Bilingualism: Psycholinguistic Approaches.* New York: Oxford University Press.

Kroskrity, P. (2000) Identity. *Journal of Linguistic Anthropology* 9 (1–2), 111–114.

Kroskrity, P. (2004) Language ideologies. In A. Duranti (ed.) *A Companion to Linguistic Anthropology* (pp. 496–517). Malden MA: Blackwell.

Kurtzleben, D. (2017) Fact check: Are DACA recipients stealing jobs away from other Americans? *NPR.org,* 6 September. See https://www.npr.org/2017/09/06/548882071/fact-check-are-daca-recipients-stealing-jobs-away-from-other-americans.

Lambert, W.E. (1975) Culture and language as factors in learning and education. In A. Wolfgang (ed.), *Education of jmmigrant students.* Toronto: Ontario Institute for Studies in Education.

Lambert, W.E., Frankle, H. and Tucker, G.R. (1966) Judging personality through speech: A French-Canadian example. *Journal of Communication* 16 (4), 305–321.

Landry, R. and Bourhis, R.Y. (1997) Linguistic landscape and ethnolinguistic vitality: An empirical study. *Journal of Language and Social Psychology* 16 (1), 23–49.

Leeman, J. (2004) Racializing language: A history of linguistic ideologies in the US census. *Journal of Language and Politics* 3 (3), 507–534.

Leeman, J. (2005) Engaging critical pedagogy: Spanish for native speakers. *Foreign Language Annals* 38, 35–45.

Leeman, J. (2007) The value of Spanish: Shifting ideologies in United States language teaching. *ADFL Bulletin* 38 (1–2), 32–39.

Leeman, J. (2010) The sociopolitics of heritage language education. In S. Rivera-Mills and D. Villa (eds) *Spanish of the US Southwest: A Language in Transition* (pp. 309–317). Madrid: Iberoamericana.

Leeman, J. (2012a) Illegal accents: Qualifications, discrimination and distraction in Arizona's monitoring of teachers. In *Arizona Firestorm* (pp. 145–166). Lanham, MD: Rowman & Littlefield.

Leeman, J. (2012b) Investigating language ideologies in Spanish as a heritage language. In S.M. Beaudrie and M. Fairclough (eds) *Spanish as a Heritage Language in the United States: The State of the Field* (pp. 43–59). Washington, DC: Georgetown University Press.

Leeman, J. (2013) Categorizing Latinos in the history of the US Census: The official racialization of Spanish. In J.D. Valle (ed.) *A Political History of Spanish: The Making of a Language* (pp. 305–323). Cambridge: Cambridge University Press.

Leeman, J. (2014) Critical approaches to the teaching of Spanish as a local-foreign language. In M. Lacorte (ed.) *The Handbook of Hispanic Applied Linguistics* (pp. 275–292). New York: Routledge.

Leeman, J. (2015) *Cognitive Testing of the American Community Survey: Language Questions in Spanish.* Center for Survey Measurement Study Series No. 2015-02.Washington, DC : US Census Bureau, Research and Methodology Directorate. See https://www.census.gov/srd/papers/pdf/ssm2015-02.pdf.

Leeman, J. (2017). Censuses and Large-Scale Surveys in Language Research. In K.A. King, Y.-J. Lai and S. May (eds), *Research Methods in Language and Education* (pp. 83–97). https://doi.org/10.1007/978-3-319-02249-9_8

Leeman, J. (2018a) Becoming Hispanic: The negotiation of ethnoracial identity in US census interviews. *Latino Studies* 16 (4), 432–460. https://doi.org/10.1057/s41276-018-0147-6

Leeman, J. (2018b) Critical language awareness and Spanish as a heritage language: Challenging the linguistic subordination of US Latinxs. In K. Potowski (ed.) *Handbook of Spanish as a Minority/Heritage Language* (pp. 345–358). New York: Routledge.

Leeman, J. (2018c) It's all about English: The interplay of monolingual ideologies, language policies and the U.S. Census Bureau's statistics on multilingualism. *International Journal of the Sociology of Language* 252, 21–43.

Leeman, J. and King, K. (2015) Heritage language education: Minority language speakers, second language instruction, and monolingual schooling. In M. Bigelow and J. Ennser-Kananen (eds) *The Routledge Handbook of Educational Linguistics* (pp. 210–223). New York: Routledge.

Leeman, J. and Martínez, G. (2007) From identity to commodity: Ideologies of Spanish in heritage language textbooks. *Critical Inquiry in Language Studies* 4, 35–65.

Leeman, J. and Modan, G. (2010) Selling the city: Language, ethnicity and commodified space. In E. Shohamy, E. Ben-Rafael and M. Barni (eds) *Linguistic Landscape in the City* (pp. 182–198). Bristol: Multilingual Matters.

Leeman, J. and Rabin, L. (2007) Reading language: Critical perspectives for the literature classroom. *Hispania* 90, 304–315.

Leeman, J. and Serafini, E.J. (2016) Sociolinguistics for heritage language educators and students: A model for critical translingual competence. In M. Fairclough and S.M. Beaudrie (eds) *Innovative Strategies for Heritage Language Teaching* (pp. 56–79). Washington, DC: Georgetown University Press.

Leeman, J. and Serafini, E.J. (2020) 'It's not fair': Discourses of deficit, equity, and effort in mixed HL/L2 Spanish classes. *Journal of Language, Identity & Education.*

Leeman, J., Rabin, L. and Román-Mendoza, E. (2011) Critical pedagogy beyond the classroom walls: Community service-learning and Spanish heritage language education. *Heritage Language Journal* 8 (3), 293–314.

Lepore, J. (2002) *A is for American: Letters and Other Characters in the Newly United States.* New York: Alfred A. Knopf.

Lewis, L.A. (2000) Blacks, Black Indians, Afromexicans: The dynamics of race, nation, and identity in a Mexican 'moreno' community (Guerrero). *American Ethnologist* 27 (4), 898–926.

Lichter, S.R. and Amundson, D.R. (1997) Distorted reality: Hispanic characters in TV entertainment. In C.E. Rodríguez (ed.) *Latin Looks: Images of Latinas and Latinos in the U.S. Media* (pp. 57–72). Boulder, CO: Westview Press.

Liebler, C.A., Rastogi, S., Fernandez, L.E., Noon, J.M. and Ennis, S.R. (2017) America's churning races: Race and ethnic response changes between Census 2000 and the 2010 Census. *Demography* 54 (1), 259–284.

Lindholm-Leary, K. (2001) *Dual Language Education.* Clevedon: Multilingual Matters.

Lindholm-Leary, K. (2014) Bilingual and biliteracy skills in young Spanish-speaking low-SES children: Impact of instructional language and primary language proficiency. *International Journal of Bilingual Education and Bilingualism* 17 (2), 144–159.

Lindholm-Leary, K. (2016) Bilingualism and academic achievement in children in dual language programs. In E. Nicoladis and S. Montanari (eds) *Bilingualism Across the Lifespan: Factors Moderating Language Proficiency* (pp. 203–223). Washington, DC: APA Books.

Lindholm-Leary, K. and Hernández, A. (2011) Achievement and language proficiency of Latino students in dual language programmes: Native English speakers, fluent English/previous ELLs, and current ELLs. *Journal of Multilingual and Multicultural Development* 32 (6), 531–545.

Linton, A. (2004) A critical mass model of bilingualism among U.S.-born Hispanics. *Social Forces* 83 (1), 279–314.

Lippi-Green, R. (1994) Accent, standard language ideology, and discriminatory pretext in the courts. *Language in Society* 23, 163–198.

Lippi-Green, R. (2012) *English with an Accent: Language, Ideology and Discrimination in the United States* (2nd edn). London: Routledge.

Lipski, J. (1993) Creoloid phenomena in the Spanish of transitional bilinguals. In A. Roca and J. Lipski (eds) *Spanish in the United States: Linguistic Contact and Diversity* (pp. 155–182). Berlín: Mouton de Gruyter.

Lipski, J.M. (2002) Rethinking the place of Spanish. *PMLA* 117 (5), 1247–1251.

Lipski, J.M. (2003) La lengua española en los Estados Unidos: Avanza a la vez que retrocede. *Revista Española de Lingüística* 33 (2), 231–260.

Lipski, J.M. (2005) *A History of Afro-Hispanic Language: Five Centuries, Five Continents.* Cambridge: Cambridge University Press.

Lipski, J.M. (2007) The evolving interface of U.S. Spanish: Language mixing as hybrid vigor. http://citeseerx.ist.psu.edu/viewdoc/summary?doi=10.1.1.131.7959

Lipski, J.M. (2008) *Varieties of Spanish in the United States.* Washington, DC: Georgetown University Press.

Liu, A.H., Sokhey, A.E., Kennedy, J.B. and Miller, A. (2014) Immigrant threat and national salience: Understanding the 'English official' movement in the United States. *Research & Politics* 1 (1), 1–8.

Livingston, G. and Brown, A. (2017) *Intermarriage in the U.S. 50 Years After Loving v. Virginia.* Washington, DC: Pew Research Center. See https://www.pewsocialtrends.org/wp-content/uploads/sites/3/2017/05/Intermarriage-May-2017-Full-Report.pdf.

Llamoca, J. (2019) Dora the Explorer and the quest for authentic Indigenous representations. *The New York Times*, 23 August. See https://www.nytimes.com/2019/08/23/movies/dora-the-explorer-peru.html.

Long, D. and Preston, D.R. (eds) (2002) *Handbook of Perceptual Dialectology, Vol. 2*. Amsterdam: John Benjamins.

Looney, D. and Lusin, N. (2018) *Enrollments in Languages Other than English in United States Institutions of Higher Education, Summer 2016 and Fall 2016: Preliminary Report*. New York: Modern Language Association.

Lope Blanch, J. (1986) *El estudio del español hablado culto: Historia de un proyecto*. México, DF: UNAM.

Lope Blanch, J. (2001) La norma lingüística hispánica. Presented at the Congreso Internacional de la Lengua Española: El español en la Sociedad de la Información, 16 October. See https://revistas-filologicas.unam.mx/anuario-letras/index.php/al/article/viewFile/3/3.

López, G. and González-Barrera, A. (2016) Afro-Latino: A deeply rooted identity among U.S. Hispanics. *Fact Tank*, 1 March. Washington, DC: Pew Research Center. See http://www.pewresearch.org/fact-tank/2016/03/01/afro-latino-a-deeply-rooted-identity-among-u-s-hispanics/.

López, G. and Patten, E. (2015) *The Impact of Slowing Immigration: Foreign-born Share Falls among 14 Largest U.S. Hispanic Origin Groups*. Washington, DC: Pew Research Center.

López, I. (2005) Borinkis and chop suey: Puerto Rican identity in Hawai'i, 1900 to 2000. In C.T. Whalen and V. Vázquez-Hernández (eds) *Puerto Rican Diaspora* (pp. 43–67). Philadelphia, PA: Temple University Press.

Lopez, M.H. and Gonzalez-Barrera, A. (2013) A growing share of Latinos get their news in English. *Hispanic Trends*, 23 July. Washington, DC: Pew Research Center.

Lopez, M.H., Gonzalez-Barrera, A. and López, G. (2017) Hispanic identity fades across generations as immigrant connections fall away. *Hispanic Trends*, 20 December. Washington, DC: Pew Research Center. See http://www.pewhispanic.org/2017/12/20/hispanic-identity-fades-across-generations-as-immigrant-connections-fall-away.

Lopez, M.H., Krogstad, J.M. and Flores, A. (2018) Hispanic parents' Spanish use with children falls as generations pass. *Fact Tank*, 2 April. Washington, DC: Pew Research Center. See http://www.pewresearch.org/fact-tank/2018/04/02/most-hispanic-parents-speak-spanish-to-their-children-but-this-is-less-the-case-in-later-immigrant-generations/.

López, M.M. (2012) Children's language ideologies in a first-grade dual-language class. *Journal of Early Childhood Literacy* 12 (2), 176–201.

López, N. (2013) Killing two birds with one stone? Why we need two separate questions on race and ethnicity in the 2020 census and beyond. *Latino Studies* 11 (3), 428–438.

López, V. (2018) 'Todes les diputades': El lenguaje inclusivo avanza entre los jóvenes y genera polémica. *Clarín*, 6 December. See https://www.clarin.com/sociedad/todes-diputades-lenguaje-inclusivo-avanza-jovenes-genera-polemica_0_Sy6mQt6em.html.

Loveman, M. (2014) *National Colors: Racial Classification and the State in Latin America*. Oxford: Oxford University Press.

Lowenthal, A.F. (1970) The United States and the Dominican Republic to 1965: Background to intervention. *Caribbean Studies* 10 (2), 30–55.

Lowther Pereira, K. (2015) Developing critical language awareness via service-learning for Spanish heritage speakers. *Heritage Language Journal* 12 (2), 159–185.

Loza, S. (2017) Transgressing standard language ideologies in the Spanish heritage language (SHL) classroom. *Chiricù Journal: Latina/o Literature, Art, and Culture* 1 (2), 56–77. https://doi.org/10.2979/chiricu.1.2.06

Lozano, R. (2018) *An American Language: The History of Spanish in the United States*. Oakland, CA: University of California Press.

Lutz, A. (2006) Spanish maintenance among English-speaking Latino youth: The role of individual and social characteristics. *Social Forces* 84 (3), 1417–1433.

Lynch, A. (2000) The subjunctive in Miami Cuban Spanish: Bilingualism, contact, and language variability. PhD dissertation, University of Minnesota.

Lynch, A. (2018) A historical view of US Latinidad and Spanish as a heritage language. In K. Potowski (ed.) *Handbook of Spanish as a Minority/Heritage Language* (pp. 17–35). New York: Routledge.

Lynch, A. and Potowski, K. (2014) La valoración del habla bilingüe en los Estados Unidos: Fundamentos sociolingüísticos y pedagógicos en 'Hablando bien se entiende la gente'. *Hispania* 97 (1), 32–46.

Lyons, K. and Rodríguez-Ordóñez, I. (2015) Public legacies: Spanish-English (in) authenticity in the linguistic landscape of Pilsen, Chicago. *University of Pennsylvania Working Papers in Linguistics* 21 (2), 14.

Macedo, D. (1997) English only: The tongue-tying of America. In A. Darder, R.D. Torres and H. Gutierrez (eds) *Latinos and Education: A Critical Reader* (pp. 269–278). New York: Routledge.

MacGregor-Mendoza, P. (2000) Aqui no se habla español: Stories of linguistic repression in southwest schools. *Bilingual Research Journal* 24 (4), 355–367.

Macías, R.F. (2014) Spanish as the second national language of the United States: Fact, future, fiction, or hope? *Review of Research in Education* 38 (1), 33–57.

MacSwan, J. (2014) *A Minimalist Approach to Intrasentential Code Switching*. New York: Routledge.

Makoni, S. and Pennycook, A. (2005) Disinventing and (re)constituting languages. *Critical Inquiry in Language Studies* 2, 137–156.

Malavé, I. and Giordani, E. (2015) *Latino Stats: American Hispanics by the Numbers*. New York: The New Press.

Mangual Figueroa, A. (2012) 'I have papers so I can go anywhere!': Everyday talk about citizenship in a mixed-status Mexican family. *Journal of Language, Identity & Education* 11 (5), 291–311.

Markert, J. (2010) The changing face of racial discrimination: Hispanics as the dominant minority in the USA – a new application of power-threat theory. *Critical Sociology* 36 (2), 307–327.

Markham, L. (2019) How climate change is pushing Central American migrants to the US. *The Guardian*, 6 April. See https://www.theguardian.com/commentisfree/2019/apr/06/us-mexico-immigration-climate-change-migration.

Mar-Molinero, C. and Paffey, D. (2011) Linguistic imperialism: Who owns Global Spanish? In M. Díaz-Campos (ed.) *The Handbook of Hispanic Sociolinguistics* (pp. 747–764). Malden, MA: John Wiley.

Márquez, C. (2018) Becoming Pedro: 'Playing Mexican' at South of the Border. *Latino Studies* 16 (4), 461–481.

Márquez Reiter, R. and Martín Rojo, L. (2014) Introduction: Exploring Latin American communities across regions and communicative arenas. In R. Márquez Reiter and L. Martín Rojo (eds) *A Sociolinguistics of Diaspora* (pp. 1–11). New York: Routledge.

Martinez, D. (2015) *Jane the Virgin* proves diversity is more than skin deep. *The Atlantic*, 19 October. See https://www.theatlantic.com/entertainment/archive/2015/10/jane-the-virgin-telenovelas/409696/.

Martinez, D. (2017) Op-Ed: The case against 'Latinx'. *Los Angeles Times*, 17 December. See http://www.latimes.com/opinion/op-ed/la-oe-hernandez-the-case-against-latinx-20171217-story.html.

Martínez, G. (2003) Classroom based dialect awareness in heritage language instruction: A critical applied linguistic approach. *Heritage Language Journal* 1.

Martínez, G. (2007) Writing back and forth: The interplay of form and situation in heritage language composition. *Language Teaching Research* 11 (1), 31–41.

Martínez, G. (2008) Language-in-healthcare policy, interaction patterns, and unequal care on the U.S.-Mexico border. *Language Policy* 7 (4), 345–363.

Martínez, G. (2009) Language in healthcare policy and planning along the U.S. Mexico border. In M. Lacorte and J. Leeman (eds) *Español en Estados Unidos y otros Contextos de Contacto: Sociolingüística, Ideología y Pedagogía* (pp. 255–269). Madrid: Iberoamericana.

Martínez, G. (2010) Language and power in healthcare: Towards a theory of language barriers among linguistic minorities in the United States. In J. Watzke, P. Chamness and M. Mantero (eds) *Readings in Language Studies: Language and Power* (Vol. 2, pp. 59–74). Lakewood, FL: International Society for Language Studies.

Martínez, G. (2014) Vital Signs: A photovoice assessment of the linguistic landscape in Spanish in healthcare facilities along the US-Mexico border. *International Journal of Communication and Health* 14, 18–24.

Martínez, G. and Schwartz, A. (2012) Elevating 'low' language for high stakes: A case for critical, community-based learning in a medical Spanish for heritage learners program. *Heritage Language Journal* 9, 37–49.

Martínez, R. A., Hikida, M. and Durán, L. (2015). Unpacking ideologies of linguistic purism: How dual language teachers make sense of everyday translanguaging. *International Multilingual Research Journal* 9 (1), 26–42.

Martínez-Roldán, C.M. (2013) The representation of Latinos and the use of Spanish: A critical content analysis of Skippyjon Jones. *Journal of Children's Literature* 39 (1), 5–14.

Martínez-Roldán, C.M. (2015) Translanguaging practices as mobilization of linguistic resources in a Spanish/English bilingual after-school program: An analysis of contradictions. *International Multilingual Research Journal* 9 (1), 43–58.

Massey, D.S. (2016) The Mexico-U.S. border in the American imagination. *Proceedings of the American Philosophical Society* 160 (2), 160–177.

Mastro, D.E. and Bohm-Morazvifz, E. (2005) Latino representation on primetime television. *Journalism & Mass Communication Quarterly* 82 (1), 110–130.

May, S. (2001) *Language and Minority Rights: Ethnicity, Nationalism and the Politics of Language.* Harlow: Longman.

McCarty, T.L. (2016) Policy and politics of language revitalization in the USA and Canada. In S.M. Coronel-Molina and T.L. McCarty (eds) *Indigenous Language Revitalization in the Americas* (pp. 15–34). New York: Routledge.

McCarty, T.L. and Lee, T. (2014) Critical culturally sustaining/revitalizing pedagogy and Indigenous education sovereignty. *Harvard Educational Review* 84 (1), 101–124.

McKay Wilson, D. (2011) Dual language programs on the rise: 'Enrichment' model puts content learning front and center for ELL students. *Harvard Education Letter* 27 (2).

Meador, E. (2005) The making of marginality: Schooling for Mexican immigrant girls in the rural southwest. *Anthropology and Education Quarterly* 36 (2), 149–164.

Megenney, W.W. (1983) Common words of African origin used in Latin America. *Hispania* 66 (1), 1–10.

Mendible, M. (ed.) (2010) *From Bananas to Buttocks: The Latina Body in Popular Film and Culture.* Austin, TX: University of Texas Press.

Mendoza-Denton, N. (2008) *Homegirls: Language and Cultural Practice among Latina Youth Gangs.* Malden, MA: Blackwell.

Menjívar, C. and Gómez Cervantes, A. (2018, August 27) El Salvador: Civil war, natural disasters, and gang violence drive migration. *MPI Profile*, 27 August. See https://www.migrationpolicy.org/article/el-salvador-civil-war-natural-disasters-and-gang-violence-drive-migration.

Menken, K. and Solorza, C. (2014) No child left bilingual: Accountability and the elimination of bilingual education programs in New York City schools. *Educational Policy* 28 (1), 96–125.

Mersha, T.B. and Abebe, T. (2015) Self-reported race/ethnicity in the age of genomic research: Its potential impact on understanding health disparities. *Human Genomics* 9 (1), 1.

Metcalf, A. (1979) *Chicano English.* Washington, DC: Center for Applied Linguistics.

Migration Policy Institute (n.d.) *Countries of Birth for U.S. Immigrants, 1960–Present.* Washington, DC: Migration Policy Institute. See https://www.migrationpolicy.org/programs/data-hub/charts/immigrants-countries-birth-over-time.

Milroy, J. (2007) The ideology of the standard language. In C. Llamas, L. Mullany and P. Stockwell (eds) *Routledge Companion to Sociolinguistics* (pp. 133–139). London: Routledge.

Milroy, J. and Milroy, L. (1999) *Authority in Language* (3rd edn). London: Routledge.

Milroy, L. (2002) Social networks. In J.K. Chambers, P. Trudgill and N. Schilling-Estes (eds) *The Handbook of Language Variation and Change* (pp. 549–572). Oxford: Blackwell.

Misra, T. (2016) Yes, the Fair Housing Act protects non-English speakers. *CityLab*, 15 September. See http://www.citylab.com/housing/2016/09/yes-the-fair-housing-act-protects-non-english-speakers/500210/.

Mitchell, T.D., Jaworski, A. and Thurlow, C. (2010) A Latino community takes hold': Reproducing semiotic landscapes in media discourse. *Semiotic landscapes: Language, image, space* 168–186.

Mithun, M. (2001) *The Languages of Native North America.* Cambridge: Cambridge University Press.

Mize, R.L. and Swords, A.C.S. (2010) *Consuming Mexican Labor: From the Bracero Program to NAFTA.* Toronto: University of Toronto Press.

Molina-Guzmán, I. (2010) *Dangerous Curves: Latina Bodies in the Media.* New York: New York University Press.

Montes-Alcalá, C. (2000) Attitudes towards oral and written codeswitching in Spanish-English bilingual youths. In A. Roca (ed.) *Research on Spanish in the U.S.* (pp. 218–227). Somerville, MA: Cascadilla Press.

Montes-Alcalá, C. (2011) ¿Mejor o peor español? Actitudes lingüísticas de universitarios hispanohablantes en Estados Unidos. *Studies in Hispanic and Lusophone Linguistics* 4 (1), 35–54.

Montgomery, D. (2006) An anthem's discordant notes: Spanish version of 'Star-Spangled Banner' draws strong reactions. *The Washington Post*, 28 April. See https://www.washingtonpost.com/archive/politics/2006/04/28/an-anthems-discordant-notes-span-classbankheadspanish-version-of-star-spangled-banner-draws-strong-reactionsspan/5885bf36-cf07-4c56-a316-f76e7d17c158/.

Montoya, M.C. (2011) Expression of possession in Spanish in contact with English: A sociolinguistic study across two generations in the greater New York metropolitan area. PhD thesis, University at Albany, State University of New York.

Montrul, S. (2004) Subject and object expression in Spanish heritage speakers: A case of morphosyntactic convergence. *Bilingualism: Language and cognition* 7 (2), 125–142.

Montrul, S. (2007) Interpreting mood distinctions in Spanish as a heritage language. In K. Potowski and R. Cameron (eds) *Spanish in Contact: Policy, Social and Linguistic Inquiries* (pp. 23–40). Philadelphia, PA: John Benjamins.

Mora, G.C. (2014) *Making Hispanics: How Activists, Bureaucrats, and Media Constructed a New American*. Chicago, IL: University of Chicago Press.

Mora, G.C. and Rodríguez-Muñiz, M. (2017) Latinos, race, and the American future: A response to Richard Alba's 'The likely persistence of a White majority'. *New Labor Forum* 26 (2), 40–46.

Mora, M.T., Dávila, A. and Rodríguez, H. (2017) Education, migration, and earnings of Puerto Ricans on the island and US mainland: Impact, outcomes, and consequences of an economic crisis. *Migration Studies* 5 (2), 168–189.

Morales, H.L. (2003) *Los Cubanos de Miami: Lengua y Sociedad*. Miami, FL: Ediciones Universal.

Morales, P.Z. (2016) Transnational practices and language maintenance: Spanish and Zapoteco in California. *Children's Geographies* 14 (4), 375–389.

Moran, K.C. (2007) The growth of Spanish-language and Latino-themed television programs for children in the United States. *Journal of Children and Media* 1 (3), 294–300.

Moran, R.F. (2009) The untold story of Lau v. Nichols. In M. Lacorte and J. Leeman (eds) *Español en Estados Unidos y Otros Contextos de Contacto: Sociolingüística, ideología y pedagogía* (pp. 277–302). Madrid: Iberoamericana.

Moran, R. (2015) Undone by law: The uncertain legacy of Lau v. Nichols. *Berkeley La Raza Law Journal* 16 (1). https://doi.org/10.15779/Z38J94M

Moreno, M. and Benavides, M. (2019) Dynamics of ethnic and racial self-identification in contemporary Peru. *Ethnic and Racial Studies* 42 (10), 1686–1707.

Moreno-Fernández, F. (2009) *La Lengua Española en su Geografía*. Madrid: Arco/ Libros.

Moreno-Fernández, F. (ed.) (2018) U.S. Spanish in the Spotlight. *Informes Del Observatorio/ Observatorio Reports* 043-09/2018EN. https://doi.org/10.15427/OR043-09/2018EN

Morning, A. (2008) Ethnic classification in global perspective: A cross-national survey of the 2000 census round. *Population Research and Policy Review* 27 (2), 239–272.

Morse, P. (2018) Six facts about the Hispanic market that may surprise you. *Forbes*, 9 January. See https://www.forbes.com/sites/forbesagencycouncil/2018/01/09/six-facts-about-the-hispanic-market-that-may-surprise-you/.

Motschenbacher, H. and Stegu, M. (2013) Queer linguistic approaches to discourse. *Discourse & Society* 24 (5), 519–535.

Murji, K. and Solomos, J. (2005) Introduction: Racialization in theory and practice. In K. Murji and J. Solomos (eds) *Racialization: Studies in Theory and Practice* (pp. 1–27). Oxford: Oxford University Press.

Myers, D. and Levy, M. (2018) Racial population projections and reactions to alternative news accounts of growing diversity. *The Annals of the American Academy of Political and Social Science* 677 (1), 215–228.

Myers-Scotton, C. (1993a) *Social Motivations for Codeswitching: Evidence from Africa.* Oxford: Clarendon Press.

Myers-Scotton, C. (1993b) *Duelling Languages: Grammatical Structure in Codeswitching.* Oxford: Clarendon Press.

Myers-Scotton, C. (2006) *Multiple Voices: An Introduction to Bilingualism.* Oxford: Blackwell.

NBC News (2019) Meet the press. *NBC News*, 27 January. See https://www.nbcnews.com/meet-the-press/meet-press-january-27-2019-n963321.

Ndulue, E.B., Bermejo, F., Ramos, K., Lowe, S.E., Hoffman, N. and Zuckerman, E. (2019) *The Language of Immigration Reporting: Normalizing vs. Watchdogging in a Nativist Age.* Cambridge, MA: MIT Center for Civic Media. See https://defineamerican.com/journalismreport/.

Negrón, R. (2014) New York City's Latino ethnolinguistic repertoire and the negotiation of latinidad in conversation. *Journal of Sociolinguistics* 18 (1), 87–118.

Negrón, R. (2018) Ethnic identification and New York City's intra-Latina/o hierarchy. *Latino Studies* 16, 185–212.

Negrón-Muntaner, F. (2014) *The Latino Media Gap.* New York: Center for the Study of Ethnicity and Race. See https://media-alliance.org/2016/05/the-latino-media-gap/.

Ngai, M.M. (2004) *Impossible Subjects: Illegal Aliens and the Making of Modern America.* Princeton, NJ: Princeton University Press.

Nieto, S. (2010) *Language, Culture, and Teaching: Critical Perspectives.* New York: Routledge.

Nieto-Phillips, J. (2000) Spanish American ethnic identity and New Mexico's statehood struggle. In E. Gonzales-Berry and D.R. Maciel (eds) *The Contested Homeland: A Chicano History of New Mexico* (pp. 97–142). Albuquerque, NM: University of New Mexico Press.

Nieto-Phillips, J. (2004) *The Language of Blood.* Albuquerque, NM: University of New Mexico.

Niño-Murcia, M. (2001) Late-stage standardization and language ideology in the Colombian press. *International Journal of the Sociology of Language* 149, 119–144.

Nobles, M. (2000) *Shades of Citizenship.* Stanford, CA: Stanford University Press.

Nuñez, I. and Palmer, D. (2017) Who will be bilingual? A critical discourse analysis of a Spanish-English bilingual pair. *Critical Inquiry in Language Studies* 14 (4), 294–319.

Oboler, S. (1998) Hispanics? That's what they call us. In R. Delgado and J. Stefancic (eds) *The Latino/a Condition: A Critical Reader* (pp. 3–5). New York: New York University Press.

Ochs, E. (1992) Indexing gender. In A. Duranti (ed.) *Rethinking Context: Language as an Interactive Phenomenon* (pp. 335–359). Cambridge: Cambridge University Press.

Olivas, M.A. (2006) *'Colored Men' and 'Hombres Aquí': Hernandez v. Texas and the Emergence of Mexican-American Lawyering.* Houston, TX: Arte Público Press.

OMB (Office of Management and Budget) (1997) *Revisions to the Standards for the Classification of Federal Data on Race and Ethnicity.* Federal Register Notice, 30 October. Washington, DC: Executive Office of the President.

Omi, M. (2001) The changing meaning of race. In N.J. Smelser, W.J. Wilson and F. Mitchell (eds) *America Becoming: Racial Trends and their Consequences, Vol. 1.* (pp. 243–263). Washington, DC: National Academies Press.

Omi, M. and Winant, H. (1994) *Racial Formation in the United States* (2nd edn). New York: Routledge.

Oquendo, Á. (1995) Re-imagining the Latino/a race. *Harvard Blackletter Law Journal* 12, 93–129.

Orellana, M.F. (2009) *Translating Childhoods: Immigrant Youth, Language, and Culture.* New Brunswick, NJ: Rutgers University Press.

Ornstein-Galicia, J. (ed.) (1984) *Form and Function in Chicano English.* Rowley, MA: Newbury House.

Otheguy, R. (1993) A reconsideration of the notion of loan translation in the analysis of U.S. Spanish. In A. Roca and J.M. Lipski (eds) *Spanish in the United States: Linguistic Contact and Diversity* (pp. 21–45). Berlin: Mouton de Gruyter.

Otheguy, R. (2013) Convergencia conceptual y la sobrestimación de la presencia de elementos estructurales ingleses en el español estadounidense. In D. Dumitrescu and G. Piña-Rosales (eds) *El español en los Estados Unidos: E Pluribus Unum? Enfoques Multidisciplinarios* (pp. 129–149). New York: Academia Norteamericana de la Lengua Española.

Otheguy, R. and Stern, N. (2010) On so-called Spanglish. *International Journal of Bilingualism* 15 (1), 85–100.

Otheguy, R. and Zentella, A.C. (2011) *Spanish in New York: Language Contact, Dialectal Leveling, and Structural Continuity.* Oxford: Oxford University Press.

Otheguy, R., Zentella, A.C. and Livert, D. (2007) Language and dialect contact in Spanish in New York: Toward the formation of a speech community. *Language* 83 (4), 770–802.

Ovando, C.J. (2003) Bilingual education in the United States: Historical development and current issues. *Bilingual Research Journal* 27 (1), 1–24.

Paffey, D. (2012) *Language Ideologies and the Globalization of 'Standard' Spanish: Raising the Standard.* London: Bloomsbury.

Painter, N.I. (2010) *The History of White People.* New York: W.W. Norton.

Palmer, D. (2007) A dual immersion strand program in California: Carrying out the promise of dual language education in an English-dominant context. *International Journal of Bilingual Education and Bilingualism* 10 (6), 752–768.

Palmer, D. (2009) Middle-class English speakers in a two-way immersion bilingual classroom: 'Everybody should be listening to Jonathan right now ...'. *TESOL Quarterly* 43 (2), 177–202.

Parada, M. (2016) Ethnolinguistic and gender aspects of Latino naming in Chicago: Exploring regional variation. *Names* 64 (1), 19–35.

Paris, D. (2012) Culturally sustaining pedagogy: A needed change in stance, terminology, and practice. *Educational Researcher* 41 (3), 93–97.

Parra, M.L. (2016) Understanding identity among Spanish heritage learners: An interdisciplinary endeavor. In D. Pascual y Cabo (ed.) *Advances in Spanish as a Heritage Language* (pp. 177–204). Amsterdam: John Benjamins.

Pascual y Cabo, D. and Prada, J. (2018) Redefining Spanish teaching and learning in the United States. *Foreign Language Annals* 51 (3), 533–547.

Pascual y Cabo, D., Prada, J. and Lowther Pereira, K. (2017) Effects of community service-learning on heritage language learners' attitudes toward their language and culture. *Foreign Language Annals* 50 (1), 71–83.

Pauwels, A. (2016) *Language Maintenance and Shift*. Cambridge: Cambridge University Press.

Pavlenko, A. (2002) 'We have room but for one language here': Language and national identity at the turn of the 20th century. *Multilingua* 21, 163–196.

Pavlenko, A. (2003) 'Language of the enemy': Foreign language education and national identity. *International Journal of Bilingual Education and Bilingualism* 6 (5), 313–331.

Pease-Alvarez, L. (2003) Transforming perspectives on bilingual language socialization. In R. Bayley and S.R. Schecter (eds) *Language Socialization in Bilingual and Multilingual Societies* (pp. 9–24). Clevedon: Multilingual Matters.

Pease-Alvarez, L. and Winsler, A. (1994) Cuando el maestro no habla Espanol: Children's bilingual language practices in the classroom. *TESOL Quarterly* 28 (3), 507–535.

Penfield, J. and Ornstein-Galicia, J.L. (1985) *Chicano English: An Ethnic Contact Dialect*. Amsterdam: John Benjamins.

Penny, R. (2000) *Variation and Change in Spanish*. Cambridge: Cambridge University Press.

Petrovic, J.E. (2005) The conservative restoration and neoliberal defenses of bilingual education. *Language Policy* 4 (4), 395–416.

Petrucci, P.R. (2008) Portraying language diversity through a monolingual lens: On the unbalanced representation of Spanish and English in a corpus of American films. *Sociolinguistic Studies* 2 (3), 405–425.

Pew Research Center (2006) America's immigration quandary. *Hispanic Trends*, 30 March. See https://www.pewhispanic.org/2006/03/30/v-views-and-perceptions-of-immigrants/.

Pew Research Center (2013) A growing share of Latinos get their news in English. *Hispanic Trends*, 23 July. See http://www.pewhispanic.org/2013/07/23/a-growing-share-of-latinos-get-their-news-in-english/.

Pew Research Center (2017) Demographics of self-identified Hispanics and non-Hispanics. *Hispanic Trends*, 20 December. See http://www.pewhispanic.org/chart/demographics-of-self-identified-hispanics-and-non-hispanics/.

Pfaff, C.W. (1979) Constraints on language mixing: Intrasentential code-switching and borrowing in Spanish/English. *Language* 55 (2), 291–318.

Piller, I. (2015) Language ideologies. In K. Tracy, T. Sandel and C. Ilie (eds) *The International Encyclopedia of Language and Social Interaction*. Malden, MA: John Wiley. https://doi.org/10.1002/9781118611463.wbielsi140

Piñón, J. and Rojas, V. (2011) Language and cultural identity in the new configuration of the US Latino TV industry. *Global Media and Communication* 7 (2), 129–147.

Poggi, J. (2019) Verizon to debut new campaign starring real customers during Oscars. *AdAge*, 22 February. See https://adage.com/article/media/verizon-debuts-campaign-oscars/316717.

Pomada, A. (2008) Puerto Rico, school language policies. In J.M. González (ed.) *Encyclopedia of Bilingual Education* (pp. 701–704). Los Angeles, CA: SAGE.

Pomerantz, A. (2002) Language ideologies and the production of identities: Spanish as a resource for participation in a multilingual marketplace. *Multilingua* 21, 275–302.

Pomerantz, A. and Huguet, A. (2013) Spanish language education in US public schools: Bilingualism for whom? *Infancia y Aprendizaje* 36 (4), 517–536.

Pomerantz, A. and Schwartz, A. (2011) Border talk: Narratives of Spanish language encounters in the United States. *Language and Intercultural Communication* 11 (3), 176–196.

Poplack, S. (1980) Sometimes I'll start a sentence in Spanish y termino en Espanol: Toward a typology of code-switching. *Linguistics* 18 (7–8), 581–618.

Porcel, J. (2006) The paradox of Spanish among Miami Cubans. *Journal of Sociolinguistics* 10 (1), 93–110.

Portes, A. and Rumbaut, R.G. (2001) *Legacies: The Story of the Immigrant Second Generation*. Berkeley, CA: University of California Press.

Portes, A. and Rumbaut, R.G. (2005) Introduction: The second generation and the Children of Immigrants Longitudinal Study. *Ethnic and Racial Studies* 28, 983–999.

Potowski, K. (2004) Student Spanish use and investment in a dual immersion classroom: Implications for second language acquisition and heritage language maintenance. *The Modern Language Journal* 88 (1), 75–101.

Potowski, K. (2007) *Language and Identity in a Dual Immersion School*. Clevedon: Multilingual Matters.

Potowski, K. (2010) *Language Diversity in the USA*. Cambridge: Cambridge University Press.

Potowski, K. (2011) Linguistic and cultural authenticity of 'Spanglish' greeting cards. *International Journal of Multilingualism* 8 (4), 324–344.

Potowski, K. (2016) *IntraLatino Language and Identity: MexiRican Spanish*. Amsterdam: John Benjamins.

Potowski, K. and Shin, N.L. (2018) *Gramática Española: Variación Social*. Routledge.

Potowski, K. and Torres, L. (forthcoming) *Spanish in Chicago*. Oxford: Oxford University Press.

Prada Pérez, A.D. (2018) Subject pronoun expression and language mode in bilingual Spanish. *Studies in Hispanic and Lusophone Linguistics* 11 (2), 303–336.

Preston, D.R. (ed.) (1999) *Handbook of Perceptual Dialectology, Vol. 1*. Amsterdam: John Benjamins.

Proposition 227 (1998) See http://vigarchive.sos.ca.gov/1998/primary/propositions/227text.htm.

Quiroz, P.A. (2001) The silencing of Latino student 'voice': Puerto Rican and Mexican narratives in eighth grade and high school. *Anthropology & Education Quarterly* 32 (3), 326–349.

Rabin, L. (2013) Literacy narratives for social change: Making connections between service-learning and literature education. *Enculturation* 6.

Rabin, L. and Leeman, J. (2015) Critical service-learning and literary study in Spanish. In L. Grobman and R. Rosenberg (eds) *Service Learning and Literary Studies in English* (pp. 128–137). New York: Modern Language Association.

Radford, J. (2019) Key findings about U.S. immigrants. *Fact Tank*, 17 June. Washington, DC: Pew Research Center. See https://www.pewresearch.org/fact-tank/2019/06/17/key-findings-about-u-s-immigrants/.

RAE/Real Academia Española (2014) Estadounidismo. *Diccionario de la lengua española, Edición del Tricentenario*. See http://dle.rae.es/?id=GjyFPOD.

Rael-Gálvez, E. (2017) Raising consciousness and imagining reconciliation. *Green Fire Times*, November.

Rahel, K.O. (2014) Why the Sixth Amendment right to counsel includes an out-of-court interpreter. *Iowa Law Review* 99, 2299–2333.

Ramírez, J.D., Yuen, S.D. and Ramey, D.R. (1991) *Final Report: Longitudinal Study of Structured English Immersion Strategy, Early-exit and Late-exit Programs for Language Minority Children*. Report submitted to the US Department of Education. San Mateo, CA: Aguirre International.

Ramirez Berg, C. (2002) *Latino Images in Film: Stereotypes, Subversion, & Resistance*. Austin, TX: University of Texas Press.

Ramos, R. (2019) The Alamo is a rupture. *Guernica*, 19 February. See https://www.guernicamag.com/the-alamo-is-a-rupture-texas-mexico-imperialism-history/.

Ramsey, P.J. (2010) *Bilingual Public Schooling in the United States: A History of America's 'Polyglot Boardinghouse'*. New York: Palgrave Macmillan.

Rangel, N., Loureiro-Rodríguez, V. and Moyna, M.I. (2015) 'Is that what I sound like when I speak?': Attitudes towards Spanish, English, and code-switching in two Texas border towns. *Spanish in Context* 12 (2), 177–198.

Raschka, C., Wei, L. and Lee, S. (2006) Bilingual development and social networks of British-born Chinese children. *International Journal of the Sociology of Language* 2002 (153), 9–25.

Raymond, C.W. (2016) Reconceptualizing identity and context in the deployment of forms of address. In M.I. Moyna and S. Rivera-Mills (eds) *Forms of Address in the Spanish of the Americas* (pp. 267–288). Amsterdam: John Benjamins.

Relaño Pastor, A.M. (2014) *Shame and Pride in Narrative: Mexican Women's Language Experiences at the U.S.-Mexico Border*. New York: Palgrave Macmillan.

Rey Agudo, R. (2019) There is nothing wrong with Julián Castro's Spanish. *The New York Times*, 27 July. See https://www.nytimes.com/2019/07/27/opinion/sunday/julian-castro-spanish.html.

Reyes, A. (2016) The voicing of Asian American characters: Korean linguistic styles at an Asian American cram school. In H.S. Alim, J.R. Rickford and A.F. Ball (eds) *Raciolinguistics: How Language Shapes our Ideas about Race* (pp. 309–326). Oxford: Oxford University Press.

Reynolds, J.F. and Orellana, M.F. (2009) New immigrant youth interpreting in White public space. *American Anthropologist* 111 (2), 211–223.

Rhodes, N. and Pufahl, I. (2014) *An Overview of Spanish Teaching in US Schools: National Survey Results.* Cambridge, MA: Instituto Cervantes at Harvard University – FAS.

Ricento, T. (2005) Problems with the 'language-as-resource' discourse in the promotion of heritage languages in the USA. *Journal of Sociolinguistics* 9 (3), 348–368.

Ricento, T. (ed.) (2009) *An Introduction to Language Policy: Theory and Method.* Malden, MA: John Wiley.

Ricento, T.K. and Hornberger, N.H. (1996) Unpeeling the onion: Language planning and policy and the ELT professional. *TESOL Quarterly* 30 (3), 401.

Ríos, M., Romero, F. and Ramírez, R. (2014) Race reporting among Hispanics: 2010. Working Paper No. 102, Population Division, U.S. Census Bureau, Washington, DC.

Rivadeneyra, R. (2011) Gender and race portrayals on Spanish-language television. *Sex Roles* 65 (3–4), 208–222.

Rivera-Mills, S. (2001) Acculturation and communicative need: Language shift in an ethnically diverse Hispanic community. *Southwest Journal of Linguistics* 20 (2), 211–223.

Rivera-Mills, S.V. (2011) Use of voseo and Latino identity: An intergenerational study of Hondurans and Salvadorans in the western region of the US. In L.A. Ortiz-López (ed.) *Selected Proceedings of the 13th Hispanic Linguistics Symposium* (pp. 94–106). Somerville, MA: Cascadilla Proceedings Project.

Rivera-Mills, S.V. (2012) Spanish heritage language maintenance: Its legacy, its future. In S.M. Beaudrie and M.A. Fairclough (eds) *Spanish as a Heritage Language in the United States: The State of the Field* (pp. 21–42). Washington, DC: Georgetown University Press.

Rivera Ramos, E. (1996) The legal construction of American colonialism: The Insular Cases (1901–1922). *Revista Jurídica Universidad de Puerto Rico* 65 (2), 225–328.

Rivero, Y.M. (2012) Interpreting Cubanness, Americanness, and the sitcom: WPBT-PBS's ¿Qué pasa U.S.A.? (1975–1980). In S. Shahaf and T. Oren (eds) *Global Television Formats: Understanding Television Across Borders.* New York: Routledge.

Robbins, L. (2018) Man threatens Spanish-speaking workers: 'My next call will be to ICE'. *The New York Times,* 17 May. See https://www.nytimes.com/2018/05/16/nyregion/man-threatens-spanish-language-video.html.

Rodríguez, A. (2007) *Diversity.* Mountain View, CA: Floricanto Press.

Rodríguez, C. (2000) *Changing Race: Latinos, the Census, and the History of Ethnicity in the United States.* New York: New York University Press.

Rodríguez, C.E. (1997) Visual retrospective: Latino film stars. In C.E. Rodríguez (ed.) *Latin Looks: Images of Latinas and Latinos in the U.S. Media* (pp. 80–84). Boulder, CO: Westview Press.

Rodríguez, J.M. (2003) *Queer Latinidad: Identity Practices, Discursive Spaces.* New York: New York University Press.

Rodriguez-Arroyo, S. (2013) The never ending story of language policy in Puerto Rico. *Comunicación, Cultura & Política* 4 (1), 79–98.

Román-Mendoza, E. (2018) *Aprender a aprender en la era digital: Tecnopedagogía crítica para la enseñanza del español LE/L2* (1st edn). London: Routledge.

Ronkin, M. and Karn, H.E. (1999) Mock Ebonics: Linguistic racism in parodies of Ebonics on the internet. *Journal of Sociolinguistics* 3 (3), 360–380.

Roosevelt, T. (1919) *Letter from Theodore Roosevelt to Richard M. Hurd*, 3 January. See http://www.theodorerooseveltcenter.org/Research/Digital-Library/Record.aspx?libID=o265602.

Rosa, J. (2014) Learning ethnolinguistic borders: Language and diaspora in the socialization of US Latinas/os. In R. Rolón-Dow and J.G. Irizarry (eds) *Diaspora Studies in Education: Toward a Framework for Understanding the Experiences of Transnational Communities* (pp. 39–60). New York: Peter Lang.

Rosa, J. (2016a) Racializing language, regimenting Latinas/os: Chronotope, social tense, and American raciolinguistic futures. *Language & Communication* 46, 106–117.

Rosa, J. (2016b) Standardization, racialization, languagelessness: Raciolinguistic ideologies across communicative contexts. *Journal of Linguistic Anthropology* 26 (2), 162–183.

Rosa, J. (2016c) From mock Spanish to inverted Spanglish. In J. Rosa, H.S. Alim, J.R. Rickford and A.F. Ball (eds) *Raciolinguistics: How Language Shapes our Ideas about Race* 65–80. Oxford: Oxford University Press.

Rosa, J. (2019) *Looking Like a Language, Sounding Like a Race*. Oxford: Oxford University Press.

Rosa, J. and Flores, N. (2017) Unsettling race and language: Toward a raciolinguistic perspective. *Language in Society* 46 (5), 621–647.

Roth, W.D. (2012) *Race Migrations: Latinos and the Cultural Transformation of Race*. Palo Alto, CA: Stanford University Press.

Roth, W.D. and Ivemark, B. (2018) Genetic options: The impact of genetic ancestry testing on consumers' racial and ethnic identities. *American Journal of Sociology* 124 (1), 150–184.

Roy, S. (2005) Language and globalized discourse: Two case studies of Francophone minorities in Canada. *Sociolinguistic Studies* 6 (2), 243–268.

Ruíz, R. (1984) Orientations in language planning. *NABE Journal* 8 (2), 15–34.

Ruíz, R. (2010) Reorienting language-as-resource. In J.E. Petrovic (ed.) *International Perspectives on Bilingual Education: Policy, Practice, and Controversy* (pp. 155–172). Charlotte, NC: Information Age.

Rumbaut, R.G. (2009) A Language graveyard? The evolution of language competencies, preferences and use among young adult children of immigrants. In T.G. Wiley, J.S. Lee and R. Rumberger (eds) *The Education of Language Minority Immigrants in the United States* (pp. 35–71). Multilingual Matters.

Rumbaut, R.G., Massey, D.S. and Bean, F.D. (2006) Linguistic life expectancies: Immigrant language retention in Southern California. *Population and Development Review* 32 (3), 447–460.

Sallabank, J. (2010) The role of social networks in endangered language maintenance and revitalization: The case of Guernesiais in the Channel Islands. *Anthropological Linguistics* 52 (2), 184–205.

Sánchez Munoz, A. (2016) Heritage language healing? Learners' attitudes and damage control in a heritage language classroom. In D. Pascual y Cabo (ed.) *Advances in Spanish as a Heritage Language* (pp. 205–218). Amsterdam: John Benjamins.

Sánchez-Muñoz and Amezcua, A. (2019) Spanish as a tool of Latinx resistance against repression in a hostile political climate. *Chiricú Journal: Latina/o Literatures, Arts, and Cultures* 3 (2), 59–76.

San Miguel, G. (2001) *Let All of Them Take Heed: Mexican Americans and the Campaign for Educational Equality in Texas, 1910–1981.* College Station, TX: Texas A&M University Press.

Santa Ana, O. (1993) Chicano English and the nature of the Chicano language setting. *Hispanic Journal of Behavioral Sciences* 15 (1), 3–35.

Santa Ana, O. (2002) *Brown Tide Rising: Metaphors of Latinos in Contemporary American Public Discourse.* Austin, TX: University of Texas Press.

Santa Ana, O. (2013) *Juan in a Hundred: The Representation of Latinos on Network News.* Austin, TX: University of Texas Press.

Santa Ana, O. and Bayley, R. (2004) Chicano English phonology. In B. Kortmann, K. Burridge, R. Mesthrie, E.W. Schneider and C. Upton (eds) *A Handbook of Varieties of English, Vol. 1: Phonology* (pp. 417–434). Berlin: Mouton de Gruyter.

Santiago, B. (2008) *Pardon my Spanglish.* Philadelphia, PA: Quirk Books.

Saperstein, A. and Penner, A.M. (2012) Racial fluidity and inequality in the United States. *American Journal of Sociology* 118 (3), 676–727.

Schachner, J. (2003) *Skippyjon Jones.* New York: Puffin Books.

Schecter, S.R. and Bayley, R. (2002) *Language as Cultural Practice: Mexicanos en el Norte.* Mahwah, NJ: Lawrence Erlbaum.

Schiffman, H.F. (1996) *Linguistic Culture and Language Policy.* London: Routledge.

Schiller, N.G., Basch, L. and Blanc, C.S. (1995) From immigrant to transmigrant: Theorizing transnational migration. *Anthropological Quarterly* 68 (1), 48.

Schmid, C. (2001) *The Politics of Language: Conflict, Identity and Cultural Pluralism in Comparative Perspective.* Oxford: Oxford University Press.

Schmidt, R. (2000) *Language Policy and Identity Politics in the United States.* Philadelphia, PA: Temple University Press.

Schmidt Sr., R. (2002) Racialization and language policy: The case of the USA. *Multilingua* 21 (2/3), 141–162.

Schmidt Sr., R. (2007) Defending English in an English-dominant world: The ideology of the 'Official English' movement in the United States. In A. Duchêne and M. Heller (eds) *Discourses of Endangerment: Ideology and Interest in the Defence of Languages* (pp. 197–215). New York: Continuum.

Schwartz, A. (2008) Their language, our Spanish: Introducing public discourses of 'Gringoism' as racializing linguistic and cultural reappropriation. *Spanish in Context* 5 (2), 224–245.

Schwartz, A. (2011) Mockery and appropriation of Spanish in White spaces: Perceptions of Latinos in the United States. In M. Díaz-Campos (ed.) *The Handbook of Hispanic Sociolinguistics* (pp. 646–663). Malden, MA: John Wiley.

Schwartz, A. (2016) Trump relies on Mock Spanish to talk about immigration. *Latino Rebels*, 20 October. See http://www.latinorebels.com/2016/10/20/trump-relies-on-mock-spanish-to-talk-about-immigration-opinion/.

Schwartz, M. (2010) Family language policy: Core issues of an emerging field. *Applied Linguistics Review* 1 (1), 171–192.

Serafini, E.J., Winsler, A. and Rozell, N. (2018) Long-term outcomes of bilingual education models: What does the research tell us? *Teachers' Hub Magazine*, March. See https://www.teachershubmag.com/longterm-outcomes.html.

Serna, L.I. (2017) Latinos in Film. In *Oxford Research Encyclopedia of American History*.

Shannon, S.M. (1999) The debate on bilingual education in the US: Language ideology as reflected in the practice of bilingual teachers. In J. Blommaert (ed.) *Language Ideological Debates* (pp. 171–199). Berlin: Mouton de Gruyter.

Shenk, P.S. (2007) 'I'm Mexican, remember?' Constructing ethnic identities via authenticating discourse. *Journal of Sociolinguistics* 11, 194–220.

Shin, H. and Ortman, J. (2011) *Language Projections: 2010 to 2020*. Presented at the Federal Forecasters Conference, Washington, DC, 21 April.

Shohamy, E. (2006) *Language Policy: Hidden Agendas and New Approaches*. New York: Routledge.

Showstack, R.E. (2015) Institutional representations of 'Spanish' and 'Spanglish': Managing competing discourses in heritage language instruction. *Language and Intercultural Communication* 15 (3), 341–361.

Showstack, R.E. (2016) Stancetaking and language ideologies in heritage language learner classroom discourse. *Journal of Language, Identity & Education* 16 (5), 271–284.

Showstack, R. (2018) Spanish and identity among Latin@s in the US. In K. Potowski (ed.) *The Routledge Handbook of Spanish as a Heritage Language* (pp. 106–120). London: Routledge.

Silva-Corvalán, C. (1994) *Language Contact and Change: Spanish in Los Angeles*. Oxford: Oxford University Press.

Silva-Corvalán, C. (2004) Spanish in the southwest. In E. Finnegan and J. Rickford (eds) *Language in the USA: Themes for the Twenty-first Century* (pp. 205–229). Cambridge: Cambridge University Press.

Silverstein, M. (1996) Monoglot 'standard' in America: Standardization and metaphors of linguistic hegemony. In D. Breinneis and R. Macaulay (eds) *The Matrix of Language: Contemporary Linguistic Anthropology* (pp. 284–306). Boulder, CO: Westview.

Silverstein, M. (2003) The whens and wheres – as well as hows – of ethnolinguistic recognition. *Public Culture* 15 (3), 531–557. See https://muse.jhu.edu/article/47190.

Skutnabb-Kangas, T. (2013) Role of linguistic human rights in language policy and planning. In C.A. Chapelle (ed.) *The Encyclopedia of Applied Linguistics*. https://doi.org/10.1002/9781405198431.wbeal1026

Slobe, T. (2018) Style, stance, and social meaning in mock white girl. *Language in Society* 47 (4), 541–567.

Smead, R.N. (2000) Phrasal calques in Chicano Spanish: Linguistic or cultural innovations? In A. Roca (ed.) *Research on Spanish in the U.S.* (pp. 162–172). Somerville, MA: Cascadilla Press.

Smith, S.L., Choueiti, M., Pieper, M., Yao, K., Case, A. and Choi, A. (2019) *Inequality in 1,200 Popular Films: Examining Portrayals of Gender, Race/Ethnicity, LGBTQ & Disability from 2007 to 2018*. Los Angeles, CA: Annenberg Foundation.

Smokoski, H.L. (2016) Voicing the other: Mock AAVE on social media. MA thesis, City University of New York.

Sniderman, P.M., Piazza, T., Tetlock, P.E. and Kendrick, A. (1991) The new racism. *American Journal of Political Science* 35 (2), 423–447.

Sowards, S.K. and Pineda, R.D. (2011) *Latinidad* in Ugly Betty: Authenticity and the paradox of representation. In M.A. Holling and B.M. Calafeel (eds) *Latina/o Discourse in Vernacular Spaces: Somos de Una Voz?* New York: Rowman & Littlefield.

Spell, J. (1927) Spanish teaching in the United States. *Hispania* 10, 141–159.

Stack, L. (2019) A border agent detained two Americans speaking Spanish. Now they have sued. *The New York Times*, 14 February. See https://www.nytimes.com/2019/02/14/us/border-patrol-montana-spanish.html.

Stannard, D.E. (1993) *American Holocaust: The Conquest of the New World*. Oxford: Oxford University Press.

Stavans, I. (2000) The gravitas of Spanglish. *The Chronicle of Education*, 13 October.

Stavans, I. (2003) *Spanglish: The Making of a New American Language*. New York: Harper Collins.

Stavans, I. and Albin, V. (2007) Language and empire: A conversation with Ilan Stavans. In N. Echávez-Solano and K.C. Sworkin y Méndez (eds) *Spanish and Empire* (pp. 219–243). Nashville, TN: Vanderbilt University Press.

Steinberg, B. (2019) Disney open to running more Spanish-language ads on English-language TV. *Variety*, 7 March. See https://variety.com/2019/biz/news/disney-spanish-language-commercials-abc-espn-1203157198/.

Stevens, M. (2017) New Jersey teacher who told students to 'Speak American' returns to school. *The New York Times*, 24 October. See https://www.nytimes.com/2017/10/24/nyregion/speak-american-high-school.html.

Stoessel, S. (2002) Investigating the role of social networks in language maintenance and shift. *International Journal of the Sociology of Language* 153, 93–132.

Stolz, T., Bakker, D. and Palomo, R.S. (2008) *Hispanisation: The Impact of Spanish on the Lexicon and Grammar of the Indigenous Languages of Austronesia and the Americas*. Munich: Walter de Gruyter.

Strom, M. (2015) Intersemiotic relationships in Spanish-language media in the United States: A critical analysis of the representation of ideology across verbal and visual modes. *Discourse & Communication* 9 (4), 487–508.

Stroud, C. and Mpendukana, S. (2009) Towards a material ethnography of linguistic landscape: Multilingualism, mobility and space in a South African township. *Journal of Sociolinguistics* 13 (3), 363–386.

Subtirelu, N.C. (2017) Raciolinguistic ideology and Spanish-English bilingualism on the US labor market: An analysis of online job advertisements. *Language in Society* 46 (4), 477–505.

Subtirelu, N.C., Borowczyk, M., Thorson Hernández, R. and Venezia, F. (2019) Recognizing *whose* bilingualism? A critical policy analysis of the Seal of Biliteracy. *The Modern Language Journal* 103 (2), 371–390. https://doi.org/10.1111/modl.12556

Tavernise, S. (2018) Why the announcement of a looming White minority makes demographers nervous. *The New York Times*, 22 November. See https://www.nytimes.com/2018/11/22/us/white-americans-minority-population.html.

Taylor, A. (2002) *American Colonies*. New York: Penguin.

Taylor, A. (2013) *Colonial America: A Very Short Introduction*. Oxford: Oxford University Press.

Taylor, P., Lopez, M.H., Martínez, J.H. and Velasco, G. (2012) When labels don't fit: Hispanics and their views of identity. *Hispanic Trends*, 4 April. Washington, DC: Pew Research Center. See http://www.pewhispanic.org/2012/04/04/when-labels-dont-fit-hispanics-and-their-views-of-identity/.

Telles, E.E. (2014) *Pigmentocracies: Ethnicity, Race, and Color in Latin America*. Chapel Hill, NC: UNC Press Books.

Telles, E. and Bailey, S. (2013) Understanding Latin American beliefs about racial inequality. *American Journal of Sociology* 118 (6), 1559–1595.

Thomas, W. and Collier, V. (1997) *School Effectiveness for Language Minority Students*. Washington, DC: National Clearinghouse for Bilingual Education.

Thomas, W. and Collier, V. (2000) Accelerated schooling for all students: Research findings on education in multilingual communities. In S. Shaw (ed.) *Intercultural Education in European Classrooms* (pp. 15–36). Hernden, VA: Stylus.

Thomas, W. and Collier, V. (2002) *A National Study of School Effectiveness for Language Minority Students' Long-term Academic Achievement*. Final Report, Center for Research on Education, Diversity and Excellence, UC Berkeley. See http://escholarship.org/uc/item/65j213pt.

Tollefson, J. (1991) *Planning Language, Planning Inequality: Language Policy in the Community*. London: Longman.

Tollefson, J.W. (2006) Critical theory and language policy. In T. Ricento (ed.) *An Introduction to Language Policy: Theory and Method* (pp. 42–57). Malden, MA: Blackwell.

Toribio, A.J. (2000) Nosotros somos dominicanos: Language and self-definition among Dominicans. In A. Roca (ed.) *Research on Spanish in the United States: Linguistic Issues and Challenges* (pp. 252–270). Somerville, MA: Cascadilla Press.

Toribio, A.J. (2004) Spanish/English speech practices: Bringing chaos to order. *International Journal of Bilingual Education and Bilingualism* 7 (2–3), 133–154.

Torres, J., Pascual y Cabo, D. and Beusterien, J. (2018) What's next? Heritage language learners shape new paths in Spanish teaching. *Hispania* 100 (5), 271–276.

Torres, L. (2018) Latinx? *Latino Studies* 16 (3), 283–285.

Torres Torres, A. (2010) El español de América en los Estados Unidos. In M. Aleza Izquierdo and J.M. Enguita Utrilla (eds) *La Lengua española en América normas y usos actuales* (pp. 403–427). Valencia: Universitat de València. See http://www.uv.es/aleza/.

Torrez, J.E. (2013) 'Somos mexicanos y hablamos mexicano aquí': Rural farmworker families' struggle to maintain cultural and linguistic identity in Michigan. *Journal of Language, Identity & Education* 12 (4), 277–294.

Torruella, J.R. (2007) The Insular Cases: The establishment of a regime of political apartheid. *University of Pennsylvania Journal of International Law* 29 (2), 283–348.

Trujillo-Pagán, N. (2018) Crossed out by LatinX: Gender neutrality and genderblind sexism. *Latino Studies* 16 (3), 396–406.

Tukachinsky, R., Mastro, D. and Yarchi, M. (2017) The effect of prime time television ethnic/racial stereotypes on Latino and Black Americans: A longitudinal national level study. *Journal of Broadcasting & Electronic Media* 61 (3), 538–556.

Ullman, C. (2010) Consuming English: How Mexican transmigrants form identities and construct symbolic citizenship through the English-language program *Inglés sin Barreras [English without Barriers]*. *Linguistics and Education* 21 (1), 1–13.

Ullman, C. (2015) Performing the Nation: Unauthorized Mexican migration and the politics of language use and the body along the US–Mexico border. *Ethnos* 80 (2), 223–247.

Urciuoli, B. (1996) *Exposing Prejudice: Puerto Rican Experiences of Language, Race, and Class*. Boulder, CO: Westview.

Urciuoli, B. (2008) Whose Spanish? The tension between linguistic correctness and cultural identity. In M. Niño-Murcia and J. Rothman (eds) *Bilingualism and Identity: Spanish at the Crossroads with Other Languages* (pp. 257–278). Amsterdam: John Benjamins.

Urciuoli, B. (2009) Talking/not talking about race: The enregisterments of culture in higher education discourses. *Journal of Linguistic Anthropology* 19 (1), 21–39.

Urciouli, B. (2015) Politics of language and identity. In S. Oboler and D.J. Gonzales (eds) *Oxford Encyclopedia of Latinos and Latinas in Contemporary Politics, Law and Social Movements* (pp. 541–545). Oxford: Oxford University Press.

US Citizenship and Immigration Services, US Department of Homeland Security (2018) *DACA Characteristics Data: Approximate Active DACA Recipients as of Aug. 31, 2018*. See https://www.uscis.gov/sites/default/files/USCIS/Resources/Reports%20and%20Studies/Immigration%20Forms%20Data/All%20Form%20Types/DACA/DACA_Population_Data_August_31_2018.pdf.

Valdeón, R.A. (2013) Hispanic or Latino: The use of politicized terms for the Hispanic minority in US official documents and quality news outlets. *Language and Intercultural Communication* 13 (4), 433–449.

Valdés, G. (1981) Pedagogical implications of teaching Spanish to the Spanish-speaking in the United States. In G. Valdés, A.G. Lozano and R. García-Moya (eds) *Teaching Spanish to the Hispanic Bilingual* (pp. 3–20). New York: Teacher's College.

Valdés, G. (1995) The teaching of minority languages as academic subjects: Pedagogical and theoretical challenges. *The Modern Language Journal* 79 (3), 299–328.

Valdés, G. (2005) Bilingualism, heritage language learners, and SLA research: Opportunities lost or seized? *The Modern Language Journal* 89 (3), 410–426.

Valdés, G. (2015) Latin@s and the intergenerational continuity of Spanish: The challenges of curricularizing language. *International Multilingual Research Journal* 9 (4), 253–273.

Valdés, G., González, S.V., García, D.L. and Márquez, P. (2003) Language ideology: The case of Spanish in departments of foreign languages. *Anthropology & Education Quarterly* 34 (1), 3–26.

Valdez, V.E., Freire, J.A. and Delavan, M.G. (2016a) The gentrification of dual language education. *The Urban Review* 48 (4), 601–627.

Valdez, V.E., Delavan, G. and Freire, J.A. (2016b) The marketing of dual language education policy in Utah print media. *Educational Policy* 30 (6), 849–883.

Valenzuela, A. (1999) *Subtractive Schooling: U.S.-Mexican Youth and the Politics of Caring*. Ithaca, NY: State University of New York Press.

Van Deusen-Scholl, N. (2003) Toward a definition of heritage language: Sociopolitical and pedagogical considerations. *Journal of Language, Identity & Education* 2 (3), 211–230.

Van Dijk, T. (1993) *Elite Discourse and Racism*. Newbury Park, CA: Sage.

Van Dijk, T.A. (2005) *Racism and Discourse in Spain and Latin America*. Amsterdam: John Benjamins.

Vann, R.J, Bruna, K.R., and Escudero, M.D.P. (2006) Negotiating identities in a multilingual science class. In T. Omoniyi and G. White (eds) *The Sociolinguistics of Identity* (pp. 201–216). New York: Continuum.

Vargas, N. (2015) Latina/o whitening: Which Latinas/os self-classify as White and report being perceived as White by other Americans? *Du Bois Review: Social Science Research on Race* 12 (1), 119–136.

Varghese, M.M. and Park, C. (2010) Going global: Can dual-language programs save bilingual education? *Journal of Latinos and Education* 9 (1), 72–80.

Vega, D., Moore III, J.L. and Miranda, A.H. (2015) In their own words: Perceived barriers to achievement by African American and Latino high school students. *American Secondary Education* 43 (3), 36.

Velázquez, I. (2012) Mother's social network and family language maintenance. *Journal of Multilingual and Multicultural Development* 34 (2), 189–202.

Velázquez, I. (2014) Maternal perceptions of agency in intergenerational transmission of Spanish: The case of Latinos in the U.S. Midwest. *Journal of Language, Identity & Education* 13 (3), 135–152.

Velázquez, I. (2018) *Household Perspectives on Minority Language Maintenance and Loss: Language in the Small Spaces*. Bristol: Multilingual Matters.

Vélez-Ibáñez, C.G. (2017) *Hegemonies of Language and their Discontents: The Southwest North American Region since 1540*. Tucson, AZ: University of Arizona Press.

Veltman, C. (1998) Quebec, Canada, and the United States: Social reality and language rights. In T. Ricento and B. Burnaby (eds) *Language and Politics in the United States and Canada: Myths and Realities* (pp. 301–316). Mahwah, NJ: Lawrence Erlbaum.

Veltman, C. (2000) The American linguistic mosaic. In S.L. McKay and S.C. Wong (eds) *New Immigrants in the United States* (pp. 59–93). Cambridge: Cambridge University Press.

Verhovek, S.H. (1995) Mother scolded by judge for speaking in Spanish. *The New York Times*, 30 August. See http://www.nytimes.com/1995/08/30/us/mother-scolded-by-judge-for-speaking-in-spanish.html.

Vespa, J., Armstrong, D.M. and Medina, L. (2018) *Demographic Turning Points for the United States: Population Projections for 2020 to 2060*. No. 2550 2099. Washington, DC: US Census Bureau.

Vidal-Ortiz, S. and Martínez, J. (2018) Latinx thoughts: Latinidad with an X. *Latino Studies* 16 (3), 384–395.

Villa, D.J. (2002) The sanitizing of US Spanish in academia. *Foreign Language Annals* 35 (2), 222–230.

Villa, D. and Rivera-Mills, S. (2009) An integrated multi-generational model for language maintenance and shift: The case of Spanish in the Southwest. *Spanish in Context* 6 (1), 26–42.

Villa, L. and del Valle, J. (2014) The politics of Spanish in the world. In M. Lacorte (ed.) *The Routledge Handbook of Hispanic Applied Linguistics* (pp. 571–587). New York: Routledge.

Villenas, S.A. (2012) Ethnographies de lucha (of struggle) in Latino education: Toward social movement. *Anthropology & Education Quarterly* 43 (1), 13–19.

Wade, P. (2008) Race in Latin America. In D. Poole (ed.) *A Companion to Latin American Anthropology* (pp. 175–192). Oxford: Blackwell.

Walsh, C. (1991) *Pedagogy and the Struggle for Voice: Issues of Language, Power and Schooling for Puerto Ricans.* New York: Bergin & Garvey.

Waltermire, M. (2014) The influence of English on US Spanish: Introduction. *Sociolinguistic Studies* 8 (1), 1.

Walters, J. (2006) Come sing along, Señor Bush. *The Guardian*, 30 April. See https://www.theguardian.com/world/2006/apr/30/usa.joannawalters.

Weber, D.J. (2000) The Spanish frontier in North America. *OAH Magazine of History* 14 (4), 3–4.

Wei, L. (2018) Translanguaging as a practical theory of language. *Applied Linguistics* 39 (1), 9–30.

Weisman, E.M. (2001) Bicultural identity and language attitudes: Perspectives of four Latina teachers. *Urban Education* 36, 203–225.

Welch, K. (2007) Black criminal stereotypes and racial profiling. *Journal of Contemporary Criminal Justice* 23 (3), 276–288.

Whalen, C.T. (2005) Colonialism, citizenship, and the making of the Puerto Rican diaspora: An introduction. In V. Vázquez-Hernández and C.T. Whalen (eds) *The Puerto Rican Diaspora: Historical Perspectives* (pp. 1–42). Philadelphia, PA: Temple University Press.

Wildsmith, E., Alvira-Hammond, M. and Guzman, L. (2016) *A National Portrait of Hispanic Children in Need.* Publication No. 2016-15. Bethesda, MD: National Research Center on Hispanic Children and Families. See https://www.hispanicresearchcenter.org/wp-content/uploads/2018/04/Hispanics-in-Need-Errata-11.29-V2.pdf.

Wiley, T.G. (1998) The imposition of World War I era English-only policies and the fate of German in North America. In T. Ricento (ed.) *Language and Politics in the United States and Canada* (pp. 211–241). Mahwah, NJ: Lawrence Erlbaum.

Wiley, T.G. (2000) Continuity and change in the function of language ideologies in the United States. In T. Ricento (ed.) *Ideology, Politics and Language Policies: Focus on English* (pp. 67–85). Philadelphia, PA: John Benjamins.

Wiley, T.G. (2004) Language planning, language policy, and the English-Only Movement. In E. Finegan and J.R. Rickford (eds) *Language in the USA: Themes for the Twenty-first Century* (pp. 319–338). Cambridge: Cambridge University Press.

Wiley, T.G. (2010) The United States. In J.A. Fishman and O. García (eds) *Handbook of Language and Ethnic Identity: Disciplinary and Regional Perspectives, Vol. 1* (pp. 302–322). Oxford: Oxford University Press.

Wiley, T.G. (2014) Policy considerations for promoting heritage, community, and Native American languages. In T.G. Wiley, J.K. Peyton, D. Christian, S.C.K. Moore and N. Liu (eds) *Handbook of Heritage, Community, and Native American Languages in the United States: Research, Policy, and Educational Practice* (pp. 45–53). New York: Routledge.

Wiley, T.G. and García, O. (2016) Language policy and planning in language education: Legacies, consequences, and possibilities. *The Modern Language Journal* 100 (S1), 48–63.

Wiley, T.G. and Wright, W.E. (2004) Against the undertow: Language-minority education policy and politics in the 'age of accountability'. *Educational Policy* 18 (1), 142–168.

Wilkerson, M.E. and Salmons, J. (2008) 'Good old immigrants of yesteryear' who didn't learn English: Germans in Wisconsin. *American Speech* 83 (3), 259–283.

Wilson, C. (1997) *The Myth of Santa Fe: Creating a Modern Regional Tradition.* Albuquerque, NM: New Mexico University Press.

Woolard, K.A. (1998) Language ideology as a field of inquiry. In B.B. Schieffelin, K.A. Woolard and P.V. Kroskrity (eds) *Language Ideologies: Practice and Theory* (pp. 3–47). Oxford: Oxford University Press.

Woolard, K. (2005) Language and identity choice in Catalonia: The interplay of contrasting ideologies of linguistic authority. UCSD Linguistic Anthropology Working Paper, University of San Diego.

Woolard, K.A. (2016) *Ideologies of Linguistic Authority: Authenticity, Anonymity, and Naturalism.* Oxford: Oxford University Press.

Woolley, S. (2016) 'Out gay boys? There's, like, one point seven five': Negotiating identity in superdiversity. *International Journal of the Sociology of Language* 241, 39–68.

Yagmur, K. and Ehala, M. (2011) Tradition and innovation in the Ethnolinguistic Vitality theory. *Journal of Multilingual and Multicultural Development* 32 (2), 101–110.

Yamauchi, L.A., Ceppi, A.K. and Lau-Smith, J.A. (2000) Teaching in a Hawaiian context: Educator perspectives on the Hawaiian language immersion program. *Bilingual Research Journal* 24 (4), 385–403.

Yrigoyen Fajardo, R.Z. (2015) The panorama of pluralist constitutionalism: From multiculturalism to decolonization. In C.R. Garavito (ed.) *Law and Society in Latin America: A New Map* (pp. 157–174). New York: Routledge.

Zayas, L.H. (2015) *Forgotten Citizens: Deportation, Children, and the Making of American Exiles and Orphans.* Oxford: Oxford University Press.

Zelinsky, W. (2001) *The Enigma of Ethnicity: Another American Dilemma.* Iowa City, IA: University of Iowa Press.

Zentella, A.C. (1997a) *Growing Up Bilingual.* Oxford: Blackwell.

Zentella, A.C. (1997b) The hispanophobia of the Official English movement in the US. *The International Journal of the Sociology of Language* 127, 71–86.

Zentella, A.C. (2003) José, can you see? In D. Sommer (ed.) *Bilingual Games* (pp. 51–66). New York: Palgrave Macmillan.

Zentella, A.C. (2007) 'Dime con quién hablas, y te diré quién eres': Linguistic (in)security and Latina/o unity. In J. Flores and Renato Rosaldo (eds) *A Companion to Latina/o Studies* (pp. 25–38). Oxford: Blackwell.

Zentella, A.C. (2014) TWB (Talking While Bilingual): Linguistic profiling of Latina/os, and other linguistic torquemadas. *Latino Studies* 12 (4), 620–635.

Zentella, A.C. (2017) 'Limpia, fija y da esplendor': Challenging the symbolic violence of the Royal Spanish Academy. *Chiricú Journal* 1 (2), 21.

Zong, J. and Batalova, J. (2018) Dominican immigrants in the United States. *MPI Spotlight*, 9 April. See https://www.migrationpolicy.org/article/dominican-immigrants-united-states.

Zyzik, E. (2016) Toward a prototype model of the heritage language learner: Understanding strengths and needs. In M. Fairclough and S. Beaudrie (eds) *Innovative Strategies for Heritage Language Teaching: A Practical Guide for the Classroom* (pp. 19–38). Washington, DC: Georgetown University Press.

Index

Accent, 81, 130, 133, 142, 145, 158, 159, 164, 186
As basis for discrimination (ch 8), 190–192
Academia Noreteamericana de la Lengua Española (ANLE), 74–75, 175, 254, 264, 265, 267–268
Acoma massacre, 37, 47–48
Acquisition planning, 175
Additive bilingualism, 28, 205, 207, 218, 265, 271
Affirmative language rights, 177, 271
African American English (AAE), 139, 191
Definition, 271
Related to Latinx Englishes, 245
Americanization, 195–196, 203
Anglo, definition, 6, 42, 150, 181, 271
Anglophone, definition, 143, 155, 157, 271
Appropriation, 143, 271
Assimilation, 77, 87, 100, 102, 126–127, 152, 155, 159, 160, 176, 180, 183, 203, 207, 215, 241, 261
cultural, 127, 152, 155
linguistic, 183, 203, 207, 241
Attitudes towards language, language attitudes, 22, 24, 86, 135, 149, 169, 175, 226, 242, 245–248
Authentic [identities], Authenticity, 10, 20, 22, 47, 87, 125–126, 129–130, 139, 143, 154, 157, 159, 166, 246, 254–255,

Bilingual Education Act, 185, 203
Binary race system, 271
Black Legend, 45–46, 271
Borrowing, 37, 39, 128, 140, 228, 230–231, 233–235, 249, 271
Bracero program, 53

Calque, syntactic calque, 235, 271–272
Casta, 39, 101, 272
Census Bureau, US, 1, 9, 11–15, 17, 25–27
Census Bureau's language question, 11, 14–15,
Chicano/a/x, definition, 110, 272
Chicanx English, 73, 243–244, 267, 272
Circumstantial bilingualism, 218, 272
Civil Rights, 3, 53, 59, 105, 108, 182, 184–186
Class, social, 4, 22, 23, 43, 45, 56, 57, 59, 70, 72–73, 78, 86, 116, 121, 123–124, 132, 134, 138–139, 140–141, 151–152, 159, 167, 180, 202, 209, 215–217, 222
identity, 260–262

Codeswitching, 82–83, 134–135, 160, 175, 212, 216, 219, 230–232, 234, 235–238, 240, 248–249, 267, 272 (*see also* translanguaging)
Cognate, 157–158, 272
Colonialism, colonial rule, 34–42, 44–48, 60, 91, 100–103, 106, 115, 127, 179–180, 183
Colorism, 104, 151, 272
Commodification, commodifying discourses, 47, 83–84, 87, 164, 166, 178, 217–218, 258, 261, 266–267, 272
Corpus planning, 175
Covert prestige, 247, 272
Critical pedagogy, 212, 219–220, 266, 269, 273
Cubans, 11–12, 51, 55–56
Cuban varieties [of Spanish], 245–247
Cyclical bilingualism, 29, 273

DACA, 49–50, 54
Deportation, 50, 53, 155
Differential bilingualism, 84–85, 218, 222, 258, 261, 266, 273
Dominicans, 11–12, 51, 58–59, 106, 110, 114, 129, 247
Dream Act, Dreamers, 137, 257
Double monolingualism, 83, 273
Dual monolingualism, 83, 214, 273

Elective bilingualism, 218, 272
Elite bilingualism, 273
Endogamy, 21, 273
English-only, 30, 66, 158, 183, 190–191, 193, 195, 197, 213, 273
English Plus, 195
Erasure, 48, 69, 70, 73, 77–78, 85–87, 102, 115, 116, 128, 150, 152, 156, 161, 179, 194, 202, 214, 257, 262, 273
Essentialism/essentialist, 87, 94, 125, 132, 255, 273
Ethnic identity, 100, 114, 134–135, 261–262
Ethnolinguistic vitality, 21–23, 25, 28, 166, 176, 181, 256, 274
Ethnoracial, 92, 99–100, 274
Executive Order 13166, 187–189, 264, 274
Exogamy, 21, 255, 274
Exoticization, 47, 55, 151, 153–154, 161, 166

Family language policy, 24, 176, 274
First-generation Americans, 30, 274, 278

First-generation immigrants, 274, 278
Filibuster, 42
Florida, 10, 11, 35–38, 41–42, 55–56, 179, 187, 189, 226
Fresas, 134

Generation 1.5, 30–31, 274
Grammatical gender, 140, 274
Guise, matched or verbal, 245–248
Guadalupe Hidalgo, Treaty of (*see* Treaty of Guadalupe Hildalgo)

Hegemonic discourses and/or ideologies, 65–68, 71–72, 88, 96, 122–123, 149, 163, 169, 219, 222, 231, 259, 266, 273, 274
Hegemony, 65–68, 157, 167, 174, 194, 213–214, 218, 221, 242, 248, 256, 261, 275
Heritage language education, 212, 275
Heritage (language) speakers, 8, 29, 201, 211–212, 215, 219, 247–248, 275
Heteroglossia, 275
Heteroglossic ideology, 275
Hispanophilia, 46–47

Iconicity, 69, 275
i-word, 50–51
illegal alien, as discriminatory term, 50–51, 97, 156
Immigration and Nationality Act of 1965, 182
Immigration quotas, 50, 53, 182
Index, 7, 69, 76, 86–88, 118
Indexicality, 68–69, 78–80, 88, 116–118, 125–127, 132–134
Indian Removal Act, 180
Indigenous languages, 15, 59–60, 70, 95, 102–103, 192, 195, 228, 241–242, 264
Instituto Cervantes, 25, 30, 74, 217, 265, 268
Instrumentalist ideologies, 83–84, 217, 266, 275
Intersectionality, 22, 137, 140, 154, 275

Jim Crow, 182
Jotería Studies, 140

Language choice, 24, 125, 135–136, 180, 191, 219
Language-as-problem orientation, 177, 204, 217, 276
Language-as-resource orientation, 178–179, 217
Language-as-right orientation, 178
Language planning and policy (LPP), 173–177, 276
Language maintenance and/or shift, 9, 21, 176
Lateralization (of /r/), 229, 276
'Latin Look', 163
Latinidad, 8, 132, 139, 149–150, 152, 155, 159, 162, 164, 169, 198, 213, 254, 276
Latinx, definition and use (ch 1 ch 5), 2, 6–7, 91–92, 95–97
Lau v. Nichols, 185–186, 204, 206
Linguistic profiling, 190, 276
Linguistic repertoire, 81–83, 89, 134, 150, 161, 226, 230, 241–243, 267, 276
Linguistic landscape, 166–169, 170, 247
Linguistic variation and varieties, 3–4, 73, 95, 124, 164–165, 212, 220, 225–230, 238–241, 245–247, 266

Maintenance bilingual education, 205, 265
Manifest Destiny, 40, 44, 276
Marielitos, 56
Matched guise, *see* guise, matched
Medium of instruction, 175, 196, 203, 205, 211–212, 265, 276
Mestizaje, 46, 100, 102–103, 276
Mestizos, 39, 46, 102
Mexicans, 11–12, 43–44, 46–50, 51–54
Mexican varieties [of Spanish], 13, 46, 163–164, 247
Mexico, 3, 10, 13, 16, 37–43, 45–54
Mexiricans, 241
Minority or minoritized languages, 178, 194, 258, 273, 277
'mixed race', 13, 40, 97, 99, 101–102, 113, 260, 272
Mock Spanish, 69–70, 97, 117, 141–145, 158, 168–170, 261, 277
Monoglossic ideologies, 81, 83, 205, 214, 216–218, 249, 277
Mulatos, 39
Multilingual discourse, 82–83, 135, 226, 231–233, 235–237, *see also* translanguaging

Nativism, nativists, 50, 52, 56, 77, 182, 255, 277
Naturalization/Naturalized of ideologies or categories, 65, 66, 75, 79, 92, 277
Naturalization Act, the, 182
Nebraska v. Myers, 203
Negative language rights, 177, 192, 277
New Mexico, 43, 45, 47–48, 114, 181–183, 192, 203, 267
Non-standard varieties, 63, 65, 76, 157
  Of English, 191, 202
  Of Spanish, 134
Normative monolingualism, 80–81, 83, 157, 178, 194, 210, 214, 221, 231, 256, 277

Official English, 192–195
Oñate, Juan de, 47–48
One-drop rule, 99, 260, 277
One nation–one language ideology, 65–66, 68, 70–72, 76–80, 174, 193, 209, 277
Operation Wetback, 53
Othering, 45, 94, 108, 143, 195, 278

Perceptual dialectology, 245–246
Performance (of identity), 125, 132, 135, 248, 267, 269
Pew Center, 12, 18, 25, 26, 61, 87, 110, 116, 163, 259
Phenotype, 92, 102, 104, 107, 110, 117, 278
Pluricentrism, 74–75
Pronunciation
  Spanish, 126–127, 261, 270
  Anglicized, 126, 142, 145
Puerto Rico, 3, 18, 28, 35–36, 40, 44–45, 54–55, 102, 104–106, 179, 183, 195–196, 203, 229, 246, 253
Puerto Ricans, 11, 20, 24, 27–28, 37, 44–45, 54–55, 58–59, 81, 91, 100, 106, 135, 187, 196, 228, 241, 247
Puerto Rican varieties [of Spanish], 226, 229, 246
Pueblo Revolt, 39, 47
Pull factors, 49, 51, 53, 54, 60, 61, 257, 278
Push factors, 49, 278

Queer, 28, 116, 139–140
  Identities, 139–140
  Theory, 136, 140

Racial category/racial group, 92, 94, 99, 108, 110, 113, 198
Racial identity, 13, 37, 60, 72, 92–95, 97–98, 101–117
Racial profiling, 95, 105
Racialization, 16, 28, 37, 40, 43, 45, 51, 60, 80, 88, 91, 94–97, 100–103, 105–108, 111, 113, 117–118, 132, 139, 141, 143–145, 156, 159, 164, 168, 181, 183, 185, 194–195, 197, 202, 210, 213, 215–216, 218, 220–222, 231, 242, 247, 253, 256–257, 260–261, 266, 278
Real Academia Española (RAE), 74, 117, 175, 232, 254
Rhotacization, rhotacism (of /l/), 229, 278
Romance languages, 227, 278
Roosevelt, Theodore, 44, 78, 182

Salvadorans, 11, 51, 56–58, 128, 228
Seal of Biliteracy, 205, 266, 278
Second-generation immigrants, 30, 278
Segregation, 47, 94, 96, 99, 103, 181–185, 203, 206
Slave codes, 180, 279
Social class, *see* class, social
Social network theory, 23, 279
Social constructionism, 4–5, 92–94, 97, 99–100, 106, 111, 117, 122, 140, 259, 279
Spanglish, 135, 144–145, 231
Spanglish, definition and usage of term (ch. 10), 231–233, 264–265, 279
Spanish identity, 12, 45–48, 60, 108–109, 111, 113–114
Stance, stance-taking, 69, 125, 127–128, 141, 145, 236, 279
Standard language ideology, 63–68, 72, 73–76, 80, 87, 164, 191, 212, 215–216, 221–222, 231–232, 279
Standard variety or language, 67, 73, 82, 165, 175, 216, 279
Status planning, 175–176
Subtractive bilingualism, 205, 207, 215, 218, 279
Supreme Court, 44, 184–186, 189, 203–204
Symbolic domination, 65–68, 280

Texas, 10, 13, 19, 27, 40, 42–44, 46, 56, 203, 244, 248, 256
TPS, Temporary Protected Status, 49–50, 58
Transitional bilingual education, 207, 215
Translanguaging, 82–83, 134–135, 165, 175, 212, 214, 216, 218–220, 230–231, 233, 235–237, 259, 262, 267
Transnationalism, 2, 24, 136, 163
Treaty of Guadalupe Hidalgo, 43, 181, 280
Treaty citizens, 43, 46, 49, 51, 52, 106, 181, 257, 280
Two-way immersion (TWI) programs, 207–210, 217, 265–266, 280

UN Declaration on the Rights of Persons Belonging to National or Ethnic, Religious and Linguistic Minorities, 177–178

Velarization (of /n/), 229, 280
Verbal guise, *see* guise, verbal
Vos, voseo 4, 128–129, 229, 241
Voting Rights Act, the, 15, 22, 105, 108, 184, 186–187, 264

Webster, Noah, 180

Xenophobia, 5, 22, 140, 182, 280

Zero-sum ideology, 80–81, 178, 183, 194, 215, 218, 280